National Audubon Society
Field Guide to

North American Wildflowers

A Chanticleer Press Edition

National Audubon Society
Field Guide to

North American Wildflowers

Western Region

Revised Edition

Richard Spellenberg
Professor Emeritus of Biology
New Mexico State University

Alfred A. Knopf, New York

This is a Borzoi Book.
Published by Alfred A. Knopf, Inc.

Copyright © 2001 by Chanticleer Press, Inc. All rights reserved under International and Pan-American Copyright Conventions. Published in the United States by Alfred A. Knopf, Inc., New York, and simultaneously in Canada by Random House of Canada, Limited, Toronto. Distributed by Random House, Inc., New York.

www.randomhouse.com

Knopf, Borzoi Books, and the colophon are registered trademarks of Random House, Inc.

Prepared and produced by
Chanticleer Press, Inc., New York.

Printed and bound by Dai Nippon Printing Co., Ltd., Hong Kong.

Published July 1979
Second edition, fully revised, March 2001
First printing

Library of Congress Cataloging-in-Publication Data available.
ISBN: 0-679-375-40233-0

National Audubon Society® is a registered trademark of National Audubon Society, Inc., all rights reserved.

CONTENTS

NATIONAL AUDUBON SOCIETY

The mission of NATIONAL AUDUBON SOCIETY, *founded in 1905, is to conserve and restore natural ecosystems, focusing on birds, other wildlife, and their habitats for the benefit of humanity and the earth's biological diversity.*

One of the largest, most effective environmental organizations, AUDUBON has nearly 550,000 members, numerous state offices and nature centers, and 500+ chapters in the United States and Latin America, plus a professional staff of scientists, educators, and policy analysts. Through its nationwide sanctuary system AUDUBON manages 160,000 acres of critical wildlife habitat and unique natural areas for birds, wild animals, and rare plant life.

The award-winning *Audubon* magazine, which is sent to all members, carries outstanding articles and color photography on wildlife, nature, environmental issues, and conservation news. AUDUBON also publishes *Audubon Adventures,* a children's newsletter reaching 450,000 students. Through its ecology camps and workshops in Maine, Connecticut, and Wyoming, AUDUBON offers nature education for teachers, families, and children; through *Audubon Expedition Institute* in Belfast, Maine, AUDUBON offers unique, traveling undergraduate and graduate degree programs in Environmental Education.

AUDUBON sponsors books and on-line nature activities, plus travel programs to exotic places like Antarctica, Africa, Baja California, the Galápagos Islands, and Patagonia. For information about how to become an AUDUBON member, subscribe to *Audubon Adventures,* or to learn more about any of our programs, please contact:

NATIONAL AUDUBON SOCIETY
Membership Dept.
700 Broadway
New York, NY 10003
(800) 274-4201
(212) 979-3000
http://www.audubon.org/

THE AUTHOR

Richard Spellenberg is Professor Emeritus of Biology at New Mexico State University. He is a specialist in the plant species of the western United States and the Sierra Madre Occidental in Mexico.

ACKNOWLEDGMENTS

This revised guide builds upon the original edition's success in aiding the public to appreciate the marvelous wildflower diversity of western North America. I therefore wish to express my sincere appreciation to all of those whose help and encouragement I acknowledged in the first edition.

More than 20 years after the first edition was published, another fine group of people helped make this thorough revision a reality. I especially thank my wife, Naida Zucker, for her patience as I spent many nights and weekends at the computer. Phil Jenkins, Assistant Curator of the Herbarium at the University of Arizona, is a good friend and fine botanist; he reviewed manuscripts and provided many helpful comments and corrections, as did another great colleague, Dr. John Thieret, who was simultaneously revising the companion volume for eastern wildflowers.

I am very grateful to the highly skilled staff at Chanticleer Press. I express special thanks to Miriam Harris, senior editor, who guided this project to fruition, and to Lisa Lester, whose intensive editing work in the final months greatly improved the quality and useability of this guide. Photo editors Ruth Jeyaveeran and Meg Kuhta did an outstanding job of gathering and sorting through thousands of images to find the accurate and beautiful photographs that are so essential to this field guide; illustrator Bobbi Angell contributed lovely renderings of many species; and art director Drew Stevens and designer Bernadette Vibar brought the text and images together splendidly. Tremendous assistance throughout the final copyediting and proofreading stages of the project came from editorial assistant Mee-So Caponi, proofreader Linda Eger, and editors Lisa Leventer, Pamela Nelson, and Marian Appellof. Alicia Mills and Katherine Thomason saw the guide through the complex production and printing processes. In earlier stages of the project, Mary Sutherland helped with editing, and further assistance came from Edie Locke, Lauren Weidenman, and Amy Oh. I thank Amy Hughes for getting this project off the ground during her tenure as editor-in-chief. Thanks also to her successor, George Scott, for seeing the project through to completion. Finally, to the photographers, thanks for your keen eyes and superb skills in obtaining beautiful photographs.

INTRODUCTION

What is a wildflower? What one person considers a wild-flower may be a weed to another. All we can safely say is that wildflowers are wild plants with flowers and that they may be found almost anywhere, from cracks in city sidewalks to vast empty deserts, pristine forests, seashores, old fields, prairies, or mountain meadows. This guide is directed toward the reader whose interest in wildflowers is new as well as toward the nature devotee who knows many of the common or showy western wildflowers but desires to learn more. Because space in a single book is necessarily limited, only a portion of the thousands of western wildflowers can be discussed or illustrated. Therefore, it is the aim of this guide to cover most of the flowers of western North America that attract attention because they are showy or because of their unusual nature, to represent the floral diversity of all regions of the West more or less equally, to illustrate with at least one example most genera of western wildflowers, and to represent the variation found among species of some of the huge western groups, such as lupines, beardtongues, and evening primroses.

Geographic Scope
Many field guides covering eastern and western North America use the 100th meridian as a dividing line between the two regions. We have chosen, instead, a more natural boundary (see map), which extends southeastward from the Arctic along the eastern base of the Rocky Mountains to the Big Bend region of Texas at the Mexican border. This line marks a pronounced change in the kinds of native plants, with few species extending very far beyond on either side. This guide covers the entire region from this line westward to the Pacific Coast.

Major Western Habitats
The topographical variety of the western United States has resulted in a wide range of habitats, which accounts for the great number and diversity of native plants. Near the

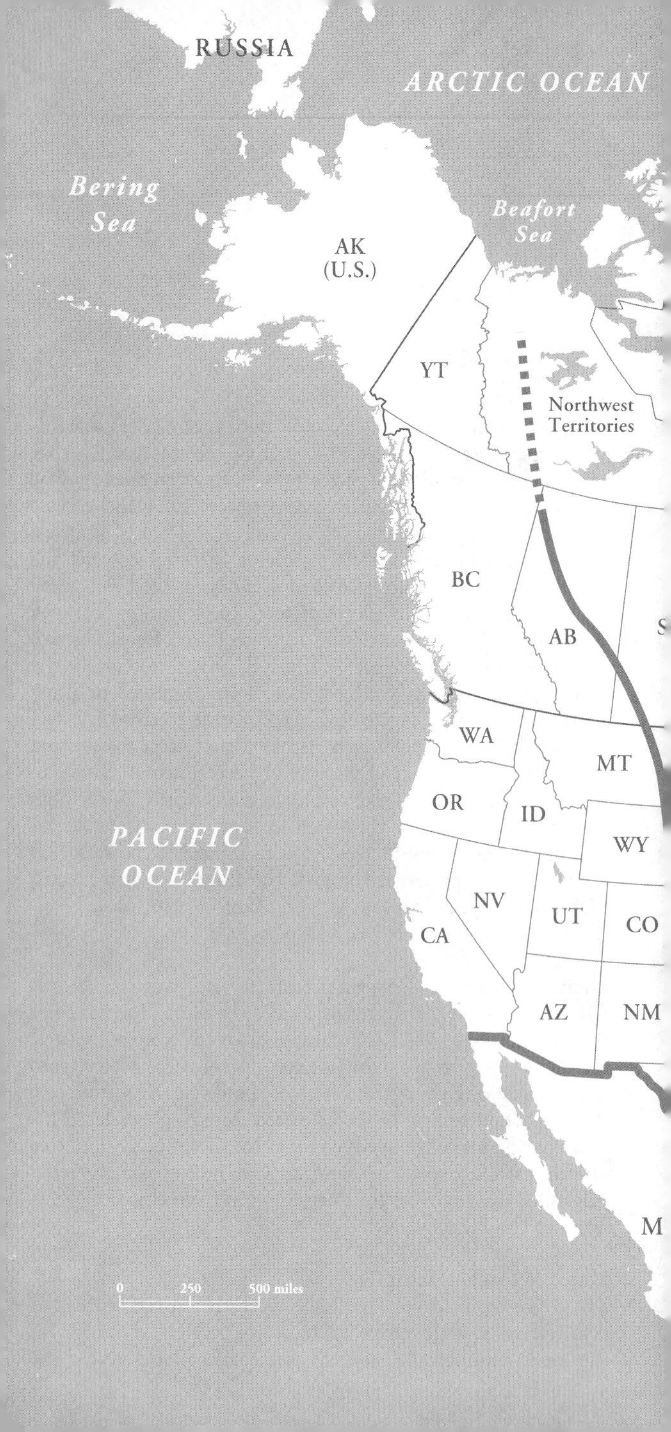

RUSSIA

ARCTIC OCEAN

*Bering
Sea*

*Beaufort
Sea*

AK
(U.S.)

YT

Northwest
Territories

BC

AB

S

*PACIFIC
OCEAN*

WA

MT

OR

ID

WY

NV

UT

CO

CA

AZ

NM

M

0   250   500 miles

Pacific Coast moist conditions prevail, with a drier, warmer climate to the south and wetter, cooler conditions to the north, creating a general division between plant species approximately at the California–Oregon border. In the mountains there are dense coniferous forests, most with few wildflowers, some surrounding meadows that bloom with a profusion of colorful species. The high Pacific mountains (the Sierra Nevada and the Cascade and Olympic Ranges), some with cold, wind-swept, tundra-like habitat on their ridges, receive most of the rainfall from the west. As a result, there are virtual rain forests on the slopes that face the prevailing winds, but a slight bit eastward, on the lee-ward side of the mountains, is a wide area of arid grasslands and deserts. To the north at lower elevations lies a cold desert with many gray shrubs, especially sagebrush. To the south the hot Mojave, Sonoran, and Chihuahuan Deserts have mostly Creosote Bush, an olive green shrub, and a completely different set of plants from those in the cold desert.

Ponds, streams, and coastal salt marshes provide habitats for many kinds of marshland and aquatic plants. Species growing along the Pacific Coast and inland in low desert pools must be tolerant of salty conditions. Strongly selective habitats, such as sand along the coast or in the deserts, have their own peculiar sets of plants.

Photographs

Although many flower books are illustrated with drawings or paintings, we have chosen to use color photographs because they show flowers as seen in nature, rather than as interpreted by an artist. In presenting the work of expert wildflower photographers, we believe we provide any naturalist, amateur and professional alike, an excellent means of arriving at an accurate identification of many of our western plants. A good photograph captures the true color of a wildflower in its natural setting, facilitating identification. In addition, the beauty of pictures taken by outstanding photographers makes this useful guide a delight to the eye.

The photographs we have chosen usually emphasize the flowers themselves, but leaves and other identifying features are also often shown. Where useful, line drawings are included among the text descriptions.

Captions

The caption under each photograph gives the plate number, the plant's main common name, height data for the plant, and one of the following dimensions: the approximate flower width (*w.*) or flower length (*l.*), or the approximate cluster length (*cl.*) or cluster width (*cw.*). This information is especially helpful for the photographs showing flowers larger or smaller than life-size. Plant height is not given for plants classified as aquatics, vines, or creepers (the term creeper is used here loosely to describe any trailing or sprawling plant). The caption ends with the page number of the species description in the text.

Arrangement by Color
Although we realize that any identification technique has its limitations, we have grouped the photographs of the flowers by color, since that is the feature most of us notice first. Note that colors may intergrade, that is, they may blend into one another, resulting in intermediate hues. Thus, if you are looking for a specific plant in the yellow color group and do not find it there, check the orange and green groups as well, since yellow often intergrades with these hues. The color groups are arranged in the following order:

Green
Green intergrades into white, yellow, and sometimes blue; intermediate-hued flowers should be sought here or among those colors.

White
White intergrades into many colors, particularly very pale pink, lavender, blue, green, and yellow. Pale pastel flowers should also be sought among those colors.

Yellow
Yellow intergrades especially into orange and green.

Orange
Orange intergrades into brown, red, and yellow.

Brown
A number of western wildflowers are brownish, brown-maroon, or rust in color. These hues intergrade into purple (through maroon), red, orange, and occasionally yellow.

Red
Red intergrades into pink, orange, and purple.

Pink
Here, pink is considered to be a pastel red, without any blue hue to it. Nevertheless, it intergrades into purple through lavender, and as the color becomes denser it intergrades into red.

Purple

Among all the colors, purple is perhaps the most difficult to define. Colors mixing blue and red may be differently perceived from one person to the next. As used here, purple ranges from lavender through red-violet to violet-blue. Flowers with some mixture of red or pink, blue, or blue and violet may be grouped in the pink or the blue category.

Blue

Blue intergrades into purple or lavender and through pastel hues into white.

A plant that has flowers with more than one prominent color may be included in two different color sections; also, when a plant has a conspicuously colored or unusual fruit, the fruit may be shown as well.

Flower Subgroups

Within the color groups we have further organized the plants so those that have flowers or flower clusters with similar structure occur together.

To accomplish this, we have devised six basic subgroups: radially symmetrical flowers; daisy- and dandelion-like flowers; bilaterally symmetrical flowers; elongated clusters; rounded clusters; and fruit. (Not all subgroups are present in every color group.) These subgroups are discussed in more detail in "How to Identify a Flower," below. First, however, we will review the structure of a flower and other parts of a plant so that the subgroups are better understood.

Flower Symmetry

The overall symmetry of a flower is evident when you look directly into its "face." If its flower parts are of equal length and radiate outward from the center, in spoke-like fashion, it is termed radially symmetrical, or regular (below, left); such a flower can be divided into equal halves along several lines that run through the center. If flower parts are of unequal length on one side relative to the other, and the flower can be divided into equal halves along only one line through the center, the flower is termed bilaterally symmetrical, or irregular (below, right). For accurate identification, it is most helpful to observe a flower's type of symmetry.

Radially symmetrical

Bilaterally symmetrical

Flower Parts

Most flowers consist of four series of parts. The outer, often green series is the calyx, composed of sepals. The next, usually showy series is the corolla, composed of petals. Generally it is the corolla that most clearly reveals the symmetry of a flower. The calyx and the corolla together are called the perianth. In some plants sepals and petals may look alike. In others petals may be missing, and only green, sepal-like structures are present. In a very few plants there are no petals, but the sepals are petal-like and sometimes very showy, which is understandably confusing to the beginner. Sepals may be joined to one another and form a dish, bell, or tube; petals may also be joined in such shapes. If petals are separate, a gentle tug on one will remove only it; if they are joined, all petals will be removed at once. In our description of a flower with separate petals, the number of petals is given; in a flower with joined petals, the number of lobes of the corolla is given.

Just inside the petals, and often attached to the corolla in plants with joined petals, are the stamens. Each stamen consists of a relatively slender stalk (filament) and a pollen-bearing body called the anther. In the very center of the flower is at least one pistil. The pistil has a swollen basal portion, the ovary, containing ovules, each ovule harboring an egg; ovules grow into seeds. All these flower parts may be attached at the top of the ovary or at its base. The ovary matures into a dry or fleshy fruit. Above the ovary is a stout or slender, sometimes branched style, topped by a pollen-receiving stigma. The pollen inside the anther is transferred to the stigma by insects or other animals (e.g., hummingbirds), wind, or water. This is pollination. Soon the pollen will produce the sperm that fertilizes the egg deep within the flower.

Flower Clusters

Flowers may be borne singly at the end of the stem (terminal) or singly all along the stem in the leaf axils (the angle formed by the stem and the upper side of the leaf). Frequently, flowers are arranged in clusters (inflorescences) set apart from the rest of the plant. These clusters may be flat-topped, elongated, or more or less round, and they may be relatively loose or dense. Technical names for flower clusters have been avoided in our text wherever possible, but some are very helpful in identification. For example, in the carrot family (Apiaceae) the flower cluster usually has a number of branches all attached at one point, an inflorescence called an umbel. Also, many members of the aster family (Asteraceae) have a cluster of tiny flowers, some forming the button-like, central disk, others forming the petal-like rays; all are collectively called the head, which resembles a single radially symmetrical flower. Reduced

Parts of a Flower

Generalized Flower

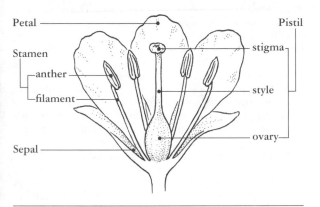

Petal

Pistil

Stamen
- anther
- filament

stigma
style
ovary

Sepal

Flowers in a Composite Head

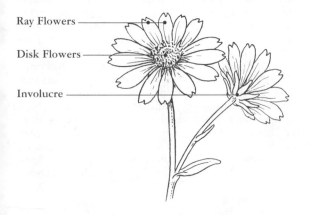

Ray Flowers

Disk Flowers

Involucre

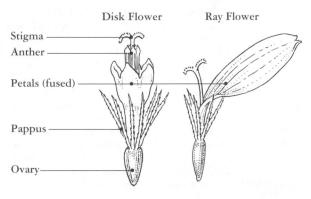

Disk Flower   Ray Flower

Stigma
Anther

Petals (fused)

Pappus

Ovary

Pea Flower

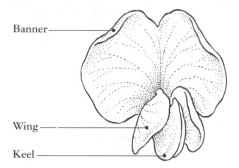

Banner

Wing

Keel

Iris

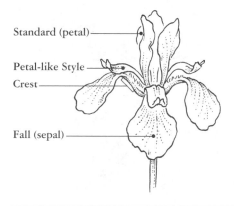

Standard (petal)

Petal-like Style

Crest

Fall (sepal)

Arum

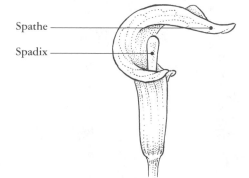

Spathe

Spadix

Flower Cluster Types

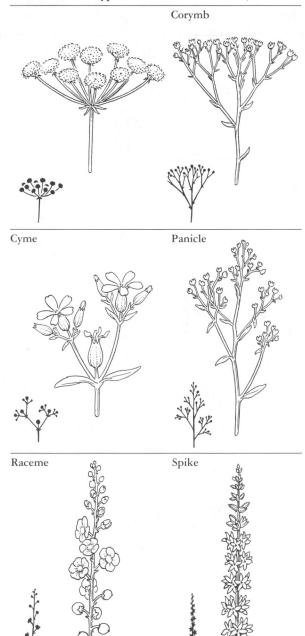

Corymb

Cyme

Panicle

Raceme

Spike

leaves near the flower or in or near the flower cluster are called bracts. (Commonly used botanical terms are explained in the Glossary and also appear in labeled drawings.)

Leaves

Leaves can be an important aid in identifying a wildflower. Each leaf has two parts, a stalk (petiole) and a blade. A leaf may be simple, with the blade all in one piece, or it may be compound. In a compound leaf the blade is composed of separate parts, the leaflets, either arranged along a central stalk (pinnately compound), or attached at the end of a stalk, spreading like the fingers of a hand (palmately compound). The edges of leaves and leaflets may be smooth, toothed, or more or less deeply lobed.

There are several common arrangements of leaves on plants. In the most common arrangement, called alternate, each leaf is attached at a different level on the stem. If two leaves are attached at one level but on opposite sides of the stem, they are said to be opposite. If three or more are attached in a ring, at one level and equally spaced, the leaves are described as whorled. Leaves that appear at ground level are called basal; if there are many, they form a basal rosette. In the text, if the leaf arrangement is not mentioned, you may assume it is alternate.

Classification and Names

Common names of plants are highly variable and often differ from one region to the next. A geographically widespread plant may have several common names or, if well known, perhaps just one, whereas a plant that has a more restricted distribution may have no common name at all. In addition, the same name often refers to more than one species, which may or may not resemble one another. Each plant, however, has only one scientific name. In the mid–18th century, the great Swedish botanist Carl von Linné (Carolus Linnaeus) developed the scientific nomenclature in use today. The names are structured in Latin, and many have Greek roots. The first part of the scientific name is the genus (plural, genera); it is always capitalized and is usually assigned to a number of species with many characteristics in common. The second part is the species name; it is not capitalized and often tells something about the particular plant, such as its flower color, size, where it grows, or whom its name honors. The two parts together form the plant's scientific name, which is used uniformly around the world. (In some cases, there is debate among authorities about which genus certain species belong to.) Just as species may be grouped in genera according to shared characteristics, so genera may be grouped in larger aggregations called families.

Parts of a Leaf

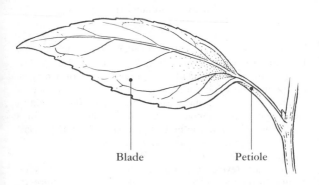

Blade Petiole

Leaf Margins

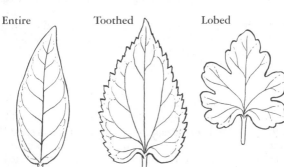

Entire Toothed Lobed

Leaf Shapes

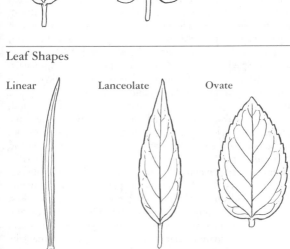

Linear Lanceolate Ovate

Leaf Arrangements

Simple Leaves

Opposite   Basal   Alternate

Whorled   Clasping   Perfoliate

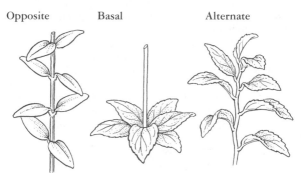
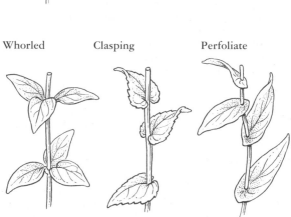

Compound Leaves

Palmate   Once Pinnate   Twice Pinnate

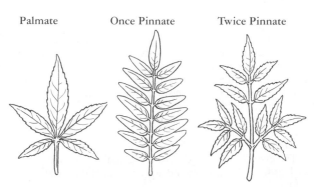

The scientific names in this book are based primarily on modern regional sources, books that compile, describe, and often illustrate all the plants that grow naturally within a defined geographic region.

Occasionally we use the terms subspecies and variety, which are formal categories below the species level. These subdivisions mean about the same thing biologically; the categories are maintained for historical and practical purposes. Both terms refer to geographic populations of a given species that differ somewhat from one another genetically, but not enough to warrant the designation of each as a separate species.

We also sometimes use informal terms such as race, phase, form, and variant, which are descriptive of population structure or geographic variation and relate to differences that are not represented in formal classification. Race refers to a population of a given species that differs genetically from other populations of the same species. Phase, a very casual term, signifies some alternate condition in a plant's appearance (for example, a yellow-flowered individual in a normally orange-flowered species). The terms form and variant, both used here nontechnically, simply refer to the appearance of an individual plant or of a particular population that may differ from that of another individual plant or population of the same species.

Wildflower Descriptions

The text contains descriptions of each wildflower species shown in the color plates. The accounts are arranged alphabetically by scientific name, first by family, then by genus within each family, and finally, by species within each genus. This arrangement tends to put closely related species near one another, thus allowing for easy comparison of similar species. The following details are given in each of the species accounts:

Description

The entry for each species begins with a statement describing the conspicuous features of the plant, so that the user of this guide can quickly decide whether he or she is on the right track. Detailed information then follows about the plant's flowers, leaves (in the case of cacti, stems and spines), and fruit (if applicable). As an additional aid, diagnostic features of the plant are italicized.

Height

The overall height of the plant is given, or, in some cases, such as for trailing vines and aquatic plants, the length.

Flowering

Each entry includes the plant's blooming period, which may vary considerably depending on latitude, elevation, and climatic conditions. The period given applies to the entire geographic range; in one locality, the plant may flower for only a portion of the time stated in the text. Plants that occur in southern locations tend to bloom earlier than those growing in more northerly sites; likewise, plants found at low elevations tend to bloom earlier than those at higher altitudes.

Habitat

Knowing the general environment in which a plant occurs is often very helpful in its identification, for most plants grow only in certain situations. This section may also mention commonly associated trees or shrubs, such as Ponderosa Pine, piñon (a bushy pine), juniper (also called "cedar" in parts of the West), Creosote Bush, and sagebrush; it helps to become familiar with these to fully understand some habitat descriptions.

Range

The listing of geographic range begins as far as practical in the northwestern part of the plant's range and proceeds from north to south, then west to east. (When the range is given as "Throughout," this indicates that the plant occurs across the West, as defined in "Geographic Scope," above.)

Comments

These notes give additional items of interest about the plant, such as whether it is native to North America or was introduced from Europe or Asia, other related or similar species, the origin of the plant's names, its uses, and various legend and lore. This may include mention that a certain plant or some part of it is poisonous. However, because this book is not intended as a guide to edible plants, information about toxicity is not always given, and some plants that are poisonous may not be noted as such. Thus, we must urge that you never ingest any part of a wild plant unless you are absolutely certain of its identification and know that you are not allergic or otherwise sensitive to it.

This section may also include information as to whether the plant or its relatives are rare and/or endangered. Populations of many native wildflowers have been depleted because of land development, lumbering, farming, intensive grazing, and, in a few instances, by private and commercial collecting. By 1973, humankind's impact on the environment had become so severe that Congress passed, and has since repeatedly renewed, the Endangered Species Act to give some protection to plants and other organisms faced with extinction. State laws, which vary widely, offer additional protection for many plants and are often strictly enforced. Therefore, the reader is advised to check the laws of his or her state carefully before removing any plant from the environment. However, in the wide open spaces of the West, these laws are often difficult—if not impossible—to enforce. Conscience is the best guide if we are to save our rarest wildflowers from extinction.

How to Identify a Flower

First determine which of the major color groups the flower of the plant you are observing belongs to. (To make it easy to locate each color group, and the flower shapes within them, thumb tabs showing the color and shape are provided within the color plate section.) Then turn to that color section and look for a photograph that matches the flower; if you do not find it there, check the color groups into which the flower may intergrade (see "Arrangement by Color," above).

The color sections are further divided into subgroups according to flower or flower cluster shape and fruit. Flowers are complicated structures and not every flower will fit precisely into any one grouping; therefore, if you fail to find your flower in one likely subgroup, try another subgroup in the same color category. The subgroups are:

Radially Symmetrical Flowers

These flowers are mostly borne separately among or above the foliage; when viewed face on (looking into the center of the flower), they have the symmetry of a wheel. The individual flower parts are equal in size and radiate out from the center, and the flower can be divided into equal halves along several lines running through the center.

Daisy- and Dandelion-like Flowers

A daisy-like flower appears to be a single radially symmetrical flower but is actually composed of many tiny flowers forming a button-like, central disk from which radiate numerous showy, petal-like flowers. A dandelion-like flower is similarly constructed but lacks the button-like center; here the central flowers are surrounded by larger petal-like flowers.

Bilaterally Symmetrical Flowers

These flowers are mostly borne separately among or above the foliage; when viewed face on (looking into the center of the flower), one vertical half forms the mirror image of the other, and there is only one dividing line that gives equal halves. Most often the flower parts on the lower side of the

flower are longer than those on the upper, but exceptio\
occur.

Elongated Clusters
For the most part these flowers are held above the foliage
and are arranged loosely or tightly in an elongated mass on
a central stalk. Even if among the foliage, the central stalk
and the flower cluster are apparent. Often the cluster is very
tight, the individual flowers packed together and sometimes almost individually indistinguishable. Flowers may
be radially or bilaterally symmetrical.

Rounded Clusters
For the most part, these flowers are held above the foliage
and are arranged loosely or tightly in a rounded (sometimes
flat-topped) mass atop a main stalk. Even if among the
foliage, the main stalk and the flower cluster are apparent.
When the cluster is loose, the slender stalks of the individual
flowers all attach at a common point, or nearly so, atop the
main stalk. Often the cluster is very tight, the individual
flowers packed together and sometimes almost individually
indistinguishable. Flowers may be radially or bilaterally
symmetrical.

Fruit
Some plants are spectacular when in fruit, during which
time the dry or fleshy, mature, seed-bearing portion of the
flower is evident.

If the photograph and the plant you have found seem to
match, read the caption beneath the picture and refer to the
text description to confirm your identification.

An inexpensive hand lens is useful in studying wildflowers, and will also expand your appreciation of the
minute structure and beauty of the individual flower parts.

HOW TO USE THIS GUIDE

Example 1: Red Flower in Woodland
You have found a plant with bright red, tubular, radially
symmetrical flowers in rounded clusters.

Turn to the color plates labeled Red Rounded Clusters
and look for a flower with the form described. You note several flowers of this type, all grouped together, and Firecracker Flower seems to be the closest match. The
caption under the photograph gives information about the
plant height and the size of the flower, as well as the page
number of the text description.

You check the text description and find that your plant matches Firecracker Flower (*Dichelostemma ida-maia*), which is a woodland plant.

Example 2: Blue-violet Flower in Grassland

You have found a plant in open grassland with blue-violet flowers in a rounded cluster atop a long leafless stalk with a few grass-like leaves at the base.

Turn to the color plates labeled Purple Rounded Clusters. You think your plant looks like the photograph of Ookow (*Dichelostemma congestum*).

Turning to the description in the text, you find it does resemble Ookow, but you note that your flower has flattened scales with round ends between the stamens. From reading the Comments section at the end of the text description you discover that your plant is the related species Roundtooth Ookow (*D. multiflorum*).

Example 3: Green Fruit Along a Roadside

You have found a round green fruit with spiny projections growing on a leafy weed along a roadside.

Turn to the color plates labeled Green Fruit. Among the four photographs in this section, only one resembles your specimen: Buffalo Bur (*Solanum rostratum*).

Upon reading the species description, you find that another plant, Melonleaf Nightshade (*S. citrullifolium*), also grows in the same habitat. Since the flowers on the plant you are observing are blue-violet, not yellow (as are those of Buffalo Bur), you correctly identify your specimen as Melonleaf Nightshade.

PART I
COLOR PLATES

KEY TO THE COLOR PLATES

The color plates on the following pages are divided into nine color groups (see "Arrangement by Color" on page 19 of the Introduction for explanation):

Green
White
Yellow
Orange
Brown
Red
Pink
Purple
Blue

Within the color groups, the flowers are further divided by shape and form into up to five subgroups:

Radially Symmetrical Flowers
Daisy- and Dandelion-like Flowers
Bilaterally Symmetrical Flowers
Elongated Clusters
Rounded Clusters

Thumb Tabs
Each subgroup is indicated by a colored symbol on a thumb tab at the left edge of each double-page of plates. The red and green color groups have an additional thumb tab for fruit.

Symbol	Subgroup

Radially Symmetrical Flowers
Viewed face-on, flowers have a wheel-like symmetry, with individual parts radiating from center, so that they can be divided into equal halves along several lines. Usually 4–5 petals, occasionally 3 or 6.

Daisy- and Dandelion-like Flowers
Flower head with a button-like center and many radiating, strap-like petals (actually ray flowers), or with many ray flowers and no button-like center.

Bilaterally Symmetrical Flowers
Viewed face-on, flowers have a bilateral symmetry: One half forms mirror image of other, so that they can be divided into equal halves only along one line through the center. Usually 4–5 petals or lobes, sometimes 3 or 6.

Elongated Clusters
Elongated masses of flowers arranged along a central stalk. Cluster is often very dense, with individual flowers packed tightly together. Individual flowers may be radially or bilaterally symmetrical.

Rounded Clusters
Rounded masses of flowers atop a central stalk. Cluster is often so dense that individual flowers, which may be radially or bilaterally symmetrical, are almost indistinguishable.

Fruit
The dried or fleshy, seed-bearing part of the flower.

Examples

Poppy

Phlox

Trillium

Daisy

Desert Dandelion

Dandelion

Pea

Dayflower

Violet

Goldenrod

Larkspur

Purple Loosestrife

Milkweed

Wild Carrot

Field Mint

Buffalo Bur

Western Redbud

Bittersweet Berries

How to Read the Captions Under the Plates

Example:
454   Western Sea Purslane, 1–2′, *w.* ½″, *p. 319*
1—   2 ————————— 3 — 4— 5 ——

w. (width)	Refers to average *width* of the flower. In sunflowers and clovers it is the width of the entire flower head.
l. (length)	Refers to average *length* of the flower. Given for some tubular and nodding or hanging flowers as well as some extremely recurved flowers where the length of the flower in profile is its most noticeable dimension. In sunflowers and clovers it is the length of the entire flower head.
cw. (cluster width)	Refers to range of *cluster width*. Given for broad clusters, usually umbels, compound umbels, corymbs, and cymes.
cl. (cluster length)	Refers to range of *cluster length*. Given for elongated clusters, usually spikes, racemes, and panicles.

1 Plate number.
2 Common name of plant.
3 Height of typical mature plant. Usually a range is given; if only one figure is shown, it refers to maximum height.
4 Dimensions of the flower (see chart below left).
5 Page number of species description.

Sunflower   Lily   Bunchberry

Coneflower   Orchid (lip)   Fairybell

Buckwheat   Wild Carrot   Fairy Duster

Smartweed   Corn Lily   White Sweet Clover

1   Green Passionflower, *vine, w.* ¾", *p. 664*

2   Teddybear Cholla, 3–9', *w.* 1–1½", *p. 447*

3 Green Pitaya, 1–10″, *w.* ¾–1″, *p. 443*

4 California Pitcher Plant, 3′, *l.* 2½″, *p. 737*

5   Early Coral Root, 3–12″, *l.* ¼″, *p. 641*

6   Alaska Rein Orchid, 8–31″, *l.* ⅛″, *p. 647*

7 Broad-leaved Twayblade, 2–14″, *l.* ½″, *p. 645*

8 Green False Hellebore, 2–7′, *w.* ½–¾″, *p. 600*

9   Leafy Spurge, 8–36″, *w.* ⅛″, *p. 494*

10   Five-point Bishop's Cap, 4–16″, *w.* ¼″, *p. 743*

11   Sotol, 6–17′, *cl.* 5–8′, *p. 326*

Green Fruit

13   Flatpod, 1–5″, *w.* ⅛″, *p.* 429

14   Spectacle Pod, 2′, *cw.* 1½–2½″, *p.* 425

15   Bladderpod, 2–8′, *w.* 1″, *p. 457*

16   Buffalo Bur, 16–31″, *w.* ¾–1″, *p. 792*

17 Tufted Phlox, 2–6″, *l.* ¼–½″, *p. 675*

18 Nuttall's Linanthus, 1′, *w.* ½″, *p. 674*

19 Coast Boykinia, 6–24″, *w.* ¼″, *p.* 739

21   Beautiful Sandwort, 2–12″, *w.* ½″, *p. 461*

22   Meadow Chickweed, 2–20″, *w.* 1″, *p. 462*

24   Broad-leaved Claytonia, 4–16″, *l.* ½″, *p. 685*

25   Bladder Campion, 3′, *w.* ½″, *p. 467*

27   **Rattlesnake Weed,** *creeper, w.* ⅛″, *p. 493*

28   **Quail Plant,** *creeper, w.* ¼–⅜″, *p. 418*

29 Popcorn Flower, 6–20″, *w.* ¼″, *p. 421*

30 Lance-leaved Draba, 2–10″, *cw.* ¾–1″, *p. 426*

31   Western Serviceberry, 4–30′, *w.* 1–2″, *p.* 723

32   Dwarf Bramble, 4″, *w.* ½″, *p.* 734

33   Dwarf Hesperochiron, 1–2″, *w.* ½–1¼″, *p.* 542

34 White Mountain Avens, *creeper*, w. 1", p. 725

35 Bunchberry, 2–8", *w. 4"*, p. 476

37   Beach Strawberry, *creeper, w.* ¾″, *p.* 726

38   Apache Plume, 7′, *w.* 1–1½″, *p.* 725

39   Mock Orange, 4–10′, *w.* ¾–1¼″, *p.* 540

40 Velvety Nerisyrenia, 8–24″, *w.* ¾″, *p. 432*

41 Round-leaved Sundew, 10″, *w.* ⅜″, *p. 485*

42 Crystalline Ice Plant, *creeper, w.* 1″, *p. 331*

43 Matilija Poppy, 3–8′, *w.* 4–7″, *p. 662*

44 Great Desert Poppy, 8–20″, *w.* 2–3″, *p. 656*

45 Prickly Poppy, 4′, *w.* 3″, *p.* 657

46 Birdcage Evening Primrose, 2–12″, *w.* 1½–3″, *p.* 636

47 Wood Nymph, 2–6″, *w.* ¾″, *p.* 699

49 Marsh Marigold, 1–8″, *w.* ½–1¼″, *p. 708*

50 Water Buttercup, *aquatic, w.* ½–¾″, *p. 718*

51 Desert Anemone, 4–16″, *w.* 1–1½″, *p.* 704

52 White Globeflower, 4–20″, *w.* 1–1½″, *p.* 720

53 Western Pasque Flower, 8–24", *w.* 1¼–2", *p. 716*

55 Elegant Cat's Ears, *2–8″, w. 1″, p. 577*

56 Fringed Water Plantain, *aquatic, w. ¾″, p. 333*

58 Sego Lily, 6–18″, *w.* 1–2″, *p.* 579

59 Fringed Grass-of-Parnassus, 6–20″, *w.* 1″, *p.* 744

61   Sweet-scented Heliotrope, 4–16″, *w.* ½–1″, *p.* 417

62   Cascade Lily, 2–7′, *w.* 3–4″, *p.* 591

63 Queen's Cup, 2½–6″, *w.* 1–1½″, *p. 582*

64 Wavy-leaved Soap Plant, 2–10′, *w.* 1–1½″, *p. 580*

65 Wartberry Fairybell, 1–2', *l.* ⅜–⅝", *p.* 584

66 Avalanche Lily, 6–10", *w.* 2½", *p.* 586

67   Star Lily, 8″, *w.* 1¼″, *p.* 589

68   Alpine Lily, 2–6″, *w.* ¾″, *p.* 592

69 Desert Lily, 1–6′, *l.* 2½″, *p.* 589

70 Night-blooming Cereus, 1–3′, *w.* 2–3″, *p.* 451

71 Southwestern Thorn Apple, 5′, *l.* 6″, *p. 786*

72 Bindweed, 1–3′, *w.* 1″, *p. 472*

73 White Heather, 2–12″, *l.* ¼″, *p. 488*

74 White Globe Lily, 1–2′, *l.* 1″, *p. 575*

75 White Rhododendron, 3–7′, *w.* ½–¾″, *p. 491*

76   Miner's Lettuce, 1–14″, *w.* ⅛–¼″, *p.* 687

77   Western Spring Beauty, 2–10″, *w.* ¼–¾″, *p.* 686

78   White Shooting Star, 6–16″, *l.* 1″, *p.* 693

79 Sweet Four O'Clock, 1½–5′, *l. 3–7″, p. 623*

80 Angel Trumpets, *creeper, l. 3½–6½″, p. 621*

81 Desert Tobacco, 1–3′, *l. ½–¾″, p. 788*

82   Indian Pipe, 2–10″, *l.* ¾″, *p. 616*

83   Green-flowered Macromeria, 3′, *l.* 1½″, *p. 420*

84   Coville's Columbine, 8–14″, *w.* 1½″, *p. 708*

85 English Daisy, 2–8″, *w.* 1″, *p.* 359

86 White-rayed Mule's Ears, 6–31″, *w.* 2½–5″, *p.* 407

87 Blackfoot Daisy, 6–20″, *w.* 1″, *p.* 389

88 Oxeye Daisy, 8–31″, *w. 3″*, *p. 383*

89 Desert Star, 1–2″, *w. ¾″*, *p. 390*

91   Yerba Mansa, 1′, *cl.* 1–2″, *p. 738*

92   Desert Chicory, 6–20″, *w.* 1–1½″, *p. 393*

93   Stemless Daisy, 1–2″, *w.* 1–2″, *p. 402*

94 Engelmann Aster, 1½–5′, *w.* 1½–2½″, *p. 356*

95 Spreading Fleabane, 4–28″, *w.* 1″, *p. 371*

97   Canada Violet, 4–16″, *w.* 1″, *p.* 799

98   Southwestern Ringstem, 4′, *l.* 1¼–1½″, *p.* 622

99　Naked Broomrape, 1¼–4″, *l.* 1″, *p. 652*

101   Grass-leaved Sagittaria, *aquatic, w. ½", p. 334*

102   Arrowhead, *aquatic, w. ¾–1½", p. 335*

103 Elegant Camas, 6–28″, *w.* ¾″, *p. 601*

105 Spectacle Pod, 2′, *cw.* 1½–2½″, *p. 425*

106 Bedstraw, 8–31″, *cw.* 1–3″, *p. 736*

107   False Mitrewort, 8–16″, *cl.* 3–8″, *p. 750*

109   Partridge Foot, 2–6″, *cl.* 1–2″, *p. 730*

110   Enchanter's Nightshade, 4–20″, *w.* ⅛″, *p. 631*

111 Lonely Lily, 6–12″, *w.* ¾–1″, *p.* 585

113 Hot Rock Penstemon, 8–24", *l.* ½–¾", *p.* 774

114 White Snapdragon, 4½', *l.* ½", *p.* 751

115 Plains Larkspur, 5′, *w.* 1″, *p. 712*

116 Northern Inside-out Flower, 6–20″, *l.* ¼″, *p. 411*

117 California Lady's Slipper, 1–4′, *l.* ¾″, *p.* 642

118 Elegant Rein Orchid, 8–16″, *l.* ⅜″, *p.* 646

120   Bog Rein Orchid, 6–52″, *l.* ⅜″, *p. 648*

121   Hooded Ladies' Tresses, 4–24″, *l.* ⅜–½″, *p. 649*

White Elongated Clusters

123   Blue Yucca, 5′, *cl.* 3′, *p. 327*

124   Our Lord's Candle, 4–11′, *cl.* 3–9′, *p. 328*

125 Mojave Yucca, 4–15′, *l.* 1¼–2½″, *p. 328*

127   **Fringe Cups,** 31″, *w.* ½″, *p. 749*

128   **White Milkwort,** 8–14″, *cl.* ¾–3″, *p. 678*

129 Case's Fitweed, 2–7′, *l.* ¾–1″, *p. 528*

130 White Locoweed, 3–16″, *l.* ¾–1″, *p. 518*

131   White Sweet Clover, 2–10′, *l.* ¼″, *p. 516*

132   Saltmarsh Clubflower, 8–16″, *l.* ¾″, *p. 758*

133   Parry's Nolina, 10′, *cl. 2′, p. 327*

135   Rocky Mountain Rockmat, 3″, *cw.* ¾–1¼″, *p.* 730

136   English Plantain, 6–24″, *cl.* ¾–3″, *p.* 665

137   Western Bistort, 8–28″, *cl.* 1–2″, *p.* 683

138 Vanilla Leaf, 10–20″, *cl.* 1–2″, *p. 409*

139 White Prairie Clover, 1–2′, *cl.* 2½″, *p. 503*

140 Bear Grass, 5′, *cl.* 4–24″, *p. 601*

141   **False Lily-of-the-valley,** 6–14", *cl.* 1–2", *p. 593*

142   **False Solomon's Seal,** 1–3', *cl.* 1–8", *p. 594*

144   Western Goatsbeard, 3–7′, *w.* ⅛″, *p. 723*

145   Salal, 4–48″, *l.* ⅜″, *p. 488*

147   Cow Parsnip, 10′, *cw.* 1′, *p. 340*

149 Wild Carrot, 1–4′, *cw.* 6″, *p. 338*

150 Yarrow, 12–39″, *cw.* 2–5″, *p. 352*

151 Snowball, *4–20″, cw. 1–3″, p. 619*

152 Beach Silvertop, *2½″, cw. 3–4″, p. 340*

153 Pearly Everlasting, 8–36″, *l.* ¼″, *p. 354*

154 Ranger's Button, 1½–7′, *cw.* 4″, *p. 342*

155 Ballhead Gilia, 8–12″, *l.* ¼″, *p. 669*

156 Climbing Milkweed, *vine, cw.* 4″, *p. 350*

157 White-stemmed Milkweed, 3–10′, *cw.* 2″, *p. 347*

159   Buckbean, *aquatic, w. ½", p. 615*

160   Downy-fruited Valerian, *4–24", l. ¼", p. 794*

161   Water Plantain, *aquatic, w. ¼–½", p. 333*

162   Sierran Mountain Misery, 8–24″, *w.* ¼″, *p. 724*

163   Mexican Thistle, 8–24″, *cw.* ¼–⅜″, *p. 338*

164   White Brodiaea, 10–28″, *w.* ½″, *p. 598*

165   Shepherd's Purse, 6–16″, *w.* ⅛″, *p. 423*

166   Western Peppergrass, 16″, *cw.* 1–1½″, *p. 430*

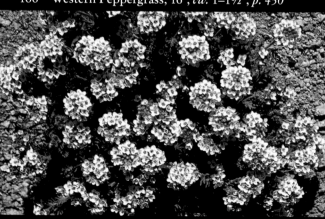

167   Western Smelowskia, 2–8″, *cw.* 1–1½″, *p. 437*

168 Hoary Cress, 8–20″, *cw.* 1–1½″, *p. 424*

169 Wild Candytuft, 1¼–16″, *cw.* ¾–1¼″, *p. 438*

171   Northern Fairy Candelabra, 1–10″, *w.* ⅛″, *p. 691*

172   Bouncing Bet, 1–3′, *w.* 1″, *p. 464*

173   White Virgin's Bower, *vine, w.* ¾″, *p. 710*

174 Watercress, *creeper, cw.* 1–1½", *p. 434*

175 Trapper's Tea, 2–7', *w.* ½", *p. 490*

177　Alpine Saxifrage, 1–3″, *cw.* 1–2″, *p. 748*

178　Diamondleaf Saxifrage, 2–12″, *cw.* ¾″, *p. 748*

179　Leatherleaf Saxifrage, 2–10″, *cw.* ¾–1″, *p. 742*

180   Yerba de Selva, *creeper, cw.* ½–1″, *p. 541*

181   Yerba Buena, *creeper, l.* ¼″, *p. 566*

182   Baneberry, 1–3′, *cl.* 2–4″, *p. 703*

183   Freckled Milkvetch, 4–16″, *l.* ³⁄₈–¾″, *p. 498*

184   White Clover, *creeper, w.* ½″, *p. 523*

185 Clammyweed, 4–31″, *cw.* 1½–2½″, *p.* 457

186 Cotton Grass, 8–40″, *cw.* 2–3″, *p.* 483

187 Sticky Cinquefoil, 20″, *w.* ½–¾″, *p.* 732

188 Shrubby Cinquefoil, 6–36″, *w.* 1″, *p.* 732

189   Common Silverweed, *creeper, w. ¾″, p. 731*

190   Bigleaf Avens, 3′, *w. ½″, p. 727*

191 Rough Menodora, 5–14″, *w.* ½–¾″, *p.* 628

192 Rain Lily, 9″, *l.* ¾–1″, *p.* 336

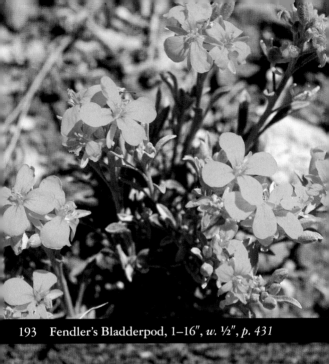

193 Fendler's Bladderpod, 1–16″, *w. ½″, p. 431*

195 Beach Primrose, *creeper, w. ½–1¼", p. 629*

196 Hooker's Evening Primrose, *2–3', w. 2–3", p. 637*

197   Fringed Loosestrife, 1–4′, *w.* ¾″, *p.* 695

198   Flannel Bush, 5–30′, *w.* 1½–2½″, *p.* 793

199   Klamath Weed, *1–3′, w. 1″, p. 550*

200   Tinker's Penny, *creeper, w. ¼″, p. 549*

201   Common Purslane, *creeper, w. ¼″, p. 688*

202 Sagebrush Buttercup, 2–8″, *w.* ¾–1¼″, *p. 719*

203 Subalpine Buttercup, 2–10″, *w.* ¾–1½″, *p. 718*

205 White-bracted Stickleaf, 6–12″, *l.* 1–1¼″, *p. 606*

206 Desert Rock Nettle, 1–2′, *w.* 1–2″, *p. 605*

207 Peak Rushrose, 8–12″, *w.* 1″, *p. 468*

208   Alpine Poppy, 2–6″, *w.* ¾–1½″, *p. 661*

209   Tree Poppy, 4–20′, *w.* 1–2½″, *p. 658*

210   Cream Cup, 4–12″, *w.* ½–1″, *p. 662*

211 **Plains Prickly Pear**, 3–6″, *w.* 2–3″, *p.* 449

213 California Barrel Cactus, 3–10′, *w.* 1½–2½″, *p. 444*

214 Great Plains Paintbrush, 4–12″, *l.* 1¼–2½″, *p. 756*

215   Hottentot Fig, *creeper, w. 3–4″, p. 330*

216   Fragrant Water Lily, *aquatic, w. 3–6″, p. 626*

217　Blazing Star, 1–3′, *w.* 2–5″, *p. 606*

218　Douglas's Meadow Foam, 4–16″, *w.* ¾″, *p. 602*

219   Desert Rosemallow, 4′, *w.* 1–2″, *p.* 609

220   Yellow Mariposa Lily, 8–24″, *w.* 1–1½″, *p.* 578

221   Chihuahua Flax, 4–20″, *w.* ¾″, *p.* 604

222   Flower-of-an-hour, 1–2′, *w.* 1½″, *p.* 610

223   Desert Gold, 2–4″, *w.* ¼–½″, *p.* 672

225 Dingy Chamaesaracha, *creeper, w. ½", p.* 786

226 Ivyleaf Groundcherry, *4–10", w. ½", p.* 789

227   Yellow Willow Herb, 8–28″, *w.* 1–1½″, *p. 634*

228   Buffalo Gourd, *creeper, w.* 2–3″, *p. 482*

229 Fringed Gromwell, 2–12″, *w.* ½–1¼″, *p. 418*

230 Melon Loco, *creeper, w.* 1½″, *p. 481*

231   Tansy-leaved Evening Primrose, *1–4″, w. 1″, p. 630*

232   Indian Pond Lily, *aquatic, w. 2½–4″, p. 626*

233   Fiddleneck, *1–3′, w. ⅛–⅜″, p. 413*

234 Whispering Bells, 6–20″, *l. ½″, p. 542*

235 Yellow Bell, 4–12″, *l. ½–1″, p. 588*

237 Tiger Lily, 2–4′, w. 2–3″, p. 590

238 Yellow Fawn Lily, 6–12″, l. 2″, p. 585

239   Golden Columbine, 1–4′, *w.* 1½–3″, *p. 705*

240   Yellow Globe Lily, 8–20″, *l.* 1″, *p. 576*

241 Mexican Hat, 1–4′, *l.* 1–3″, *p.* 394

242 Cut-leaved Coneflower, 2–7′, *w.* 3–6″, *p.* 395

243 Threadleaf Groundsel, 1–3', *w. 1¼", p. 396*

245 Goldfields, 4–10″, *w.* ¾–1″, *p. 382*

246 Greeneyes, 1–4′, *w.* 1½″, *p. 360*

247   Common Sunflower, 2–13′, *w.* 3–5″, *p.* 378

248   Arrowleaf Balsam Root, 8–31″, *w.* 4–5″, *p.* 358

249   Golden Aster, 8–20″, *w.* 1″, *p.* 379

250   Mule's Ears, 12–31″, *w.* 3–5″, *p.* 406

251   Heartleaf Arnica, 4–24″, *w.* 2–3½″, *p. 355*

252   Five-needle Fetid Marigold, 4–8″, *w.* ¼–½″, *p. 401*

253 Stemless Golden Weed, ½–6″, *w.* 1½″, *p. 399*

255 Yellow Spiny Daisy, 6–14″, *w.* 1″, *p. 385*

257   Desert Sunflower, 1–3′, *w. 2″, p. 376*

258   Sunray, 6–18″, *w. 4″, p. 370*

259   Chinchweed, 2–8″, *w. ½″, p. 391*

260 Golden Yarrow, 4–24″, *w.* 2½″, *p.* 373

261 Woolly Daisy, ½–4″, *w.* ¼″, *p.* 374

262 Cowpen Daisy, 4–60″, *w.* 1½–2″, *p.* 405

263   Giant Coreopsis, 1–10′, w. 3″, p. 367

264   Brittlebush, 3–5′, w. 2–3″, p. 369

266 Rosin Weed, 1–4′, *w.* 1″, *p. 361*

267 Little Golden Zinnia, 3–9″, *w.* 1–1½″, *p. 408*

269   Desert Marigold, 12–20″, *w.* 1½–2″, *p. 358*

270   Alpine Gold, 6–14″, *w.* 2–3½″, *p. 380*

271 Stemless Hymenoxys, 3–12″, *w.* 1–2″, *p. 381*

273   Curlycup Gumweed, 1–3′, *w.* 1½″, *p.* 376

274   Snakehead, 4–20″, *w.* 1–1½″, *p.* 387

275   Desert Dandelion, 6–14″, *w.* 1–1½″, *p.* 388

276   Common Dandelion, 2–20″, *w.* ¾–1½″, *p. 400*

277   Pale Agoseris, 4–28″, *w.* ½–1¼″, *p. 353*

279 Douglas's Violet, 2–6″, *w.* ½–¾″, *p. 800*

280 Stream Violet, 2–12″, *w.* ½–¾″, *p. 801*

281 Goosefoot Violet, 2–6″, *w.* ½–¾″, *p. 802*

282   Redwood Violet, *creeper, w.* ½″, *p. 803*

283   Yellow Wood Violet, 4–14″, *w.* ¾–1″, *p. 801*

284   Twinleaf, 4–16″, *w.* ½″, *p. 500*

285   Bladderpod, 2–8′, *w.* 1″, *p. 457*

286   Blue Palo Verde, 33′, *w.* ¾″, *p. 500*

287   Seep-spring Monkeyflower, 3', *l.* ½–1½", *p.* 765

288   Yellow Twining Snapdragon, *vine, l.* ½", *p.* 752

289   Devil's Claw, *creeper, l.* 1–1½", *p. 614*

291   Dwarf Lousewort, 4″, l. ¾″, p. 771

293   Hill Lotus, *creeper, l. ¼", p. 510*

295 Scotch Broom, 10′, *l.* ¾″, *p. 502*

296 Common Bladderwort, *aquatic, l.* ½–¾″, *p. 571*

297 Large-flowered Brickelbush, 1–3′, *l.* ⅜–½″, *p. 360*

298 Western Wallflower, 6–36″, *w.* ¾″, *p. 427*

299 Menzies's Wallflower, 1–8″, *w.* ½–¾″, *p. 429*

301 Moth Mullein, 1–5′, *w.* 1″, *p.* 783

303   Mountain Jewel Flower, 8–39″, *l.* ½″, *p. 438*

305 Butter-and-eggs, 4″, *l.* 1–1½″, *p.* 762

306 Tree Lupine, 2–9′, *l.* ½″, *p.* 512

308 Yellow Rattle, 6–31″, *l.* ½″, *p. 780*

309 Golden Smoke, 4–24″, *l.* ½–¾″, *p. 527*

311   Hog Potato, 4–12″, *w.* ¾″, *p.* 507

313   Yellow Owl's Clover, 4–16″, *l.* ½″, *p.* 768

315 Golden Ear-drops, 1½–5′, *l.* ½″, *p. 528*

316 Poker Heuchera, 6–36″, *cl.* 1–4″, *p. 741*

318 Yellow Skunk Cabbage, 12–20″, *l.* 8″, *p. 344*

319 Nodding Groundsel, 1–3′, *w.* ½″, *p. 395*

321 Meadow Goldenrod, 1–5′, *l.* ⅛″, *p.* 397

323 Lecheguilla, 7–10′, *cl.* ¾–1½″, *p. 325*

325 Golden Alexanders, 8–24", *cw. 2½", p. 342*

327   Spring Gold, 4–20″, *cw.* 2–4″, *p. 341*

329 Snakeweed, 6–36″, *l.* ¼″, *p.* 377

331 Golden-eyed Grass, 8–24″, *w.* ½–¾″, *p.* 556

333   Dune Tansy, 8–24″, *w.* ½″, *p. 400*

334   Yellow Head, 2–8″, *w.* ½″, *p. 404*

336   Silvery Luina, 6–16″, *l.* ⅜″, *p. 384*

337   Silvercrown Luina, 1–3′, *cl.* ½–¾″, *p. 361*

338   Yellow Star Thistle, 4–30″, *w.* ½–⅝″, *p. 364*

339   Hedge Mustard, 1–3′, *cw.* ½–1″, *p. 436*

340   Charlock, 1–3′, *cw.* 1–2″, *p. 435*

341   Alpine Wallflower, 2–8″, *w.* ½–¾″, *p. 428*

342 Wayside Gromwell, 8–24″, *w.* ¼–½″, *p.* 419

343 Yellow Bee Plant, 1½–5′, *cw.* 1–2″, *p.* 455

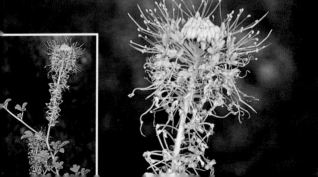

345   **Canyon Dudleya**, *4–8", l. ½", p. 478*

346   **Powdery Dudleya**, *4–14", w. ⅜", p. 479*

348   Turtleback, 2–5″, *w.* ¼″, *p. 392*

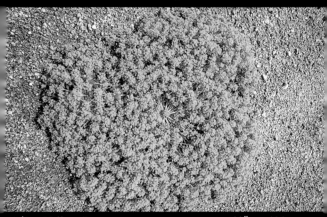

349   Yellow Peppergrass, *creeper, cw.* 1–1½″, *p. 430*

350   Rydberg Twinpod, 1¼–8″, *w.* ¾–½″, *p. 433*

351   Golden Stars, 6–24″, *w.* ½–1″, *p.* 574

352   Pretty Face, 4–18″, *w.* ¾″, *p.* 599

353   Gordon's Ivesia, 8″, *cw.* ½–¾″, *p.* 729

354 Desert Primrose, 1–30″, w. ¼–1½″, p. 629

355 Yellow Cryptantha, 3–10″, w. ⅜″, p. 414

356 Spotted Saxifrage, 2–6″, w. ⅜″, p. 745

357 Oregon Grape, *4–8″, w. ½″, p. 410*

358 Yellow Sand Verbena, *creeper, cw. 1–2″, p. 619*

359 Northern Buckwheat, *4–20″, cw. 1–4″, p. 679*

360   Tufted Loosestrife, 8–31″, *l.* ¼″, *p.* 696

361   Desert Trumpet, 8–40″, *cw.* ¼–½″, *p.* 680

362   Bigleaf Trefoil, ⅛–5″, *p.* 508

363   Winged Dock, *6–20″, l. ½–1½″, p. 683*

364   Scarlet Pimpernel, *creeper, w. ¼″, p. 691*

365   Flame Flower, *6–14″, w. 1″, p. 689*

366 Scarlet Globemallow, 20″, *w. 1–1¼″, p. 612*

367 Coulter's Globemallow, 8–60″, *w. ¾–1″, p. 613*

368 Fire Poppy, 1–2′, *w. 1″, p. 660*

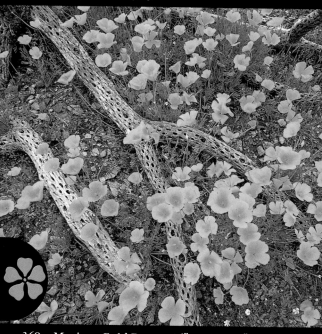

369   Mexican Gold Poppy, 16″, *w.* ¾–1½″, *p.* 659

370   California Poppy, 8–24″, *w.* 1–2″, *p.* 659

371 Desert Poppy, *creeper, w. 2", p. 805*

372 Desert Mariposa Lily, *4–20", w. 1–2", p. 577*

373   Orange Agoseris, *4–24″, w. 1″, p. 353*

374   Butterfly Weed, *3′, cw. 3″, p. 349*

375   Orange Bush Monkeyflower, 2–4′, *l.* 1¼–2″, *p.* 763

376   Snub Pea, 2–3′, *l.* ½″, *p.* 508

Brown Radially Symmetrical

377 Western Meadow Rue, 1–3′, *w.* ⅜″, *p.* 720

378 Western Stenanthium, 4–20″, *l.* ½–¾″, *p.* 595

379 Mission Bells, 1–4′, *l.* ¾–1½″, *p.* 586

380 Western Peony, 8–24″, *w.* 1–1½″, *p. 655*

381 Long-tailed Wild Ginger, *creeper, w.* 1½–5″, *p. 345*

382 Fetid Adder's Tongue, 8″, *w.* 1″, *p. 593*

383 Stream Orchid, 1–3′, *w.* 1–1½″, *p. 644*

384 Clustered Lady's Slipper, 2–8″, *w.* 1½″, *p. 643*

385 Spotted Coral Root, 8–31″, *w.* ¾″, *p. 640*

387 Red Cinquefoil, 1–2½′, *w.* 1″, *p.* 733

389   Scarlet Creeper, *vine, l. ¾–1½", p. 473*

391   Crimson Columbine, 6–36″, w. 2″, p. 707

392   Scarlet Fritillary, 1–3′, l. ¾–1¼″, p. 588

394 Rocky Mountain Lily, 12–28″, *w.* 2–2½″, *p.* 590

395 Indian Pink, 6–16″, *w.* 1–1½″, *p.* 465

397 Red Four O'Clock, 1–3′, *l.* ½–¾″, *p.* 623

398 Red Shrubby Penstemon, 12–20″, *l.* 1–1½″, *p.* 760

400 California Fuchsia, 1–3′, *l.* 1½–2½″, *p. 634*

401 Crimson Woolly Pod, 4–8″, *l.* 1½″, *p. 497*

403 Coral Bells, 10–20″, *l.* ¼–½″, *p. 741*

404 Candystick, 4–12″, *cl.* 3–9″, *p. 616*

406   Snow Plant, 8–24″, *l.* ½–¾″, *p. 618*

407   Texas Betony, 3′, *l.* ¾–1″, *p. 568*

409 Cardinal Flower, 1–3', *l.* 1–1½", *p. 454*

411 Crimson Sage, 20″, *l.* 1½″, *p. 565*

413   Giant Red Paintbrush, 1–3′, *l.* ¾–1½″, *p. 754*

415   Scarlet Bugler, 1–4′, *l.* 1–1¼″, *p.* 772

417 Scarlet Bouvardia, 3′, *l.* ½–1¼″, *p. 736*

418 Red Monardella, 4–20″, *l.* 1¼–2″, *p. 560*

420　Red Clintonia, 10–20″, *cw.* 1–2″, *p. 581*

421　Roseroot, 1¼–12″, *l.* ⅛″, *p. 480*

422　Snowy Thistle, 2–4′, *l.* 1½–2½″, *p. 366*

423 **Desert Christmas Cactus**, *3', w. ½–1", p. 449*

424 **Cut-leaved Globe Berry**, *vine,* w. ½", *p. 482*

425 Baneberry, 1–3′, *cl.* 2–4″, *p.* 703

427   Sticky Geranium, 1–3′, *w.* 1″, *p. 538*

428   Filaree, 1′, *w.* ½″, *p. 536*

430 Bridge's Gilia, 2–14″, *l.* ⅜–¾″, *p. 667*

431 Alpine Collomia, *creeper, w.* ¾″, *p. 667*

432 Few-flowered Shooting Star, 4–24″, *l.* ¾–1″, *p. 694*

433   Prickly Phlox, 1–3′, *w.* 1″, *p.* 671

434   False Baby Stars, 2–12″, *w.* ½–¾″, *p.* 672

435   **Long-leaved Phlox,** 4–16″, *w.* 1″, *p. 675*

437   Moss Pink, 1–2½″, *w. ½″*, *p. 465*

439 Corn Cockle, 1–3′, *w.* 1″, *p. 460*

441 Bitterroot, ½–2″, *w.* 1½–2½″, *p.* 688

443 Pygmy Talinum, 1–3″, *w.* ¾″, *p. 690*

444 Prairie Star, 20″, *w.* ½–1″, *p. 742*

445 Mountain Four O'Clock, *3′, w. ½″, p. 624*

446 Trailing Four O'Clock, *creeper, cw. ⅛–1″, p. 621*

447   Western Sea Purslane, *1–2', w. ⅜", p. 332*

448   Sea Fig, *creeper, w. 1½–2½", p. 330*

449   Smooth Douglasia, *creeper, w. ⅜", p. 694*

450   Western Starflower, *4–10", w. ½", p. 698*

451 Northern Gentian, 2–16″, *w.* ½–¾″, *p. 533*

453   Adobe Lily, 1–18″, *l.* 1–1½″, *p.* 587

455 Western Clematis, *vine, l.* 1¼–2½", *p.* 711

456 Alpine Laurel, 4", w. ¼", p. 489

457 **Purple Saxifrage,** 2″, *w.* ¼″, *p.* 747

458 **Violet Suksdorfia,** 4–8″, *l.* ⅜″, *p.* 749

460   Redwood Sorrel, 2–7″, *w.* ½–¾″, *p.* 653

461   Nootka Rose, 2–13′, *w.* 2–3″, *p.* 734

463 **Fishhook Cactus,** 6″, *w.* ¾–1″, *p. 445*

465　Cushion Cactus, 1½–6″, *w.* 1–2″, *p.* 441

467 **Rainbow Cactus,** 4–12″, *w.* 2½–5½″, *p. 442*

468 **Beavertail Cactus,** 6–12″, *w.* 2–3″, *p. 446*

470   **Pale Face**, 1–3′, *w.* 1–1½″, *p. 609*

471   **Farewell to Spring**, 6–36″, *w.* 1¼″, *p. 632*

472   **Desert Five Spot**, 4–24″, *w.* ¾–1¼″, *p. 608*

473   Shrubby Tiquilia, 4–20″, *l.* ⅜″, *p. 421*

474   Bush Morning Glory, 4′, *w.* 2–2½″, *p. 474*

475 Beach Morning Glory, *creeper, w.* 1½–2½″, *p.* 472

477 Spreading Dogbane, 8–20", *l.* ¼–⅜", *p. 343*

479 Twinflower, *creeper, l. ½", p.* 459

480 Kinnikinnick, *creeper, l. ¼", p.* 486

481   Philadelphia Fleabane, 8–28″, *w.* 1″, *p. 372*

482   Seaside Daisy, 4–16″, *w.* 2½″, *p. 371*

483   Showy Daisy, 1–3′, *w.* 2″, *p. 373*

484   Leafy Aster, 8–20″, *w.* 1–2″, *p. 356*

485   Showy Palafoxia, 1–2′, *w.* 1–1½″, *p. 390*

486   Spotted Knapweed, 12–39″, *w.* ⅜″, *p. 363*

487   Fremont's Monkeyflower, 1–8″, *w.* ¾–1″, *p. 764*

488   Steer's Head, 1–4″, *l.* ½″, *p. 530*

489   Texas Purple Spike, 1′, *w.* 1–1¼″, *p. 645*

490 Calypso, 8″, *l.* 1¼″, *p.* 638

491 Western Bleeding Heart, 8–18″, *l.* ¾″, *p.* 529

492 Silky Beach Pea, 8–24″, *l.* ¾″, *p.* 508

493   Desert Willow, 4–30′, *l. ¾–1½″, p. 412*

494   Cliff Penstemon, *creeper, l. 1–1½″, p. 778*

495 Texas Silverleaf, 8′, *l.* ¾–1″, *p. 761*

496 Mountain Pride, 6–12″, *w.* ¾–1¼″, *p. 776*

497   Mountain Globemallow, 3–7′, *w. 1–2″, p. 610*

498   Checkermallow, 1–3′, *w. 1–1½″, p. 611*

499   Fireweed, 2–7′, *w. ¾–1¼″, p. 630*

500   Scarlet Gaura, 6–24″, *w.* ½″, *p. 635*

501   Elegant Clarkia, 6–36″, *w.* 1–1½″, *p. 633*

503   Bog Wintergreen, 6–16″, *w.* ½″, *p. 701*

504   Parry's Penstemon, 4′, *l.* ¾″, *p. 777*

506   Elephant Heads, 31″, *l.* ½″, *p.* 770

507   Balloon Flower, 2–7′, *l.* 1–1½″, *p.* 777

509　Nettleleaf Horsemint, 1–5′, *cl.* 1¼–6″, *p. 558*

511 Autumn Sage, 3′, *l.* 1–1¼″, *p. 564*

513   Purple Locoweed, 4–16″, l. ½–1″, p. 517

515 Western Sweetvetch, 16–31", *l.* ¾", *p. 506*

517 Showy Locoweed, 4–16″, *l.* ½″, *p.* 519

519   Common Owl's Clover, 4–16″, *l.* ½–1¼″, *p. 754*

520   Dotted Gayfeather, 6–31″, *l.* ¾″, *p. 384*

521 Sierra Primrose, *creeper, w.* ¾″, *p. 697*

522 Parry's Primrose, 3–16″, *w.* ½–1¼″, *p. 697*

523 Umbrella Plant, 2–6′, *cw.* 2–7″, *p.* 740

524 Western Pink Vervain, 8–16″, *w.* ¼–½″, *p.* 796

525   Daggerpod, 2–8″, w. ½″, p. 433

526   California Thrift, 2–16″, cw. ¾–1″, p. 666

527   Shaggy Tuft, 2½", *w.* ½", *p. 324*

529   Showy Milkweed, 1–4′, w. ¾″, p. 348

531 **Desert Four O'Clock,** 1½', *w.* 1", *p. 625*

532 **Lewis's Monkeyflower,** 1–3', *l.* 1¼–2", *p. 765*

533   Pink Mountain Heather, 4–16″, *l.* ¼″, *p. 491*

534   Cushion Buckwheat, 1–12″, *cw.* 1″, *p. 680*

535   **Pussy Paws,** *creeper, cw. 1½–2½", p. 685*

537 Bighead Clover, 4–12″, *w.* 1¼–2″, *p. 522*

538 Red Clover, 1–3′, *w.* 1–1½″, *p. 523*

540 Fairy Duster, *8–20″, w. 2″, p. 499*

541 Nuttall's Pussytoes, *6″, l. ½″, p. 354*

543   Rocky Mountain Bee Plant, 6–60″, *l.* ½″, *p. 456*

545 Coyote Mint, 6–14″, *l.* ½″, *p. 561*

546 Honesty, 20–40″, *w.* ¾″, *p. 432*

547   Nodding Onion, 4–20″, l. ¼″, p. 573

548   Hooker's Onion, 4–12″, l. ½″, p. 572

549 Western Redbud, 6–16½′, *l.* ½″, *p. 501*

551 Crescent Milkvetch, 2–10″, *l.* ¾–1″, *p. 496*

553   Field Milkvetch, 2–12″, *l.* ½–¾″, *p.* 495

554   Cow Clover, 4–31″, *w.* ¾–1¼″, *p.* 524

555 Threadleaf Phacelia, 4–20″, *w.* ⅜–¾″, *p.* 548

556 Wild Heliotrope, 8–31″, *w.* ¼″, *p.* 546

557   Scalloped Phacelia, 6–30″, *w.* ¼″, *p. 547*

558   Prairie Gentian, 10–28″, *l.* 1¼–1½″, *p. 531*

559   Spotted Langloisia, 1½–6″, *w.* ½″, *p.* 670

560   Red Maids, 2–16″, *w.* ½″, *p.* 684

561 Grass Widow, 4–12", *w.* 1¼–2", *p. 554*

563 **Baby Blue Eyes,** 4–12″, *w.* ½–1½″, *p. 545*

565   Common Morning Glory, *vine, w.* 1½–2½″, *p.* 474

567 Hound's Tongue, 12–31″, *w. ½″, p. 415*

569   White Horsenettle, *3′, w. ¾–1¼″, p. 791*

570   Limestone Columbine, *2–5″, w. 1½–2″, p. 707*

571 Tough-leaved Iris, 16″, *w.* 3–4″, *p. 554*

572 Douglas's Iris, 6–31″, *w.* 3–4″, *p. 551*

573 Rocky Mountain Iris, 8–20″, *w.* 3–4″, *p. 553*

574　**Ground Iris,** 6–8″, *w.* 2½–4″, *p.* 552

575　**Pasque Flower,** 14″, *w.* 1½–2″, *p.* 717

577 Pale Trumpets, 2′, *l.* 1–1½″, *p.* 670

578 Sky Pilot, 4–16″, *w.* ½–¾″, *p.* 677

580 Alpine Shooting Star, 4–12″, *l.* ¾–1″, *p. 692*

581 Vase Flower, 8–24″, *l.* 1″, *p. 709*

582 Bittersweet, *vine, w.* ½–¾″, *p. 791*

583   Sticky Aster, 1–3′, *w.* 1½″, *p.* 385

584   Mojave Aster, 1–2½′, *w.* 2″, *p.* 407

585   Tahoka Daisy, 4–16″, *w.* 1¼–2½″, *p. 386*

587   Western Dayflower, 20″, *w.* ¾″, *p. 469*

588   Western Pansy Violet, 2–5″, *w.* ½–¾″, *p. 798*

590 Dwarf Purple Monkeyflower, *4″, l. ½–1″, p. 766*

591 Pima Ratany, *6–24″, w. ¾″, p. 557*

593   Desert Calico, 1–2″, *w.* ½″, *p.* 674

595   Net-cup Snapdragon Vine, *vine, l. 1″, p. 763*

597 Lowbush Penstemon, 6–16″, *l.* 1–2″, *p.* 775

599   **Marsh Skullcap,** 4–31″, *l.* ½–¾″, *p. 567*

600   **Austin's Skullcap,** 4–12″, *l.* 1–1½″, *p. 568*

601   Chaparral Pea, 7′, *l.* ¾″, *p.* 519

602   Bladder Sage, 2–3′, *l.* ¾″, *p.* 561

603   Wright's Birdbeak, 2′, *l.* ¾–1¼″, *p. 759*

605 New Mexico Vervain, 3′, *w.* ¼″, *p.* 796

607   Western Polemonium, 1–3′, *w.* ½–¾″, *p.* 676

609   Vinegar Weed, 2–5′, *l.* ½″, *p.* 569

610   Purple Fringe, 16″, *l.* ¼″, *p.* 548

611 Purple Chinese Houses, 1–2′, *l.* ¾″, *p.* 757

613   Rydberg's Penstemon, 8–24″, *l.* ½–¾″, *p.* 779

614   Cascade Penstemon, 8–28″, *l.* ¾–1″, *p.* 779

615   Whipple's Penstemon, 4–28″, *l.* ¾–1¼″, *p.* 780

617   Alpine Besseya, 6″, *l.* ¼″, *p.* 752

618   Cooper's Spike Broomrape, 4–16″, *l.* ¾–1¼″, *p.* 65

619   Bird Vetch, 4–7′, *l.* ½–¾″, *p.* 525

620   Stinging Lupine, 8–40″, *l.* ½″, *p. 514*

621   Blue-pod Lupine, 2–5′, *l.* ½″, *p. 515*

623 Fendler's Waterleaf, 8–31″, *w.* ¼–⅜″, *p. 544*

625 Ookow, 1–3′, *l.* ½–¾″, *p.* 582

626 Snow Queen, 6″, *l.* ¼″, *p.* 782

627   **Gray-ball Sage,** 8–31″, *l.* ½″, *p.* 563

628   **Chia,** 4–20″, *l.* ½″, *p.* 563

629 Wild Teasel, 1½–7', *w.* 1¼–2", *p. 484*

630 Desert Sand Verbena, *creeper cw. 2–3", p. 620*

631   Wild Blue Flax, 6–31″, *w. ¾–1½″, p. 604*

632   Alpine Forget-me-not, 4″, *w. ¼″, p. 415*

633   Many-flowered Stickseed, 1–3′, *w. ¼″, p. 416*

635   Blue-eyed Grass, 4–20″, w. ½–1½″, p. 555

636   Blue Anemone, 4–12″, w. 1–1½″, p. 704

638   Desert Bell, 8–30″, *l. ¾–1½″, p. 546*

639   Bluebell, 4–40″, *l. ½–1″, p. 452*

640   Explorer's Gentian, 2–12″, *l. 1–1½″, p. 532*

641   Chicory, 1–6', *w. 2", p. 366*

642   Blue Violet, *4", w. ½–¾", p. 798*

643   Slender Dayflower, 1', *w.* 1", *p.* 470

645 Camas, 8–28″, *w.* 1½–2½″, *p.* 580

646 Cusick's Speedwell, 2–8″, *w.* ½″, *p.* 785

648　Southwestern Blue Lobelia, 8–28″, *l.* ½–1″, *p. 453*

649　Narrowleaf Penstemon, 6–16″, *l.* ¾″, *p. 776*

651 Western Monkshood, 1–7′, *l.* 1″, *p.* 702

652 Nuttall's Larkspur, 4–16″, *w.* 1″, *p.* 714

654   Miniature Lupine, 4–16″, *l.* ⅜″, *p. 513*

655   Coulter's Lupine, 8–16″, *l.* ½″, *p. 515*

657   Silverleaf Phacelia, 8–20″, *l.* ¼″, *p. 547*

659   Douglas's Triteleia, 8–28″, *w.* ¾″, *p. 598*

660   Mountain Bluebell, 6–60″, *l.* ½–¾″, *p. 421*

PART II
FAMILY AND SPECIES DESCRIPTIONS

ACANTHUS FAMILY
Acanthaceae

Herbs or shrubs with showy flowers often held in large, often showy bracts.

Flowers: Usually bilaterally symmetrical. Sepals 4–5; petals 4–5, united, usually forming 2-lobed upper lip and 3-lobed lower lip; stamens 2 or 4; all these parts attached at base of ovary.
Leaves: Opposite, simple, often with pale streaks or bumps, sometimes with smooth edges.
Fruit: 2-celled capsule, with seeds borne on characteristic, small, hooked stalks.

There are about 230 genera and 2,500 species, native to temperate and tropical regions. Many are cultivated as ornamentals. Several plants are used medicinally, particularly in the Old World. In the West, most species are restricted to the warmer parts of the southwestern United States.

399 Chuparosa; Beleperone
Justicia californica

Description:	Numerous *tubular, dull red flowers* on a *mostly leafless, densely branched, grayish-green shrub.*
Flowers:	Corolla 1–1½″ (2.5–4 cm) long, deeply cleft into 2-lobed upper lip and 3-lobed lower lip.
Leaves:	About ½″ (1.5 cm) long, ovate, finely hairy, deciduous.
Height:	To 5′ (1.5 m); nearly as wide.
Flowering:	February–June.
Habitat:	Along desert watercourses, mostly below 2,500′ (750 m) elevation.
Range:	Southeastern California, southern Arizona, and northwestern Mexico.
Comments:	Very few species of the huge tropical genus *Justicia* extend north into the United States. The common name Chuparosa is Spanish for "hummingbird"; these birds frequently visit the nectar-rich plants, pollinating flower after flower as they feed. Linnets and sparrows bite off the flowers and eat the nectar-filled bases. Sometimes known locally as Honeysuckle, Chuparosa is said to have been eaten by Native Americans of the Southwest.

527 Shaggy Tuft
Stenandrium barbatum

Description:	A dwarf, *tufted, grayish plant* with *short spikes of rose-pink flowers* nestled among leaves.
Flowers:	Corolla about ½" (1.5 cm) wide, with 5 lobes flaring from a narrow tube, upper 2 lobes slightly darker than lower 3.
Leaves:	To 1½" (4 cm) long, narrowly lanceolate, broader above middle, densely shaggy with gray hairs.
Height:	To 2½" (6.5 cm).
Flowering:	March–June.
Habitat:	Open, limestone flats and rocky or clay banks.
Range:	Southern New Mexico and western Texas south to northern Mexico.
Comments:	The bright rose-pink flowers of this species are conspicuous against the gray limestone; it is one of the first wildflowers to bloom in the normally dry spring of western Texas.

AGAVE FAMILY
Agavaceae

Stout plants, with woody stems or stem-bases, often tall or even tree-like, with stout, rapidly growing flower stalks rising from crowded rosettes of long narrow leaves at stem or branch ends.

Flowers: Usually radially symmetrical. Sepals and petals 3 each, colored alike, often thick and fleshy, separate or united to form a tube at base; stamens 6; all these parts attached at top of ovary in some genera, at base of ovary in others.

Leaves: Strongly thickened, leathery, or firm-succulent (rarely soft-succulent), parallel-veined, usually very fibrous, often prickly or with stout teeth on edges, often with a sturdy, terminal spine.

Fruit: Usually a capsule, sometimes a firm berry.

There are about 20 genera and 700 species, found in tropical or warm regions, often where it is arid. Some supply valuable fiber, such as sisal hemp from Sisal *(Agave sisalana)*. Despite their common name, century plants *(Agave)* do not take 100 years to flower, but it may take several decades to store enough food reserves to supply the rapidly growing flower stalk and mature the seeds, after which time the rosette dies. The liquors pulque, mescal, sotol, and tequila are made from fermented extracts of the large fleshy bases of *Agave* species in Mexico. Members of Agavaceae are sometimes included in the complex lily family (Liliaceae).

323 Lecheguilla
Agave lecheguilla

Description: *A tall narrow cluster of flowers* growing from a basal rosette of *erect, rigid, sharply pointed leaves.*

Flowers: ¾–1½" (2–4 cm) long, in small clusters along main stalk; petal-like segments 6, yellow to red or purplish, narrow, spreading.

Leaves: 12–20" (30–50 cm) long, about 1" (2.5 cm) wide, straight or slightly curved.

Height: 7–10' (2.1–3 m).

Flowering: May–July.

Habitat: Rocky, limestone slopes.

Range: Southern New Mexico and western Texas south to Mexico.

Comments: This formidable plant was a dangerous obstacle in the early exploration of the Southwest. The sharp leaves pierced horses' legs, and a rider who fell could be impaled. Today, leaves of small plants puncture tires of off-road vehicles. Native Americans obtained fiber from the leaves. The common name is sometimes spelled Lechuguilla.

324 Palmer's Century Plant
Agave palmeri

Description: A tall *stout flower stalk, resembling a huge candelabrum,* growing from center of a *compact rosette of thick, rigid, narrowly lanceolate, grayish-green leaves.*

Flowers: Buds purplish, *open flowers yellowish,* facing upward in clusters near branch ends; petal-like segments 6, each about 1¼ " (3 cm) long, united to form a tube

at base; stamens 6; petal-like segments
and stamens attached near upper edge of
flower tube.

Leaves: 1–2½′ (30–75 cm) long, concave on
upper side, each bearing a dangerously
sharp terminal spine and numerous
smaller spines along edges.

Height: 10–16′ (3–5 m).

Flowering: June–August.

Habitat: Dry rocky slopes and flats.

Range: Southeastern Arizona and southwestern
New Mexico south to northwestern
Mexico.

Comments: Century plants such as this provided
Native Americans in the Southwest with
food, beverages, fiber, soap, medicine,
and lances.

11 Sotol; Desert Spoon
Dasylirion wheeleri

Description: *Thousands of tiny, greenish-white flowers
in a long narrow cluster* growing from
a dense bunch of *many slender, spiny
leaves.*

Flowers: Cluster 5–8′ (1.5–2.4 m) long; petal-
like segments 6.

Leaves: To 3′ (90 cm) long, ½–1″ (1.5–2.5 cm)
wide, with teeth on edges curving
forward.

Height: Flower stalk 6–17′ (1.8–5.1 m); trunk
to 3′ (90 cm).

Flowering: May–July.

Habitat: Rocky, desert slopes.

Range: Southern Arizona east to western Texas;
also northern Mexico.

Comments: This species may be treated in the same
manner as agaves to produce food and
liquor (sotol). The tough leaves can be
woven into mats and baskets and used
for thatching. The broad, spoon-like
base is often used in dried flower
arrangements. The smaller Smooth-
leaved Sotol *(D. leiophyllum),* which
grows on limestone in southern New
Mexico, western Texas, and northern
Mexico, has leaves with teeth that curve
toward the base.

133 Parry's Nolina; Bear Grass
Nolina parryi

Description: *A very dense cluster of tiny, whitish flowers* growing from a *rosette of many long leaves atop a short, trunk-like stem.*

Flowers: About ¼" (6 mm) long; cluster about 2' (60 cm) long, almost as wide, on a stalk 3–5' (90–150 cm) high.

Leaves: 2–3' (60–90 cm) long, less than ¾" (2 cm) wide, flexible, concave on upper surface.

Height: To 10' (3 m).

Flowering: April–June.

Habitat: Dry brushy slopes.

Range: Southern California.

Comments: This is one of the largest and showiest of 25 species in this southwestern genus. Many are much smaller, resembling thick tufts of coarse grass on dry hillsides, and are often called Sacahuista (pronounced *sac-ah-wees-tah*), the Native American name for this plant. The leaves were woven into baskets or mats, and the young stems were prepared as food.

123 Blue Yucca; Banana Yucca; Datil
Yucca baccata

Description: *Rigid, spine-tipped leaves* in 1 or several rosettes, and a long cluster of *large whitish flowers* on a stalk about as tall as leaves.

Flowers: Petal-like segments 6, each 2–4" (5–10 cm) long, white or cream and often purplish-tinged, waxy.

Leaves: To 3' (90 cm) long, with few whitish fibers at edges.

Fruit: Fleshy, cylindrical pod, 2½–10" (6.5–25 cm) long, round at ends.

Height: To 5' (1.5 m); trunk to 20" (50 cm).

Flowering: April–July.

Habitat: Rocky soil in deserts, grasslands, and open woods.

Range: Southeastern California east through southern Nevada and Utah to southwestern Colorado and western Texas, and south to northern Mexico.

Comments: The baked fruit of Blue Yucca tastes somewhat like sweet potato. Yucca flowers are still eaten by rural Mexicans to such an extent that some species now rarely show mature pods. Identification of the many *Yucca* species is often difficult. Those with broad leaves are sometimes called Spanish Daggers, a name generally applied to the tree-like species of western Texas. Plain's Yucca (*Y. angustifolia*), common from the eastern edge of the Rocky Mountains eastward almost throughout the plains and prairies of the central United States, is a small species with narrow, gray-green leaves.

125   Mojave Yucca
Yucca schidigera

Description: Rosettes of *stiff, narrow, spine-tipped leaves* on branched or unbranched trunks, topped by long broad clusters of *many cream, bell-like flowers.*

Flowers: 1¼–2½″ (3–6.5 cm) long, nearly spherical; petal-like segments 6.

Leaves: 1–5′ (30–150 cm) long, with pale fibers peeling and curling on edges.

Height: Trunk 4–15′ (1.2–4.5 m); flower stalk and cluster to 4′ (1.2 m).

Flowering: April–May.

Habitat: Brushy slopes, flats, and open deserts.

Range: Southern California, southern Nevada, northwestern Arizona, and Baja California.

Comments: This is a common yucca in the Mojave Desert, often growing with Joshua Tree (*Y. brevifolia*), a tree-like species that often forms "forests." Joshua Tree's stiff leaves are 8–14″ (20–35 cm) long.

124   Our Lord's Candle
Yucca whipplei

Description: *Several thousand white or cream flowers,* often tinged with purple, in a long massive cluster on a stout stalk growing from a *dense basal rosette of gray-green, rigid, spine-tipped leaves.*

Flowers: Petal-like segments 6, each 1–1½″ (2.5–4 cm) long, forming a bell.

Leaves: 3′ (90 cm) long.

Height: 4–11′ (1.2–3.3 m).

Flowering: April–May.

Habitat: Stony slopes in chaparral.

Range: Southern California and northern Baja California.

Comments: This is the showiest of the yuccas; hundreds in bloom provide a spectacular sight on brushy slopes. The plants die after flowering. All yuccas have a reciprocal relationship with Yucca Moths. After gathering pollen from the flowers and rolling the pollen into little balls, the moths lay their eggs in the ovaries of other flowers and then pack the pollen into holes on the stigma, thus both pollinating the flower and ensuring seed production. The larvae feed on a fraction of the developing seeds, then burrow out of the fruit when mature.

ICE PLANT FAMILY
Aizoaceae

Usually fleshy herbs with showy flowers and simple leaves.

Flowers: Radially symmetrical; commonly solitary or in small open clusters. Sepals 5–8, often brightly colored and petal-like; petals technically absent, but in many species sterile, brightly colored, outer stamens resemble numerous narrow petals; stamens many; all these parts attached at either base or top of ovary.

Leaves: Opposite or alternate.

Fruit: Capsule, with at least 2 chambers; rarely berry-like, fleshy, edible.

There are about 130 genera and 2,500 species, mostly in South Africa. In the United States members of this family are most common in the West, especially near the warm coast. Several genera are cultivated as ground-cover and as dune stabilizers (especially *Carpobrotus* and *Mesembryanthemum*), and a few as succulent novelties, such as the diminutive and almost invisible pebble plants (*Lithops*). The family is often divided by botanists into the

Mesembryanthemaceae, containing ice plants, pebble plants, and similarly succulent species, and the Aizoaceae, which contains weedier species such as sea purslanes.

---

448 Sea Fig; Ice Plant
Carpobrotus chilensis

Description: A mat-forming plant with *trailing, rooting stems,* bearing large, deep reddish-lavender flowers nestled among *erect, narrow, succulent leaves.*

Flowers: 1½–2½″ (4–6.5 cm) wide; sepals of varying lengths, larger ones leaf-like; petals numerous, very narrow.

Leaves: 1½–3″ (4–7.5 cm) long, mostly opposite, straight, 3-sided, rather roundish-triangular in cross section, outer angle smooth.

Fruit: Green, fleshy, plump, flat at top, with 8–10 chambers, edible.

Height: Creeper; flowering branches to 5″ (12.5 cm), trailing stems to 6′ (1.8 m) long.

Flowering: April–September.

Habitat: Coastal sands and bluffs.

Range: Southern Oregon south to Mexico.

Comments: Flowers open only in full sun. The original home of Sea Fig is lost to history. It is thought to be native to South Africa. It will hybridize with Hottentot Fig *(C. edulis)* on coastal dunes and along roads near the coast. Both species have flowers ranging in color from yellow to magenta. Both commonly known as Ice Plant, they were formerly placed in the genus *Mesembryanthemum.* Other cultivated species, rather similar but in different genera, have escaped cultivation in parts of California; they have flat or nearly cylindrical leaves.

---

215 Hottentot Fig; Ice Plant
Carpobrotus edulis

Description: Long, trailing, rooting stems with *pink or yellow flowers* among *slender, erect, succulent leaves.*

Flowers: 3–4″ (8–10 cm) wide; sepals of varying
lengths, larger ones similar to leaves;
petals numerous, very narrow.

Leaves: 2½–4″ (6–10 cm) long, mostly opposite,
somewhat curved, sharply triangular in
cross section, outer angle with fine teeth
near tip.

Fruit: Green, maturing to yellow, plump, flat
at top, with several chambers, edible.

Height: Creeper; flowering branches to about 8″
(20 cm), trailing stems to 9′ (2.7 m)
long.

Flowering: April–October.

Habitat: Sandy roadsides, bluffs, and dunes along
coast.

Range: California south to Mexico.

Comments: Hottentot Fig is extensively planted
on slopes along coastal freeways to
reduce erosion and on dunes for
stabilization of loose sand. Flowers are
on short stout stalks, unlike the nearly
stalkless flowers of the closely related
Sea Fig *(C. chilensis),* with which the
species hybridizes.

---

42 **Crystalline Ice Plant**
Mesembryanthemum crystallinum

Description: A succulent plant with branched,
reclining stems covered with tiny,
glistening beads; white or reddish flowers
in upper leaf axils.

Flowers: 1″ (2.5 cm) wide; *petals many,* each
¼–⅜″ (6–9 mm) long, *narrow;* stamens
many.

Leaves: ¾–4″ (2–10 cm) long, ovate or spatula-
shaped, wavy.

Height: Creeper; flowering branches about 3″
(7.5 cm), reclining stems 8–24″ (20–60
cm) long.

Flowering: March–October.

Habitat: Open, sandy flats and slopes near coast
and inland in deserts.

Range: Southern half of California,
southwestern Arizona, and Baja
California.

Comments: This plant, found also in southern
Europe and Africa, was introduced to

North America from South Africa, the home of many *Mesembryanthemum* species. The tongue-tangling genus name means "blooming at midday." The beads on the stems are actually swollen with water; easily crushed, the beads exude their contents and give the plant a moist feel. The species name refers to the crystalline look of the water cells.

447 Western Sea Purslane
Sesuvium verrucosum

Description: A succulent, grayish-green plant with branched, prostrate or ascending stems bearing *star-like, pink flowers* in upper leaf axils.

Flowers: About ⅜" (1 cm) wide; *sepals 5*, green on outside, pink on inside, joined to form a bell-shaped base, with small green horn on back of each pointed tip; *petals absent;* stamens many.

Leaves: ⅜–1½" (1–4 cm) long, opposite, narrow or lanceolate, broadest above middle.

Height: 1–2' (30–60 cm).

Flowering: April–November.

Habitat: Open low spots in salty or alkaline soil.

Range: Southern half of California east through southern Utah, Colorado, and Kansas to Missouri, and south to Mexico.

Comments: This is the only *Sesuvium* species in the West. Other sea purslanes grow to the east or south, most in saline soil, some near the coast (hence the common name).

WATER PLANTAIN FAMILY
Alismataceae

Aquatic or marsh herbs with long-stalked, simple, basal leaves and a leafless stalk bearing whorls of small flowers in a raceme or an often much-branched panicle.

Flowers: Radially symmetrical. Sepals 3, green; petals 3, delicate, white or pinkish; stamens 6 to many; all these parts attached at base of 6 to many separate pistils.

Leaves: Prominently veined, with bases sheathing stem.

Fruit: Hard, 1-seeded; in clusters.

There are about 12 genera and 75 species, widely distributed in shallow freshwater, brackish, or muddy habitats in warm and temperate climates. Many provide food for wildlife.

161 Water Plantain
Alisma plantago-aquatica

Description: A tall *spindly plant* with basal leaves and a flower stalk with umbel-like clusters of *small, white or pale pink flowers* near ends of whorled branches.

Flowers: ¼–½″ (6–13 mm) wide; sepals 3; petals 3; stamens several; pistils 10–25, in a ring.

Leaves: Those above water 1–6″ (2.5–15 cm) long, ovate blades on long stalks; those underwater often narrow and grass-like.

Fruit: Small, seed-like, arranged in a ring; several in each flower.

Height: Aquatic; flower clusters 3–4′ (90–120 cm) above water.

Flowering: June–August.

Habitat: Shallow water, marshy places, and muddy shores.

Range: Much of North America.

Comments: According to some authorities, *A. plantago-aquatica* is restricted to Eurasia. By that view, North America has two species, both called Water Plantain: *A. trivale* has petals ⅛–¼″ (3–5 mm) long; *A. subcordatum* has petals ¹⁄₁₆–⅛″ (1–3 mm) long. The submerged fleshy portion of several species of *Alisma* was dried and eaten by Native Americans. Narrow-leaved Water Plantain *(A. gramineum)*, with grass-like leaves and smaller pink petals, occurs across southern Canada and the northern United States.

56 Fringed Water Plantain
Damasonium californicum

Description: Several basal leaves and 1 or few flower stalks with *white or pink, fringed flowers* often in clusters on whorled branches.

Flowers: Sepals 3; petals 3, each about ¾" (2 cm) wide, broad, with *small, sharp, uneven teeth across ends.*

Leaves: 1–3" (2.5–7.5 cm) long, ovate blades on long stalks.

Fruit: Needle-pointed, arranged like wheel spokes; several in each flower.

Height: Aquatic; flower clusters 8–18" (20–45 cm) above water.

Flowering: April–August.

Habitat: Shallow water or mud in open areas.

Range: Northern half of California and adjacent regions of Oregon and Nevada east to southwestern Idaho.

Comments: This was once considered the sole species in a small western American genus, *Machaerocarpus.* It has now been placed in a wide-ranging but still small genus, which also occurs in Eurasia and Australia.

101 Grass-leaved Sagittaria
Sagittaria graminea

Description: *Long, grass-like leaves* emerging from water and surrounding shorter, spindly flower stalks with *white flowers on whorled branches.*

Flowers: About ½" (1.5 cm) wide, each on a hair-like, ascending stalk; sepals 3, broad; petals 3, broad; upper flowers usually only with stamens; lower flowers usually only with pistils.

Leaves: Blades absent, or long-stalked and to 8" (20 cm) long and 1" (2.5 cm) wide.

Fruit: Many, seed-like; in a head about ½" (1.5 cm) wide.

Height: Aquatic; flower clusters about 2' (60 cm) above water.

Flowering: April–November, occasionally throughout year.

Habitat: Shallow water or mud in ditches, marshes, streams, and ponds.

Range: Great Plains and south-central Texas east throughout eastern United States.

Comments: Grass-leaved Sagittaria has consistently narrow leaves. It barely enters the eastern edge of this book's range.

102 Arrowhead; Tule Potato; Wapato
Sagittaria latifolia

Description: *Arrowhead-shaped, basal leaves* surrounding a taller flower stalk with *small white flowers* at ends of short whorled branches; sap milky.

Flowers: ¾–1½" (2–4 cm) wide; sepals 3, spreading out or bent back; petals 3; stamens 20 or more in some flowers, in others *many pistils form a sphere.*

Leaves: Conspicuously veined, with long petiole attached in V at base of blade; blades 4–20" (10–50 cm) long.

Height: Aquatic; flower clusters to 3′ (90 cm) above water.

Flowering: July–September.

Habitat: Ditches, ponds, and swampy areas.

Range: Most of United States south to South America.

Comments: In mud, rhizomes produce starchy tubers, once an important source of food for Native Americans. Early settlers called this plant Duck Potato. The genus name comes from *sagitta,* Latin for "arrow," referring to the shape of the leaves of some species of *Sagittaria.*

AMARYLLIS FAMILY
Amaryllidaceae

Herbs, or rarely woody plants, growing from underground stems or bulbs, with narrow, basal leaves and a long leafless flower stalk.

Flowers: Radially symmetrical. Sepals and petals 3 each, colored alike, united below into a tube, sometimes with additional parts in center forming a crown; stamens 6; all these parts attached at top of ovary.

Leaves: Grass-like or strap-shaped, sometimes with few teeth.

Fruit: Capsule or berry.

There are about 65 genera and 900 species, mostly native to tropical and warm regions. Daffodils and jonquils (both of which are groups in the genus *Narcissus*) as well as species of *Amaryllis* are highly prized ornamentals. Members of Amaryllidaceae are sometimes included in the complex lily family (Liliaceae).

192 Rain Lily
Zephyranthes longifolia

Description:	*1 yellow, funnel-shaped flower* held erect on a slender stem; *resembling a crocus* but much smaller and more delicate.
Flowers:	¾–1″ (2–2.5 cm) long; petal-like parts 6, yellow inside, copper-tinged outside, joined above ovary.
Leaves:	To 9″ (22.5 cm) long, few, basal, very narrow, often absent at flowering.
Fruit:	Nearly spherical, 3-chambered capsule, about ¾″ (2 cm) wide, filled with flat, black, D-shaped seeds.
Height:	To 9″ (22.5 cm).
Flowering:	April–July.
Habitat:	Sandy deserts and grasslands.
Range:	Southern Arizona east to western Texas and south to northern Mexico.
Comments:	*Zephyranthes* means "flower of the west wind." Flowers of this species appear very soon after substantial rains, hence its common name.

CARROT FAMILY
Apiaceae

Usually aromatic herbs with hollow stems, sometimes fern-like leaves, and small flowers usually in umbels, further grouped into compound umbels.

Flowers: Radially symmetrical; those near edge of compound umbel sometimes bilaterally symmetrical. Sepals 5, small, or absent; petals 5; stamens 5; all these parts attached at top of ovary.
Leaves: Simple or pinnately or palmately compound.
Fruit: Splitting into halves, each 1-seeded.

There are about 300 genera and 3,000 species, mostly in the Northern Hemisphere. Nearly a quarter of the genera are native to the United States, with several large genera in the West. The family is important for such food as carrots *(Daucus carota),* parsnips *(Pastinaca sativa),* and celery *(Apium graveolens),* and such spices and seasonings as coriander seeds and cilantro (both obtained from *Coriandrum sativum*), caraway *(Carum carvi),* anise *(Pimpinella anisum),* parsley *(Petroselinum crispum),* and dill *(Anethum graveolens).* Certain native species, some of which very closely resemble domesticated plants, are quite poisonous. Flower clusters often resemble umbrellas. Apiaceae has also been known as the parsley family (Umbelliferae).

148 Water Hemlock
Cicuta douglasii

Description:	A tall plant with *flat-topped compound umbels of tiny white flowers* atop a stout, hollow, leafy stem.
Flowers:	Compound umbel to 5″ (12.5 cm) wide; petals 5.
Leaves:	5–14″ (12.5–35 cm) long, pinnately divided; those near leaf base again pinnately divided into lanceolate leaflets, each 1¼–4″ (3–10 cm) long, with sharp teeth on edges, the vein ending in notch between teeth.
Fruit:	Small, flat, round, with corky, roundish ridges.
Height:	1½–7′ (45–210 cm).
Flowering:	June–September.
Habitat:	Marshes, edges of streams and ditches, and wet low places.
Range:	Pacific Coast east to Rocky Mountain region from Alberta to New Mexico and northern Mexico.
Comments:	The swollen bases of the stems and usually the thick roots have horizontal chambers inside, a feature that helps identify this deadly poisonous species.

Water Hemlock

Its toxin rapidly affects the nervous
system, causing severe convulsions and
usually death. Another tall member of
this family, with white flowers, fern-like
leaves, and purple-spotted stems, is
Poison Hemlock *(Conium maculatum);*
judging from the symptoms, it was an
extract of this hemlock that poisoned
Socrates, and children have been fatally
poisoned by blowing whistles made
from its hollow stems.

149 Wild Carrot; Queen Anne's Lace
Daucus carota

Description: Few large, *flat-topped umbels of tiny white
flowers* atop a hairy or sometimes nearly
smooth *lacy-leaved stem.*

Flowers: Umbel about 6″ (15 cm) wide; central
flower commonly purple or pink
(sometimes all flowers pink); branches
of older umbels curl inward, resembling
birds' nests.

Leaves: Lacy blades 2–6″ (5–15 cm) long,
repeatedly pinnately divided into
narrow segments.

Fruit: Oval, with minute barbed prickles along
every other rib.

Height: 1–4′ (30–120 cm).

Flowering: May–September.

Habitat: Roadsides, fields, and old lots.

Range: Most of North America.

Comments: Native to Europe, this is the ancestor
of the cultivated carrot. The flowering
heads served 18th-century English
courtiers as "living lace," hence the
common name.

163 Mexican Thistle
Eryngium heterophyllum

Description: *Prickly white bracts* surrounding tiny,
pale blue flowers in *dome-like heads* atop
a *thistle-like plant.*

Flowers: Head about ¼–½″ (7–15 mm) high,
¼–⅜″ (5–10 mm) wide, spiny;
surrounded by 8–14 rigid, spiny,

narrowly lance-shaped, white bracts,
each ¾–1″ (2–2.5 cm) long.

Leaves: Those at base 2½–4½″ (6–12 cm) long,
narrow, edges with many spine-tipped
teeth; those on stem smaller, also spiny,
from deeply toothed to pinnately
divided.

Height: 8–24″ (20–60 cm).

Flowering: July–October.

Habitat: Sandy soil in grasslands, open woods,
and along watercourses, usually in
mountains.

Range: Southeastern Arizona east to western
Texas and south to Mexico.

Comments: This large genus of mostly temperate
regions resembles the thistles of the
aster family (Asteraceae) in their
prickliness, but the flowers reveal that
these species belong to the carrot family.
In Europe roots of some species are
candied, and in South America the fiber
caraguata is obtained from the leaves of
one. In North America curative powers
have been ascribed to some species.

326 Sweet Fennel
Foeniculum vulgare

Description: A tall plant with *feathery leaves* and *tiny,
yellow flowers in compound umbels* on upper
branches.

Flowers: Umbel 2–7″ (5–17.5 cm) wide; sepals
absent; petals 5.

Leaves: 12–16″ (30–40 cm) long, triangular,
pinnately divided several times into
hair-like segments.

Fruit: ¼″ (5 mm) long, cylindrical, bluntly
tapered at ends, ribbed.

Height: 3–7′ (90–210 cm).

Flowering: May–September.

Habitat: Roadsides, old lots, and fields.

Range: Most frequent west of Cascade Range
and Sierra Nevada.

Comments: All parts are edible and have a mild
anise or licorice flavor. Introduced from
Europe, Sweet Fennel is used in French,
Italian, and other cuisines. Young shoots
are eaten cooked or raw as a vegetable;

leaves are used in salads and for seasoning; seeds are used as a flavoring in cooking and in candy and liqueurs. This species is sometimes called Wild Anise, although true Anise is of the genus *Pimpinella*.

152   Beach Silvertop
Glehnia littoralis subsp. *leiocarpa*

Description: A low spreading plant with rosettes of *pinnate leaves lying on sand;* small, tight, round, short-stemmed umbels rising from center and bearing *numerous tiny white flowers.*

Flowers: Umbel 3–4″ (7.5–10 cm) wide, with few stout woolly branches; conspicuous bracts beneath umbel.

Leaves: 1–6″ (2.5–15 cm) long, fleshy, hairy beneath, divided 3 times into *3-lobed leaflets.*

Fruit: ¼–½″ (6–13 mm) long, with corky wings on edges and each flat side.

Height: 2½″ (6.5 cm).

Flowering: May–July.

Habitat: Beach sands and dunes.

Range: Pacific Coast from Alaska south to northern California.

Comments: The genus name probably honors P. von Glehn, a 19th-century curator at the St. Petersburg Botanic Garden. There is only one species of *Glehnia;* the other subspecies is Asian.

147   Cow Parsnip
Heracleum lanatum

Description: *A tall, leafy, stout plant* topped by large *umbels of tiny white flowers.*

Flowers: Umbel to 1′ (30 cm) wide, often in groups; petals 5, those at edge of umbel larger, each about ¼″ (6 mm) long, cleft in middle.

Leaves: 6–16″ (15–40 cm) long, round, divided into 3 lobes or parts, edges coarsely toothed.

Fruit: Flat, oval, broader above middle, the broad sides with 4 dark lines extending

halfway down, alternating with 3
fine ribs.

Height: To 10′ (3 m).
Flowering: February–September.
Habitat: Moist, partially shaded places to 9,000′
(2,700 m) elevation.
Range: Most of Canada and United States,
except Florida.
Comments: This is the largest native species of the
carrot family in North America. The
genus is named for Heracles (Hercules),
who reputedly used it for medicine.
Early each year, Native Americans
peeled and ate the young, sweet,
aromatic leaf and flower stalks.
However, before eating any wild plants
of the carrot family, one should be sure
of their identity, for some are deadly.
This species, although edible, can cause
dermatitis.

327 Spring Gold
Lomatium utriculatum

Description: *Little spheres of tiny, bright yellow flowers*
in umbels above *finely divided, carrot-like
leaves.*
Flowers: Umbel in flower about 2–4″ (5–10 cm)
wide, with 5–20 main branches of
unequal lengths; umbel in fruit to 10″
(25 cm) wide.
Leaves: Blade 2–6″ (5–15 cm) long, divided 3
times into very fine, narrow segments,
on a stalk ¾–4″ (2–10 cm) long,
sheathing stem.
Fruit: ¼–⅜″ (5–10 mm) long, seed-like, rather
flat, oblong, with thin wings on edges.
Height: 4–20″ (10–50 cm).
Flowering: February–June.
Habitat: Grassy slopes, meadows, and woodlands.
Range: British Columbia south to California
west of Cascade Range and Sierra
Nevada.
Comments: The genus *Lomatium* is composed of
about 80 species restricted to western
North America. The genus name,
derived from the Greek *loma* ("a
border"), refers to the wings on the fruit.

In California Native Americans ate the leaves raw in the early spring, when they are still crisp.

154 Ranger's Button; Swamp White Head
Sphenosciadium capitellatum

Description: A stout tall plant with numerous tiny white *flowers in compact, separate, white "buttons"* at ends of hairy branches.

Flowers: Umbel to 4″ (10 cm) wide; sepals absent; petals 5.

Leaves: 4–16″ (10–40 cm) long, broad, pinnately divided, lower segments again divided; leaflets 1–3″ (2.5–7.5 cm) long, lanceolate, *edges with few teeth above middle.*

Height: 1½–7′ (45–210 cm).

Flowering: July–August.

Habitat: Wet meadows, swamps, and streambanks from foothills to moderate elevations.

Range: Eastern Oregon and central Idaho south to southern California mountains.

Comments: The genus name comes from the Greek *sphen* ("wedge") and *skias* ("umbrella"), probably referring to the shape of the flower cluster.

325 Golden Alexanders
Zizia aptera

Description: A cluster of several leafy stems bearing bright yellow flowers in *compound umbels.*

Flowers: Umbel to 2½″ (6.5 cm) wide; sepals and petals 5 each.

Leaves: Basal leaves 1–4″ (2.5–10 cm) long, long-stalked, ovate blades indented at base, edges with teeth; *upper leaves pinnately divided into 3 segments* with several narrow lobes, edges with teeth.

Fruit: Elliptical, slightly flat, with low ribs.

Height: 8–24″ (20–60 cm).

Flowering: May–July.

Habitat: Moist meadows and open woods, streambanks, and low ground.

Range: Western Canada south to eastern
Washington, northwestern Oregon,
and northeastern Nevada, and east
to Colorado; also in much of eastern
United States.

Comments: The genus is named for the German
botanist Johann Ziz, who lived around
the turn of the 19th century.

DOGBANE FAMILY
Apocynaceae

Herbs or shrubs (trees in tropical regions) with flowers
borne singly or in clusters and often with milky sap.

Flowers: Radially symmetrical. Calyx with 5 united sepals;
corolla with 5 united petals; corolla lobes often twisted in
bud; stamens 5; all these parts attached at base of ovary.
Leaves: Opposite, whorled, or alternate; simple.
Fruit: 2 pods, often attached at tips by style.

There are about 200 genera and 2,000 species, most
abundant in the tropics and subtropics. Oleander *(Nerium
oleander)* and several species of periwinkle *(Vinca)* are popular ornamentals. Many, including Oleander, are poisonous.
Some species are sources of medicine and others produce
valuable fruit or commercial rubber.

477 Spreading Dogbane
Apocynum androsaemifolium

Description: A branched bushy plant with *drooping
pairs of leaves* and fragrant, *small, pink,
bell-shaped flowers* in short open clusters
at ends of stems or in leaf axils; *sap milky.*

Flowers: Corolla ¼–⅜" (6–9 mm) long, with 5
outward-curved tips on rim.

Leaves: 1–2½" (2.5–6.5 cm) long, ovate.

Fruit: *2 slender pods,* each 5–7" (12.5–17.5 cm)
long, containing many seeds with long
silky hairs.

Height: 8–20" (20–50 cm), usually less than
1′ (30 cm).

Flowering: June–September.

Habitat: Dry soil, mostly in coniferous forests
from low to medium elevations.

Range: Most of Canada and United States,
except Florida.

Comments: The common name Dogbane is derived
from the Greek *apocynum,* meaning
"noxious to dogs." Distasteful and
poisonous, these plants are avoided by
animals. Native Americans used the
stems of Indian Hemp *(A. cannabinum),*
a plant 1–4′ (30–120 cm) high with
greenish or white corollas, as a source of
fiber for cords, nets, and cloth.

ARUM FAMILY
Araceae

Erect, prostrate, or climbing herbs with numerous small
flowers crowded on a fleshy spike (spadix), usually surrounded by an often showy bract (spathe).

Flowers: Bisexual or unisexual. Sepals and petals absent, or
represented by 4–6 segments (tepals); stamens usually
4–6; all these parts attached at base of ovary.
Leaves: Simple or compound, mostly long-stalked.
Fruit: Usually a berry.

There are about 110 genera and 1,800 species, found in
shady, damp or wet places, most numerous and varied in the
tropics. Many, such as Calla Lily *(Zantedeschia aethiopica),*
Philodendron species, and *Dieffenbachia picta* and *D. seguine,*
both known by the common name Dumbcane, are cultivated
as ornamentals. Without proper treatment, many species
are poisonous. Once treated, the roots of some tropical
species are an important starch supply; for instance, the root
of Taro *(Calocasia esculenta)* is the source of Hawaiian poi.

318 Yellow Skunk Cabbage
Lysichiton americanus

Description: A spike of minute flowers surrounded by
a large, conspicuous, *yellow or cream bract*
open on one side; spike borne on a stout
stalk rising from a cluster of giant, *erect
leaves.*
Flowers: Bract to 8″ (20 cm) long, often
appearing before leaves fully develop;
individual flowers inconspicuous.
Leaves: 1–5′ (30–150 cm) long, with stalks
usually much shorter than oval blades.
Height: 12–20″ (30–50 cm).
Flowering: March–July, often as snow melts.

Habitat: Swampy soil.
Range: Alaska south to central California near the coast, and east to Montana.
Comments: The common name refers to the skunk-like odor of the sap and the fetid odor of the flowers, which draws flies as pollinators. The peppery sap was once used as a treatment for ringworm. The short, fleshy, underground stem is eaten by animals. Baked, it supplemented the winter diets of Native Americans.

BIRTHWORT FAMILY
Aristolochiaceae

Herbs or woody vines with commonly heart-shaped leaves and medium to large, bizarre, often carrion-scented flowers.

Flowers: Bilaterally or radially symmetrical. Calyx 3-lobed or bent, with red, purple, or brown, united sepals; petals absent; stamens usually at least 6; all these parts attached at top of ovary.
Leaves: Alternate or basal, stalked, commonly with smooth edges.
Fruit: Capsule, with 4–6 chambers.

There are about 10 genera and 600 species, widely distributed in tropical and temperate regions. Some are aromatic; a few are cultivated.

381 Long-tailed Wild Ginger
Asarum caudatum

Description: 1 peculiar, *brown-purplish to yellowish or greenish flower hidden by heart-shaped leaves* growing in pairs from dense patches of trailing, rooting stems.
Flowers: 1½–5″ (4–12.5 cm) wide, 1 in each leaf axil; petal-like lobes 3, each ¾–3″ (2–7.5 cm) long, tapering out from bowl-like base to slender tips; stamens 12, tipped with scale-like appendages shorter than anthers.
Leaves: ¾–4″ (2–10 cm) long.
Height: Creeper; leafstalks 6″ (15 cm).
Flowering: April–July.
Habitat: Moist shaded woods below 5,000′ (1,500 m) elevation.

Range: British Columbia and western Montana to northeastern Oregon and south on western side of Cascade Range and Sierra Nevada to central California near the coast.

Comments: The flowers are not easily visible, as they rest on the ground under the leaves. The aromatic stems and roots were used by early settlers as a substitute for tropical ginger, to which it is not closely related. There are three other western species. Lemmon's Wild Ginger *(A. lemmonii),* found in the southern Sierra Nevada and northwestern California, has uniformly green leaves; in this respect, it is similar to *A. caudatum,* but its calyx lobes are only ½″ (1.5 cm) long or less. The other two species both have leaves mottled with white along the major veins. Hartweg's Wild Ginger *(A. hartwegii),* found in southwestern Oregon, northern California, and southward along the Sierra Nevada, has a calyx tube that is white on the inner surface with several red stripes covered by bands of white hairs. Marbled Wild Ginger *(A. marmoratum)* has a dark maroon calyx tube with scattered dark hairs; it occurs in southwestern Oregon and northwestern California.

MILKWEED FAMILY
Asclepiadaceae

Herbs, shrubs, or vines usually with thick milky sap, opposite or whorled leaves, flowers in flat or round, umbel-like clusters (cymes), and tufted seeds in pods.

Flowers: Radially symmetrical. Sepals 5; corolla of 5 united petals, with reflexed lobes; stamens 5, united with style to form a central columnar structure; often a central crown (corona) of 5 inflated sacs or scoop-shaped hoods between petals and stamens (*Asclepias* species with hoods usually enclosing a curved, horn-like appendage); all these parts attached at base of 2 ovaries.

Leaves: Simple, mostly opposite or in whorls.

Fruit: 2 pods, often joined at tips by style, containing many silky-haired seeds.

There are about 250 genera and 2,000 species, widely distributed but most abundant in tropical and subtropical regions. The rather elaborate central crown is especially characteristic of milkweed flowers. Several popular houseplants, such as those in the genera *Hoya* and *Stapelia,* belong to this family. Some species are a source of commercial rubber. In milkweeds *(Asclepias)* and others, the unusual structure of the flower regulates pollination. Pollen, contained in minute masses located in slits in the side of the central column, become attached to an insect when one of its legs enters a slit; as the insect visits another flower, the pollen must be left in precisely the right place on the column for pollination to be successful. This complicated mechanism may explain why so few fruits develop from each many-flowered cluster. Insects unable to pull free die trapped on the flower.

157 White-stemmed Milkweed; Wax Milkweed
Asclepias albicans

Description: Tall, *leafless, waxy-white stems* with woolly umbels of whitish, star-like flowers on branches near top; sap milky.

Flowers: Umbel about 2″ (5 cm) wide; each flower about ½″ (1.5 cm) wide; sepals 5, greenish, small; petals 5, *greenish white,* tinged brown or pink, bent back; 5 *round, yellowish hoods* with short horns curving toward center.

Leaves: ½–¾″ (1.5–2 cm) long, hair-like, 3 at each node, dropping soon after development.

Fruit: Smooth plump pod, about 4″ (10 cm) long, containing many seeds with silky hairs.

Height: 3–10′ (90–300 cm).

Flowering: March–May.

Habitat: Dry rocky places in deserts.

Range: Southeastern California and southwestern Arizona south to northwestern Mexico.

Comments: The genus was named in honor of Asclepiades, a physician in ancient Greece, undoubtedly because some species have long been used to treat a variety of ailments. The similar Rush Milkweed *(A. subulata)* is found in the same region in desert washes and on sandy flats; it is distinguished by its narrow, erect hoods, which are about as long as its petals.

---

529 Showy Milkweed
Asclepias speciosa

Description: *A grayish, velvety plant* with erect, leafy stems and *umbels of star-like, pinkish flowers* in upper leaf axils and at top; sap milky.

Flowers: Each flower about ¾″ (2 cm) wide; sepals 5, reddish; *petals 5, each about ½″* (1.5 cm) long, *pink or reddish purple,* bent back; 5 pink *erect hoods* with horns curving toward center.

Leaves: 4–8″ (10–20 cm) long, opposite, broadly lanceolate or ovate, with conspicuous veins from midrib to edge.

Fruit: Plump pod, 2–4″ (5–10 cm) long, covered with velvet and *small soft spines.*

Height: 1–4′ (30–120 cm).

Flowering: May–August.

Habitat: Dry, gravelly slopes, sandy areas, along watercourses, brush, and open forests.

Range: British Columbia south to California east of Cascade Range, and east to central United States.

Comments: There are recipes for preparing this species as a vegetable, but the plants should be positively identified. Some of the milkweeds are highly poisonous, and eating them can result in death.

---

158 Poison Milkweed;
Horsetail Milkweed
Asclepias subverticillata

Description: A plant forming feathery clumps or patches and bearing *white, star-like flowers in round umbels* and 3–5 very *narrow leaves in whorls* at nodes; sap milky.

Flowers: Umbel ¾–1¼″ (2–3 cm) wide; each flower almost ½″ (1.5 cm) wide; sepals 5, tiny; petals 5, bent back; 5 roundish hoods with long horns arching toward center.

Leaves:	¾–5″ (2–12.5 cm) long, with dwarf branches, very small leaves in axils.
Fruit:	Broad smooth pod, 2–4″ (5–10 cm) long, containing many seeds with long silky hairs.
Height:	To 4′ (1.2 m).
Flowering:	May–September.
Habitat:	Sandy or rocky plains and desert flats and slopes; common along roadsides.
Range:	Central Arizona and much of Utah east to Kansas and south to Mexico.
Comments:	This unpalatable species is very poisonous to livestock. When better forage is unavailable, animals may eat Poison Milkweed, often with fatal results.

374 Butterfly Weed; Orange Milkweed; Chiggerflower
Asclepias tuberosa

Description:	Umbels of *star-like, orange, yellow, or red flowers* in upper leaf axils and atop leafy, hairy, clustered stems.
Flowers:	Umbel to 3″ (7.5 cm) wide; each flower about ½″ (1.5 cm) wide; sepals 5, small; *petals 5, bent back; 5 erect, scoop-shaped hoods* with slender horns arching toward center.
Leaves:	1¼–4½″ (3–11 cm) long, almost opposite on stem, narrowly or broadly

Butterfly Weed

lanceolate, base of some indented, underside hairy.

Fruit: Narrow, tapered pod, 3–6″ (7.5–15 cm) long, containing many seeds with silky hairs.

Height: To 3′ (90 cm).

Flowering: April–September.

Habitat: Dry places, especially in prairies and canyons, and in brush or open woods.

Range: Arizona and Utah northeast to South Dakota and south to Texas, New Mexico, and Mexico; also in much of East.

Comments: This milkweed does not have milky sap. The thick, tuberous root was once used as a treatment for pleurisy, hence this plant is sometimes also known as Pleurisy Root.

156 Climbing Milkweed
Sarcostemma cynanchoides

Description: *A smooth vine with umbels of pale white, star-like flowers and long twining stems* often clambering over tops of bushes; sap milky.

Flowers: Umbel to 4″ (10 cm) wide; each flower about ½″ (1.5 cm) wide; sepals 5; petals 5, white, purplish, or pink, pointed, spreading; *5 white, spherical hoods* near center.

Leaves: To 2½″ (6.5 cm) long, opposite; blades narrow, lanceolate, or narrowly triangular, with at least 1 gland on midrib near base.

Fruit: Plump downy pod, to 3″ (7.5 cm) long, containing many seeds with silky hairs.

Height: Vine; stems to 10′ (3 m) long.

Flowering: April–August.

Habitat: Sandy or rocky soil, mostly in deserts but also on dry plains and in brush near coast.

Range: Southern California east through southern Utah to Oklahoma and Texas, and south to Mexico.

Comments: *Sarcostemma,* from the Greek *sarx* ("flesh") and *stemma* ("crown"), refers to the fleshy inner portion of the corona.

There are several similar species of this
genus in the Southwest, all hairy or
downy and with foliage that smells
somewhat like hot rubber.

ASTER FAMILY
Asteraceae

Herbs, sometimes shrubs or vines, rarely trees, with simple
or compound, alternate or opposite leaves, some species
with milky sap; flowers small and often organized into
larger, flower-like heads resembling 1 radially symmetrical
flower cupped by a ring of bracts (involucre).

Flower-like heads: Tiny, radially symmetrical flowers (disk
   flowers) forming a central disk; larger, strap-shaped,
   petal-like flowers (rays) surrounding central disk; flower
   head may be composed of all disk flowers (as in ragweeds)
   or all rays (as in dandelions).

Flowers: Calyx absent or represented by hairs, bristles, scales,
   or a crown, often persisting atop fruit; corolla with 4–5
   united petals; stamens 4–5; all these parts attached at top
   of ovary.

Leaves: Opposite, alternate, or whorled; simple or compound.

Fruit: 1-seeded, seed-like, with a hard shell; often topped
   with a pappus.

There are about 1,100 genera and 20,000 species in this
large, worldwide family, making it and the orchid family
(Orchidaceae) the two largest plant families. Many garden
varieties of Common Sunflower *(Helianthus annuus),* horticultural variants of species in the genera *Cosmos, Zinnia,* and
Dahlia, and several other plants are grown as ornamentals.
Many kinds of lettuce seen in the grocery store are obtained
from *Lactuca sativa,* and artichokes are from *Cynara scolymus.*
Common Sunflower provides sunflower oil and sunflower
seeds; Safflower *(Carthamus tinctorius)* is the source of safflower oil. Pollen from ragweeds *(Ambrosia)* is a major cause
of hay fever. When ingested, a number of species are poisonous to grazing animals; among these are snakeroots
(Eupatorium), broomweeds *(Gutierrezia),* certain sneezeweeds *(Dugaldia* and *Helenium),* bitterweeds *(Hymenoxys),*
and groundsels *(Senecio).* The family contributes tremen-
dously to the diversity, and thus to the stability, of arid
woodland and shrubland ecosystems throughout the world,
as in the sagebrush-dominated areas of the western United
States. Asteraceae has also been known as the daisy or sunflower family (Compositae).

150 Yarrow; Milfoil
Achillea millefolium

Description: An aromatic plant bearing *feathery, fern-like leaves* on a tough fibrous stem topped with a *flattish cluster of small white flower heads.*

Flowers: Head with 3–5 roundish white (sometimes pinkish) rays, each ⅛″ (3 mm) long; disk flowers 10–30.

Leaves: To 1½″ (4 cm) wide, blades repeatedly pinnately divided into fine segments.

Height: 12–39″ (30–100 cm).

Flowering: March–October.

Habitat: Open areas from lowlands to mountain highlands.

Range: Most of temperate North America.

Comments: This plant also occurs in Eurasia. Among its several common names, Milfoil and Plumajillo ("little feather") refer to the divided leaves, and Sneezeweed and Nosebleed may derive from its irritating odor. Spanish Californians once used leaves steeped in water to treat cuts and bruises and to stop bleeding.

Yarrow

373 Orange Agoseris
Agoseris aurantiaca

Description: Several leafless stalks, each topped with
1 *coppery-orange flower head,* growing
from a basal cluster of leaves; *sap milky.*

Flowers: Head about 1″ (2.5 cm) wide; *flowers all
rays,* those in center of head very short.

Leaves: 2–14″ (5–35 cm) long, narrow, broadest
above middle, often with few large
teeth.

Fruit: Seed-like, stalk at tip about as long as
body, tipped by fine silvery bristles.

Height: 4–24″ (10–60 cm).

Flowering: June–August.

Habitat: Meadows and grassy openings in
coniferous forests in mountains.

Range: Western Canada south to California
and New Mexico.

Comments: This plant is easily recognized. It is the
only orange-flowered *Agoseris.* Others
are yellow.

277 Pale Agoseris
Agoseris glauca

Description: Several leafless stalks, each topped with
1 *yellow flower head,* growing from a
basal cluster of leaves; *sap milky.*

Flowers: Head ½–1¼″ (1.5–3 cm) wide; *flowers
all rays,* those in center of head very
short.

Leaves: 2–14″ (5–35 cm) long, very narrow to
broadly lanceolate, broader above
middle; without teeth, with few teeth,
or sometimes deeply pinnately divided.

Fruit: Seed-like, with fine ridges at tip, stalk
tipped by fine white hairs.

Height: 4–28″ (10–70 cm).

Flowering: May–September.

Habitat: Open areas in coniferous forests and in
sagebrush.

Range: Western Canada south through
California mountains and east to New
Mexico, South Dakota, and Minnesota.

Comments: Several other yellow-flowered species of
Agoseris, all called False Dandelion or
Mountain Dandelion, are distinguished

from this one by technical features of the fruit. True dandelions *(Taraxacum)* are also similar but have minute pegs all over the top of the fruit and bracts usually curved back beneath the involucre.

153 Pearly Everlasting
Anaphalis margaritacea

Description: Several evenly leafy, woolly stems in a small patch, topped by a crowded, roundish cluster of rayless flower heads with *pearly white bracts,* sometimes with a dark spot at base of each outer bract.

Flowers: Head about ¼″ (6 mm) long; disk flowers minute; some plants bearing heads of disk flowers with stamens and lacking pistils, some bearing heads of disk flowers with pistils and lacking stamens.

Leaves: To 5″ (12.5 cm) long, narrowly lanceolate, underside densely hairy, top less hairy or smooth and dark green.

Height: 8–36″ (20–90 cm).

Flowering: June–September.

Habitat: Along roadsides and in fields from lowlands to high in mountains; commonly in forest openings.

Range: Much of North America south to southern California, Arizona, New Mexico, South Dakota, Minnesota, and North Carolina.

Comments: This plant also occurs in Eurasia. The dried stalks, with their pearly white flower heads, are attractive in flower arrangements.

541 Nuttall's Pussytoes
Antennaria parvifolia

Description: An erect, sparsely leaved stalk with *clusters of small, rayless, whitish to pinkish flower heads,* rising from a small, *grayish, basal rosette.*

Flowers: Head about ½″ (1.5 cm) long; bracts translucent, scale-like, barely darkened at base.

Leaves: ½–¾" (1.5–2 cm) long, equally hairy on
both sides; those in rosettes lanceolate
but obviously broader near top; those on
flower stalk much narrower.

Fruit: Seed-like, with 5 white bristles at tip.

Height: To 6" (15 cm).

Flowering: July–September.

Habitat: Openings in dry forests and on plains.

Range: Western Canada south to eastern
Washington and through Rocky
Mountains and western Plains states to
Arizona and New Mexico.

Comments: Some plants in this species produce seed
in the usual manner, by fertilization of
eggs in the ovary; others do not require
fertilization. The tightly clustered, basal
leaves and the near absence of dark bases
on the bracts of the flower heads help
distinguish Nuttall's Pussytoes from
other members of this large genus.

251 Heartleaf Arnica
Arnica cordifolia

Description: A plant forming patches with stems
bearing *2–4 pairs of heart-shaped leaves* and
topped by *1–3 broad yellow flower heads.*

Flowers: Head 2–3½" (5–9 cm) wide; rays
10–15; disk flowers many, tiny; bracts
with long spreading hairs.

Leaves: Those on separate short shoots largest,
1½–5" (4–12.5 cm) long, with long
petioles attached at notch; those on
flowering stem with short or no petioles.

Fruit: Seed-like, with a tuft of white or pale
tan hairs at tip.

Height: 4–24" (10–60 cm).

Flowering: April–June, occasionally to September.

Habitat: Lightly shaded woods.

Range: Alaska south to southern California and
east to Rocky Mountains from Canada to
New Mexico; also in northern Michigan.

Comments: In alpine areas or in open places along
roads, the leaves may be narrower and
without the notch at the base of the
blade. This species has heart-shaped
leaves; all western species have opposite
leaves on the stems.

94   Engelmann Aster
Aster engelmannii

Description: Stems, leafy in middle but not below,
branched near top and bearing *flower
heads with few white or pinkish rays* at
branch ends.

Flowers: Head with about 13 rays surrounding
a yellow central disk about 1½–2½″
(4–6.5 cm) wide; bracts with a
strong, raised midvein, pale and stiff
at base.

Leaves: 2–4″ (5–10 cm) long, lanceolate,
without stalks, not hairy or only lightly
hairy, hairs densest on lower side.

Fruit: Seed-like, hairy, with few fine bristles
at tip.

Height: 1½–5′ (45–150 cm).

Flowering: June–September.

Habitat: Open places and woodland clearings.

Range: Western Canada south to northwestern
California, northeastern Nevada, and
northern Colorado.

Comments: This is one of a number of tall asters; its
stems are straight, erect, with few in a
bunch, and branched only near the top.
Its flower heads, with a few often
slightly curled rays, have a ragged
appearance.

484   Leafy Aster
Aster foliaceus

Description: Leafy stems with ascending branches
terminated by several flower heads, each
with *many narrow, lavender or purple to
pink rays.*

Flowers: Head 1–2″ (2.5–5 cm) wide; rays
surrounding a *yellow central disk;*
involucre bracts overlapping; additional
outer, rather leafy, large bracts often
present.

Leaves: 5–8″ (12.5–20 cm) long; basal ones
lanceolate, gradually narrowing to stalk-
like base; those at midstem with bases
partly surrounding and clasping stem.

Fruit: Seed-like, smooth or sparsely hairy on
surface, tipped by a tuft of fine hairs.

Height: 8–20″ (20–50 cm).
Flowering: July–September.
Habitat: Moist places in woods, along road banks, and in mountain meadows.
Range: Alaska south to central California, Arizona, and New Mexico.
Comments: The genus name means "star" in Greek. Asters have flower heads that resemble those of fleabanes *(Erigeron),* another large and complex western genus. The bracts of plants in the genus *Aster,* however, usually vary in length, overlapping like shingles on a roof. Many asters are tall and leafy; few fleabanes are. As the great assemblage called *Aster* is studied and better understood, it is clear that there are several groups within it worthy of generic recognition. Botanists anticipate that Leafy Aster, along with nearly 80 other species now in the genus *Aster,* will be placed in the genus *Symphyotrichum.*

90 Tobacco Weed; Parachute Plant
Atrichoseris platyphylla

Description: A smooth, gray-green plant with a *flat rosette* of basal leaves and tall spindly stems, openly branched in upper half, with *white or pale pink flower heads* at branch ends.
Flowers: Head 1–2″ (2.5–5 cm) wide; *flowers all rays,* those in center of head smaller.
Leaves: 1¼–4″ (3–10 cm) long, ovate, often purple-spotted; edges with uneven, tiny, spine-tipped teeth.
Fruit: Seed-like, shaped like a 5-sided club, lacking hairs.
Height: 12–28″ (30–70 cm).
Flowering: February–May.
Habitat: Sandy, desert washes.
Range: Southwestern Utah and northwestern Arizona southwest to southeastern California.
Comments: The scientific name means the "flat-leaved" *(platyphylla)* "chicory plant without hairs" *(Atrichoseris),* referring to the absence of hairs on the fruit.

269   Desert Marigold
Baileya multiradiata

Description: A grayish, woolly plant, branched and
leafy mostly in lower half, with *brilliant
yellow flower heads,* 1 borne atop each of
many nearly leafless stalks.

Flowers: Head 1½–2″ (4–5 cm) wide; rays
25–50, oblong, after seed-set becoming
papery and remaining on head; lacking
scales among disk flowers.

Leaves: Blades 1½–3″ (4–8 cm) long, broadly
ovate, pinnately divided into broad
lobes, which are again divided or with
roundish teeth.

Fruit: Seed-like, pale tan or chalky white,
lacking bristles or scales at tip.

Height: 12–20″ (30–50 cm).

Flowering: April–October.

Habitat: Sandy or gravelly areas in deserts;
common along roadsides.

Range: Southern Utah south to southeastern
California, western Texas, and northern
Mexico.

Comments: Dense patches often form solid strips
of yellow along miles of desert roads.
In gardens a single plant grows into a
perfect hemisphere of yellow, blooming
throughout the hot summer and into the
fall. The common name marigold, given
to several species of Asteraceae with
sunny yellow or orange flowers, comes
from "Mary's Gold," in honor of the
Virgin Mary.

248   Arrowleaf Balsam Root
Balsamorhiza sagittata

Description: An almost leafless stalk topped with 1
large, *bright yellow flower head* growing
from a *basal cluster of large, silvery-gray
leaves* covered with felt-like hairs.

Flowers: Head 4–5″ (10–12.5 cm) wide; rays 8–25,
each 1–1½″ (2.5–4 cm) long; disk flowers
many, each enfolded by a parchment-
like scale; bracts densely woolly.

Leaves: Blades to 1′ (30 cm) long, on petioles of
about equal length.

Fruit:	Seed-like, lacking hairs or scales at tip.
Height:	8–31″ (20–80 cm).
Flowering:	May–July.
Habitat:	Open hillsides and flats in grasslands, sagebrush, and open pinewoods.
Range:	British Columbia south through Sierra Nevada and east to western Montana, western South Dakota, and Colorado.
Comments:	Native Americans prepared medicine from the roots. The very similar Deltoid Balsam Root *(B. deltoidea),* found in open places in Washington, western Oregon, and California, is only sparsely hairy, is much greener, and drops its rays soon after flowering. Several species of *Balsamorhiza* have pinnately divided leaves.

85 English Daisy
Bellis perennis

Description:	Short, slender, leafless stalks, each bearing 1 flower head with *many narrow, white or pinkish rays* and yellow disk flowers, growing from a *basal rosette of leaves.*
Flowers:	Head about 1″ (2.5 cm) wide; bracts of equal length.
Leaves:	To 1½″ (4 cm) long, blades elliptical or round, with small teeth on edges, tapering at base to broad petioles of about equal length.
Fruit:	Seed-like, lacking hairs or scales at tip.
Height:	2–8″ (5–20 cm).
Flowering:	March–September.
Habitat:	Lawns, fields, and roadsides.
Range:	Scattered throughout United States; in West, most frequent from Washington to California.
Comments:	It may be that the word daisy originated with this plant. It means "day's eye" and comes from the Anglo-Saxon *daeges ege.* English Daisy folds up its rays at night and opens them again at dawn—the "eye of the day." Introduced from Europe, this pretty flower is a common weed in lawns, especially in cool moist regions near the coast. A doubled form is planted as an ornamental.

246 Greeneyes; Chocolate Flower
Berlandiera lyrata

Description: A leafy plant, often with many short branches at base and longer, leaning branches ending in leafless stalks topped by flower heads with *yellow rays surrounding a maroon central disk.*

Flowers: Head about 1½" (4 cm) wide; rays 5–12 (usually 8), each ½" (1.5 cm) long, broad, underside yellowish maroon or with maroon veins; each disk flower enfolded by a scale; *bracts broadly ovate, nearly flat;* involucre bracts, fruit of ray flowers, 2 nearby bracts, and disk flowers all dropping off together when mature.

Leaves: 2–6" (5–15 cm) long, velvety, with scalloped edges or pinnately divided into scalloped-edged segments, *end segment largest.*

Fruit: Seed-like, lacking scales or hairs at tip.

Height: 1–4' (30–120 cm).

Flowering: April–October.

Habitat: Grassy areas in gravelly or rocky soil; common along roadsides.

Range: Southeastern Colorado and southern Kansas south through western Texas and New Mexico to Mexico.

Comments: The genus name honors Jean-Louis Berlandier, a French-Swiss physician who collected plants in northern Mexico and Texas in the early 1800s. A chocolate odor may be detected when the rays are plucked from the flower head.

297 Large-flowered Brickelbush
Brickellia grandiflora

Description: Clusters of *creamy-yellow, rayless flower heads* hanging from short branches at tips of leafless stalks borne in upper axils of leafy stems.

Flowers: Head ⅜–½" (9–13 mm) long; outer bracts ovate, with long slender tips; inner bracts long, narrow; *all bracts straw-colored, striped with green.*

Leaves:	¾–5″ (2–12.5 cm) long, blades triangular, angles near base rounded, edges scalloped.
Fruit:	Seed-like, slender, with 10 ribs and fine hairs at tip.
Height:	1–3′ (30–90 cm).
Flowering:	July–October.
Habitat:	Banks, cliffs, and canyons at moderately high elevations, mostly in forests.
Range:	Eastern Washington south to Baja California and east to western Texas, Arkansas, Missouri, and Nebraska.
Comments:	This large and complex genus consists mostly of shrubs. Some were used medicinally by Native Americans.

337 Silvercrown Luina
Cacaliopsis nardosmia

Description:	*Golden yellow, rayless flower heads* in a narrow cluster atop stout stems growing from a cluster of basal leaves.
Flowers:	Head ½–¾″ (1.5–2 cm) long; *bracts of about equal length, lined up side by side,* barely overlapping.
Leaves:	Blades to 8″ (20 cm) long, *nearly round, palmately cleft,* coarsely toothed, long-stalked.
Fruit:	Seed-like, slender, with numerous fine bristles at tip.
Height:	1–3′ (30–90 cm).
Flowering:	May–July.
Habitat:	Meadows and open woods in mountains.
Range:	Washington south along Cascade Range to northern California, and south in northern Coast Ranges to upper San Francisco Bay.
Comments:	This is the only species in the genus *Cacaliopsis.* It is sometimes included in *Luina,* a small genus of western North America.

266 Rosin Weed
Calycadenia truncata

Description:	A slender, odorous plant with *yellow flower heads* in a narrow cluster and *very*

362 Aster Family

narrow leaves; each upper leaf tipped with a broad, *dish-shaped gland.*

Flowers: Head about 1″ (2.5 cm) wide; rays 3–8, each about ¼–½″ (6–13 mm) long, *broad,* with *3 teeth at end,* central tooth narrowest.

Leaves: ¾–3½″ (2–9 cm) long.

Fruit: Seed-like; those of disk flowers slender, sparsely hairy, topped by several short scales; those of rays short, squat, wrinkled, lacking hairs or scales.

Height: 1–4′ (30–120 cm).

Flowering: June–October.

Habitat: Dry, sunny, sparsely grassy slopes.

Range: Southern Oregon south to central California.

Comments: The genus name comes from the Greek *kalyx* ("cup") and *adenos* ("gland"), referring to the peculiar glands that distinguish all but one species of this genus found primarily in California. Rays on some species are white, changing to rose as they age.

---

542 **Musk Thistle; Bristle Thistle; Nodding Thistle**
Carduus nutans

Description: A tall leafy plant, *prickly on leaf edges and on thin ribs along stem,* topped by large, handsome, *deep pink to reddish-lavender, rayless flower heads.*

Flowers: Head 1½–3″ (4–7.5 cm) wide; bracts prickly, lower ones bent back.

Leaves: To 16″ (40 cm) long, stalkless, pinnately lobed, the lobes jagged.

Fruit: Seed-like, with fine, long, white bristles at tip.

Height: 1–9′ (30–270 cm).

Flowering: June–October.

Habitat: Roadsides, pastures, and rangelands.

Range: Throughout much of United States; frequent in Rocky Mountain region.

Comments: Native to Europe and western Asia, this plant has become increasingly frequent in disturbed areas and can crowd out native vegetation. Lovely as the flower heads may be, the plant is a noxious

weed. The more common *Cirsium*
thistles are very similar but have
tiny hairs along the bristles at the fruit
tip, giving the bristles a feathery
appearance.

486 Spotted Knapweed
Centaurea maculosa

Description: *A slender, repeatedly branched, open, broom-like plant with many pink-lavender, rayless flower heads at ends of stiff stems.*

Flowers: Head about ⅜″ (10 mm) wide, slightly longer and tapered toward top, with bright pink-lavender (rarely white) disk flowers at top, those around edge of head each ½–1″ (1.5–2.5 cm) long; corolla of each disk flower with 5 long slender lobes; *bracts on side of head with blackish fringed tip.*

Leaves: Those at base 4–6″ (10–15 cm) long, deeply pinnately divided into narrow lobes, often with glandular spots; those on stem smaller, uppermost ones often not lobed.

Height: 12–39″ (30–100 cm).

Flowering: July–September.

Habitat: Disturbed areas, often along roadsides.

Range: Washington south to California and east across much of southern Canada and northern United States.

Comments: If this noxious weed is extensively handled, gloves are advised; there is some evidence that it causes tumors on the hands. It grows in thick stands, crowding out other vegetation. In an unsuccessful attempt to control the plant, flies have been introduced whose grubs feed upon the developing seeds. Even though seed production is reduced 30–85 percent by the grubs, there are still hundreds of seeds to spread the species. There is some recent evidence that the correct name for this introduced species is *C. biebersteinii,* there being possibly an early nomenclatural mix-up of plants in these two variable European species.

338 Yellow Star Thistle
Centaurea solstitialis

Description: A slender, branched, *grayish-hairy plant with wing-like ridges along stem* and small, rayless, *bright yellow flower heads* with *lustrous, sharp, golden spines.*

Flowers: Head about ½–⅝" (12–16 mm) wide, slightly longer; spines each ⅜–1" (1–2.5 cm) long, spreading.

Leaves: Those at base 2–3" (5–8 cm) long, deeply lobed; those on stem smaller, not lobed, bases continuing down stem with wing-like ridges.

Height: 4–39" (10–100 cm).

Flowering: May–October.

Habitat: Disturbed areas, pastures, and dry grasslands and hillsides.

Range: Washington south to California and east to Utah and Idaho.

Comments: Native to Europe, this invasive plant is spreading across the western United States. It grows in dense stands that are painful to walk through because of the piercing spines. If continually eaten, it is poisonous to horses. A virtue, however, is that it produces a fine light honey. This unloved weed is a relative of Bachelor's Button *(C. cyaneus).* A similar but less showy plant, Tocolote *(C. melitensis),* has smaller spines on the flower heads, the longest only about ¼–⅜" (5–10 mm) long; it, too, has been introduced from Europe and is rapidly spreading in western North America.

170 Desert Pincushion; Esteve's Pincushion
Chaenactis stevioides

Description: A small, openly branched plant with flower heads of all *white disk flowers,* those around edge larger and somewhat ray-like.

Flowers: Head about 1" (2.5 cm) wide, sometimes tinged with pink.

Leaves: ½–1½" (1.5–4 cm) long, *lightly woolly, pinnately divided,* segments again

pinnately divided into short narrow
lobes.

Fruit: Seed-like, club-shaped, hairy, with 4
lanceolate scales at tip.

Height: 4–10″ (10–25 cm).

Flowering: March–June.

Habitat: Rocky or sandy deserts.

Range: Southeastern Oregon east through
southern Idaho to western Wyoming
and Colorado, and south to California,
Arizona, New Mexico, and northwestern
Mexico.

Comments: Other common names sometimes used
are False Yarrow and Broad-leaved
Chaenactis. There are several *Chaenactis*
species with white flowers.

330 Rubber Rabbit Brush
Chrysothamnus nauseosus

Description: A shrub with *erect, slender, flexible
branches* covered with dense, felt-like,
matted hairs (visible when surface
lightly scraped), very narrow leaves, and
small, rayless, yellow flower heads in dense
clusters at stem ends.

Flowers: Head ¼–½″ (6–13 mm) long, slender;
bracts oriented in 5 vertical rows, outer
bracts short.

Leaves: ¾–3″ (2–7.5 cm) long.

Rubber Rabbit Brush

Fruit:	Seed-like, with fine hairs at tip.
Height:	To 7′ (2.1 m).
Flowering:	August–October.
Habitat:	Grasslands, open woodlands, and dry open areas with sagebrush.
Range:	Western Canada south to California, Texas, and northern Mexico.
Comments:	Rubber Rabbit Brush is a common and variable species in a genus found only in western North America. Some races are light green; others have silvery hairs. The Navajo obtained a yellow dye from the flower heads.

641 Chicory
Cichorium intybus

Description:	Wiry branched stems with few leaves on upper part and *pale blue flower heads* along main branches; *sap milky.*
Flowers:	Head about 2″ (5 cm) wide; *flowers all rays,* each with 5 small teeth across blunt end.
Leaves:	Those near base 3–10″ (7.5–25 cm) long, lanceolate, pinnately toothed or lobed, edged with small sharp teeth; upper leaves smaller.
Fruit:	Seed-like, with tiny scales at tip.
Height:	1–6′ (30–180 cm).
Flowering:	March–October.
Habitat:	Roadsides, fields, and city lots.
Range:	Throughout most of United States; more common in regions with ample rain.
Comments:	Introduced from Eurasia, Chicory is grown for its roots; ground and roasted, they are added to or substituted for coffee. Young leaves may be used in salads or as a vegetable. Endive *(C. endivia),* a close relative, is cultivated as a salad plant.

422 Snowy Thistle
Cirsium occidentale var. *candidissimum*

Description:	*A white, woolly, prickly plant* with *rayless, crimson flower heads* atop few upper branches terminating main stem.

Flowers:	Head 1½–2½″ (4–6.5 cm) long; disk flowers bright red, extending about 1″ (2.5 cm) beyond bracts; bracts of equal length, tipped with spines.
Leaves:	4–12″ (10–30 cm) long, narrow, pinnately lobed, edges prickly and continuing down stem as narrow, wing-like ridges.
Fruit:	Seed-like, with long white hairs at tip, each hair lined with many smaller hairs.
Height:	2–4′ (60–120 cm).
Flowering:	June–September.
Habitat:	Dry open slopes in brushy or grassy areas and in open woods.
Range:	Southern Oregon, northern California, southwestern Idaho, and western Nevada.
Comments:	With its blaze of red flowers accentuated by white foliage, this is perhaps the handsomest thistle among a genus considered to be composed of aggressive weeds. Snowy Thistle is one of an intergrading complex of forms all in *C. occidentale,* some with less densely hairy foliage, others with grayer hairs; some have white, rose, or purple disk flowers. These various forms occur from northern to southern California.

263 Giant Coreopsis
Coreopsis gigantea

Description:	A soft woody stem branching near top bearing *feathery leaves* and clusters of *large yellow flower heads* atop long leafless stalks; *plant resembles a small tree.*
Flowers:	Head to 3″ (7.5 cm) wide; rays two-tone yellow, more deeply colored at base; bracts in 2 series, outer ones lanceolate and shorter, inner ones broader.
Leaves:	To 1′ (30 cm) long, broadly ovate, repeatedly pinnately divided into fine, fleshy, very narrow lobes; stems about 4″ (10 cm) thick.
Height:	1–10′ (30–300 cm).
Flowering:	March–May.
Habitat:	Coastal dunes and bluffs.
Range:	San Luis Obispo County south to Los Angeles County, California.

Comments: Another species, Sea Dahlia (*C. maritima*), stout but not woody and with heads borne singly on stalks, is found in coastal San Diego County and Baja California. It is not a true dahlia, a popular ornamental developed from *Dahlia* wildflowers found in the mountains of Mexico.

254 Hawk's Beard
Crepis acuminata

Description: A loose, flattish or round-topped cluster of many *narrow flower heads of yellow rays* atop a branched *leafy stem; sap milky*.

Flowers: Head about ½–1″ (1.5–2.5 cm) wide; flowers all rays, 5–10 per head; inner bracts each ⅜–½″ (9–15 mm) long, at least twice as long as outer bracts.

Leaves: 4–16″ (10–40 cm) long, lightly and softly downy, pinnately lobed, edges often with teeth.

Fruit: Seed-like, with slender white hairs at tip.

Height: 8–28″ (20–70 cm).

Flowering: May–August.

Habitat: Open dry places in sagebrush and coniferous forests.

Range: Eastern Washington south to eastern California and east to northern New Mexico, Colorado, and central Montana.

Comments: *Crepis* is Greek for "sandal"; the reason for its application to this genus is apparently lost in history. *Crepis* species have races that reproduce asexually, adding to the variation within the genus and making identification sometimes difficult.

256 Orange Sneezeweed; Owl Claws
Dugaldia hoopesii

Description: 1 or several stout leafy stems bearing *orange-yellow flower heads with drooping rays* atop nearly leafless stalks.

Flowers: Head 2–3″ (5–7.5 cm) wide; rays each ¾–1″ (2–2.5 cm) long, narrow, with 3 teeth at tip, surrounding a *nearly spherical central disk.*

Leaves: To 1′ (30 cm) long, lanceolate, progressively smaller higher on stem.

Fruit: Seed-like, densely covered with tan hairs, with several sharply pointed scales at tip.

Height: 2–4′ (60–120 cm).

Flowering: July–September.

Habitat: Wet places in mountain meadows.

Range: Southern Oregon and northern California south along Sierra Nevada and east to New Mexico, Colorado, and Wyoming.

Comments: The round, deep yellow flower heads with rays hanging around the edge distinguish sneezeweeds. The heads of some species are much smaller. This species, previously known as *Helenium hoopesii,* has leaves with edges that do not continue down the stem. Similar species in the now more narrowly circumscribed genus *Helenium* have leaves that are narrow and thread-like or are broader, but then the edges continue down the stem as narrow, wing-like ridges. Orange Sneezeweed, which has become increasingly frequent in heavily grazed areas, causes a sheep poisoning called "spewing sickness." The common name sneezeweed, equally correct for *Dugaldia* or *Helenium,* refers to the allergic irritation caused by the pollen. Preparations made from the root have been used to treat rheumatic pains, stomach disorders, and, in infants, colic and diarrhea.

264 Brittlebush; Incienso
Encelia farinosa

Description: A round, *silvery-gray, leafy bush* with *bright yellow flower heads* in loosely branched clusters on branched stalks well above foliage.

Flowers: Head 2–3″ (5–7.5 cm) wide; rays 8–18, each ¼–½″ (6–15 mm) long, yellow; central disk yellow (brown in southern part of range), with disk flowers enfolded by scales.

Leaves: 1¼–4″ (3–10 cm) long, ovate, hairy, with petioles.

Fruit: Seed-like, lacking hairs or scales at tip.

Height: 3–5′ (90–150 cm).

Flowering: March–June.

Habitat: Dry slopes and washes in deserts.

Range: Southwestern Utah south through western Arizona, southern Nevada, and southeastern California to northwestern Mexico.

Comments: In full flower, this plant seems a solid hemisphere of brilliant yellow. The stems exude a fragrant resin that was chewed by Native Americans and used as incense in churches in Baja California, hence the common name Incienso. A similar species, California Encelia *(E. californica),* which grows near the southern California coast, has only one head on each stalk.

---

258 **Sunray**
Enceliopsis nudicaulis

Description: 1 or several *leafless stalks,* each topped with a *broad yellow flower head,* growing from a *basal cluster of gray-green leaves.*

Flowers: Head 3–4″ (7.5–10 cm) wide; rays about 20; central disk broad, with each small disk flower enfolded in a stiff bract.

Leaves: Blades ½–2½″ (1.5–6.5 cm) long, ovate, tapered to long flat stalks.

Fruit: Seed-like, flat, hairs on sides nearly hiding 2 stiff bristles at tip.

Height: 6–18″ (15–45 cm).

Flowering: May–August.

Habitat: Among desert brush.

Range: Central Idaho south to Nevada, Utah, northern Arizona, and southeastern California.

Comments: Its beauty—golden flower heads held high above a tuft of gray foliage—makes Sunray a worthwhile ornamental in dry regions.

95 Spreading Fleabane
Erigeron divergens

Description:
A well-branched plant covered with *short grayish hairs,* those on stems standing straight out; each of many branches topped by a flower head with *many narrow, white, pink, or lavender rays* surrounding a yellow central disk.

Flowers:
Head about 1″ (2.5 cm) wide; rays each ¼–⅜″ (6–10 mm) long; *bracts very narrow, mostly lined up side by side,* not overlapping.

Leaves:
Those at base ½–1″ (1.5–2.5 cm) long, in tufts, with a lanceolate blade evenly tapered to a stalk-like base; those on stem numerous, slightly smaller.

Fruit:
Seed-like, with numerous fine fragile bristles at tip.

Height:
4–28″ (10–70 cm).

Flowering:
April–September.

Habitat:
Open, sandy areas in deserts, plains, valleys, and foothills.

Range:
Southern British Columbia south to California and Mexico, and east to western Texas, Colorado, and Montana.

Comments:
This is one of a large number of similar species. Most usually can be recognized as *Erigeron* by their low form, many white, pink, or lavender rays, and bracts around the head all of about the same length. Occasionally, Spreading Fleabane may lack rays and have only yellow disk flowers.

482 Seaside Daisy
Erigeron glaucus

Description:
Bristly-hairy, sticky stems growing from a basal rosette, each long branch topped by a flower head with *many narrow, pale pink or lavender rays* surrounding a yellowish central disk.

Flowers:
Head 1½–2½″ (4–6.5 cm) wide; rays about 100; bracts shaggy-hairy.

Leaves:
To 5″ (12.5 cm) long, broadly spatula-shaped, sometimes with teeth on edges near top, tapering to a broad flat stalk.

Fruit:	Seed-like, with numerous fine fragile bristles at tip.
Height:	4–16″ (10–40 cm).
Flowering:	April–August.
Habitat:	Coastal bluffs, hills, and old dunes.
Range:	Oregon south to southern California.
Comments:	This daisy is slightly succulent, a common feature of seaside plants but unusual in this genus.

481 Philadelphia Fleabane
Erigeron philadelphicus

Description:	1 leafy stem, branched mostly in upper half, with each branch topped by a flower head with *150–400 very slender, white or pink rays;* plant covered with sparse, long, spreading hairs.
Flowers:	Head ½–1″ (1.5–2.5 cm) wide; rays each ¼–⅜″ (6–10 mm) long, surrounding a yellow central disk; *bracts of about equal length, mostly lined up side by side,* not overlapping.
Leaves:	To 6″ (15 cm) long, *spatula-shaped,* bases on most continuing around point of attachment and *clasping stem;* lower leaves tapering to stalks.
Fruit:	Seed-like, with numerous fine fragile bristles at tip.
Height:	8–28″ (20–70 cm).
Flowering:	May–September.
Habitat:	Most common in moist, often partly shaded sites with disturbed soil.
Range:	Throughout United States and most of Canada.
Comments:	In this especially pretty species, the many thread-like rays form a delicate fringe around the central disk. The common name fleabane comes from the old belief that these plants repelled fleas. Fleabanes are very similar to members of the genus *Aster,* but asters usually bloom late in the season and have bracts on the flower head of different lengths, overlapping like shingles.

96, 483 Showy Daisy
Erigeron speciosus

Description: A leafy stem branching near top into
leafless stalks, each topped by 1 flower
head with *many narrow, pink, lavender, or
white rays* surrounding a yellow central
disk.

Flowers: Head 1½–2″ (4–5 cm) wide; rays each
½–¾″ (1.5–2 cm) long; *bracts of about
equal length, lined up side by side,* not
overlapping.

Leaves: Lower ones 3–6″ (7.5–15 cm) long,
lanceolate, smooth, commonly with 3
veins, bases joined to stem about
halfway around and slightly clasping.

Fruit: Seed-like, with fine fragile bristles at tip.

Height: 1–3′ (30–90 cm).

Flowering: June–September.

Habitat: Woodland openings and lightly wooded
areas at moderate elevations in mountains.

Range: Southern British Columbia south to
Arizona and east to New Mexico, South
Dakota, and Montana.

Comments: This fleabane has one of the showiest
heads, reflected in the species name,
which means "pretty." The similar Hairy
Showy Daisy *(E. subtrinervis)* has
spreading hairs over most of the stem
and leaves.

260 Golden Yarrow
Eriophyllum lanatum

Description: *A grayish, woolly, leafy plant* with several
branched stems ending in short leafless
stalks and *golden yellow flower heads.*

Flowers: Head 1½–2½″ (4–6.5 cm) wide; rays
8–12, each ½–¾″ (1.5–2 cm) long,
broad, surrounding disk flowers; bracts
broadly lanceolate, with prominently
ridged backs.

Leaves: 1–3″ (2.5–7.5 cm) long, irregularly
divided into narrow lobes.

Fruit: Seed-like, narrow, smooth, with a low
crown of scales at tip.

Height: 4–24″ (10–60 cm).

Flowering: May–July.

Habitat:	Dry thickets and dry open places.
Range:	British Columbia south to southern California and western Nevada, and east to northeastern Oregon, western Montana, and western Wyoming; perhaps also in Utah.
Comments:	This common and variable species often colors road banks with a blaze of yellow in drier portions of the West. The plant's white hairs conserve water by reflecting heat and reducing air movement across the surface of the leaves.

261   Woolly Daisy
Eriophyllum wallacei

Description:	*A tiny, gray, woolly, tufted plant* with small, *golden yellow flower heads.*
Flowers:	Head about ¼″ (6 mm) wide; rays 5–10, each about ⅛″ (3 mm) long, oval, surrounding few disk flowers.
Leaves:	To ¾″ (2 cm) long, ovate, tapering to short stalks.
Fruit:	Seed-like, narrow, black, with few short scales at tip.
Height:	½–4″ (1.5–10 cm).
Flowering:	March–June.
Habitat:	Sandy deserts.
Range:	Southwestern Utah and northwestern Arizona south through southeastern California to northern Baja California.
Comments:	In desert annuals, such as Woolly Daisy, seed production is vital for yearly survival. During drought, plants often grow only about ¼″ (6 mm) before producing one flower head, ensuring at least some seeds. In more moist conditions, plants repeatedly branch near the base, producing taller stems, many heads, and abundant seeds.

396   Indian Blanket; Firewheel; Gaillardia
Gaillardia pulchella

Description:	Branched stems, mostly leafy near base, topped by showy flower heads with *rays*

*red at base, tipped with yellow, each with 3
teeth at broad end.*

Flowers: Head 1½–2½″ (4–6.5 cm) wide; rays
each ½–¾″ (1.5–2 cm) long; central
disk reddish maroon, dome-like, with
bristly scales among disk flowers.

Leaves: To 3″ (7.5 cm) long, oblong, edges
toothed or plain.

Fruit: Seed-like, with tapered, translucent,
white scales at tip.

Height: 1–2′ (30–60 cm).

Flowering: May–July.

Habitat: Sandy plains and deserts; common along
roadsides.

Range: Nebraska and southeastern Colorado
south to central and southern California,
Arizona, New Mexico, Texas, and
Mexico; also in much of eastern Canada
and United States.

Comments: Frequent along roadsides in the
Southwest, these wildflowers stand like
hundreds of showy Fourth of July
pinwheels at the tops of slender stalks.
Aptly, this species is sometimes also
called Showy Gaillardia. Varieties are
popular in cultivation, as they tolerate
heat and dryness; they often escape into
disturbed areas. Some of the several
species in the Southwest have entirely
yellow flower heads.

Indian Blanket

257 Desert Sunflower
Geraea canescens

Description: A slender, *hairy plant* with few leaves, and *golden yellow flower heads* at ends of several branches.

Flowers: Head about 2″ (5 cm) wide; rays 10–20, each ¾″ (2 cm) long, oblong, surrounding disk flowers; bracts with long, stiff, white hairs on edges.

Leaves: To 3″ (7.5 cm) long, lanceolate or ovate, often with few teeth.

Fruit: Seed-like, flat, hairy, tip with 2 pointed scales, edges with a strong white margin; each tightly enfolded by a parchment-like bract.

Height: 1–3′ (30–90 cm).

Flowering: February–May; sometimes October–November, depending on rains.

Habitat: Sandy, barren, flat deserts.

Range: Southwestern Utah south through western Arizona and southeastern California to northwestern Mexico.

Comments: *Geraea* comes from the Greek *geraios* ("old man"), referring to the white hairs on the fruit. After adequate rain, this species may bloom for mile after mile along hot, dry, desolate roadsides.

273 Curlycup Gumweed; Stickyheads
Grindelia squarrosa

Description: A dark green, leafy plant, openly branched in upper parts, with *many yellow flower heads; tips of bracts around flower heads strongly rolled back.*

Flowers: Head about 1½″ (4 cm) wide; rays 25–40, surrounding a small central disk.

Leaves: To 3″ (7.5 cm) long, oblong, clasping stem at bases; edges with sharp, forward-pointing teeth.

Fruit: Seed-like, plump, brownish, usually with 4 angles; several narrow scales at tip easily dropping off.

Height: 1–3′ (30–90 cm).

Flowering: July–September.

Habitat: Dry open areas, often in old fields and waste places.

Range: Frequent throughout much of the arid West; also in much of East.

Comments: The toxicity of gumweeds *(Grindelia),* especially Curlycup Gumweed, depends upon the soil in which each species grows. When the plants absorb the element selenium, they become poisonous and pose considerable problems for cattle and horse ranchers. However, species have been used medicinally for centuries. Influenced by magical numbers, Spanish New Mexicans would boil three flower buds in three pints of water three times until only one pint of liquid remained, and then would drink a glassful three times daily for kidney disorders. Extracts were used for a wide variety of complaints, from skin irritations to asthma and rheumatic pains.

---

329 Snakeweed; Matchweed; Matchbush
Gutierrezia sarothrae

Description: *Many slender green branches forming a round plant, woody at base,* with *hundreds of tiny, yellow flower heads* in loose clusters.

Flowers: Head ⅛–¼″ (3–6 mm) long, narrow; rays 3–7, each about ⅛″ (3 mm) long; disk flowers 2–6, tiny.

Leaves: ¼–2½″ (6–63 mm) long, less than ⅛″ (3 mm) wide, resinous.

Fruit: Seed-like, hairy, plump, with low scales at tip.

Height: 6–36″ (15–90 cm).

Flowering: August–September.

Habitat: Deserts, plains, and among piñon and juniper.

Range: Eastern Oregon and southern Idaho south to southern California and Mexico, and east to Texas and the western plains as far north as central Canada.

Comments: The names Matchweed and Matchbush refer to this plant's match-like flower heads. Bundled dried stems made primitive brooms, hence its other common names Broom Snakeweed and Broomweed. It is also known as

Turpentine Weed, referring to its odor.
A very similar species, Littlehead
Snakeweed *(G. microcephala),* which may
grow in the same area, has 1–3 rays and
1–3 disk flowers. As with many
aromatic plants, these species were used
medicinally, occasionally as a treatment
for snakebite, hence the common name
snakeweed. Both species pose serious
problems as range weeds. More frequent
under improper range management,
they now cover thousands of square
miles of once good grassland. They are
poisonous, occasionally killing grazing
livestock but more commonly causing
miscarriages.

---

247 Common Sunflower; Mirasol
Helianthus annuus

Description: *A tall, coarse, leafy plant* with a hairy
stem commonly branched in upper half
and bearing several to many flower
heads with many *bright yellow rays*
surrounding a *maroon central disk.*

Flowers: Head 3–5″ (7.5–12.5 cm) wide; disk

Common Sunflower

flowers among stiff scales; bracts ovate, abruptly narrowing to a slender tip.

Leaves: Lowest ones ovate, often heart-shaped, edges usually with irregular teeth; upper ones smaller, narrower.

Fruit: Seed-like, flattish but plump; 2 scales above 2 sharp edges, readily dropping off.

Height: 2–13′ (60–390 cm).

Flowering: June–September.

Habitat: Dry open plains and foothills; especially common along roadsides and edges of fields.

Range: Throughout most of North America.

Comments: This is the state flower of Kansas. Mirasol, the Spanish name, means "looks at the sun"; the flower heads follow the sun each day, facing east in the morning and west at sunset. The plant has been cultivated in the Americas since pre-Columbian times; yellow dye obtained from the flower heads, and a black or dull blue dye from the seeds, were once important in Native American basketry and weaving. In the United States and Eurasia, seeds from cultivated forms are now used for cooking oil and livestock feed. Many variants have been developed, some with one huge flower head topping a stalk 10–16½′ (3–5 m) tall, others with maroon rays. Prairie Sunflower *(H. petiolaris)*, similar to the wild forms of Common Sunflower, has scales tipped by white hairs in the central disk, easily visible when the disk flowers are spread apart.

---

249 Golden Aster
Heterotheca villosa

Description: A round plant with erect or spreading, leafy stems, covered with *rough grayish hairs,* and *yellow flower heads in branched clusters.*

Flowers: Head about 1″ (2.5 cm) wide, with yellow rays surrounding a yellow central disk.

Leaves:	Those at midstem ½–1¼″ (1.5–3 cm) long, lanceolate.
Fruit:	Seed-like, with dingy white bristles at tip, outer bristles shorter.
Height:	8–20″ (20–50 cm).
Flowering:	May–October.
Habitat:	Open plains, rocky slopes, and cliffs from low elevations into coniferous forests.
Range:	Canada south to southern California and Mexico, and east to Texas, Nebraska, and Wisconsin.
Comments:	This species and its close relatives, distinguished by their hairiness, are very common in the West; they are found in dry places everywhere, often in quite showy displays. The species are variable and often difficult to identify precisely; Golden Aster alone has five named varieties.

270 Alpine Gold; Alpine Hulsea
Hulsea algida

Description:	*A low, tufted, densely glandular-hairy plant* with sparsely leaved stems, each topped by a flower head with 25–60 *short, narrow, yellow rays* surrounding a yellow central disk.
Flowers:	Head 2–3½″ (5–9 cm) wide; central disk broad; *bracts of about equal length,* narrow, overlapping.
Leaves:	Lower ones to 6″ (15 cm) long, succulent, lanceolate, often with scalloped or lobed edges.
Fruit:	About ½″ (1.5 cm) long, seed-like, narrow, with 4 scales at tip.
Height:	6–14″ (15–35 cm).
Flowering:	July–September.
Habitat:	Sandy or gravelly soil and rock crevices high in mountains.
Range:	Northeastern Oregon and eastern California mountains east to Idaho and southwestern Montana.
Comments:	The similar Dwarf Hulsea *(H. nana),* found in the mountains of Washington, Oregon, and northern California, is more compact, rarely more than 4″

(10 cm) high, with a usually leafless flower stalk and a flower head with only about 21 rays.

---

271 Stemless Hymenoxys
Hymenoxys acaulis

Description: Short leafless stalks growing from *tufted basal leaves,* each stalk topped with 1 *yellow flower head.*

Flowers: Head 1–2″ (2.5–5 cm) wide; rays usually 8–13, broad, with 3 teeth; disk flowers many, each about ⅛″ (4 mm) long.

Leaves: To 3″ (7.5 cm) long, ½″ (1.5 cm) wide, hairy or smooth.

Fruit: Seed-like, hairy, usually with few pointed scales at tip.

Height: 3–12″ (7.5–30 cm).

Flowering: June–September.

Habitat: Open dry hillsides and dry plains.

Range: Southern Idaho south to southeastern California and east to central Canada, North Dakota, Ohio, and Texas.

Comments: This common species is highly variable, reaching its greatest complexity in Wyoming and western Colorado. A few plants may lack rays; most have no stems below the flower stalk. Some are very hairy, while others are nearly hairless.

---

272 Old-man-of-the-mountain; Alpine Sunflower
Hymenoxys grandiflora

Description: *A whitish, hairy plant with feather-like leaves* mostly near base and 1 *large yellow flower head* borne on each of 1 or several stout stems.

Flowers: Head 3–4½″ (7.5–11.5 cm) wide; rays at least 20, surrounding a broad central disk; bracts numerous, very narrow, woolly.

Leaves: 3–4″ (7.5–10 cm) long, pinnately divided into very narrow segments.

Fruit: Seed-like, 5-sided, densely hairy, narrow, with 5–8 stiff narrow scales at tip.

Height: 1–12″ (2.5–30 cm).

Flowering: June–August.

Habitat: Rocky slopes, high meadows, and tundra.

Range: Central Idaho and southwestern Montana south to Colorado and eastern Utah.

Comments: In a complicated genus of about 20 species in western North America, this plant has the largest and prettiest flower heads; *grandiflora* means "large-flowered."

---

245 Goldfields
Lasthenia californica

Description: A small slender annual with reddish stems, *very narrow opposite leaves,* and a small, *golden yellow flower head* atop each branch.

Flowers: Head ¾–1″ (2–2.5 cm) wide; rays about 10, oblong, surrounding a cone-shaped central disk.

Leaves: ½–2½″ (1.5–6.5 cm) long, stiffly hairy at base.

Fruit: Seed-like, slender, with several narrow, brownish, pointed scales at tip; scales sometimes absent.

Height: 4–10″ (10–25 cm).

Flowering: March–May.

Habitat: Open fields and slopes at low elevations.

Range: Southwestern Oregon south to central Arizona and Baja California.

Comments: In open areas with poor soil, where grass is sparse, this plant will form carpets of gold if moisture is ample. It is sometimes placed in the genus *Baeria. Crocidium multicaule* (not to be confused with *Lomatium utriculatum* of the carrot family, Apiaceae, which shares the common name Spring Gold) looks very much like Goldfields but has most leaves in a basal rosette; leaves on the stem are alternate, with tufts of hair in the axils.

88 Oxeye Daisy
Leucanthemum vulgare

Description: A *dark green, leafy plant* with a cluster
of several stems topped by nearly
leafless branches, each bearing 1
flower head with *many white rays*
surrounding a yellow central disk;
*each bract of flower head with a narrow
brown line near margin.*

Flowers: Head about 3″ (7.5 cm) wide; rays each
½–¾″ (1.5–2 cm) long.

Leaves: Lower ones 1½–6″ (4–15 cm) long,
broadly lanceolate, with long petioles;
upper ones smaller, lacking petioles;
all with edges lobed or cleft and
scalloped.

Fruit: Seed-like, lacking scales or hairs at tip.

Height: 8–31″ (20–80 cm).

Flowering: May–October.

Habitat: Fields, pastures, and roadsides.

Range: Throughout much of southern Canada
and United States; more common in
north.

Comments: Introduced from Europe and naturalized
throughout much of North America,
this plant was once considered to be
among the very close relatives of our
cultivated chrysanthemums; it was
formerly classified as *Chrysanthemum
leucanthemum.* Botanical research
indicates that it is best placed in a
genus of about 25 species separate
from *Chrysanthemum. L. maximum,* a
parent of the commonly cultivated
Shasta Daisy, also grows wild west
of the Cascade Range and in California
at or near the coast; it resembles
Oxeye Daisy but generally has
rays ¾–1¼″ (2–3 cm) long. The
chrysanthemum sold by florists, *C.
morifolium,* derives from eastern Asian
sources, but the precise history of its
many variations in size and of the
doubling of its flower head is unknown.
The genus name *Chrysanthemum* means
"golden flower."

520 Dotted Gayfeather
Liatris punctata

Description: Several stems bearing *narrow, crowded heads of rose-lavender disk flowers in slender, elongated clusters.*

Flowers: Head about ¾" (2 cm) long; disk flowers 4–8.

Leaves: 3–6" (7.5–15 cm) long, very narrow, stiff, minutely dotted.

Fruit: Seed-like, narrow, hairy, with many small plumes at tip.

Height: 6–31" (15–80 cm).

Flowering: August–September.

Habitat: Dry open places, plains, and among piñon and juniper, often in sandy soil.

Range: Central Canada south along eastern base of Rocky Mountains to western Texas and northern Mexico, and east to Michigan, Iowa, and Arkansas.

Comments: Rayless heads of purple flowers and slender, often plume-like bristles on the fruit generally distinguish this complex genus mostly of the eastern United States.

336 Silvery Luina
Luina hypoleuca

Description: A leafy plant with several *stems in a clump, covered with white wool* densest on stems and undersides of leaves, and *dull yellowish, rayless flower heads* in a branched cluster at each stem tip.

Flowers: Head about ⅜" (9 mm) long; bracts of equal length, side by side, barely overlapping.

Leaves: 1–2½" (2.5–6.5 cm) long, broadly ovate.

Fruit: Seed-like, with soft white bristles at tip.

Height: 6–16" (15–40 cm).

Flowering: June–October.

Habitat: Rocky places and cliffs.

Range: Central British Columbia south to central California.

Comments: Each leaf has a white underside, as the species name suggests (*hypo* means "beneath" and *leuca* means "white"), often contrasting with the upper surface, which may be darker. The plant must have reminded the botanist who named this genus of another, *Inula*, also white and woolly (*Luina* is an obvious anagram).

583 Sticky Aster
Machaeranthera bigelovii

Description: Leafy branched stems topped by flower heads with *many narrow, bright reddish-lavender or purple rays* surrounding a *yellow central disk.*

Flowers: Head about 1½″ (4 cm) wide; *bracts glandular-hairy,* pale and stiff at base, green at *bent or curled-back tip.*

Leaves: 2–4″ (5–10 cm) long, oblong, with *sharp teeth on edges.*

Fruit: Seed-like, with many slender bristles at tip.

Height: 1–3′ (30–90 cm).

Flowering: August–October.

Habitat: Plains and openings in coniferous forests.

Range: Western Colorado south to New Mexico and Arizona.

Comments: These wildflowers of late summer often color entire banks and roadsides with vibrant purple. In the afternoon, as flower heads become shaded, the rays fold upward in the "sleep position." Sticky Aster resembles true asters *(Aster)* but has spiny or divided leaves.

255 Yellow Spiny Daisy
Machaeranthera pinnatifida

Description: A slender plant with *small, weakly bristly leaves* and 1 *yellow flower head* at tip of each of many upper branches.

Flowers: Head about 1″ (2.5 cm) wide; rays each about ⅜″ (9 mm) long, surrounding disk flowers.

Leaves: ⅛–¾″ (3–20 mm) long, narrow, lowest ones sometimes with few lobes, angled upward or pressed against stem, edges with a *spiny bristle at tip of each tooth.*

Fruit:	Seed-like, densely covered with short hairs, with numerous slender, pale tan bristles at tip.
Height:	6–14″ (15–35 cm).
Flowering:	August–October.
Habitat:	Open places in arid grasslands and deserts and among piñon and juniper.
Range:	Alberta south through Rocky Mountain region and much of the Plains states to New Mexico, Arizona, southern California, and northern Mexico.
Comments:	The classification of this species, once known as *Haplopappus spinulosus,* has perplexed botanists; *Haplopappus* in the strictest sense is a southern South American genus. North American plants related to Yellow Spiny Daisy may be better placed in *Machaeranthera.* The very similar but annual species *M. gracilis,* also called Yellow Spiny Daisy, has the lowest chromosome number known in plants, with only four chromosomes in each cell; most plants have 14–30.

585 Tahoka Daisy
Machaeranthera tanacetifolia

Description:	Branched stems with *fern-like leaves* ending in *flower heads with many bright purple, very narrow rays* surrounding a *yellow central disk.*
Flowers:	Head 1¼–2½″ (3–6.5 cm) wide.
Leaves:	2–5″ (5–12.5 cm) long, pinnately divided, main segments also pinnately divided.
Fruit:	Seed-like, covered with short hairs lying flat on surface, with many slender bristles at tip.
Height:	4–16″ (10–40 cm).
Flowering:	May–September.
Habitat:	Sandy, open ground on plains and deserts.
Range:	Alberta south to southeastern California, Arizona, New Mexico, Texas, and Mexico.
Comments:	The fern-like leaves of this beautiful species make it one of the easiest to identify in a complex group. False Tahoka Daisy *(M. parviflora)* is similar

but has smaller flower heads, each with a central disk only ¼–½″ (6–13 mm) wide, and less elaborately divided leaves; it occurs from Utah south to Arizona, New Mexico, Texas, and Mexico.

268 Common Madia
Madia elegans

Description: Slender, erect, leafy stems with mostly *yellow flower heads* at ends of branches in upper part.

Flowers: Head 1¼–2″ (3–5 cm) wide; rays about 13, each ½–¾″ (1.5–2 cm) long, yellow, with *3 teeth* at broad end and often a maroon patch near base; erect hairs among disk flowers; *bracts completely enfolding adjacent fruit.*

Leaves: To 8″ (20 cm) long, narrow.

Fruit: Seed-like, flat, dark, produced only by ray flowers.

Height: 1–4′ (30–120 cm).

Flowering: July–September.

Habitat: Dry, open, usually grassy places, often along roadsides.

Range: Southwestern Washington south to Baja California.

Comments: Species of *Madia* (a Chilean name for a species once grown for the oil in its seeds) are covered with sticky, glandular hairs and are often called Tarweed. The flower heads of many, including those of Common Madia, close at night. It is estimated that there are about 11 species of *Madia* in California.

274 Snakehead
Malacothrix coulteri

Description: Pale, smooth, branched stems with most leaves near base and *pale yellow flower heads* at tips; *sap milky.*

Flowers: Head 1–1½″ (2.5–4 cm) wide; *flowers all rays,* those in center of head smaller.

Leaves: Those near base 2–4″ (5–10 cm) long, lanceolate, edges coarsely toothed; those on stem ovate, with bases clasping stem.

Fruit:	Seed-like, narrow, pale greenish brown, with 4–5 sharp angles and 2 fine lines between angles; slender bristles at tip, most of which break off easily.
Height:	4–20″ (10–50 cm).
Flowering:	March–May.
Habitat:	Open flats and hills in grasslands or deserts.
Range:	Central California south to Baja California and east to southwestern Utah and southern Arizona.
Comments:	The flower head of this species has broad round bracts with parchment-like edges and a purplish or greenish central band that resembles a serpent's scales, and the bud resembles a fanciful snake head, hence the common name. Among similar species, Yellow Tackstem (*Calycoseris parryi*) has small, tack-shaped glands on the bracts and upper stem, and Scalebud (*Anisocoma acaulis*) has seed-like fruits with feathery bristles at the tip, the outer bristles half the length of the inner bristles.

275   Desert Dandelion
Malacothrix glabrata

Description:	A smooth plant with *few pinnately divided leaves* and *canary yellow flower heads* on branched stems.
Flowers:	Head 1–1½″ (2.5–4 cm) wide; flowers all rays.
Leaves:	2½–5″ (6.5–12.5 cm) long, divided into few thread-like lobes.
Fruit:	Seed-like, with several soft bristles at tip, 2 of which do not drop off.
Height:	6–14″ (15–35 cm).
Flowering:	March–June.
Habitat:	Sandy deserts, plains, and washes.
Range:	Eastern Oregon and southwestern Idaho south through Nevada and eastern Utah to southeastern California, much of Arizona, southwestern New Mexico, and northwestern Mexico.
Comments:	In wet years this showy wildflower will form masses of yellow in sandy deserts. There are about 15 species of

Malacothrix in western North America; all have dandelion-like flower heads.

87 Blackfoot Daisy
Melampodium leucanthum

Description: A low, round, bushy plant with flower heads of *8–10 broad white rays* surrounding a small yellow central disk.

Flowers: Head about 1″ (2.5 cm) wide; *broad outer bracts 5,* joined along one-half to two-thirds their length.

Leaves: ¾–2″ (2–5 cm) long, opposite, narrow.

Fruit: Seed-like, with several narrow scales at tip.

Height: 6–20″ (15–50 cm).

Flowering: March–November.

Habitat: Rocky soil in deserts and on dry plains.

Range: Kansas southwest to Arizona and Mexico.

Comments: At first glance, Blackfoot Daisy appears to be the twin of White Zinnia *(Zinnia acerosa),* but flower heads of the latter species have 4–6 broad white rays and a narrow base of several overlapping scales. Both may be found in the same habitat, but the range of White Zinnia does not extend as far south as Blackfoot Daisy.

Blackfoot Daisy

89 Desert Star
Monoptilon bellioides

Description: A *small low plant* with flower heads of *white rays* often tinged with rose surrounding a *yellow central disk;* longer branches tending to lie on ground.

Flowers: Head ¾″ (2 cm) wide; rays about 20.

Leaves: To ½″ (1.5 cm) long, few, narrow, stiffly hairy.

Fruit: Seed-like, plump, hairy, with *several short scales and longer bristles* at tip.

Height: 1–2″ (2.5–5 cm); 1–10″ (2.5–25 cm) wide.

Flowering: January–May; sometimes September, depending on rains.

Habitat: Sandy or gravelly, desert flats.

Range: Southern California, western Arizona, and northwestern Mexico.

Comments: As is often characteristic of desert annuals, this species' growth depends upon the amount of rainfall. If winter rains are ample, it and other spring wildflowers grow in profusion, even obscuring the surface of the ground; if rainfall is scant, the plant will be only a fraction of an inch tall, with one head disproportionately large in comparison to the rest of the plant. Daisy Desert Star *(M. bellidiforme),* a very similar species from the same region, has only one plume-tipped bristle atop the fruit.

485 Showy Palafoxia
Palafoxia sphacelata

Description: A slender, erect, sparsely leaved plant, usually glandular-hairy on upper parts, with few *pink flower heads* at ends of upper branches.

Flowers: Head 1–1½″ (2.5–4 cm) wide; each ray with a narrow base and a *broad tip with 3 narrow lobes;* disk flowers many; bracts of about equal length.

Leaves: 1½–3″ (4–7.5 cm) long, lanceolate.

Fruit: Seed-like, slender, narrow, with several *slender, pointed scales* at tip.

Height: 1–2′ (30–60 cm).

Flowering: May–October.

Habitat: Sandy plains, deserts, piñon and juniper rangeland, and dunes.

Range: Kansas south and southwest to Texas, New Mexico, and Mexico.

Comments: The related Spanish Needles *(P. arida)* has only very pale lavender disk flowers; on top of the fruit are four slender, pointed scales (the "Spanish needles"). It is common on sandy flats and in washes from southeastern California west to southwestern Utah and western Arizona.

---

259 Chinchweed
Pectis papposa

Description: Slender stems branching many times in a forked manner and forming a low, small, leafy plant with *small yellow flower heads* in bundles at branch ends.

Flowers: Head about ½″ (1.5 cm) wide; rays 7–9, surrounding a small central disk; bracts each less than ¼″ (6 mm) long, narrow, lined up side by side, not overlapping, with 3–7 conspicuous *glands.*

Leaves: To 1½″ (4 cm) long, less than ⅛″ (3 mm) wide, dotted with glands, bases broad, edges translucent with few bristle-tipped lobes.

Fruit: Seed-like, narrow; tipped with a low crown of few scales, 1–2 sometimes much longer than others.

Height: 2–8″ (5–20 cm).

Flowering: July–October.

Habitat: Open areas on arid plains and deserts, especially on sandy soil; frequent along roadsides.

Range: Southern California east to western Texas and south to Mexico.

Comments: On a hot summer afternoon in areas where these plants are numerous, the air is saturated with a heavy lemon odor reminiscent of furniture polish. A look-alike, Lemonweed *(P. angustifolia),* is often found with Chinchweed but is denser and has only one gland at the tip of each bract.

335 Pericome
Pericome caudata

Description: *Rayless, yellow flower heads in branched clusters* above several branched leafy stems forming large rounded masses of foliage.

Flowers: Head about ½″ (1.5 cm) wide; bracts numerous, lined up side by side.

Leaves: 2–5″ (5–12.5 cm) long, *arrowhead-shaped, tapered to a long slender tip.*

Height: 2–5′ (60–150 cm).

Flowering: August–October.

Habitat: Slopes in coniferous forests.

Range: Mountains of east-central California and central Colorado south to western Texas, New Mexico, Arizona, and northern Mexico.

Comments: A common late-season wildflower along mountain road banks, this plant was called Yerba de Chivato (the "herb of the he-goat") by early Spaniards because of its odor.

348 Turtleback; Desert Velvet
Psathyrotes ramosissima

Description: *A low, compact, round, gray, velvety plant* with a strong *turpentine odor* and tiny, yellow flower heads.

Flowers: Head about ¼″ (6 mm) wide, of all disk flowers, held erect just above leaves.

Leaves: To ¾″ (2 cm) long, *thick, roundish,* with *prominent veins* and coarsely toothed edges.

Fruit: Seed-like, densely silky-hairy, with yellow-brown bristles at tip.

Height: 2–5″ (5–12.5 cm).

Flowering: March–June.

Habitat: Desert flats and ledges.

Range: Southwestern Utah south through western Arizona and southeastern California to northwestern Mexico.

Comments: The plants form mounds resembling the shape of a turtle's shell, and the intermeshed leaves are even fancied to represent its scales, hence one of this species' common names.

265 Paperflower
Psilostrophe cooperi

Description: Many well-branched, leafy stems, woolly at base, forming a *nearly round plant covered with loose wool* and usually bearing 1 yellow flower head at each branch end.

Flowers: Head ½–1″ (1.5–2.5 cm) wide; *rays 3–5, very broad,* each with *3 shallow teeth* at end, surrounding few small disk flowers.

Leaves: 1–2½″ (2.5–6.5 cm) long, very narrow.

Fruit: Seed-like, with several pointed scales at tip.

Height: 4–20″ (10–50 cm).

Flowering: April–October.

Habitat: Deserts and plains.

Range: Southeastern California east to southwestern Utah and southwestern New Mexico, and south to Mexico.

Comments: Paperflower forms brilliant yellow globes. Its rays become dry and papery, remaining on the plant long after flowering. There are several closely related species, all poisonous to livestock.

92 Desert Chicory; Plumeseed
Rafinesquia neomexicana

Description: A smooth, sparsely leaved, grayish-green plant with *white flower heads* at ends of few branches; *sap milky.*

Flowers: Head 1–1½″ (2.5–4 cm) wide; *flowers all rays,* longest ones each ½″ (1.5 cm) long, often purplish on back; outer bracts short, with slender, curled back tips.

Leaves: Those at base 2–8″ (5–20 cm) long, pinnately divided into narrow lobes; upper leaves much smaller.

Fruit: Seed-like, narrow, with a *slender, rigid stalk tipped with feathery hairs,* stalk not quite as long as body.

Height: 6–20″ (15–50 cm).

Flowering: March–May.

Habitat: Sandy or gravelly desert flats and slopes, often supported by shrubs.

Range: Southeastern California and southern Utah east to tip of western Texas and south to Mexico.

Comments: The genus name honors C. S.
Rafinesque, an eccentric early
naturalist. Two similar species in
the same region are California
Plumeseed *(R. californica),* with
smaller flower heads and the stalk
on the fruit longer than the body,
and White Tackstem *(Calycoseris
wrightii),* with tack-shaped, glandular
hairs beneath the flower head.

241 Mexican Hat
Ratibida columnifera

Description: A plant branched and leafy in
lower part with long leafless
stalks bearing flower heads of
*3–7 yellow or yellow and red-brown,
drooping rays* surrounding a *long,
red-brown central disk.*

Flowers: Head 1–3″ (2.5–7.5 cm) long;
rays each ½–¾″ (1.5–2 cm) long,
either yellow, yellow with red-brown
base, or red-brown with small
yellow tip; central disk ½–2½″
(1.5–6.5 cm) high, ½″ (1.5 cm)
thick, bluntly conical; outer
bracts about twice as long as
inner bracts.

Leaves: 1–6″ (2.5–15 cm) long, pinnately
cleft into few very narrow segments.

Fruit: Seed-like, with a fringe on one edge,
tipped with a low crown and 2 tooth-
like projections.

Height: 1–4′ (30–120 cm).

Flowering: July–October.

Habitat: Open, limestone soil; common
along roadsides and on prairies.

Range: Most of Great Plains and along
eastern base of Rocky Mountains
west to Arizona and south to Mexico.

Comments: The colorful flower heads, resembling
the traditional broad-brimmed, high-
centered hat worn during Mexican
fiestas, often bloom by the thousands.
Prairie Coneflower *(R. tagetes)* has a
spherical or oblong central disk and
leaves closer to the flower head.

242 **Cut-leaved Coneflower**
Rudbeckia laciniata

Description: A tall leafy plant with erect branches ending in *large flower heads with yellow, downward-arching rays surrounding a brown central disk.*

Flowers: Head 3–6″ (7.5–15 cm) wide; rays 6–16, each 1–2½″ (2.5–6.5 cm) long, slender; *central disk cylindrical or conical.*

Leaves: 3–8″ (7.5–20 cm) long, deeply divided into 3, 5, or 7 variously cut and toothed lobes, lower ones on long stalks.

Fruit: Seed-like, 4-sided, with a low crown at tip.

Height: 2–7′ (60–210 cm).

Flowering: July–October.

Habitat: Moist mountain meadows, slopes, and valleys.

Range: Canada south through Rocky Mountain region to Arizona, New Mexico, and Texas, and east to Atlantic Coast.

Comments: This plant is mildly toxic to livestock. Black-eyed Susan *(R. hirta),* an eastern species introduced in many places in the West, has a dark brown or brown-maroon, hemispherical central disk surrounded by orange-yellow, somewhat drooping rays; its lanceolate leaf blades sometimes have teeth, and there is no crown or ring of scales on the fruit.

319 **Nodding Groundsel**
Senecio bigelovii

Description: An erect, leafy stem with *nodding, rayless, yellow flower heads* on usually bent stalks and arranged in a narrow branched cluster.

Flowers: Head ½″ (1.5 cm) wide; bracts each ½–¾″ (1.5–2 cm) long, *side by side, not overlapping.*

Leaves: 4–8″ (10–20 cm) long, lanceolate, with teeth on edges.

Fruit: Seed-like, with a *tuft of fine white hairs at tip.*

Height: 1–3′ (30–90 cm).

Flowering: July–September.

Habitat: Rich moist soil on grassy mountain
            hillsides and forests.
Range: Western Colorado south to Arizona and
            New Mexico.
Comments: *Senecio,* as traditionally constructed, was
            one of the largest genera of plants, with
            2,000–3,000 species worldwide. The
            genus is unwieldy, and several of its
            definable subunits have been raised to
            the level of genus (these name changes
            affect none of the species in this book).
            Nearly 100 species occur in the West.
            Olympic Mountains Groundsel *(S.
            neowebsteri),* found in the Olympic
            Mountains in western Washington, and
            Showy Alpine Senecio *(S. amplectens),*
            found in the Rocky Mountains, both
            also have nodding flower heads, but
            these species have rays.

243   Threadleaf Groundsel
Senecio flaccidus

Description: *A bluish-green, bushy, leafy plant covered
                with close white wool* and bearing *yellow
                flower heads* in branched clusters.
Flowers: Head about 1¼″ (3 cm) wide; rays each
                about ½″ (1.5 cm) long, surrounding a
                narrow central disk; bracts of about
                equal length, *lined up side by side, not
                overlapping.*
Leaves: 1–5″ (2.5–12.5 cm) long, *divided into few
                very narrow lobes;* upper leaves often
                simple, very narrow.
Fruit: Seed-like, with a tuft of slender white
                hairs at tip.
Height: 1–3′ (30–90 cm).
Flowering: April–September.
Habitat: Dry rocky plains, deserts, and piñon-
                juniper rangelands.
Range: California east to Utah and southern
                Colorado, and south to western Texas,
                Arizona, and Mexico.
Comments: This is one of the range plants most
                toxic to livestock, especially the tender
                new growth; because it is generally
                avoided by cattle, it tends to increase on
                overstocked ranges. It was used

medicinally by southwestern Native Americans. This species has several varieties, ranging from hairless annuals to woolly shrubs.

244 Arrowleaf Groundsel
Senecio triangularis

Description: *Broadly or narrowly triangular or arrowhead-shaped leaves with many sharp teeth on edges* on several leafy stems topped by *yellow flower heads* in a branched flattish cluster.

Flowers: Head 1–1½" (2.5–4 cm) wide; rays about 8, each ½" (1.5 cm) long, surrounding a small central disk; bracts each about ½" (1.5 cm) long, lined up side by side, not overlapping.

Leaves: 2–8" (5–20 cm) long.

Fruit: Seed-like, with a tuft of slender white hairs at tip.

Height: 1–5' (30–150 cm).

Flowering: June–September.

Habitat: Streambanks and other moist places in mountains.

Range: Alaska and western Canada south to southern California, western Nevada, northern Utah, and northern New Mexico.

Comments: As indicated by the common and species names, the triangular leaves of this species are distinctive.

321 Meadow Goldenrod;
Canada Goldenrod
Solidago canadensis

Description: A tall, leafy, *finely hairy stem* topped by *tiny, yellow flower heads* in a long or flat-topped cluster on *arching branches.*

Flowers: Head about ⅛" (3 mm) long; rays 3, short.

Leaves: 2–5" (5–12.5 cm) long, lanceolate, finely hairy, with 3 prominent veins.

Fruit: Seed-like, sparsely hairy, with numerous pale bristles at tip.

Meadow Goldenrod

Height:	1–5′ (30–150 cm).
Flowering:	May–September.
Habitat:	Meadows and open forests.
Range:	Throughout most of North America.
Comments:	This handsome species produces showy displays, usually late in the summer. Although goldenrods are commonly blamed for hay fever, this discomfort is usually caused by pollen from ragweeds *(Ambrosia),* which are less conspicuous plants with greenish flower heads that bloom at the same time. Missouri Goldenrod *(S. missouriensis)* is similar but usually smaller, with smooth stems; it is also found throughout much of the West.

322 Narrow Goldenrod; Coast Goldenrod
Solidago spathulata

Description:	Generally several stems in a clump with largest leaves at base and many *small yellow flower heads in a narrow long cluster.*
Flowers:	Head about ¼″ (6 mm) long; *rays 5–10 (usually 8),* surrounding a small central disk.
Leaves:	To 6″ (15 cm) long, lanceolate, smooth, tapering to a smooth, stalk-like base.

| Fruit: | Seed-like, slender, with a tuft of fine white bristles at tip. |

Height: 2–31″ (5–80 cm).

Flowering: June–September.

Habitat: Coastal sand dunes and open mountain slopes and valleys.

Range: Canada south to central California coast, and in mountains to Arizona and New Mexico; also in eastern United States.

Comments: This species can be found in a wide range of habitats and is variable. Although it occurs well into the mountains, in alpine regions it is replaced by Alpine Goldenrod *(S. multiradiata)*, which is similar but with bristly hairs on the edges of its leaf stalks.

253 Stemless Golden Weed
Stenotus acaulis

Description: Numerous nearly leafless stalks, each topped with 1 *yellow flower head*, growing from *dark green, erect, stiff leaves in dense tufts or mats.*

Flowers: Head about 1½″ (4 cm) wide; rays 6–15, each about ½″ (1.5 cm) long, surrounding disk flowers; *bracts pointed,* lanceolate.

Leaves: ½–2″ (1.5–5 cm) long, with 3 veins.

Fruit: Seed-like, with numerous pale tan bristles at tip.

Height: ½–6″ (1.5–15 cm).

Flowering: May–August.

Habitat: Dry open places from foothills to fairly high elevations.

Range: Southeastern Oregon south along eastern slopes of Sierra Nevada, east to central Idaho and Colorado, and northeast to southwestern Montana and central Canada.

Comments: The very similar Thrift Golden Weed *(S. armerioides)*, found from Montana south to Arizona and New Mexico, and east to Nebraska, can be distinguished by the round tips on its bracts.

333 Dune Tansy
Tanacetum camphoratum

Description: A leafy, lightly hairy plant, growing in patches, with *feathery leaves,* aromatic when crushed, and stems topped by *open clusters of small, button-like, yellow flower heads.*

Flowers: Head about ½″ (1.5 cm) wide; *rays inconspicuous.*

Leaves: 2–8″ (5–20 cm) long, *pinnately divided, the lobes again pinnately divided* 1–2 times.

Fruit: Seed-like, with a minute crown of tiny scales at tip.

Height: 8–24″ (20–60 cm).

Flowering: June–September.

Habitat: Coastal sand dunes.

Range: British Columbia south to northern California.

Comments: Recent interpretation suggests there are only trivial differences between this more widespread race (formerly classified as *T. douglasii*) and the race known as Camphor Dune Tansy, which grows near San Francisco, is densely hairy, and lacks any suggestion of rays around the flower head. Common Tansy *(T. vulgare),* with no hairs and a cluster of 20–200 flower heads, was widely used medicinally; it was brought from Europe to the New World, where it was planted in colonial gardens, from which it escaped into the wild. Common Tansy's poisonous oil caused miscarriages, whereas a tea made from its steeped leaves was used to prevent miscarriage, and crushed leaves were used as a poultice for sprains and bruises.

276 Common Dandelion
Taraxacum officinale

Description: 1 yellow flower head atop a *hollow, leafless stalk* rising from center of a *rosette of toothed leaves; sap milky.*

Flowers: Head ¾–1½″ (2–4 cm) wide; *flowers all rays; outer bracts short, curled back;* inner

bracts longer, curling back when
fruits mature.

Leaves: 2–16″ (5–40 cm) long, lanceolate,
broadest near tip, with jagged,
backward-pointing lobes or teeth.

Fruit: Body about ¼″ (5 mm) long, seed-like,
gray or olive-brown, rough in upper
portion; tipped by a *stalk 2–4 times
as long as body, with white, feathery
bristles* at end.

Height: 2–20″ (5–50 cm).

Flowering: Mostly winter in southern part of range,
summer in northern part.

Habitat: Lawns, pastures, fields, and roadsides.

Range: Throughout most of North America.

Comments: This common weed was introduced from
Europe. The popular name comes from
dent de lion, French for "lion's tooth,"
referring to the teeth on the leaves. The
young leaves may be used in salads and
soups; wine is made from the ray
flowers. Several species, some native to
high mountain meadows, are similar to
Common Dandelion but may have
reddish-brown fruit and outer bracts
that do not curl.

252 Five-needle Fetid Marigold
Thymophylla pentachaeta

Description: A low, tufted, dark green, *prickly plant*
with 1 small, *deep yellow flower head* on
each of several leafless stalks above foliage.

Flowers: Head ¼–½″ (6–13 mm) wide; rays
8–13, each ⅛–¼″ (3–6 mm) long,
surrounding few disk flowers; bracts
surrounding head, upper parts *dotted
with conspicuous glands.*

Leaves: About ½″ (1.5 cm) long, opposite,
pinnately divided into few needle-like lobes.

Fruit: Seed-like, slender, with pointed scales at
tip.

Height: 4–8″ (10–20 cm).

Flowering: April–October.

Habitat: Open deserts and arid, rocky plains.

Range: Southern Utah south to southeastern
California, Arizona, New Mexico, Texas,
and Mexico.

Comments: This common low plant frequently
grows near Creosote Bush
(Larrea tridentata) and Snakeweed
(Gutierrezia sarothrae) or among
piñon, juniper, and Snakeweed.
The closely related Prickly Fetid
Marigold *(T. acerosa)* is more woody
and prickly, with flower heads that
sit among undivided leaves. Both
species were once included in the
larger genus *Dyssodia. Thymophylla*
is one of dozens of western North
American genera that also have
species in southern South America
but have no species in the great
distance between these two regions.
This range distribution probably
requires the long-distance dispersal of
seeds, perhaps by migratory birds.

93 Stemless Daisy
Townsendia exscapa

Description: *A dwarf, tufted, nearly stemless plant*
with comparatively large flower
heads of many *white or pinkish rays*
surrounding a yellow central disk and
nestled among *very narrow leaves.*

Flowers: Head 1–2″ (2.5–5 cm) wide; rays each
½–¾″ (1.5–2 cm) long; bracts each
½″ (1.5 cm) long.

Leaves: ¾–2″ (2–5 cm) long, erect, densely
clustered.

Fruit: Seed-like, flat, lightly hairy, tipped
with *rigid bristles* longer than body.

Height: 1–2″ (2.5–5 cm).

Flowering: March–May.

Habitat: Dry open plains and barren places in
open piñon-juniper woodlands.

Range: Central Canada south through
Montana and North Dakota to
western Texas, and west to central
and northern Arizona.

Comments: The several species of *Townsendia*
are distinguished from the numerous,
rather similar species of *Erigeron* by
lacking the latter's fine slender bristles
atop the fruit.

278 Yellow Salsify
Tragopogon dubius

Description:	Hollow stems, branched near base, with few long, narrow, tapered leaves and topped by 1 *pale yellow flower head; sap milky.*
Flowers:	Head 1½–2″ (4–5 cm) wide; *flowers all rays,* each about ½″ (1.5 cm) long; bracts 8–13, longer than rays.
Leaves:	5–6″ (12.5–15 cm) long.
Fruit:	Seed-like, brown, rough, tapering at both ends, tipped by a slender stalk ending with *pale brown, feathery* bristles nearly 1″ (2.5 cm) long.
Height:	16–31″ (40–80 cm).
Flowering:	May–September.
Habitat:	Roadsides, old lots, and fields.
Range:	Throughout West and much of East.
Comments:	This plant was introduced from Europe. *Tragopogon,* Greek for "goat's beard," probably refers to the thin, tapering, tufted, grass-like leaves or perhaps the pale brown, feathery bristles on the fruit. The widespread Meadow Salsify *(T. pratensis)* has yellow flower heads and bracts shorter than the rays. These yellow species hybridize with each other and with the purple Salsify *(T. porrifolius).* In eastern Washington botanists have discovered new species of *Tragopogon* arising through hybridization and a subsequent doubling of the chromosome number of each cell, a process well understood and long suspected to occur in the natural world. The origin of new species by this process was first recorded in *Tragopogon* in the 1950s.

586 Salsify; Oyster Plant
Tragopogon porrifolius

Description:	1 *purple flower head* at the *swollen, hollow top* of a sparsely leaved stem; *sap milky.*
Flowers:	Head 2–3″ (5–7.5 cm) wide; *flowers all rays,* outer ones each about ¾″ (2 cm) long; bracts about 8–9, tapered.

Leaves: To 1′ (30 cm) long, narrow, tapered.
Fruit: Seed-like, brown, rough, tapering at both ends; tipped by a long stalk ending with *pale brown, feathery bristles* about ¾″ (2 cm) long, like brown parachutes arranged in a lacy hemisphere 4–5″ (10–12.5 cm) wide.
Height: 20–48″ (50–120 cm).
Flowering: June–September.
Habitat: Fields, old lots, and roadsides.
Range: Throughout West and much of East.
Comments: In the Mediterranean, Salsify has been cultivated for 2,000 years for its edible root, which has a flavor like that of an oyster (hence one of its common names) or an artichoke. When a stalk bearing a bud is picked, milky sap oozes over the hollow cut end and, to the delight of children, forms a bubble that quickly changes from white to tan when the swollen part of the stalk is gently squeezed.

334 Yellow Head
Trichoptilium incisum

Description: A low, fragrant, lightly woolly plant bearing *small, rayless, yellow flower heads* on stalks much taller than *jagged leaves* with few *forward-pointing teeth on edges.*
Flowers: Head about ½″ (1.5 cm) wide.
Leaves: ¾–2″ (2–5 cm) long, mostly near base, lanceolate, tapering to a long stalk.
Fruit: Seed-like, tipped with 5 white or pale tan scales with fringed edges.
Height: 2–8″ (5–20 cm).
Flowering: February–May; sometimes October–November, depending on rains.
Habitat: Sandy or gravelly areas in deserts.
Range: Southeastern California, southern Nevada, southwestern Arizona, and northwestern Mexico.
Comments: The genus name derives from the Greek words meaning "hair" and "feather," referring to the fruit tip's dissected scales. This is the only species in the genus.

332 **Trixis**
Trixis californica

Description: A very leafy, branched shrub, often much broader than tall, with small, *yellow, rayless flower heads among lanceolate leaves.*

Flowers: Head ¾" (2 cm) long; corolla of each disk flower 3-lobed, 2 lobes toward outside of head narrow and curled, 1 toward inside broader and often with 3 teeth at tip; leaf-like bracts surrounding disk flowers, innermost ones long and narrow.

Leaves: ¾–2" (2–5 cm) long, with smooth edges or tiny teeth.

Fruit: Seed-like, with straw-colored bristles at tip.

Height: 1–3′ (30–90 cm).

Flowering: February–October.

Habitat: Rocky, desert slopes.

Range: Southern California east to western Texas and south to northern Mexico.

Comments: The genus name, from the Greek word meaning "threefold," refers to the 3-lobed corolla.

262 **Cowpen Daisy**
Verbesina encelioides

Description: A well-branched, *grayish-green plant* with mostly *opposite, toothed, nearly triangular leaves* and *yellow flower heads.*

Flowers: Head 1½–2" (4–5 cm) wide; *rays about ½" (1.5 cm) long,* surrounding disk flowers.

Leaves: 1–4" (2.5–10 cm) long, with coarse teeth on edges, base narrowing to a broad stalk.

Fruit: Seed-like; those of disk flowers with 2 slender, rigid bristles at tip; those of rays lacking bristles.

Height: 4–60" (10–150 cm).

Flowering: June–September.

Habitat: Roadsides, pastures, rangelands, washes, and field edges.

Range: Montana south through eastern Utah and Colorado to Arizona, New Mexico,

Cowpen Daisy

Texas, and into tropical America; west
to central California; and east to Kansas
and southeastern United States.

Comments: This plant is common on disturbed
ground and sometimes colors acres or
miles of roadsides solid yellow. It was
used by Native Americans and early
settlers to treat skin ailments.

250 Mule's Ears
Wyethia amplexicaulis

Description: *Stout leafy stems,* growing from clumps of
lanceolate leaves, topped by long-stalked,
large, deep yellow flower heads; plant seems
varnished with resin.

Flowers: Head with 13–21 rays; bases of disk
flowers enfolded by scales; bracts
lanceolate, often extending past top of
central disk; on plants with several
heads, central head largest, 3–5″
(7.5–12.5 cm) wide.

Leaves: Those at base 8–24″ (20–60 cm) long,
with lanceolate blades on short stalks;
those on stem smaller, bases wrapped
partly around stem.

Fruit: Seed-like, narrow, 4-sided, with a low
crown of scales at tip.

Height: 12–31″ (30–80 cm).

Flowering: May–July.
  Habitat: Open hillsides, meadows, and woods
          from foothills to moderate elevations in
          mountains.
    Range: Central Washington east to western
          Montana and south to northwestern
          Colorado, northern Utah, and Nevada.
 Comments: All *Wyethia* species have leaves on the
          stem, distinguishing them from
          Balsamorhiza, which have leaves only at
          the base.

86 White-rayed Mule's Ears
Wyethia helianthoides

Description: *Stout, leafy, hairy stems,* growing from
            a cluster of basal leaves, each topped
            by 1 flower head with *about 13 white or
            pale cream rays* surrounding a *yellow
            central disk.*
    Flowers: Head 2½–5″ (6.5–12.5 cm) wide; bases
            of disk flowers enfolded by scales; bracts
            narrow, hairy on edges.
     Leaves: Those at base 3½–14″ (9–35 cm) long,
            elliptical, tapering to a short stalk; those
            on stem smaller.
      Fruit: Seed-like, narrow, 4-sided, with a crown
            of low scales at tip.
     Height: 6–31″ (15–80 cm).
  Flowering: May–June.
    Habitat: Moist meadows in mountains.
      Range: Central Oregon east to southwestern
            Montana and northwestern Wyoming,
            and south to northern Nevada.
   Comments: This species, the only white-rayed
            Wyethia, often forms dense patches in
            low spots in valleys.

584 Mojave Aster
Xylorhiza tortifolia

Description: *Several grayish, leafy stems,* growing
            from a woody base, with long leafless
            ends topped by flower heads with
            *many narrow, pale lavender or pale violet
            rays* surrounding a yellow central disk.

Flowers:	Head about 2″ (5 cm) wide.
Leaves:	1–2½″ (2.5–6.5 cm) long, lanceolate or narrower, usually covered with *gray hairs,* bearing *spiny teeth along edges* and a spine at tip.
Height:	1–2½′ (30–75 cm).
Flowering:	March–May; sometimes October, depending on rains.
Habitat:	Dry, rocky, desert slopes and washes.
Range:	Southwestern Utah south to western Arizona and southeastern California.
Comments:	The pastel hue of the rays seems unexpectedly delicate in the plant's harsh environment, even appearing vivid in the early light of day. A similar species, Big Bend Aster *(X. wrightii),* is found in western Texas and nearby Mexico. Desert species with a woody base (*Xylorhiza* means "woody base") have been removed from the large and complex genus *Machaeranthera,* where they were placed for many decades.

267 **Little Golden Zinnia**
Zinnia grandiflora

Description:	Several short, leafy, slightly woody stems in a low round clump bearing numerous small flower heads with *3–6 nearly round, yellow-orange rays.*
Flowers:	Head 1–1½″ (2.5–4 cm) wide; disk flowers reddish or greenish; bracts overlapping, with round, translucent tips.
Leaves:	1″ (2.5 cm) long, *opposite, very narrow,* with 3 veins at base.
Fruit:	Seed-like, usually with 1–2 spines at tip.
Height:	3–9″ (7.5–22.5 cm).
Flowering:	June–October.
Habitat:	Dry areas in deserts and on plains.
Range:	Southeastern Colorado and southwestern Kansas south through southeastern Arizona, New Mexico, and western Texas to Mexico.
Comments:	The genus is named for Johann Zinn, an 18th-century German professor who collected seeds of *Z. elegans* (from which the garden zinnia descends) in Mexico.

There he was accosted by bandits who, after searching his bag, left him alone, believing him crazy and therefore unlucky. The similar Desert Zinnia *(Z. acerosa)* has white rays and is found from Arizona east to western Texas and south to northern Mexico.

BARBERRY FAMILY
Berberidaceae

Herbs or shrubs with often spiny stems and/or leaves and flowers borne singly or in clusters or racemes.

Flowers: Radially symmetrical. Sepals 4–6, often petal-like; petals 4–6; stamens 4–18, in 2 circles, with anthers opening by little flaps; all these parts attached at base of ovary.
Leaves: Simple or compound.
Fruit: Berry or capsule.

There are about 13 genera and 650 species. A few species are cultivated as ornamentals, including Heavenly Bamboo *(Nandina domestica)*. Roots of the eastern Mayapple *(Podophyllum peltatum)* have drastic purgative and emetic properties. Common Barberry *(Berberis vulgaris)* is a necessary host in the complex life cycle of wheat rust *(Puccinia)*, a destructive parasitic fungus.

138 Vanilla Leaf; Deer Foot
Achlys triphylla

Description:	*Pairs of low slender stalks growing in patches:* one stalk actually a petiole tipped by a round leaf blade with *3 broad, fan-shaped leaflets;* other stalk ending in a narrow spike of *small white flowers.*
Flowers:	Spike 1–2″ (2.5–5 cm) long; sepals and petals absent; stamens 6–13, white, outer ones swollen toward tip.
Leaves:	Leaflets 2–4″ (5–10 cm) long, with blunt teeth on ends, central leaflet with 3–5 (or up to 8) teeth.
Height:	10–20″ (25–50 cm).
Flowering:	April–June.
Habitat:	Woods.
Range:	Southern British Columbia south through Coast Ranges of northern California.

Comments: When the leaves are dried, they
smell like vanilla. The large,
3-parted leaf is unusual, like
that of its only close relative,
California Vanilla Leaf (*A.
californica*), found nearer the coast,
but which generally has 6–8
(rarely up to 12) teeth on the
central leaflet.

357   Oregon Grape
Berberis aquifolium

Description: *Pinnately compound leaves with leathery,
holly-like leaflets* on stems ending
in dense branched clusters of *small
yellow flowers.*

Flowers: About ½″ (1.5 cm) wide; sepals 6,
in 2 whorls; petals 6, in 2 whorls,
slightly shorter than sepals; stamens 6,
lying against petals, moving toward
single style when touched; bracts 3,
small, outside sepals.

Leaves: 5–7 ovate, spiny-margined leaflets,
each 1¼–3″ (3–7.5 cm) long,
shiny above.

Fruit: Chalky blue berry, about ¼″
(6 mm) wide.

Height: 4–8″ (10–20 cm).

Flowering: March–June.

Habitat: Open pine forests.

Range: Western Canada south to northeastern
California, southern Nevada, and
northern Mexico, and east to western
Texas, Colorado, South Dakota, and
western Montana.

Comments: This plant varies from a stout shrub
with many erect stems to a creeping
form with an underground rhizome,
its erect stems surfacing here and
there in the woods. The former was
known as Oregon Grape (*B. aquifolium*),
the state flower of Oregon, and the
latter was distinguished as Creeping
Oregon Grape (*B. repens*), but these
and other forms are now understood
to represent phases of the same species.

A creeping species, Cascade Oregon Grape *(B. nervosa),* found from southwestern British Columbia south to central California, has 7–23 leaflets. The berries of all are eaten by wildlife and make good jelly. Native Americans made a yellow dye from the bark and wood of shrubby species. Several are used as ornamentals; in the nursery trade those with pinnate leaves are known as Mahonia.

---

116 **Northern Inside-out Flower**
Vancouveria hexandra

Description: A patch-forming plant with *small, pointed, white flowers* in open clusters on smooth leafless stalks surrounded by stalked, basal, *pinnately compound, leathery leaves.*

Flowers: About ½" (1.5 cm) long; *sepals 6,* remaining on open flower (more present earlier), *white, sharply bent back at base,* with tips arching outward; petals 6, white, shorter than sepals, bent back; pistil and 6 stamens form point in center.

Leaves: 4–16" (10–40 cm) long, *divided 2–3 times into 3-lobed leaflets,* each to 1½" (4 cm) long, nearly as broad.

Height: 6–20" (15–50 cm).

Flowering: May–July.

Habitat: Shady coniferous forests.

Range: Western Washington south to northwestern California.

Comments: This genus has only three species; in mild climates they make excellent groundcover for woodland gardens. Redwood Inside-out Flower *(V. planipetala),* with thick-edged leaflets and gland-tipped hairs on the flower stalks, grows in shady woods near the coast from southwestern Oregon to central California. Golden Inside-out Flower *(V. chrysantha)* is distinguished by its yellow flowers.

TRUMPET CREEPER FAMILY
Bignoniaceae

Trees, shrubs, or woody vines, occasionally herbs, with large, showy, clustered flowers.

Flowers: Bilaterally symmetrical; in clusters at ends of branches or in leaf axils. Calyx 5-lobed; corolla funnel-shaped, bell-shaped, or tubular, 5-lobed and often 2-lipped; stamens 2 or 4; all these parts attached at base of ovary.
Leaves: Usually opposite; simple or pinnately or palmately compound.
Fruit: 2-valved capsule.

There are about 100 genera and 800 species, found mostly in the tropics. Some plants are cultivated as handsome ornamentals, such as those in the genera *Catalpa, Jacaranda,* and *Tecoma.*

493 Desert Willow
Chilopsis linearis

Description: A shrub or tree with narrow leaves and *large, pinkish, bilaterally symmetrical flowers.*

Flowers: Corolla ¾–1½" (2–4 cm) long, 2-lipped, lower lip slightly longer than upper, varying from white blushed with pink to pink or pale purple, usually with purple stripes and often with a yellow hue in tube; stamens 5, all but 1 with an anther.

Leaves: 4–12" (10–30 cm) long, willow-like, slender.

Fruit: Very slender, hanging pod, 6–12" (15–30 cm) long, containing numerous flat seeds with white, membranous edges.

Height: 4–30' (1.2–9 m).

Flowering: April–September.

Habitat: Along desert washes, streams, and highways where water collects.

Range: Southern California east to southern Texas and south to northern Mexico.

Comments: The habitat and resemblance of the leaves to those of the willow give this plant its common name, although there is no relationship between them. If allowed to grow, a stout shrub or small tree develops. The large flowers resemble those of the related *Catalpa* species and attract hummingbirds all season long. Chitalpa, a tree created in Uzbekistan in 1964 and recently introduced into the nursery trade in the United States, is a hybrid between *Chilopsis* and *Catalpa;* it combines more ample foliage inherited from *Catalpa* with some of the water-use efficiency of *Chilopsis.*

BORAGE FAMILY
Boraginaceae

Generally herbs, often covered with bristly hairs.

Flowers: Radially symmetrical; often borne along one side of branches or at tip of stem coiled like a fiddleneck. Sepals 5, united at base; petals 5, united into a narrow tube and an abruptly flared top, usually with 5 small pads around small entry to corolla tube; stamens 5; all these parts attached at base of ovary.
Leaves: Simple.
Fruit: Divided into usually 4 hard, seed-like sections (nutlets); rarely a berry.

There are about 100 genera and 2,000 species, found mostly in warm or temperate regions. Some species are grown as ornamentals. Alkanet, a red dye used as a stain and to color medicine, wine, and cosmetics, is obtained from the root of the European species Common Bugloss *(Anchusa officinalis)*. Boraginaceae has also been known as the forget-me-not family.

233 Fiddleneck; Rancher's Fireweed
Amsinckia menziesii

Description: *Coils of small, yellow-orange flowers* at branch ends; leafy stems with both long, *spreading, bristly hairs* and very short, dense, downward-projecting hairs.
Flowers: Calyx with 5 narrow lobes; *corolla ⅛–⅜″ (3–10 mm) wide,* joined petals forming a funnel with a narrow tube and an abruptly flared end.
Leaves: ¾–6″ (2–15 cm) long, narrowly or broadly lanceolate.

Fruit: Divided into 4 grayish nutlets, each
about ⅛″ (3 mm) long, with a rough
surface, somewhat wrinkled on back.

Height: 1–3′ (30–90 cm).

Flowering: April–May.

Habitat: Along roadsides, fields, and other dry
open places.

Range: Washington and Idaho south to Baja
California and east to Arizona.

Comments: The common name Fiddleneck
refers to the coiled inflorescence.
This species, now introduced in many
places in the world, has large- and
small-flowered races. More than 100
scientific names were applied to these
races before they were understood to be
components of a single widespread and
variable species.

355 Yellow Cryptantha
Cryptantha flava

Description: *A hairy plant* with stems in clumps
and tipped with *coils of small yellow
flowers;* leaves at base largest.

Flowers: Corolla funnel-shaped, the narrow
tube about ½″ (1.5 cm) long, flaring
abruptly into 5 lobes about ⅜″
(9 mm) wide.

Leaves: ¾–4″ (2–10 cm) long, narrowly
lanceolate, those at base broadest.

Fruit: Divided into 4 *smooth, glossy, gray
nutlets,* each about ¼″ (5 mm) long.

Height: 3–10″ (7.5–25 cm).

Flowering: April–August.

Habitat: Open, sandy areas; common on
plains and in juniper.

Range: Southwestern Wyoming south to
northeastern Arizona and northwestern
New Mexico.

Comments: *Cryptantha* is a large genus of the
arid West with mostly white-flowered
species. There are only two yellow
species in the genus. The similar
Mojave Popcorn Flower *(C. confertiflora)*
occurs from central Utah and
northwestern Arizona west to the base
of the Sierra Nevada.

567 Hound's Tongue
Cynoglossum grande

Description: Several smooth stems with *large, ovate, long-stalked leaves* mostly near base and *loose clusters of purple or blue flowers* on branches at top.

Flowers: Corolla about ½″ (1.5 cm) wide, with 5 petals joined into a funnel and 5 *white, 2-lobed pads* around opening of tube.

Leaves: Blades 3–16″ (7.5–40 cm) long, ovate, with few hairs above, many hairs beneath.

Fruit: Divided into 4 hard, roundish nutlets, each ¼″ (6 mm) long, covered with *tiny barbed prickles.*

Height: 12–31″ (30–80 cm).

Flowering: March–June.

Habitat: Dry shaded places in woods.

Range: Western Washington south to southern California.

Comments: The common name refers to the shape of the broad leaves. Native Americans used preparations from the root to treat burns and stomachaches. There are several species, all with blue to purple or maroon flowers and large rough nutlets that stick to clothing.

632 Alpine Forget-me-not
Eritrichium nanum

Description: A low, *cushion-like plant* with *deep blue flowers* just above tufted leaves.

Flowers: Corolla about ¼″ (6 mm) wide, funnel-shaped, 5-lobed, with 5 yellow pads around opening of a narrow tube.

Leaves: To ½″ (1.5 cm) long, lanceolate, covered with loose hairs.

Fruit: Divided into 4 smooth nutlets.

Height: To 4″ (10 cm).

Flowering: June–August.

Habitat: Open, rocky places high in mountains.

Range: Alaska south through northeastern Oregon and western Montana to northern New Mexico.

Comments: The genus name comes from the Greek *erion* ("wool") and *trichos* ("hair"),

referring to the hairy leaves. Howard's
Alpine Forget-me-not *(E. howardii),*
found in western Montana and northern
Wyoming, has hairs so dense they
usually hide the leaf surface.

**633   Many-flowered Stickseed;
Wild Forget-me-not**
Hackelia floribunda

Description: *Small, pale blue, funnel-shaped flowers* in a
long, open, branched cluster atop 1 or
few leafy stems; *branches coiled at tips.*

Flowers: Corolla about ¼" (6 mm) wide, with
yellow pads around opening of a narrow
tube.

Leaves: 1½–8" (4–20 cm) long, lanceolate,
lower ones with petioles, upper ones
without petioles, progressively smaller
toward top of stem.

Fruit: Divided into 4 hard nutlets, *with barbed
prickles on edges* but none on back.

Height: 1–3' (30–90 cm).

Flowering: June–August.

Habitat: Moist thickets and meadows, commonly
in coniferous forests.

Range: Southern Canada south to northern
California, Arizona, New Mexico, and
North Dakota.

Many-flowered Stickseed

Comments: It is the prickles on the nutlets that distinguish this plant from *Myosotis* forget-me-nots. The similar Jessica's Stickseed *(H. micrantha),* found from the Sierra Nevada east to Utah and Wyoming and north to Canada, generally has several stems and several very small prickles on the back of each nutlet.

61 Sweet-scented Heliotrope
Heliotropium convolvulaceum

Description: A hairy, sparsely leaved plant with 1 erect branched stem or many long, sprawling branches and *fragrant, white, broadly funnel-shaped flowers* in small coils along upper stems.

Flowers: Corolla ½–1″ (1.5–2.5 cm) wide, with 5 low lobes; minute yellow "eye" around tiny opening of narrow corolla tube.

Leaves: To 1½″ (4 cm) long, lanceolate or ovate, with short stalks.

Fruit: Divided into 4 silky-hairy nutlets, each about ⅛″ (3 mm) long, sometimes united in pairs and appearing to be 2.

Height: 4–16″ (10–40 cm).

Flowering: March–October.

Habitat: Dunes and other sandy places in deserts and arid grasslands.

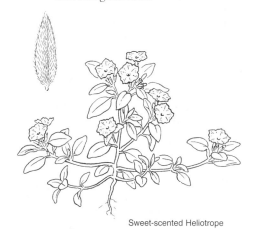

Sweet-scented Heliotrope

Range: Southeastern California east to Utah,
          Wyoming, western Nebraska, and
          western Kansas, and south through
          Arizona, New Mexico, and western
          Texas to northern Mexico.

Comments: The fragrant flowers, largest of all
          heliotropes in the West, open in the cool
          hours of the evening. The ornamental
          Common Heliotrope (H. arborescens)
          comes from Peru.

28 Quail Plant; Cola de Mico
Heliotropium curassavicum

Description: *A fleshy, bluish-green, smooth plant* with
             leafy stems mostly lying on ground,
             usually with *paired coils of small, white or
             purplish-tinged flowers.*

Flowers: Corolla ¼–⅜″ (5–9 mm) wide, funnel-
           shaped, with 5 round lobes.

Leaves: ½–1½″ (1.5–4 cm) long, spatula-
           shaped, sometimes broader toward tip.

Fruit: Divided into 4 small nutlets.

Height: Creeper; flowering branches to 16″ (40
           cm), stems to 4′ (1.2 m) long.

Flowering: March–October.

Habitat: Open, alkaline or saline soil, often in
           sand or clay; common in beds of
           dried ponds.

Range: Western United States east to Great
           Plains and across southern United States.

Comments: This plant is also found in Mexico and
           South America. In some parts of the
           West this species is called Quail Plant
           after the birds that feed on its fruit. The
           Spanish name, Cola de Mico, meaning
           "monkey tail," describes the coiled
           flower cluster.

229 Fringed Gromwell; Fringed Puccoon
Lithospermum incisum

Description: A hairy plant with several leafy stems in
             a clump and *fringed, bright yellow,
             trumpet-shaped flowers* crowded in upper
             leaf axils.

Flowers: Corolla ½–1¼″ (1.5–3 cm) long, with a

narrow tube abruptly flaring into a 5-
lobed top ½–¾" (1.5–2 cm) wide, the
lobes finely and irregularly toothed.

Leaves: ¾–2½" (2–6.5 cm) long, narrowly
lanceolate.

Fruit: Divided into *4 gray, shiny, hard nutlets,*
each about ⅛" (3 mm) long.

Height: 2–12" (5–30 cm).

Flowering: May–July.

Habitat: Dry open plains and foothills.

Range: British Columbia east to Ontario, south
to southeastern California, Arizona, New
Mexico, and Texas, and throughout Great
Plains as far east as Illinois.

Comments: The genus name means "stone seed,"
referring to the hard nutlets. This species
produces few fruits from the showy
flowers; instead, late in the season
inconspicuous flowers that remain closed
produce fruits in the lower leaf axils. There
are several species in the West, one
white-flowered, the rest with shorter,
yellow corollas.

342 Wayside Gromwell; Puccoon
Lithospermum ruderale

Description: Several or many leafy stems in a clump
and clusters of *5-lobed, light yellow flowers*
in upper leaf axils.

Flowers: Corolla ¼–½" (6–13 mm) wide, funnel-
shaped.

Leaves: 1¼–4" (3–10 cm) long, numerous,
lanceolate, hairy.

Fruit: Divided into 4 *(often only 1–2) shiny gray
nutlets,* each ⅛–¼" (3–6 mm) long.

Height: 8–24" (20–60 cm).

Flowering: April–June.

Habitat: Open places among sagebrush, juniper,
and pine.

Range: Western Canada south to northeastern
California and east to western Colorado.

Comments: The common name Puccoon, a Native
American word for plants that yield dye,
alludes to the purple dye extracted from
the roots of several species; this name is
given to more than one *Lithospermum*
species.

83 Green-flowered Macromeria
Macromeria viridiflora

Description: *A hairy, leafy plant* with several stout
stems in a clump and *pale, hairy, trumpet-
shaped flowers in large coils* at ends of
upper branches.

Flowers: Corolla 1½″ (4 cm) long, pale greenish
yellow to white, with 5 pointed lobes;
stamens 5, slightly protruding.

Leaves: 2–5″ (5–12.5 cm) long, broadly
lanceolate, largest near base,
progressively smaller toward top.

Height: To 3′ (90 cm).

Flowering: July–September.

Habitat: Rocky slopes and valleys in pinewoods
from moderate to high elevations.

Range: Eastern Arizona and southern New
Mexico south to Mexico.

Comments: The flowers of this species are long for
the family. Its leaves and flowers were
dried and mixed with wild tobacco
(Nicotiana) for Hopi "rain-bringing"
ceremonies.

660 Mountain Bluebell
Mertensia ciliata

Description: Clumps of leafy stems and loose clusters
of *narrowly bell-shaped, blue flowers turning
pink with age.*

Flowers: Corolla ½–¾″ (1.5–2 cm) long,
5-lobed, tubular part same length as
bell-like end.

Leaves: 1¼–6″ (3–15 cm) long, tapered at base,
lower ones with long petioles.

Fruit: Divided into 4 small wrinkled nutlets.

Height: 6–60″ (15–150 cm).

Flowering: May–August.

Habitat: Streambanks, seeps, and wet meadows.

Range: Central Oregon south through Sierra
Nevada and east through central Idaho
to western Montana, western Wyoming,
western Colorado, and northern New
Mexico.

Comments: Species of *Mertensia* are also called
Lungwort, after a European species with

spotted leaves that was believed to
be a remedy for lung disease. Similar
species differ in the proportions of the
corolla.

29 Popcorn Flower
Plagiobothrys nothofulvus

Description: A slender, hairy plant with most leaves
in a basal tuft and *small white flowers in a
coil* at ends of few branches or branchless
stems.

Flowers: Calyx brownish-hairy, with 5 narrow
lobes; corolla ¼" (6 mm) wide, 5-lobed,
flat top with 5 yellow pads surrounding
narrow opening of a short tube.

Leaves: Those at base in tuft ¾–4" (2–10 cm)
long, spatula-shaped; those on stem
progressively smaller toward top.

Fruit: Divided into 4 small nutlets.

Height: 6–20" (15–50 cm).

Flowering: March–May.

Habitat: Open places; common in grass.

Range: South-central Washington south to
northern Baja California.

Comments: Open flowers are clustered at the top of
the coil, resembling pieces of popcorn.
Popcorn Flower is similar to species of
Cryptantha, but Popcorn Flower is
generally more softly hairy and grows in
moister places. Many species have a
purple dye in the stem, leaves, and roots.
When they are pressed and dried in a
folded sheet of clean paper, a striking
mirror-image pattern results.

473 Shrubby Tiquilia
Tiquilia greggii

Description: A small, round, *gray shrub* with many
twigs bearing *funnel-shaped, pink or
reddish-lavender flowers in small, feathery
clusters.*

Flowers: Calyx about ⅜" (9 mm) long, with 5
very slender lobes of varying lengths
and long hairs, feathery and purplish at

maturity; corolla about ¼″ (6 mm) long, with 5 round lobes.

Leaves: About ⅜″ (9 mm) long, ovate, hairy.

Height: 4–20″ (10–50 cm).

Flowering: March–August.

Habitat: Open, limestone slopes.

Range: Southern New Mexico, western Texas, and northern Mexico.

Comments: The feathery calyx, surrounding and carrying the tiny, one-seeded fruit, is blown by the wind. This plant was once placed in the genus *Coldenia*, a genus now realized to be restricted to the Eastern Hemisphere; Western Hemisphere plants form the genus *Tiquilia*. Shaggy Tiquilia (*T. canescens*), a tufted or matted plant with pale lavender or whitish flowers, is found in southern California east to Texas and south to northern Mexico.

MUSTARD FAMILY
Brassicaceae

Herbs often with peppery-tasting sap and flowers in racemes.

Flowers: Usually radially symmetrical. Sepals 4, separate; petals 4, separate, arranged as a cross, petal bases often long and slender; stamens usually 6, outer 2 shorter than inner 4; all these parts attached at base of ovary.

Leaves: Usually simple, sometimes pinnately compound, rarely palmately compound.

Fruit: Pod, either long and narrow (silique) or short and relatively broader (silicle), divided into 2 chambers by a parchment-like partition, sometimes many-seeded.

There are about 350 genera and 3,000 species, mostly in cooler regions of the Northern Hemisphere. The family is economically important, providing vegetables, spices, and ornamentals. Thirty percent of the vegetable acreage of some European countries is planted with species of this family. Kale, cabbage, broccoli, Brussels sprouts, cauliflower, and kohlrabi are all agricultural variants of *Brassica oleracea*. Some species are unwelcome weeds, and a few are poisonous to livestock. The family's traditional name, Cruciferae, means "crossbearer," referring to the shape of the flower.

165 Shepherd's Purse
Capsella bursa-pastoris

Description: *Flat, triangular pods* attached by pointed
ends to fine stalks along main stem of a
small plant topped by *tiny white flowers.*

Flowers: About ⅛″ (3 mm) wide; petals 4, white.

Leaves: 1–2½″ (2.5–6.5 cm) long, lanceolate in
outline, shallowly or deeply lobed.

Fruit: Pod, about ¼″ (6 mm) long, shallowly
notched across broad end.

Height: 6–16″ (15–40 cm).

Flowering: Throughout year; earlier in southern
part of range than in northern.

Habitat: Gardens, lots, and field borders.

Range: Throughout Canada and United States.

Comments: Native to Europe, this plant is now
found throughout much of the world.
Its Latin name refers to its fruit: *Capsella*
means "little box" and *bursa-pastoris*
means "purse of the shepherd."

176 Heart-leaved Bittercress
Cardamine cordifolia

Description: Several or many leafy stems bearing
white flowers and growing from an
extensive system of underground
runners.

Flowers: Petals 4, each ½–¾″ (1.5–2 cm) long.

Leaves: ¾–4″ (2–10 cm) wide, blades roundish
with shallowly scalloped edges, indented
at base; leafstalks 2–5 times length of
blades.

Fruit: Slightly flat, slender pod, ¾–1½″
(2–4 cm) long.

Height: 4–31″ (10–80 cm).

Flowering: June–September.

Habitat: Mountain streambanks, in streams,
and alpine meadows.

Range: British Columbia south to northern
California and east to New Mexico,
Colorado, Wyoming, and Idaho.

Comments: Some plants in this family were reputed
to have medicinal qualities useful in the
treatment of heart ailments. Most of the
several species in the West have
pinnately parted or lobed leaves.

168   Hoary Cress; White Top
Cardaria draba

Description: Patches of leafy stems, branched near the top and bearing *numerous tiny white flowers* in racemes, growing from an extensive system of underground runners; leaves and stems grayish with dense hairs.

Flowers: Sepals 4, dropping off upon opening; petals 4, each ⅛" (3 mm) long.

Leaves: 1½–4" (4–10 cm) long, oblong, pointed at tip, edges with small teeth; *base of blade attached to stem in notch between 2 backward-projecting, pointed lobes.*

Fruit: Roundish, slightly flat, smooth, 2-lobed pod, about ¼" (6 mm) wide, each lobe 1-seeded.

Height: 8–20" (20–50 cm).

Flowering: April–August.

Habitat: Roadsides, fields, and old lots.

Range: Nearly throughout West.

Comments: Native to Eurasia, this rather showy but aggressive plant is considered a noxious weed. The less common Globe-pod Hoary Cress (*C. pubescens*) is distinguished by its downy pod.

405   Desert Candle
Caulanthus inflatus

Description: *A stout, swollen, hollow, yellow-green stem* with few leaves, mostly near base, and many narrow flowers in a raceme.

Flowers: About ½" (1.5 cm) long; sepals 4, whitish, reddish, or purplish brown; petals 4, white, narrow, crinkled near tip; buds often very purplish or reddish.

Leaves: 1¼–3" (3–7.5 cm) long, pointed, with 2 backward-projecting lobes at base on each side of stem.

Fruit: Narrow, erect pod, 2½–4" (6.5–10 cm) long.

Height: 1–2' (30–60 cm).

Flowering: March–May.

Habitat: Sandy or gravelly, dry, open slopes in brush or deserts.

Range: Southern California and southwestern
Nevada.
Comments: This weird-looking plant resembles a
candle or candelabrum. Wild Cabbage
(C. crassicaulis) is similar, but its leaves
lack backward-projecting lobes and
its sepals and petals are purplish or
brownish; it generally grows in
sagebrush from western Nevada to
southern Idaho, western Wyoming,
and northwestern Colorado.

14, 105 **Spectacle Pod**
Dimorphocarpa wislizenii

Description: A grayish, hairy plant, either branched
or unbranched, with pinnately lobed
leaves and *white flowers* in dense thick
racemes.
Flowers: Petals 4, each about ½″ (1.5 cm) long.
Leaves: Those at base to 6″ (15 cm) long, edges
deeply pinnately lobed; those on stem
shorter, generally less deeply indented.
Fruit: *Flat pod, nearly ½″ (1.5 cm) wide, with
2 round lobes.*
Height: To 2′ (60 cm).
Flowering: February–May, often again after summer
rains.
Habitat: Open, sandy soil in dry grasslands and
deserts.
Range: Southern Utah and western Arizona east
to western Oklahoma and western Texas,
and south to northern Mexico.
Comments: Species in this genus are very similar, all
usually given the name Spectacle Pod,
as their fruit resemble tiny eyeglasses.
D. candicans branches mostly above
the middle, has upper leaves that are
abruptly contracted to the stalk at the
base (rather than tapered), and has pods
⅜–½″ (8–12 mm) wide; it occurs from
southwestern Kansas south to northern
Texas and eastern New Mexico. In both
species the anthers are not held strictly
erect but are spread somewhat from one
another. A remarkable look-alike in a
different genus, California Spectacle Pod

(Dithyrea californica), has sepals and anthers held erect and yellow-green, shallowly lobed leaves; it occurs from southern Nevada and southeastern California to western Arizona and northwestern Mexico. Until recently all were considered to be in the genus *Dithyrea* (meaning "two shields" in Greek, referring to the pod).

30 Lance-leaved Draba
Draba lanceolata

Description: Small *white flowers* in open racemes growing from densely velvety, grayish, basal rosettes.

Flowers: Petals 4, each about ¼″ (5 mm) long, notched at tip.

Leaves: Those in basal rosette ½–1¼″ (1.5–3 cm) long, edges smooth or with small teeth; those on stem smaller and fewer, with teeth.

Fruit: Flat, lanceolate pod, ¼–½″ (6–13 mm) long, generally slightly twisted.

Height: 2–10″ (5–25 cm).

Flowering: May–July.

Habitat: Dry open meadows and rock crevices high in mountains.

Range: Alaska south to Nevada and east through central Colorado to northeastern United States and southeastern Canada.

Comments: There are about 300 species in this genus, distinguished mostly by technical features. Small, tufted, alpine plants with short, flat or swollen pods are likely to be *Draba*.

194 Comb Draba
Draba oligosperma

Description: A small, grayish, hairy, *densely tufted plant* with basal leaves and racemes of *small yellow flowers on leafless stalks.*

Flowers: Petals 4, each slightly more than ⅛″ (3 mm) long.

Leaves: ⅛–½″ (3–13 mm) long, very narrow.

Fruit:	Flat oval pod, ⅛–⅜″ (3–9 mm) long, smooth or bearing hairs similar to those on leaves.
Height:	½–4″ (1.5–10 cm).
Flowering:	May–July.
Habitat:	Open slopes and ridges from moderate to high mountain elevations.
Range:	Western Canada south to central Sierra Nevada, western Nevada, Utah, and Colorado.
Comments:	This is one of many tufted species of *Draba* with yellow flowers, distinguished in part by technical characteristics of the hairs. The entire surface of this plant is covered with microscopic hairs that lie flat, each with a main axis and perpendicular branches on either side (similar to two back-to-back combs).

298 Western Wallflower
Erysimum capitatum

Description:	Erect stems, unbranched or branched in upper parts, bearing narrow leaves and ending in a dense raceme of *showy, yellow, orange, burnt-orange, or orange-maroon flowers.*
Flowers:	About ¾″ (2 cm) wide; petals 4.
Leaves:	1–5″ (2.5–12.5 cm) long, in a basal rosette and along stem except uppermost parts, narrowly lanceolate, with small teeth on edges.
Fruit:	Very slender pod, 2–4″ (5–10 cm) long, 4-sided, erect or nearly so, on stalk more slender than mature pod.
Height:	6–36″ (15–90 cm).
Flowering:	March–July.
Habitat:	Dry stony banks, slopes, and open flats.
Range:	British Columbia and Idaho south to southern California, Arizona, and New Mexico.
Comments:	This handsome and variable species intergrades with the more eastern Plains Wallflower *(E. asperum),* with pods projecting from the stem at an angle on stalks that are equal in diameter to the mature pods. Pale

Wallflower *(E. occidentale)*, with flat
pods, grows in sagebrush in eastern
Washington and Oregon, southern
Idaho, and northern Nevada.

341 Alpine Wallflower
Erysimum capitatum var. *purshii*

Description: A low plant with several short stems
growing from *tufts of basal leaves and
bearing yellow or yellow-orange flowers
with rusty-backed petals* in compact
racemes.

Flowers: ½–¾" (1.5–2 cm) wide; petals 4.

Leaves: 1¼–2½" (3–6 cm) long, very narrow,
edges smooth, toothed, or shallowly
indented and with roundish teeth.

Fruit: Pod, 1¼–3" (3–7.5 cm) long, erect or
nearly so.

Height: 2–8" (5–20 cm), seldom to 20" (50 cm).

Flowering: June–July.

Habitat: Dry slopes, rocky ridges, sagebrush
flats, aspen and spruce areas, and
alpine tundra at moderate to high
elevations.

Range: Eastern Utah and Colorado south to
central Mexico.

Comments: Western Wallflower *(E. capitatum)* is one
of the West's most striking wildflowers.
It is also one of the most variable
species, with very wide ecological
tolerance. This variation has defied easy
botanical classification; some botanists
recognize no varieties, while others
attempt to demonstrate the complex
variation through nomenclature. The
very short alpine phases in the Rocky
Mountains were once recognized as a
separate species, *E. nivale* (*nivale* means
"of snow" and refers to the plant's
habitat). *E. capitatum* var. *purshii* now
includes this and numerous other short-
stemmed phases of Western Wallflower.
The short-stemmed habit, characteristic
of many alpine plants, is an adaptation
for rapid flower production and
protection from the cold.

299 Menzies's Wallflower
Erysimum menziesii

Description: Few short branches at base and 1
short erect stem ending in *dense
thick racemes of bright orange-yellow
flowers.*

Flowers: ½–¾" (1.5–2 cm) wide; petals 4.
Leaves: 1¼–3½" (3–9 cm) long, largest at
base, spatula-shaped, sometimes
very shallowly lobed, blunt at tip.
Fruit: Slender flat pod, 1½–3" (4–7.5
cm) long, standing out stiffly
from stem.
Height: 1–8" (2.5–20 cm).
Flowering: Mostly March–May.
Habitat: Coastal dunes.
Range: Northern two-thirds of California.
Comments: This lovely coastal wildflower forms
low, conical mounds of solid yellow-
orange when in full bloom. Several
other species grow along the Pacific
Coast.

---

13 Flatpod
Idahoa scapigera

Description: A tiny plant with a basal rosette of
leaves and several slender, leafless
stems, each tipped with *1 minute
white flower* or a *round, flat, green pod.*

Flowers: Petals 4, each about ⅛" (3 mm) long.
Leaves: Blades ¼–½" (6–15 mm) long, ovate,
on petioles to 3 times as long.
Fruit: Pod, ¼–½" (6–13 mm) wide, often
mottled with reddish brown.
Height: 1–5" (2.5–12.5 cm).
Flowering: February–April.
Habitat: Open places in grasslands or
sagebrush, commonly where moist
early in season.
Range: Eastern Washington south to northern
California, northern Nevada, and
southern Idaho.
Comments: When the two sides of the pod fall
away, the silvery partition remains
attached to the tip of the flower stalk.

349   Yellow Peppergrass
Lepidium flavum

Description: Several stems, brittle at joints,
lying on ground with *dense short
racemes of yellow flowers* turning
upward.

Flowers: Petals 4, each about ⅛″ (3 mm) long.

Leaves: ¾–2″ (2–5 cm) long, larger ones
pinnately lobed.

Fruit: Flat oval pod, ⅛″ (3 mm) long.

Height: Creeper; flower clusters about 2″
(5 cm), stems 4–16″ (10–40 cm)
long.

Flowering: March–June.

Habitat: Low desert flats.

Range: Southeastern California, southern
Nevada, and Baja California.

Comments: Yellow Peppergrass, often so
common it colors broad expanses
of the desert yellow, has seeds with
a peppery flavor.

166   Western Peppergrass
Lepidium montanum

Description: A round plant formed by many
slender branches, each branch ending
in a *short dense raceme of minute white
flowers.*

Flowers: Petals 4, each ⅛″ (3 mm) long.

Leaves: Those at base about 1½–3″ (4–7.5 cm)
long, deeply and sharply pinnately
lobed; those on stem smaller and often
not lobed.

Fruit: Ovate flat pod, ⅛″ (3 mm) long, style
at tip longer than tiny notch in which
it grows.

Height: To 16″ (40 cm).

Flowering: March–June, sometimes again after
summer rains.

Habitat: Dry open areas in deserts and rangelands
among Creosote Bush, sagebrush, piñon,
and juniper.

Range: Western Montana southwest to
southeastern Oregon and south on
eastern side of Cascade Range and Sierra
Nevada to southeastern California,

Wyoming, Colorado, New Mexico, and western Texas.

Comments: There are at least 15 races of this species, but in this region any perennial, rather bushy mustard with small white flowers is likely to be Western Peppergrass. The showiest peppergrass is Fremont's Peppergrass *(L. fremontii),* found from southeastern California to southwestern Utah, western Arizona, and northwestern Mexico; it has white flowers with petals ¼" (5 mm) long and pods resembling broad hearts about ¼" (6 mm) wide.

193 Fendler's Bladderpod
Lesquerella fendleri

Description: *Yellow flowers* in loose short racemes at stem ends of a low, rather *tightly tufted, silvery-gray perennial;* plant surfaces covered with tiny, star-like scales.

Flowers: Petals 4, each about ½" (1.5 cm) wide.

Leaves: To 4" (10 cm) long, lanceolate or strap-shaped; those at base sometimes with few teeth on edges.

Fruit: Nearly spherical pod, ¼–⅜" (6–9 mm) long, smooth.

Height: 1–16" (2.5–40 cm).

Flowering: March–June, often again after summer rains.

Habitat: Rocky or sandy soil, especially that derived from limestone, in arid grasslands or deserts.

Range: Southern Utah east to western Kansas and south through eastern Arizona, New Mexico, and western Texas to northern Mexico.

Comments: This is one of the earliest plants to flower in its area; its bright yellow is conspicuous against the drab ground of early spring. In the same region is the similar but annual Gordon's Bladderpod *(L. gordonii),* which has several slender stems that lie on the ground, turning up at the tips; unlike Fendler's Bladderpod, it is not tufted and has a more open appearance.

546 Honesty; Moonwort
Lunaria annua

Description: Leafy, freely branched stems with few
            pinkish- to reddish-purple flowers in
            racemes and *hanging, flat, oval pods.*
   Flowers: About ¾" (2 cm) wide; petals 4.
    Leaves: 1½–4" (4–10 cm) long, heart-shaped,
            lower ones on long stalks, upper ones
            without stalks.
     Fruit: Pod, 1½–2" (4–5 cm) long.
    Height: 20–40" (50–100 cm).
 Flowering: May–June.
   Habitat: Partly shaded, moist areas.
     Range: Central Washington south to central
            California.
 Comments: This plant is native to Europe.
            When the sides of the pod fall away,
            the glistening white, parchment-like
            partition between the halves remains,
            suggesting the genus name, from the
            Latin *luna* ("moon").

40 Velvety Nerisyrenia
Nerisyrenia camporum

Description: *A grayish, hairy plant* with clumps
            of leafy branched stems and *racemes
            of white or lavender flowers* at branch
            ends.
   Flowers: About ¾" (2 cm) wide; petals 4.
    Leaves: ½–2½" (1.5–6.5 cm) long, lanceolate,
            toothed, with short stalks.
     Fruit: Narrow, 4-sided, slightly flattened
            pod, ½–1½" (1.5–4 cm) long, held
            erect, partition in center of pod
            perpendicular to its broad sides.
    Height: 8–24" (20–60 cm).
 Flowering: February–October.
   Habitat: Gravelly or rocky soil derived from
            limestone and on limestone in
            deserts and arid grasslands.
     Range: Southwestern New Mexico, western
            Texas, and northern Mexico. ·
 Comments: This is the most common species of
            mustard with large white flowers in
            the region.

525 **Daggerpod**
Phoenicaulis cheiranthoides

Description: Several short, smooth, somewhat shiny, unbranched stems growing from grayish basal tufts of leaves and ending in dense *racemes of pink or purplish flowers.*

Flowers: About ½" (1.5 cm) wide; petals 4.

Leaves: 1¼–6" (3–15 cm) long, lanceolate, broader above middle, tapered to a slender petiole.

Fruit: Flat, narrow, pointed pod, ¾–3" (2–7.5 cm) long, *held almost straight out from stem.*

Height: 2–8" (5–20 cm).

Flowering: April–June.

Habitat: Sagebrush and Ponderosa Pine woods.

Range: Central Washington south to northern California, northern Nevada, and southern Idaho.

Comments: This is the only species in this genus. When the pods dry, the entire flowering stem breaks at the base and is tumbled away by the wind.

350 **Rydberg Twinpod; Double Bladderpod**
Physaria acutifolia

Description: *A silvery plant* with a basal rosette of leaves and prostrate to erect stems with upturned tips bearing *dense racemes of yellow flowers.*

Flowers: ⅜–½" (9–12 mm) wide; petals 4, each ⅜–½" (9–12 mm) long, angling strongly upward from center of flower.

Leaves: ¾–4" (2–10 cm) long; blades roundish, on long stalks, often with few small teeth.

Fruit: Pod, ¼–½" (7–15 mm) long, about as broad, with 2 round, swollen, papery lobes; bristle-like style between lobes about ⅛–¼" (4–7 mm) long.

Height: 1¼–8" (3–20 cm).

Flowering: June–August.

Habitat: Dry, rocky or gravelly areas in arid shrublands, aspen forests, coniferous forests, and alpine tundra.

Range: Wyoming, Utah, and Colorado; mostly within drainage of Colorado River.

Comments: *Physaria* derives from the Greek *physa,* meaning "bellows," referring to the swollen pod halves. There are about 14 species in the West, distinguished by features of mature pods. Most occur in dry mountain areas and are known as Twinpod or Double Bladderpod.

174 Watercress
Rorippa nasturtium-aquaticum

Description: Leafy branched stems, mostly floating in water or lying on mud, with upturned tips bearing *tiny white flowers in short racemes.*

Flowers: Petals 4, each about ¼" (5 mm) long.

Leaves: 1½–5" (4–12.5 cm) long, pinnate; leaflets ovate, terminal leaflet largest.

Fruit: Slender pod, ½–1" (1.5–2.5 cm) long, gently curved, pointing upward.

Height: Creeper; flower stalks about 4" (10 cm), stems to 2' (60 cm) long.

Flowering: March–October.

Habitat: Quiet streams and freshwater ponds.

Range: Throughout temperate regions worldwide.

Comments: Reflecting the difficulty of generic limits in the mustard family, technical botanical sources are not in agreement as to this plant's genus. Some put it in the inclusive genus *Rorippa,* others in the smaller genus *Nasturtium,* as *N. officinale.* Whatever its scientific name, its leaves add a mild peppery flavor to salads. *Nasturtium* comes from the Latin *nasi tortium* ("distortion of the nose"), referring to the plant's pungency. Although the large, orange-flowered garden Nasturtium *(Tropaeolum majus)* also has a sharp flavor, it is not related.

340 Charlock
Sinapis arvensis

Description: A hairy, leafy plant with *many racemes of yellow flowers* at ends of almost leafless branches.

Flowers: Petals 4, each ½" (1.5 cm) long.

Leaves: Those at base largest, 2–6" (5–15 cm) long, stalked, pinnately divided into several pairs of lobes, with teeth on edges; progressing up stem, leaves have shorter stalks, less prominent lobes, and finally none of either.

Fruit: Slender, smooth, round pod, 1¼–2½" (3–6 cm) long, with a *solid, pointed, flat beak* ½–1" (1.5–2.5 cm) long at tip.

Height: 1–3' (30–90 cm).

Flowering: January–June.

Habitat: Fields, roadsides, and old lots.

Range: Throughout temperate agricultural regions of North America, from southern Canada to Central America.

Comments: A native of Eurasia, this species was previously included in the large genus *Brassica,* as *B. kaber.* Occasionally its seeds have been used for mustard, but table mustard comes mostly from Black Mustard *(Brassica nigra).*

Charlock

339 Hedge Mustard
Sisymbrium officinale

Description: A hairy plant with most leaves in lower
half and branches in upper part ending
in *racemes of small yellow flowers.*

Flowers: Petals 4, each about ¼″ (5 mm) long.

Leaves: Lower leaves to 8″ (20 cm) long, oblong,
deeply pinnately cleft, with end lobe
largest, edges irregularly toothed; upper
leaves much smaller, narrow, with few
narrow lobes.

Fruit: Slender pod, ⅜–½″ (9–15 mm) long,
tapered from base to tip, *erect and pressed
against stem,* hairs on stem standing out
or pointing downward.

Height: 1–3′ (30–90 cm).

Flowering: March–September.

Habitat: Fields, roadsides, and vacant lots.

Range: Throughout Canada and United States;
in West, more frequent west of Cascade
Range and Sierra Nevada.

Comments: A native of Europe, Hedge Mustard has
two other common weedy relatives:
Tumble Mustard *(S. altissimum),* with
rigidly spreading pods 2–4″ (5–10 cm)
long, and Loesel Tumble Mustard *(S.
loeselii),* with slender, erect pods ¾–1½″
(2–4 cm) long, held away from the stem.
London Rocket *(S. irio),* with deeper
yellow flowers, is common in the
southwestern United States.

Hedge Mustard

167 Western Smelowskia
Smelowskia calycina

Description: *A gray matted plant with white or purplish flowers* in dense racemes held well above thick clusters of basal leaves.

Flowers: Petals 4, each about ¼" (6 mm) long.

Leaves: 1–2½" (2.5–6.5 cm) long, oblong, *pinnately divided into narrow segments,* on stiffly hairy stalks as long as blades.

Fruit: Lanceolate pod, ¼–½" (6–13 mm) long, held erect.

Height: 2–8" (5–20 cm).

Flowering: May–August.

Habitat: Dry open slopes at high elevations.

Range: Western Canada south in mountains to Washington, northern Nevada, Utah, and central Colorado.

Comments: The genus name honors T. Smielowski, an 18th-century Russian botanist. Alpine Smelowskia *(S. ovalis),* with pods ⅛–¼" (3–6 mm) long and petioles lacking stiff hairs, occurs in the mountains of central Washington south to central Oregon, and in northeastern California.

---

320 Desert Plume; Golden Prince's Plume
Stanleya pinnata

Description: *Slender wands of yellow flowers* atop tall, stout, smooth, bluish-green, leafy stems.

Flowers: Sepals 4; *petals 4,* each ⅜–½" (9–15 mm) long, densely hairy on inner side of brownish base.

Leaves: Those at base 2–6" (5–15 cm) long, pinnately divided, broadly lanceolate; those on stem smaller, often also pinnately divided.

Fruit: Very slender pod, 1¼–2½" (3–6.5 cm) long; on a slender stalk ½–¾" (1.5–2 cm) long, joined to slightly thicker stalk.

Height: 1½–5' (45–150 cm).

Flowering: May–July.

Habitat: Deserts and plains to lower mountains, often in sagebrush.

Range: Southeastern Oregon south to
southeastern California and east to
western Great Plains from North
Dakota to western Texas.

Comments: This is a conspicuous wildflower in the
arid West, as its flowers generally stand
above any nearby shrubs. All other
Stanleya species have yellow flowers
without hairs, except White Desert
Plume *(S. albescens)*, which has hairs on
the inside of its white petals and occurs
from northeastern Arizona to west-
central Colorado and northwestern
New Mexico.

303   Mountain Jewel Flower
Streptanthus tortuosus

Description: A branched plant with heart-shaped or
round leaves and racemes of *flask-shaped,
pale yellow or cream to dark brownish-purple
flowers.*

Flowers: ½" (1.5 cm) long; sepals 4; petals 4,
whitish with purple veins, crinkled.

Leaves: ¾–3½" (2–9 cm) long, clasping stem,
often slightly cupped, concave side
downward.

Fruit: Slender pod, 2½–5" (6.5–12.5 cm) long,
arched, spreading.

Height: 8–39" (20–100 cm).

Flowering: May–August.

Habitat: Dry rocky slopes.

Range: Southern Oregon south to southern
California west of Sierra Nevada.

Comments: Mountain Jewel Flower is one of the
most widespread and variable species in
this western genus. Heartleaf Jewel
Flower *(S. cordatus)* is very similar but
grows east of the Sierra Nevada and
Cascade Range.

169   Wild Candytuft
Thlaspi montanum

Description: 1 or several short unbranched stems
growing from a basal rosette of leaves,
bearing *small, arrow-shaped leaves,* and

ending in *dense racemes of tiny white flowers.*

Flowers: Petals 4, each ¼" (6 mm) long.

Leaves: Those at base ½–2½" (1.5–6.5 cm) long, with ovate blades abruptly tapering to a slender petiole; those on stem smaller, without petioles.

Fruit: Flat ovate pod, ¼–½" (5–13 mm) long, bluntly pointed at tip, distinctly notched.

Height: 1¼–16" (3–40 cm).

Flowering: February–August.

Habitat: Open slopes in mountains from moderate to high elevations.

Range: British Columbia south to northern California and east to Rocky Mountains from Alberta to southern New Mexico and western Texas; also in northern Mexico.

Comments: This species resembles some peppergrasses, but in each chamber of Wild Candytuft's tiny pods there are two seeds; peppergrass pods have a single seed.

CACTUS FAMILY
Cactaceae

Succulent, mostly leafless, commonly spiny, sometimes shrubby plants with often showy flowers and spherical, cylindrical, or flat, sometimes jointed stems.

Flowers: Radially symmetrical; borne singly on sides or near top of stem. Sepals many, separate, often petal-like; petals many, separate; bases of both sepals and petals may be fused into a long tube above ovary; stamens many; all these parts attached at top of ovary.

Stems: Varying from low and spherical to cylindrical or flat; in some genera divided into sections (joints) that may break off easily; sometimes with raised ribs or nipples.

Spines: Often developing in leaf axils (where leaves would be); needle-like or flat, in clusters, or absent; *Opuntia* species often also with minute bristles (glochids) in clusters.

Fruit: Berry-like, fleshy or dry, large or small, with many seeds.

There are about 140 genera and 2,000 species, nearly all found in the warm arid parts of the Americas. Primitive tropical species *(Pereskia)* have normal-looking leaves; in dry, hot, western habitats, leaves are very small and drop early or are entirely absent. Reduction of leaves, along with the compact shape of the stem, is a water-conserving adaptation, reducing the plant's overall surface area. There are several other adaptations aiding survival in this harsh environment. Root systems are shallow, enabling cacti to absorb water from brief showers and store it in the succulent stems. Pores (stomata) in the skin (epidermis) open during the cool night, allowing entry of carbon dioxide, which is chemically stored; during the day the pores are closed, reducing water loss, and the stored carbon dioxide is used in photosynthesis. Spines discourage eating of the plants by animals in regions where there is little other green growth for food; they also reflect light and heat, shading the surface and helping to reduce water loss by keeping the plant cool. Many species are grown as succulent novelties, and collecting cacti, a popular hobby, has brought some rarer species near extinction. Some are endangered and have strong legal protection. The flattened stems, or pads, of certain *Opuntia* species are edible; cut-up pieces, called nopalitos, are available canned or as a fresh vegetable.

48 Saguaro; Giant Cactus
Carnegiea gigantea

Description:	*Tall, thick, columnar, spiny stems* generally with several large, erect or twisted branches and white flowers.
Flowers:	2½–3″ (6.5–7.5 cm) wide, funnel-shaped, in crown-like clusters near branch ends; petals many.
Stems:	8–24″ (20–60 cm) wide; ribs 12–24.
Spines:	To 2″ (5 cm) long, stout, in clusters on ribs, 10–25 per cluster.
Fruit:	2½–3½″ (6.5–9 cm) long, fleshy, egg-shaped, green outside, red inside.
Height:	To 50′ (15 m); record plants near 80′ (24 m).
Flowering:	May–June.
Habitat:	Desert slopes and flats.
Range:	Extreme southeastern California east to southern Arizona and south to Mexico.
Comments:	Saguaro (pronounced *sah-**wah**-ro*) is often placed in the large genus *Cereus* (as *C. giganteus*). It is the state flower of Arizona, where, like all cacti and many other plants, it is protected by law. It

grows very slowly; the oldest plants
are estimated to be 150–200 years old.
Many are killed or injured by lightning
during desert storms. Its slow growth
and capacity to store great quantities
of water allow it to flower each year
regardless of drought. Its fruit was
an important source of food for
Native Americans and is still used
to some extent, the pulp eaten raw or
preserved, the sap fermented to make an
intoxicating drink, and the seeds ground
into a butter. The woody ribs of the
stems were used in building shelters.
During the night its flowers remain
open and are visited by nectar-feeding
bats and a variety of insects; by day its
flowers are visited by White-winged
doves, a major pollinator.

465 Cushion Cactus
Coryphantha vivipara

Description: *Small, nearly spherical to barrel-shaped stems,* sometimes single but often many in a mound, with pink, red, lavender, or yellow-green flowers near top.

Flowers: 1–2″ (2.5–5 cm) wide; petals many, each ¼–½″ (6–13 mm) long.

Stems: To 3″ (7.5 cm) wide; nipples 1–1½″ (2.5–4 cm) long, grooved on upper side.

Spines: In clusters; central spines 3–10, each ½–¾″ (1.5–2 cm) long, straight, tipped with pink, red, or black, surrounded by 12–40 slightly shorter, white spines.

Fruit: ½–1″ (1.5–2.5 cm) long, plump, green, smooth, with brown seeds.

Height: 1½–6″ (4–15 cm).

Flowering: May–June.

Habitat: Rocky, desert slopes and rocky or sandy soil among piñon, juniper, oaks, and Ponderosa Pine.

Range: Central Canada south to southeastern Oregon and southeastern California, and east to Great Plains from Minnesota to western Texas; also in northern Mexico.

Comments: The genus name comes from the Greek *koryphe* ("cluster") and *anthos* ("flower").

Nipple Cactus *(C. missouriensis)* is
very similar, differing in having a
single central spine in each cluster,
greenish-white flowers, and reddish
fruit with black seeds; it occurs mostly
east of the Rocky Mountains but grows
westward to central Idaho, western
Colorado, southern Utah, and northern
Arizona.

467   Rainbow Cactus; Comb Hedgehog
Echinocereus pectinatus

Description: A low, cylindrical cactus girdled
from top to bottom by *bands of colorful
spines,* pink, gray, pale yellow, brown, or
white; flowers pink, rose, lavender, or
yellow.

Flowers: 2½–5½″ (6.5–14 cm) wide, 1 or few per
plant; petals many.

Stems: To 4″ (10 cm) wide; ribs 15–22.

Spines: To ½″ (1.5 cm) long, slender, in close
clusters; point at which they attach is a
vertical oval.

Fruit: Plump, greenish, with spines eventually
dropping off.

Height: 4–12″ (10–30 cm).

Flowering: June–August.

Habitat: Rocky slopes and flats, commonly on
limestone.

Range: Central and southern Arizona east to
western Texas and south to northern
Mexico.

Comments: The banded colors of spines explain the
name Rainbow Cactus. The strikingly
beautiful flowers seem far too large for
the plant.

388   Claret Cup Cactus; King's Cup Cactus; Strawberry Cactus
Echinocereus triglochidiatus

Description: *Brilliant scarlet flowers* atop spiny,
cylindrical stems; in old plants many
stems form a hemispherical clump.

Flowers: 1¼–2″ (3–5 cm) wide; petals many.

Stems: 3–4″ (7.5–10 cm) wide; ribs 5–12.

Spines:	Larger spines 1–1¾" (2.5–4.5 cm) long, 2–16 per cluster, on ribs.
Fruit:	½–1" (1.5–2.5 cm) long, plump, red, with few clusters of spines eventually dropping off.
Height:	2–12" (5–30 cm).
Flowering:	April–May.
Habitat:	Rocky slopes in deserts and dry woodlands and open, rocky sites in mountains.
Range:	Southeastern California east to southern Utah, central Colorado, and western Texas, and south to northern Mexico.
Comments:	Among the most beautiful cacti, this large plant makes breathtaking mounds of scarlet when its many stems are in full flower. Stems are highly variable, often with two strikingly different forms growing in the same area.

3 Green Pitaya
Echinocereus viridiflorus

Description:	A small cactus with 1 cylindrical stem or several in a clump and *yellowish-green or magenta flowers.*
Flowers:	*¾–1" (2–2.5 cm) wide,* near top of stem; petals many.
Stems:	4" (10 cm) wide; ribs 6–14.
Spines:	½–1" (1.5–2.5 cm) long, red, brownish, white, gray, or greenish yellow, creating bands of color on stem.
Fruit:	*Green,* with spines eventually dropping off.
Height:	1–10" (2.5–25 cm).
Flowering:	May–July.
Habitat:	Dry plains and hills.
Range:	Southeastern Wyoming and western South Dakota south to eastern New Mexico and western Texas.
Comments:	Pitaya (pronounced *pee-**tah**-yab*) is the phonetic spelling of the original Spanish name Pitahaya, a name given to species of *Echinocereus* but more broadly applied to a number of cacti that produce sweet, edible fruit.

213   **California Barrel Cactus**
Ferocactus cylindraceus

Description: *1 large, columnar or barrel-shaped stem;* flowers yellow or reddish near base of petals.

Flowers: 1½–2½″ (4–6.5 cm) wide, in a crown near top of stem.

Stems: 1–1½′ (30–45 cm) wide; ribs 18–27, stout.

Spines: 2–5½″ (5–14 cm) long, *stout, reddish or yellowish,* in dense clusters along ribs, almost hiding stem's surface; *4 in center of cluster* in form of a cross, curved, surrounded by 12–20 similarly stout spines.

Fruit: Fleshy, yellow, scaly.

Height: 3–10′ (90–300 cm).

Flowering: April–May.

Habitat: Along washes, on gravelly slopes, and on canyon walls in deserts.

Range: Southern California east to south-central Arizona.

Comments: The genus name comes from the Latin *ferox* ("fierce"), commonly applied to very spiny plants. Candy Barrel Cactus or Fishhook Barrel Cactus (*F. wislizenii*), which grows from southern Arizona east to western Texas and south to northern Mexico, is used for making cactus candy; in each cluster it has a large spine oriented upward, then sharply curved downward at the tip, and other central spines much stouter than the slender surrounding spines.

466   **Peyote**
Lophophora williamsii

Description: *Low, gray, spineless, nearly hemispherical stems* growing singly or in broad dense clumps, topped by several pink flowers.

Flowers: ½–1″ (1.5–2.5 cm) wide; petals many, pink.

Stems: 2–3″ (5–7.5 cm) wide; ribs about 8, low.

Fruit: ½–¾″ (1.5–2 cm) long, fleshy, red.

Height: 1–3″ (2.5–7.5 cm).

Flowering: May–September.
Habitat: Limestone soil in deserts.
Range: Southern Texas and northern Mexico.
Comments: Cut and dried "buttons" of Peyote, when chewed, produce color hallucinations and are important in certain Native American religious ceremonies. A federal permit is required to possess any part of the plant. In Texas Peyote has been almost eliminated by collectors, but in areas of Mexico it is still very common.

463 Fishhook Cactus
Mammillaria grahamii

Description: A low, cylindrical cactus with 1 or several stems and *many hooked spines; flowers pink or lavender.*
Flowers: ¾–1″ (2–2.5 cm) wide, near top of stem; petals many, each about ½″ (1.5 cm) long.
Stems: Usually less than 4″ (10 cm) long, occasionally to 1′ (30 cm); 1½–3″ (4–7.5 cm) wide.
Spines: About ¼–½″ (6–13 mm) long, in clusters at tips of nipples; central spine ½″ (1.5 cm) long, hooked, surrounded by 18–28 shorter, straight, light tan or brownish-pink spines.
Fruit: ½–1″ (1.5–2.5 cm) long, broadest above middle, smooth, at first green, after several months red.
Height: To 6″ (15 cm).
Flowering: April–May.
Habitat: Dry, gravelly places in deserts and arid grasslands.
Range: Southeastern California east to western Texas and south to northern Mexico.
Comments: The genus name refers to the projections on the stems, which resemble mammary glands. Similar species of *Mammillaria* and *Coryphantha* are distinguished by the position of the flower relative to the cluster of spines. In *Coryphantha* older projections have a groove on the upper side. Both genera have some species

with hooked spines. The wild-
plant enthusiast who wishes to
find reference to Fishhook Cactus
in more technical literature must
check under two more scientific
names: the long-used *M. microcarpa*
and the recently used *M. milleri*. The
synonymy reflects historical problems
in nomenclature and the difficulty of
obtaining a satisfactory classification,
problems that are very common in the
Cactaceae.

468 Beavertail Cactus
Opuntia basilaris

Description: Flat, grayish-green, *leafless, jointed
stems* in a clump *lacking large spines,
with vivid rose-pink or reddish-lavender
flowers* on upper edges of joints.

Flowers: 2–3″ (5–7.5 cm) wide; petals many.

Stems: Joints 2–13″ (5–33 cm) long, 1–6″
(2.5–15 cm) wide, ½″ (1.5 cm) thick,
oval, widest above middle.

Spines: Major spines absent; hundreds of sharp
bristles ⅛–¼″ (3–6 mm) long, red-
brown, in many small clusters.

Fruit: 1¼″ (3 cm) long, egg-shaped, grayish
brown, dry, with many seeds.

Height: 6–12″ (15–30 cm); clump of stems 6′
(1.8 m) wide.

Flowering: March–June.

Habitat: Dry, rocky, desert flats and slopes.

Range: Southwestern Utah south to western
Arizona, southeastern California, and
northwestern Mexico.

Comments: The gray-green stems, low growth, and
brilliant flowers, which often nearly
cover the plant, make this a popular
ornamental in hot dry climates. The
bristles (glochids) easily penetrate the
skin because of their reversed barbs,
much like microscopic harpoons, but do
not pose the danger of species with long
rigid spines, such as the Plains Prickly
Pear *(O. polyacantha)*. *Opuntia* cacti need
not be dug up; a joint broken from a

plant will quickly root in dry sand.
Opuntia with flat joints are known as
prickly pears; in the Southwest, if the
fruits are juicy and edible, they are
called *tuna* by people of Spanish-
American heritage.

2 Teddybear Cholla
Opuntia bigelovii

Description: A miniature tree, upper half with
*short stubby branches densely covered with
pale golden spines;* flowers green or
yellow, petals often streaked with
lavender.

Flowers: 1–1½″ (2.5–4 cm) wide, near ends
of joints.

Stems: Joints 3–10″ (7.5–25 cm) long,
cylindrical.

Spines: ½–1″ (1.5–2.5 cm) long.

Fruit: About ¾″ (2 cm) long, yellow, egg-
shaped, knobby.

Height: 3–9′ (90–270 cm).

Flowering: March–April.

Habitat: Hot, dry, rocky slopes in deserts.

Range: Southeastern California east to central
Arizona and south to northwestern
Mexico.

Comments: Though the branches resemble the
arms and legs of a fuzzy teddy bear,
this plant is far from cuddly; its
spines stick instantly and hold tightly
by means of minute, backward-
pointing barbs. It is one of the most
formidable cacti of the Southwest.
When a joint (which seems to "jump"
when detached by a light touch or
bump) is severely stuck, the victim's
best solution is to cut the spines with
scissors or nippers and pull them from
the flesh with pliers. Jumping Cholla
(*O. fulgida*), which also has easily
detached stem segments or joints
and has fruits connected to one another
and hanging in a chain, occurs from
southern Arizona south to northwestern
Mexico.

212   Fragile Prickly Pear; Brittle Cactus
Opuntia fragilis

Description: *A low matted clump of spiny, jointed stems* and yellow or greenish flowers.

Flowers: 1½–2″ (4–5 cm) wide, near upper ends of joints.

Stems: Joints ¾–2″ (2–5 cm) long, slightly flat, broadest above middle, readily detached.

Spines: ½–1″ (1.5–2.5 cm) long, white or pale gray, 1–9 per cluster.

Fruit: About ½″ (1.5 cm) long, egg-shaped, tan when ripe.

Height: 8–10″ (20–25 cm); clump of stems 1–3′ (30–90 cm) wide.

Flowering: May–June.

Habitat: Dry open areas.

Range: British Columbia east to southwestern Manitoba and south to northern California, northern Nevada, southeastern Arizona, northern New Mexico, northern Texas, and central Kansas.

Comments: This is one of the most common low prickly pears. Most species have flatter stems.

469   Tree Cholla; Cane Cholla
Opuntia imbricata

Description: *A spiny, leafless bush or small tree* with cylindrical, jointed branches and *deep pink to reddish-lavender flowers* near ends.

Flowers: 2–3″ (5–7.5 cm) wide; petals many.

Stems: Joints 5–16″ (12.5–40 cm) long, ¾–1¼″ (2–3 cm) wide, with sharply raised, spiny knobs.

Spines: ½–1″ (1.5–2.5 cm) long, 10–30 per cluster.

Fruit: 1–2″ (2.5–5 cm) long, yellow, egg-shaped, fleshy.

Height: 3–7′ (90–210 cm).

Flowering: May–July.

Habitat: Plains, deserts, and among piñon and juniper.

Range: Southern Colorado and Kansas south to Arizona, New Mexico, Texas, and northern Mexico.

Comments: This is the first bush-like or tree-like cholla (pronounced **choy**-*yah*) encountered when traveling from the East to the Southwest. Near the Rio Grande other species appear, and in Arizona there are many, making identification more difficult. Once the flesh has weathered away, the woody stems are hollow, with many holes, and are popular souvenirs.

423 Desert Christmas Cactus
Opuntia leptocaulis

Description: A small bush formed by *many spiny, intertangled, slender branches,* with greenish, yellow, or bronze flowers.

Flowers: ½–1″ (1.5–2.5 cm) wide, along stem.

Stems: About ¼″ (6 mm) thick, branched.

Spines: 1–2½″ (2.5–6.5 cm) long, tan or gray; 1 projecting from each raised cluster of tiny, reddish bristles.

Fruit: About ½″ (1.5 cm) long, fleshy, bright red, on stem through most of winter.

Height: To 3′ (90 cm).

Flowering: May–June.

Habitat: Flats, slopes, and along washes in deserts and grasslands.

Range: Western Arizona east to southern Oklahoma and south to northern Mexico.

Comments: This plant has the slenderest stems of all southwestern chollas. During winter its bright red fruit adds attractive color to the brown desert.

211 Plains Prickly Pear
Opuntia polyacantha

Description: A *low mound of spiny, flat, nearly oval joints* with bright yellow or sometimes bright magenta flowers.

Flowers: 2–3″ (5–7.5 cm) wide, on upper edge of joints; petals many.

Stems: Joints 2–4″ (5–10 cm) long, bluish green.

Spines: 2–3″ (5–7.5 cm) long, 6–10 per cluster, mostly bent down.

Fruit: ¾–1½" (2–4 cm) long, egg-shaped, tan when ripe.

Height: 3–6" (7.5–15 cm); clump of stems 1–10' (30–300 cm) wide.

Flowering: May–July.

Habitat: Open areas on plains, in deserts, and among piñon and juniper.

Range: Southern British Columbia south to southern Utah and northern New Mexico, and east to western Great Plains from Alberta to northern Texas.

Comments: This cactus is becoming an increasingly frequent nuisance on rangeland. The spiny pads often break off and stick in the noses and throats of livestock.

464 Simpson's Hedgehog Cactus
Pediocactus simpsonii

Description: *1 or few spiny, nearly spherical stems* with several white, rose-pink, or yellow flowers near top.

Flowers: 1–1½" (2.5–4 cm) wide.

Stems: 2–3" (5–7.5 cm) wide.

Spines: Central spines ⅜–¾" (1–2 cm) long, straight, brownish, 5–11 per cluster on low tubercles, spreading in all directions from center; surrounded by 15–30 white or cream spines, each about ¼" (6 mm) long.

Fruit: About ¼" (6 mm) long, tan and dry when ripe.

Height: 2–8" (5–20 cm).

Flowering: May–July.

Habitat: Powdery soil among sagebrush, piñon, and juniper.

Range: Eastern Washington south to central Nevada and northern Arizona, and east to Idaho, western South Dakota, western Colorado, and northern New Mexico; possibly in western Montana and western Kansas.

Comments: This cactus is fairly popular with collectors. Other species of the genus are rare. Mass collecting of cacti is inexcusable, but even one person digging up only one plant has a detrimental effect, for if many take only "their share," eventually entire plant populations are depleted.

70 Night-blooming Cereus; Queen-of-the-night
Penicereus greggii

Description:	*Few angular, gray, thin, barely spiny, twiggy stems* resembling a small dead bush; *flowers large, white.*
Flowers:	2–3″ (5–7.5 cm) wide, 4–6″ (10–15 cm) long, very sweet-scented; petals many.
Stems:	About 1″ (2.5 cm) wide; ribs 4–6.
Spines:	About ⅛″ (3 mm) long, mostly lying flat, 11–13 per cluster.
Fruit:	Plump, bright red, with many seeds.
Height:	1–3′ (30–90 cm).
Flowering:	Usually June.
Habitat:	Desert flats and washes.
Range:	Southern Arizona east to western Texas and south to northern Mexico.
Comments:	This cactus, sometimes placed in the larger genus *Cereus,* is inconspicuous most of the year. When in bloom, it is easily spotted only in the evening and early morning when its spectacular night-blooming flowers are open. It is very popular in desert rock gardens and in the cactus trade; when a population is found, all too often the large, turnip-like roots are quickly dug up. It can be grown from stem cuttings, if the cut end is allowed to heal in shade for several weeks before it is planted in dry sand. The plant is legally protected in most of its range and should be left in the wild.

BELLFLOWER FAMILY
Campanulaceae

Usually herbs, rarely trees or shrubs, with blue, lavender, or white flowers borne singly or in clusters.

Flowers: Radially symmetrical, with tubular or bell-shaped, 5-lobed corolla; or bilaterally symmetrical, with conspicuously 2-lipped corolla; calyx 5-parted; stamens 5; all these parts attached at top of ovary.

Leaves: Simple, sometimes deeply divided.
Fruit: Berry or capsule.

There are about 70 genera and 2,000 species, widely distributed in northern temperate and tropical regions. Species in the tropics generally occur at higher elevations. Species of *Lobelia* and similar plants with usually 2-lipped corollas, more common in temperate and tropical regions, are sometimes placed in their own family, the Lobeliaceae. Members of both groups contribute beautiful ornamentals to gardens. An exception to the usual blue or lavender flower color is the scarlet Cardinal Flower *(Lobelia cardinalis).* Campanulaceae has also been known as the bluebell family.

639   Bluebell; Harebell
Campanula rotundifolia

Description: *Blue-violet, bell-shaped flowers hanging* along top parts of slender, mostly unbranched stems growing in small patches.

Flowers: Corolla ½–1″ (1.5–2.5 cm) long, with 5 pointed lobes gently curved back; style about as long as corolla.

Leaves: Those along stem ½–3″ (1.5–7.5 cm) long, very narrow; those at base with round blades, usually withering before plant flowers.

Bluebell

Height: 4–40″ (10–100 cm).
Flowering: June–September.
Habitat: Meadows and rocky slopes from moderate to high elevations.
Range: Most high western mountains, except Sierra Nevada; also in much of eastern Canada and United States south to North Carolina.
Comments: This plant also occurs in Eurasia. The genus name, from the Latin *campana* ("bell"), means "little bell." The name Harebell may allude to an association with witches, who were believed to be able to transform themselves into hares, portents of bad luck when they crossed a person's path. In Scotland another old name for this plant is Witches' Thimble.

648 Southwestern Blue Lobelia
Lobelia anatina

Description: Usually 1 slender, erect stem topped with few sparse, *deep blue-violet, bilaterally symmetrical flowers in an open raceme.*
Flowers: Corolla ½–1″ (1.5–2.5 cm) long, tubular portion slit only on top, 2-lipped, 3-lobed lower lip spreading sideways and downward, 2-lobed upper lip bent upward with tips touching above flower; anthers 5, 2 with tuft of white hairs, other 3 hairless.
Leaves: 1–3″ (2.5–7.5 cm) long, lanceolate, often with low blunt teeth.
Height: 8–28″ (20–70 cm).
Flowering: July–October.
Habitat: Moist meadows, streambanks, and marshes.
Range: Southern Arizona, southern New Mexico, and northern Mexico.
Comments: This slender little lobelia is one of several bluish-flowered species in the West.

409 Cardinal Flower; Scarlet Lobelia
Lobelia cardinalis

Description: Erect, leafy stems, often in clusters, with *racemes of flowers resembling flaming red spires.*

Flowers: Corolla 1–1½″ (2.5–4 cm) long, bilaterally symmetrical, tubular base slit along top and sides, 2-lipped, lower lip with 3 large lobes, upper lip with 2 small lobes.

Leaves: 2–5″ (5–12.5 cm) long, narrowly lanceolate, with fine teeth on edges.

Height: 1–3′ (30–90 cm).

Flowering: July–October.

Habitat: Moist shady slopes and sunny streambanks.

Range: Southern California east through Utah and Arizona to eastern Colorado, southern Nebraska, and western Texas, and east throughout much of East.

Comments: One of the West's handsomest wildflowers, this lobelia attracts hummingbirds, which feed on the nectar and pollinate the flowers. Sierra Madre Lobelia *(L. laxiflora)* is also found in southern Arizona; its corolla is either red with yellow lobes or all yellow.

606 Venus's Looking Glass
Triodanis perfoliata

Description: Erect, bristly-hairy, leafy stems with 1 or few *nearly flat, blue, violet, or white flowers* in axils of upper leaves.

Flowers: ½–¾″ (1.5–2 cm) wide; sepals 5, narrow, sharp; corolla usually with 5 bluntly pointed lobes.

Leaves: ½–1¼″ (1.5–3 cm) long, broadly ovate, attached to stem in notched base, edges generally scalloped.

Height: 6–24″ (15–60 cm).

Flowering: April–July.

Habitat: Rocky banks, dry woods, and plains, often where soil has been disturbed.

Range: Southern British Columbia south to northern California and southern

Arizona, and east across continent;
also in Mexico and South America.

Comments: Some of the flowers are small,
inconspicuous, and do not open;
pollination occurs entirely within
them. Such flowers generally have
only three or four sepals.

CAPER FAMILY
Capparaceae

Commonly herbs in temperate climates; mostly trees or
shrubs in tropical regions.

Flowers: Radially or bilaterally symmetrical; usually in
racemes. Sepals 4, separate; petals 4, separate, each commonly with a slender, stalk-like base; stamens 4 to many;
all these parts attached at base of stalk beneath ovary.
Leaves: Simple or often palmately compound.
Fruit: 1-chambered capsule, berry, or drupe.

There are about 45 genera and 800 species, found in
the warm regions of the world. A few are grown as ornamentals; the garden spider flowers *(Cleome)* are especially
popular. The flower buds of *Capparis* species are used as a
seasoning.

343 Yellow Bee Plant
Cleome lutea

Description: A branched plant with *palmately
compound leaves* and racemes of *small
yellow flowers* at top.
Flowers: Petals 4, each about ¼" (6 mm) long;
stamens 6, long.
Leaves: 3–7 leaflets, each ¾–2½" (2–6.5 cm)
long, lanceolate.
Fruit: Slender pod, ½–1½" (1.5–4 cm) long,
on *long arched stalk jointed at middle.*
Height: 1½–5' (45–150 cm).
Flowering: May–September.
Habitat: Desert plains and lower valleys in
mountains, commonly near water or
areas earlier filled with water.
Range: Eastern Washington south through
eastern California and east to southern
Arizona, northern New Mexico, western
Nebraska, and Montana.

Comments: The genus name was used by the
             Greek philosopher Theophrastus
             for a plant resembling mustard;
             while the flowers resemble those
             of mustards, the ovary on a jointed
             stalk and palmately compound leaves
             distinguish this species as a member of
             the Capparaceae. The similar Golden
             Spider Flower *(C. platycarpa),* found in
             eastern Oregon, southwestern Idaho,
             and adjacent regions of California and
             Nevada, has hairy stems and leaves
             tipped with glands.

543   Rocky Mountain Bee Plant
          Cleome serrulata

Description: Branched stems with *palmately*
                compound leaves and *pink or reddish-*
                purple flowers (sometimes white) in
                racemes at branch ends.
   Flowers: ½″ (1.5 cm) long; petals 4;
                stamens 6, long; ovary on a long,
                protruding stalk.
    Leaves: 3 leaflets, each ½–3″ (1.5–7.5 cm)
                long, lanceolate.
      Fruit: Slender pod, 1½–2½″ (4–6.5 cm)
                long, on *long arched stalk jointed*
                at middle.
    Height: 6–60″ (15–150 cm).
 Flowering: June–September.
   Habitat: Plains, rangelands, and foothills
                of lower mountains.
     Range: Eastern Washington south to
                northeastern California and
                central Arizona, and east to
                Great Plains from Saskatchewan
                to Texas; introduced elsewhere
                in West.
  Comments: This plant's flowers produce
                copious nectar and attract bees,
                hence the common name. Native
                Americans boiled the strong
                leaves for food and to treat
                stomachaches. In times of drought,
                early Spanish-Americans made
                tortillas from the barely palatable
                but nourishing seeds.

15, 285 Bladderpod
Isomeris arborea

Description: *Yellow flowers* in many short racemes on a *strong-smelling, dense, round shrub with palmately compound leaves.*

Flowers: About 1″ (2.5 cm) wide; petals 4; stamens 6, long.

Leaves: 3 leaflets, each ½–1½″ (1.5–4 cm) long, oblong.

Fruit: Plump pointed pod, 1–2″ (2.5–5 cm) long, hanging down on *long stalk jointed at middle.*

Height: 2–8′ (60–240 cm).

Flowering: January–November.

Habitat: Among brush and along washes, especially in alkaline soil.

Range: Southern California and Baja California from coast to western edge of desert.

Comments: The genus name derives from the Greek *isos* ("equal") and *meris* ("part"), possibly describing the equal halves of the pod.

185 Clammyweed
Polanisia dodecandra

Description: A strong-smelling, branched plant, covered with *short sticky hairs,* bearing *palmately compound leaves and racemes of white or cream flowers.*

Flowers: Petals 4, each ¼–¾″ (6–20 mm) long, notched at tip, tapered at base to slender stalk; stamens 6–20, long, *pink or purple,* of unequal length.

Leaves: 3 leaflets, each ½–1½″ (1.5–4 cm) long, broadly lanceolate.

Fruit: Plump, cylindrical pod, ¾–3″ (2–7.5 cm) long, held erect.

Height: 4–31″ (10–80 cm).

Flowering: May–October.

Habitat: Sandy slopes and flats; common along washes, in deserts, on plains, and among piñon and juniper.

Range: Southeastern Oregon east across northern United States to Minnesota and south to northeastern California, southern Arizona, New Mexico, most of Texas, and northern Mexico.

Comments: The common name refers to the sticky moist glands on the surface of this plant.

344 Jackass Clover
Wislizenia refracta

Description: An often densely branched plant with *palmately compound leaves* and many *tiny, yellow flowers in dense racemes.*

Flowers: Petals 4, each about ⅛″ (3 mm) long; stamens 6.

Leaves: 3 leaflets, each ½–1¼″ (1.5–3 cm) long, elliptical.

Fruit: Pod, about ⅛″ (3 mm) long, with *2 round lobes side by side* and a pointed style between, on *stalk jointed and sharply bent at middle.*

Height: 16–28″ (40–70 cm).

Flowering: April–September.

Habitat: Low, sandy or alkaline soil in deserts and arid grasslands; frequent along roads and washes.

Range: California's Central Valley east through southern Nevada to western Texas, and south to Mexico.

Comments: Malodorous and poisonous to livestock, this plant is probably distasteful and rarely eaten, but it is a valuable honey plant, nevertheless. The three leaflets give it a resemblance to clovers (*Trifolium*) in the pea family (Fabaceae), but the plants are not related. The origin of the word "jackass" in the common name is unknown.

HONEYSUCKLE FAMILY
Caprifoliaceae

Mostly shrubs, sometimes vines or herbs, commonly with showy flowers usually in a branched or forked cluster.

Flowers: Radially or bilaterally symmetrical. Calyx with 5 small sepals; corolla with 5 petals united into a slender tube, flared into a trumpet-shaped end or forming an upper and lower lip; stamens usually 5; all these parts attached at top of ovary.

Leaves: Opposite, simple or compound.
Fruit: Berry, drupe, or capsule.

There are about 15 genera and 400 species, found in the northern temperate region and in tropical mountains. Snowberry *(Symphoricarpo albus)*, elderberries *(Sambucus)*, and various honeysuckles *(Lonicera)* are grown as ornamentals, and the fruits of elderberries are also eaten or made into jelly and wine.

---

479 Twinflower
Linnaea borealis

Description: A matted plant with *2 pink, narrow, bell-like flowers* hanging from tops of erect, short, leafless, forked stalks.

Flowers: About ½″ (1.5 cm) long; corolla with 5 round lobes.

Leaves: ¼–1″ (6–25 mm) long, opposite, broadly elliptical, sometimes with few shallow teeth on edges.

Height: Creeper; flower stalks less than 4″ (10 cm).

Flowering: June–September.

Habitat: Moist woods and brush.

Range: Throughout western mountains south to northern California, northern Arizona, and New Mexico, and east to western South Dakota; also in much of eastern Canada and northeastern United States.

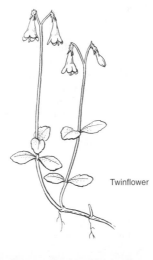

Twinflower

Comments: The genus name honors Carolus
            Linnaeus, the father of systematic
            botany, who was often depicted in
            paintings with this plant intertwined
            with his fingers. This charming plant
            makes a good groundcover in woodland
            gardens. Two other varieties occur in
            Europe and Asia.

CARNATION FAMILY
Caryophyllaceae

Herbs with swollen nodes on stems and flowers borne singly
or in branched or forked clusters.

Flowers: Sepals 5, separate or united; petals 5, each often
    with a slender portion at base, fringed or toothed at end;
    stamens 5 or 10; all these parts attached at base of ovary.
Leaves: Opposite, simple.
Fruit: Usually a capsule.

There are about 75 genera and 2,000 species, primarily in
the Northern Hemisphere, especially in cool regions. The
family simultaneously soothes us with many beautiful addi-
tions to gardens, especially pinks and carnations (both
groups in *Dianthus*) and Sweet William *(Dianthus barbatus),*
and harasses us by supplying many of the weeds found
there. Caryophyllaceae has also been known as the pink
family.

439   Corn Cockle
Agrostemma githago

Description: A slender, finely hairy, *stiffly erect plant*
              with few *branches forming narrow forks,*
              each tipped with *1 deep pink to reddish-
              lavender flower.*
    Flowers: About 1″ (2.5 cm) wide; sepals 5, each
              ¾–1½″ (2–4 cm) long, with narrow tip,
              joined at base to form a broad hard tube
              with 10 ribs; petals 5, shorter than
              sepals.
    Leaves: 2–6″ (5–15 cm) long, opposite, narrowly
              lanceolate, held nearly erect against
              stem.
    Fruit: Capsule, with 5 styles.
    Height: 1–3′ (30–90 cm).
    Flowering: May–July.

Corn Cockle

Habitat: Roadsides and other disturbed areas.
Range: Throughout Canada and United States; in West, most frequent in Washington, Oregon, and California's interior valleys.
Comments: This plant is native to Europe. In England, where "corn" generally means wheat, Corn Cockle was a weed in grain fields; before the advent of machine harvesting, the separation of its poisonous seeds from the wheat was a tedious procedure.

21 **Beautiful Sandwort**
   Arenaria capillaris

Description: *Many slender forked branches* growing on a main stalk above a leafy, matted base, with 1 *small, white, star-like flower* at end of each branch.
Flowers: Sepals 5, bluntly pointed, edges translucent; petals 5, each ¼–½" (6–13 mm) wide.
Leaves: ½–2½" (1.5–6.5 cm) long, opposite, very narrow, most on lower fourth of stem.
Fruit: Many-seeded capsule, with 3 styles.
Height: 2–12" (5–30 cm); leafy base to 8" (20 cm) wide.
Flowering: June–August.
Habitat: Sagebrush plains and rocky slopes in mountains.

Range: Alaska south to northern Oregon,
northern Nevada, and western Montana.

Comments: The genus name derives from the Latin
arena ("sand"), referring to the preferred
soil of many species. Several similar
species, distinguished by technical
characteristics, generally may be
recognized by white flowers with five
petals, three styles on the ovary, and
very narrow leaves.

23 Fendler's Sandwort
Arenaria fendleri

Description: A *tufted plant* with many slender
stems, very narrow leaves, and
numerous small white flowers in open
branched clusters.

Flowers: About ½" (1.5 cm) wide; sepals 5,
pointed, glandular; petals 5.

Leaves: ¾–3" (2–7.5 cm) long, opposite, almost
thread-like, sharply pointed.

Fruit: Small, 1-chambered capsule, with 6
teeth at tip when open.

Height: 4–12" (10–30 cm).

Flowering: July–September.

Habitat: Cliffs, ledges, and rocky banks in
mountains.

Range: Wyoming south to Arizona, New
Mexico, and western Texas.

Comments: This common southern Rocky
Mountain species gives the impression
of numerous white stars in an airy tuft.
There are a number of sandworts: Some
form tight, sometimes prickly mats;
others are tall and open but with flowers
in tight heads.

22 Meadow Chickweed
Cerastium arvense

Description: Several weak stems, each topped by a
few-branched flower cluster with 1 *white
flower* atop each nearly leafless branch.

Flowers: Nearly 1" (2.5 cm) wide; sepals 5; petals
5, each about ½" (1.5 cm) long, *deeply
notched at tip;* styles 5; bracts with stiff,

translucent edges surrounding flower cluster.

Leaves: ½–1½" (1.5–4 cm) long, opposite, narrowly lanceolate.

Fruit: Cylindrical capsule, with 10 teeth at tip when open.

Height: 2–20" (5–50 cm).

Flowering: April–August.

Habitat: Open, generally grassy areas from near coast to high in mountains.

Range: Throughout Northern Hemisphere; in West, south from Alaska and Canada to northern California, northern Arizona, and southern New Mexico; also in much of eastern United States.

Comments: The stems of Meadow Chickweed are so weak they sometimes lean on the ground. The stems bear downward-pointing hairs below the leaf nodes; the hairs on the branches of the flower cluster are tipped with glands, especially on plants in coastal areas. Those inland are often less hairy. *Cerastium,* from the Greek *keras* ("horn"), refers to the capsule, which is tapered and, in some species, bent slightly like a cow's horn. The very similar Mountain Chickweed (*C. beeringianum),* which occurs at high elevations in North America's western mountains, has green-edged bracts surrounding the flower cluster.

438 Grass Pink; Deptford Pink
Dianthus armeria

Description: 1 or several stiffly erect stems, prominently swollen at leaf nodes, with several *pink or red flowers* in a tight, forked, hairy cluster.

Flowers: Calyx about ½" (1.5 cm) wide, narrow, tubular, with 5 pointed lobes; petals 5, each ¾–1" (2–2.5 cm) long, base long and slender, upper end broad, with teeth on outer edge.

Leaves: 1½–4" (4–10 cm) long, opposite, very narrow, those on stem held erect.

Fruit: Capsule, with 2 styles.

Height: 8–24″ (20–60 cm).

Flowering: June–August.

Habitat: Roadsides, lots, and old fields.

Range: Washington south to California and east through Idaho to Montana; also throughout eastern Canada and United States, except Prairie Provinces.

Comments: Introduced from Europe, this relative of Carnation (*D. caryophyllus*) once grew in fields near Deptford, now an industrial section of London, hence one of its common names.

---

172 Bouncing Bet; Soapwort
Saponaria officinalis

Description: Leafy, unbranched *stems growing in patches* and topped with fairly dense clusters of many sweetly scented, *white or pink flowers.*

Flowers: About 1″ (2.5 cm) wide; calyx tubular, with 5 pointed teeth; petals 5, broad upper part about ½″ (1.5 cm) long, slender lower part as long as calyx; styles 2.

Leaves: 1½–5″ (4–12.5 cm) long, opposite, broadly lanceolate.

Height: 1–3′ (30–90 cm).

Flowering: June–September.

Habitat: Mostly moist places from low to moderate elevations, especially where cool.

Range: Throughout Canada and United States;

Bouncing Bet

in West, most frequent in Washington, Oregon, and California.

Comments: This old-fashioned ornamental is native to Europe. The genus name, from the Latin *sapo* ("soap"), refers to the sap, which contains saponins that produce a lather when mixed with water; saponins are poisonous when ingested.

---

437 Moss Pink; Moss Campion
Silene acaulis

Description: *Pink flowers on short stems barely above thick, moss-like mats.*
Flowers: About ½" (1.5 cm) wide; calyx ⅛–⅜" (3–9 mm) long, tubular, with 10 veins and 5 pointed lobes; petals 5, broad upper part usually notched at tip, slender lower part as long as calyx; styles 3, on ovary.
Leaves: ¼–½" (6–15 mm) long, opposite, very narrow, most at base.
Height: 1–2½" (2.5–6.5 cm); mats to 1' (30 cm) wide.
Flowering: June–August.
Habitat: Moist areas above timberline, often in rock crevices.
Range: Throughout Northern Hemisphere; in North America, from Alaska and Greenland south in mountains to Oregon, northern Arizona, northern New Mexico, and New Hampshire.
Comments: This beautiful alpine wildflower has adopted a low form as protection from frigid, drying winds. It resembles other tufted alpine plants with pink flowers, such as Purple Saxifrage *(Saxifraga oppositifolia),* with ovate leaves and only two styles, and species of *Phlox,* whose petals are united into a tube.

---

395 Indian Pink
Silene californica

Description: *Flowers with fringed, bright red petals resembling brilliant pinwheels at ends of branches on erect or trailing, leafy stems.*

Flowers:	1–1½" (2.5–4 cm) wide; calyx ½–1" (1.5–2.5 cm) long, broad, tubular, with 5 pointed teeth; petals 5, divided by small scales in middle, broad upper part with deep notches at end, slender lower part as long as calyx.
Leaves:	1¼–3" (3–7.5 cm) long, opposite, ovate.
Fruit:	Capsule, not longer than calyx.
Height:	6–16" (15–40 cm).
Flowering:	May–July.
Habitat:	Rocky, open woods.
Range:	Southwestern Oregon south to northern two-thirds of California.
Comments:	One of the showiest of western wildflowers, Indian Pink is widespread but not abundant. Cardinal Catchfly *(S. laciniata),* found from the southern third of California east to western Texas, is similar, though it has erect stems 16–40" (40–100 cm) high and the capsule is longer than the calyx.

---

440 **Stringflower**
Silene hookeri

Description:	A hairy gray plant with many short spreading stems in a cluster, few branches, and several flowers with *deeply divided petals* at branch ends.
Flowers:	1–2" (2.5–5 cm) wide; calyx ½–¾" (1.5–2 cm) long, tubular, with 5 teeth; *petals 5, white, pink, or purple,* divided by scales near middle, fan-shaped upper part ½–1" (1.5–2.5 cm) long and deeply divided into narrow lobes, slender lower part as long as calyx; styles 3.
Leaves:	1½–2½" (4–6.5 cm) long, opposite, lanceolate, widest above middle.
Height:	2–6" (5–15 cm).
Flowering:	May–June.
Habitat:	Dry rocky ground in brush and open coniferous forests.
Range:	Southwestern Oregon and northwestern California.
Comments:	The common name Stringflower best applies to the race with white petals divided into four narrow, string-like lobes.

26 White Campion; Evening Lychnis; White Cockle
Silene latifolia subsp. *alba*

Description: Several erect stems, forked in flower cluster and covered with glandular hairs, bearing *white flowers* at each branch end and leaves mostly on lower half of plant.

Flowers: About ¾″ (2 cm) wide; calyx about ¾″ (2 cm) long when flower blooms, swelling as fruit matures, narrow, tubular; petals 5, each about 1″ (2.5 cm) long, divided by several small scales near middle, upper part deeply notched at tip, lower part long and slender; some plants bearing flowers with only stamens, others bearing flowers with only ovaries.

Leaves: To 4″ (10 cm) long, opposite, lanceolate, broader above middle.

Height: 1½–4½′ (45–135 cm).

Flowering: June–August.

Habitat: Roadsides, old fields, and brushy areas.

Range: Northern California, northern Idaho, eastern Utah, and western Colorado; also in much of Canada and eastern United States.

Comments: Until recently known scientifically as *Lychnis alba,* this plant is now classified as the subspecies *alba* within the species *Silene latifolia.* White Campion is often confused with Night-flowering Catchfly (*S. noctiflora*), which has stamens and ovary in the same flower.

25 Bladder Campion
Silene vulgaris

Description: A usually smooth plant bearing several *white flowers, each with a large swollen calyx,* in an open forked cluster.

Flowers: About ½″ (1.5 cm) wide; calyx smooth, resembling a deep cup with 5 points on rim, enlarging to ¾″ (2 cm) long as fruit matures; petals 5, deeply notched at tip, with a long, stalk-like base; styles 3.

Leaves: 1¼–3″ (3–7.5 cm) long, opposite, broadly lanceolate.

Fruit: 3-celled capsule.

Height: To 3′ (90 cm).
Flowering: June–August.
Habitat: Vacant lots, fields, roadsides.
Range: Throughout West and much of Canada and eastern United States.
Comments: This plant is native to Europe. The swollen mature calyx, often tinged with purple, resembles a tiny, decorative paper lantern. Night-flowering Catchfly *(S. noctiflora),* another weedy species, has a hairy calyx. Both differ from White Campion *(S. latifolia* subsp. *alba)* by having stamens and ovary in the same flower.

ROCKROSE FAMILY
Cistaceae

Herbs or shrubs with flowers borne singly or in branched clusters.

Flowers: Radially symmetrical. Calyx with usually 3 large sepals and 2 small ones, or small ones absent; petals 5, sometimes fewer, separate, occasionally absent; stamens many; all these parts attached at base of ovary.
Leaves: Alternate or opposite, simple.
Fruit: Leathery or woody capsule, with at least 3 chambers.

There are about 8 genera and 200 species, mostly in dry sunny locations, often in chalky or sandy soil. The family is found mostly in the northern temperate region, with a few species in South America. Rockroses *(Cistus),* with vibrant pink or bright white flowers, are popular ornamentals in warmer parts of the West; a few others are also cultivated as ornamentals.

207 Peak Rushrose
Helianthemum scoparium

Description: A low, tuft-forming plant with *many spreading branches, very narrow leaves* that soon drop off, and a *yellow flower* in each upper leaf axil.
Flowers: About 1″ (2.5 cm) wide; sepals 5, each about ¼″ (6 mm) long, outer 2 much narrower and shorter than inner 3; petals 5, each ⅜–½″ (9–13 mm) long, broadly ovate; stamens many.

Leaves:	½–1¼″ (1.5–3 cm) long.
Height:	8–12″ (20–30 cm).
Flowering:	March–July.
Habitat:	Dry sandy flats near coast and inland on rocky slopes and ridges.
Range:	Northern California south to Baja California.
Comments:	The genus name, from the Greek *helios* ("sun") and *anthemon* ("flower"), refers to its flowers, which open only in the sun. Bicknell's Rushrose *(H. bicknellii),* found in eastern Wyoming and South Dakota eastward, has similar flowers but broom-like stems.

SPIDERWORT FAMILY
Commelinaceae

Herbs with more or less swollen nodes and clear, often sticky sap; flowers in clusters, sometimes enveloped in a boat-shaped bract (spathe).

Flowers: Radially symmetrical. Sepals 3; petals 3; stamens 6, filaments often with colored hairs; all these parts attached at base of ovary.
Leaves: Simple, base forming a tubular sheath around stem.
Fruit: 3-chambered capsule.

There are about 50 genera and 700 species, mostly in tropical and subtropical regions. Dayflowers *(Commelina),* Wandering Jew *(Zebrina pendula),* and Moses-in-a-boat *(Rhoeo discolor)* are cultivated as ornamentals.

587   Western Dayflower
Commelina dianthifolia

Description:	Flowers with *3 broad purple or blue petals protruding from a broad folded spathe* atop a leaning or erect, branched stem with narrow leaves.
Flowers:	About ¾″ (2 cm) wide; petals with short stalks, lower one slightly smaller; stamens 6.
Leaves:	To 6″ (15 cm) long, narrow, forming a sheath around stem at base; spathe 1–3″ (2.5–7.5 cm) long, including a long narrow tip.
Height:	To 20″ (50 cm).

Flowering: July–September.
Habitat: Rocky soil among piñon, other pines, and juniper.
Range: Eastern half of Arizona east to south-central Colorado and western Texas, and south throughout most of Mexico.
Comments: Dayflowers are so named because a single flower appears outside the leaf-like bract every few days, opening near dawn and wilting by midday.

643 Slender Dayflower; Hierba de Pollo
Commelina erecta

Description: Small clusters of flowers with *2 large, ear-like, blue petals* and 1 smaller petal; clusters borne in a spathe atop each of several erect branches.
Flowers: About 1″ (2.5 cm) wide; petals 3, upper 2 on very slender stalks, lower petal white.
Leaves: To 6″ (15 cm) long, very narrow to lanceolate, forming a sheath around stem at base; spathe ½–1½″ (1.5–4 cm) long.
Height: Branches about 1′ (30 cm); reclining stems to 3′ (90 cm) long.
Flowering: May–October.
Habitat: Sandy or rocky soil in grassy areas, open woods, and weedy places.
Range: Eastern Colorado south to southeastern Arizona, New Mexico, and Texas; also in eastern United States.
Comments: This is a highly variable species. The Spanish name, Hierba de Pollo, means "herb of the chicken."

568 Pine Spiderwort
Tradescantia pinetorum

Description: Clusters of *blue-purple, 3-petaled flowers* atop several lightly but roughly hairy stems that are mostly unbranched and erect but often bent and leaning at knee-like nodes.

Flowers:	Less than ¾″ (2 cm) wide; petals broad.
Leaves:	2–5″ (5–12.5 cm) long, sometimes much longer, very narrow.
Height:	8–20″ (20–50 cm).
Flowering:	August–September.
Habitat:	Open brush and woods.
Range:	Southern Arizona, southern New Mexico, and northern Mexico.
Comments:	This species and Western Spiderwort *(T. occidentalis)* were used by Native Americans as a cooked vegetable. Western Spiderwort, which grows from Montana south to Arizona and east to North Dakota and Texas, has smooth stems with several joints and bright blue to nearly rose-colored flowers. Wright's Spiderwort *(T. wrightii),* found on limestone slopes from central New Mexico to western Texas, has smooth stems in tufts, only about 6″ (15 cm) high, and a few glandular hairs on the sepals and individual flower stalks.

MORNING GLORY FAMILY
Convolvulaceae

Trees, shrubs, vines, or herbs, some parasitic, commonly with handsome, funnel-shaped flowers.

Flowers: Radially symmetrical. Calyx with 5 sepals; corolla with 5 united petals, almost unlobed on rim; stamens 5; all these parts attached at base of ovary.
Leaves: Simple.
Fruit: Capsule, berry, or nut.

There are about 50 genera and 1,500 species, mostly in temperate and tropical regions. A number of species are considered noxious weeds, but some are cultivated for their handsome flowers. Sweet Potato *(Ipomoea batatas)* is grown for its edible, fleshy roots, and a cathartic is extracted from the roots of Jalap *(I. purga).* *Dichondra* species provide cool groundcover in shady areas. A number of bizarre parasites in the genus *Cuscuta,* all with the common name Dodder (or Love-tangle), twining like yellow or orange strings over vegetation, are often placed in this family (if not segregated as the only genus in the family Cuscutaceae).

475   Beach Morning Glory
Calystegia soldanella

Description: *Trailing stems* growing from deep
rootstocks, with *thick, kidney-shaped leaves*
and *funnel-shaped, pale-streaked, pink or rose
flowers* on short stalks from leaf axils.

Flowers: Corolla 1½–2½" (4–6.5 cm) wide, with
5 short blunt points; bracts 2, each about
½" (1.5 cm) long, partially hiding calyx.

Leaves: 1–2" (2.5–5 cm) wide.

Height: Creeper; branches to 3" (7.5 cm), stems
to 20" (50 cm) long.

Flowering: April–September.

Habitat: Sandy beaches.

Range: Worldwide near coasts in temperate
regions; in West, along Pacific Coast
from British Columbia south to
southern California.

Comments: This fleshy plant does not seem very
similar to garden morning glories, but
the resemblance of its flower is
unmistakable. In the cool but humid
coastal climate the flowers remain open
most of the day.

72   Bindweed; Field Bindweed;
Possession Vine
Convolvulus arvensis

Description: Long, *trailing and twining stems* with rather
triangular leaves, and *white or pinkish,
funnel-shaped flowers* on short stalks.

Flowers: About 1" (2.5 cm) wide; corolla with 5
veins leading to low lobes on edge; *bracts
2,* each about ¼" (6 mm) long, *narrow,*
on stalk well below calyx.

Leaves: ¾–1½" (2–4 cm) long, generally
triangular, sometimes arrow-shaped or
ovate, short-stalked.

Height: 1–3' (30–90 cm).

Flowering: May–October.

Habitat: Fields, lots, gardens, and roadsides.

Range: Throughout West.

Comments: Bindweed is native to Europe. Its very
deep roots make it a noxious weed,
difficult to eradicate. *Calystegia,* a
common and very similar genus, has the

typical funnel-shaped corollas of
morning glories, often white or cream,
but the lobes at the end of the style are
oblong and blunt rather than narrow
and pointed. Hedge Bindweed
(*Calystegia sepium*), found in moist
places throughout much of the United
States, has two large bracts concealing
the calyx and white to cream flowers.

634 Arizona Blue-eyes; False Flax
Evolvulus arizonicus

Description: A plant with grayish hairs, slender erect
stems, and *1 shallow, bowl-shaped, blue to
purplish-blue flower* on a slender stalk in
each upper leaf axil.
Flowers: Corolla ½–¾" (1.5–2 cm) wide, with 5
round lobes; stamens 5.
Leaves: ¾–1" (2–2.5 cm) long, lanceolate.
Height: To 1' (30 cm).
Flowering: April–October.
Habitat: Open areas in deserts, grasslands, and
among piñon and juniper.
Range: Southern Arizona, southwestern New
Mexico, and northern Mexico.
Comments: In the arid parts of the Southwest, truly
blue flowers are uncommon; this flower,
often as blue as those of true flax
(*Linum*), is the prettiest of its genus in
the whole region. It is very similar to *E.
alsinoides,* a closely related species called
Ojo de Vibora (Spanish for "eye of the
viper"), which has corollas ⅛–⅜" (4–8
mm) wide; it is common from Arizona
east to Texas and south into Mexico.
Other *Evolvulus* in the West have very
short stalks beneath the flowers and
paler corollas.

389 Scarlet Creeper; Star Glory
Ipomoea cristulata

Description: A leafy vine with *scarlet, trumpet-shaped
flowers.*
Flowers: Corolla ¾–1½" (2–4 cm) long, with 5
pointed lobes; sepals ¼" (6 mm) long.

Leaves: 1¼–3″ (3–7.5 cm) long, about as wide,
            with 3 angular lobes.
Height: Vine; stems 3–7′ (90–210 cm) long.
Flowering: May–October.
Habitat: Brushy hillsides and canyons.
Range: Arizona east to western Texas and south
            to Mexico.
Comments: This plant is very similar to the
            cultivated Scarlet Creeper *(I. coccinea),*
            a southeastern species sometimes found in
            waste places in the Southwest. The
            large, tropical genus *Ipomoea* includes
            vines, shrubs, and trees.

---

474 Bush Morning Glory
Ipomoea leptophylla

Description: Smooth, erect, leafy stems, sometimes
              leaning on ground at base, forming a
              large roundish plant bearing flowers
              with *pinkish-lavender or purplish-red,
              funnel-shaped corollas* with darker centers
              in upper leaf axils.
Flowers: Corolla 2–2½″ (5–6.5 cm) wide; sepals
              5, of different lengths, joined at base.
Leaves: 1¼–3½″ (3–9 cm) long, narrowly
              lanceolate.
Height: To 4′ (1.2 m).
Flowering: May–July.
Habitat: Sandy or disturbed soil in prairies.
Range: Eastern Montana and western South
              Dakota south to northeastern New
              Mexico and western Texas.
Comments: This beautiful wildflower is
              representative of several species of
              Ipomoea that, unlike garden morning
              glories, are not vines.

---

565 Common Morning Glory
Ipomoea purpurea

Description: A vine bearing flowers with large,
              funnel-shaped corollas in axils of broad,
              often heart-shaped leaves.
Flowers: Corolla 1½–2½″ (4–6.5 cm) wide, *blue-
              violet, red, or white;* sepals 5, each about

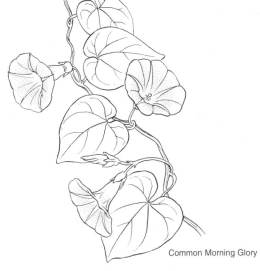

Common Morning Glory

½″ (1.5 cm) long, stiffly hairy on back, joined at base, with narrow green tips about as long as body.

Leaves: 1¼–6″ (3–15 cm) long, varying from heart-shaped to 3-lobed (if lobed, 2 at base point outward and backward).

Height: Vine; stems 3–10′ (90–300 cm) long.

Flowering: June–November.

Habitat: Fields, lots, and roadsides.

Range: California east to Texas; perhaps in Colorado; common in East and throughout tropics worldwide.

Comments: This native of tropical America is grown in much of the West as an ornamental; it is occasionally found in waste places, established as a weed. The name morning glory refers to the fact that the showy flowers that open in the morning and wilt by late afternoon. There are two similar species in the Southwest, both with the common name Morning Glory: *I. hederacea* has narrow sepal tips that curve outward and are longer than the body of the sepal; *I. nil,* from which many varieties of the garden morning glory derive, has narrow straight sepal tips.

DOGWOOD FAMILY
Cornaceae

Mostly trees or shrubs, rarely herbs, commonly with tiny flowers surrounded by petal-like bracts and resembling 1 large flower.

Flowers: Bisexual or unisexual, radially symmetrical. Sepals 4–5, small; petals 4–5; stamens 4–5; all these parts attached at top of ovary.
Leaves: Alternate or opposite, simple.
Fruit: Berry or berry-like drupe.

There are about 11 genera and 100 species, mostly in temperate regions. Many members of Cornaceae are grown as ornamentals.

35 Bunchberry
Cornus canadensis

Description: Stems growing in extensive, low patches, with *1 whorl of leaves just below a cluster of tiny, greenish flowers surrounded by 4 ovate, white or pinkish bracts; flower cluster resembling 1 large flower* held on a short stalk above leaves.

Flowers: Bracts to 4″ (10 cm) wide; each small flower in center of head with 4 sepals and 4 petals.

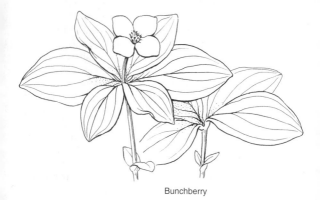

Bunchberry

Leaves:	¾–3″ (2–7.5 cm) long, narrowly ovate.
Fruit:	Tight clusters of bright red, round berries.
Height:	2–8″ (5–20 cm).
Flowering:	June–August.
Habitat:	Moist woods.
Range:	Across northern North America; in West, south near Pacific Coast and in mountains to northern California, Idaho, and northern New Mexico.
Comments:	This species is also found in northeastern Asia. Among the smallest of a genus of mostly shrubs and trees, Bunchberry makes an excellent groundcover in moist woodland gardens; it is equally attractive in flower or fruit.

36 Pacific Dogwood;
Mountain Dogwood;
Western Flowering Dogwood
Cornus nuttallii

Description:	A shrub or tree *seeming to have many large white to pinkish flowers* but actually with round heads of small greenish flowers surrounded by *4–7 conspicuous, broadly ovate, white bracts.*
Flowers:	Bracts to 4″ (10 cm) wide; each small flower in center of head with 4 sepals and 4 petals.
Leaves:	1½–4″ (4–10 cm) long, broadly lanceolate, opposite.
Fruit:	Tight clusters of red berries, each about ½″ (1.5 cm) long.
Height:	6–64′ (1.8–19.5 m).
Flowering:	April–June.
Habitat:	Open or fairly dense forests.
Range:	British Columbia south to southern California and east to western Idaho.
Comments:	In dense forests this is often an understory tree. Open and lacy, its broad white bracts seem to glitter in the filtered light. In the fall it is one of the few western trees with red foliage.

STONECROP FAMILY
Crassulaceae

Succulent herbs or small shrubs, commonly with star-like flowers in branched clusters.

Flowers: Sepals 4–5; petals 4–5, separate or united, with a scale-like gland at base of each; stamens as many, or twice as many, as petals; all these parts attached at base of 3 to several pistils.
Leaves: Alternate or opposite, simple, fleshy.
Fruit: Usually a group of 4–5 tiny pods.

There are about 25 genera and 900 species. Many are cultivated as ornamentals or succulent novelties, including Jade Tree *(Crassula arborescens),* air plants *(Kalanchoe),* and stonecrops *(Sedum).* Vegetative reproduction is common in the family; in some members, little plantlets grow along the leaf edges, drop to the ground, and root. Crassulaceae has also been known as the sedum family.

345 Canyon Dudleya
Dudleya cymosa

Description: 1 or few reddish stalks bearing *red to yellow flowers* in a flat-topped, branched, dense cluster and growing from a *basal rosette of thick, succulent, grayish-green leaves.*

Flowers: About ½" (1.5 cm) long; sepals 5, fleshy, joined at base; petals 5, erect, joined near base; flowers on stalks ¼–¾" (6–20 mm) long, along branches of cluster.

Leaves: 2–4" (5–10 cm) long, broadly lanceolate; those on flower stalk much smaller.

Height: 4–8" (10–20 cm).

Flowering: April–June.

Habitat: On rocks in brush and open woods.

Range: Much of California in Sierra Nevada and Coast Ranges.

Comments: Many species of *Dudleya* in California, and a few in Arizona, may hybridize, adding to the difficulty of identification. They resemble *Sedum,* but the latter generally have flower stalks growing from the center of the rosette or the stem tip rather than from leaf axils, and their petals are not joined near the base.

346 Powdery Dudleya
Dudleya farinosa

Description: Whitish stalks bearing *clusters of yellow flowers* and growing from a *dense rosette of ovate, succulent leaves* often covered with whitish powder.

Flowers: About ⅜" (9 mm) wide, narrow; sepals 5, short, triangular; petals 5, narrow; flowers erect on stalks ¼–½" (6–13 mm) long, on main branches of cluster.

Leaves: 1–2½" (2.5–6 cm) long, pointed; those on flower stalk much smaller.

Height: 4–14" (10–35 cm).

Flowering: May–September.

Habitat: Coastal bluffs.

Range: Southern Oregon south along Pacific Coast to southern California.

Comments: This plant often forms a large mat. In the northern part of its range it is the only coastal *Dudleya;* to the south there are several species.

347 Sierra Sedum
Sedum obtusatum

Description: *Pale yellow flowers* in branched clusters atop reddish stalks growing from *dense basal rosettes of succulent, often reddish-tinged leaves.*

Flowers: Sepals 5, blunt; petals 5, each about ⅜" (9 mm) long, narrow, pointed, united in lower fourth, yellow at first, fading to white or pinkish.

Leaves: ¼–1" (6–25 mm) long, broadest in upper half, rounded or slightly indented at tip; those on flower stalk much smaller.

Height: 1–7" (2.5–17.5 cm).

Flowering: June–July.

Habitat: Rocky slopes at moderate to high elevations.

Range: Southern Oregon south to southern Sierra Nevada.

Comments: *Sedum,* from the Latin *sedere* ("to sit"), here refers to the tendency of many species to grow low to the ground. In all plants, open pores in the leaves let in carbon dioxide, to be used in photosynthesis. However, this allows stored water to escape, a critical problem in arid environments. In many succulents, including members of *Sedum,* water loss is reduced because their pores are open only at night; the carbon dioxide that enters is stored for use in daylight, when the pores are closed.

421 Roseroot; King's Crown
Sedum roseum

Description: *A succulent, leafy plant* with erect, clustered stems topped by *small, maroon or brownish-purple flowers* in head-like bunches.

Flowers: About ⅛″ (3 mm) long; sepals 4, fleshy; petals 4, fleshy; stamens 8; no ovaries on some plants, 4 ovaries and no stamens on others; sometimes with additional parts.

Leaves: ¼–1″ (6–25 mm) long, broadly lanceolate, crowded but equally spaced along stem.

Height: 1¼–12″ (3–30 cm).

Flowering: June–August.

Habitat: Open areas high in mountains.

Range: Across northern North America; in West, south in mountains to southern California, Nevada, Utah, and Colorado.

Comments: This plant also occurs in Eurasia. The root has a rose-like fragrance, giving it one of its common names. The similar Red Orpine *(S. rhodanthum),* also known as Rose Crown, has deep pink to nearly white flowers with petals ⅜–½″ (9–13 mm) long, and each flower has stamens and ovaries; it generally grows in wet places from moderate to high elevations from south-central Montana south to northern Arizona and southern New Mexico.

CUCUMBER FAMILY
Cucurbitaceae

Herbs, often trailing or climbing by coiling tendrils.

Flowers: Radially symmetrical. Sepals 5; petals 5–6, united; some flowers (staminate) lacking an ovary and with usually 5 stamens; some flowers (pistillate) lacking stamens and with an ovary to which all parts attach at top.

Leaves: Usually simple, varying from not lobed to deeply palmately lobed.

Fruit: Berry, with a leathery rind.

There are about 90 genera and 700 species, found in warm regions. Cucurbitaceae includes many economically important genera: *Cucumis* provides muskmelons and cucumbers, *Citrullus* provides watermelons, and *Cucurbita* provides squash and pumpkins.

---

230 Melon Loco
Apodanthera undulata

Description: A malodorous, grayish, hairy plant with long, coarse, prostrate stems bearing tendrils, *kidney-shaped leaf blades,* and *yellow, funnel-shaped flowers.*

Flowers: 1½″ (4 cm) wide; petals 5, joined at base; some flowers with stamens and no ovary, others with an ovary and no stamens.

Leaves: 2–6″ (5–15 cm) wide, attached to stalk at indented side, edges shallowly toothed, lobed, or wavy.

Fruit: 2½–4″ (6–10 cm) long, oval, ribbed.

Height: Creeper; leaves to 8″ (20 cm), stems to 10′ (3 m) long.

Flowering: May–September.

Habitat: Sand dunes, gravelly flats, grasslands, and roadsides.

Range: Southern Arizona east to western Texas and south to Mexico.

Comments: Plants with the word loco in their common names are usually poisonous to some degree; several contain behavior-altering toxins.

228 Buffalo Gourd; Calabacilla Loca
Cucurbita foetidissima

Description: A malodorous plant bearing *large, gray-green, triangular leaves on long prostrate stems* and *funnel-shaped, orange to yellow flowers* mostly hidden under leaves.

Flowers: 2–3″ (5–7.5 cm) wide; corolla 5-lobed; some flowers with stamens and no ovary, others with an ovary and no stamens.

Leaves: To 1′ (30 cm) long, rough.

Fruit: 3″ (7.5 cm) wide, spherical, hard, striped, pale and dark green when immature, lemon yellow when ripe.

Height: Creeper; leaves about 1′ (30 cm), trailing stems to 20′ (6 m) long.

Flowering: April–July.

Habitat: Open areas on plains and deserts.

Range: Southern California east to Missouri and south into Mexico.

Comments: Massive roots of large specimens of this plant may weigh several hundred pounds. The fruit is easily dried and often brightly painted for decorative use. It is foul-tasting, inedible, and somewhat poisonous when mature.

424 Cut-leaved Globe Berry
Ibervillea tenuisecta

Description: *Shiny, spherical berries, resembling scarlet marbles,* hanging on a small climbing vine with tiny, yellowish-green flowers.

Flowers: About ½″ (1.5 cm) wide; some flowers with stamens and no ovary, others with an ovary and no stamens.

Leaves: 1–2¾″ (2.5–7 cm) long, deeply divided into 5 very narrow lobes again divided.

Fruit: Berry, ½″–¾″ (1.5–2 cm) wide.

Height: Vine; to 4′ (1.2 m) long.

Flowering: June–August.

Habitat: Along shallow gullies and on rocky slopes in deserts.

Range: Southeastern Arizona east to western Texas and south to northern Mexico.

Comments: Less common is Globe Berry (*I. lindheimeri*), found in Texas and southern

Oklahoma. Its leaf divisions are much
broader, and the berry is 1–1½″ (2.5–4
cm) wide.

SEDGE FAMILY
Cyperaceae

Often grass-like herbs of wet to dry sites, commonly with
3-sided stems.

Flowers: Bisexual or unisexual, radially symmetrical; each
nestled in axil of a bract, few to many aggregated into
small compact spikes or spikelets arranged in raceme-like
or head-like, dense or openly branched clusters. Sepals
and petals bristle-like or scale-like, or absent; stamens
usually 3 or 6; all these parts attached at base of ovary.
Leaves: Long, narrow, with sheaths at base enclosing stem;
leaf blade sometimes absent.
Fruit: Seed-like, lens-shaped or 3-sided.

There are about 70 genera and 4,000 species, found
nearly throughout the world. Cotton grasses *(Eriophorum),*
bulrushes and tules (both groups in *Scirpus),* and Matai
(Eleocharis tuberosa), a water chestnut, are members of
Cyperaceae. Leaves of many species are woven into mats and
baskets. Ancient Egyptians produced paper from the stems
of Papyrus or Egyptian Paper Plant *(Cyperus papyrus).*

186 Cotton Grass
Eriophorum polystachion

Description: Extensive patches of erect stems
bearing grass-like leaves and
topped by *2–8 white, cottony heads
in a cluster.*
Flowers: Cluster of heads 2–3″ (5–7.5 cm) wide,
composed of 2–8 spikes with numerous
white hairs ¾–1″ (2–2.5 cm) long and
with brownish or blackish-green scales
at base, each scale with a midrib not
reaching tip.
Leaves: 6–20″ (15–50 cm) long.
Height: 8–40″ (20–100 cm).
Flowering: July–August.
Habitat: Cold swamps and bogs.
Range: Throughout Northern Hemisphere; in
West, south to central Oregon, Idaho,

northeastern Utah, and northern New Mexico.

Comments: The genus name derives from the Greek *erion* ("wool") and *phoros* ("bearing"). The slender, cottony bristles are actually modified sepals and petals of minute flowers. There are several similar species.

TEASEL FAMILY
Dipsacaceae

Herbs with flowers clustered in dense heads.

Flowers: Bilaterally symmetrical; each associated with 2 united bracts forming a calyx-like structure. Sepals 5; petals 5, united; stamens 4; all these parts attached at top of ovary.
Leaves: Opposite, simple or sometimes deeply divided.
Fruit: Seed-like.

There are about 10 genera and 270 species, native to Eurasia. Bluebutton *(Scabiosa caucasia)* and Pincushion Flower *(S. atropurpurea)* are grown as ornamentals, and the weedy teasels *(Dipsacus)* are used in dried flower arrangements.

629 Wild Teasel
Dipsacus fullonum

Description: Angular, prickly, erect stems topped by *oval heads with many small sharp bracts.*
Flowers: Head 1¼–2″ (3–5 cm) wide, beneath which few long narrow bracts curve upward, each associated with *a small, pale purple flower.*
Leaves: To 1″ (2.5 cm) long, lanceolate, bases of each pair joined, prickly on midvein beneath.
Height: 1½–7′ (45–210 cm).
Flowering: April–September.
Habitat: Moist places, frequent on grassy hillsides.
Range: Throughout West; especially frequent west of Cascade Range and Sierra Nevada.
Comments: This is the common weedy teasel introduced from Europe. Fuller's Teasel *(D. sativus),* occasionally found in the West, has small bracts with hooked tips;

its dried flower heads were used by cloth weavers to raise the nap of, or tease, fabric, hence the common name teasel. The genus name is derived from the Greek *dipsa* ("thirst") and presumably refers to the water that can accumulate in the cup-like bases of these species' joined leaves. The progression of flowers opening on the head in all species of *Dipsacus* is unique; they start in a belt around the center, new ones opening daily in both directions, and in time forming two bands of flowers.

SUNDEW FAMILY
Droseraceae

Carnivorous herbs, mostly of acidic soil and bogs, with flowers in racemes or openly branched clusters.

Flowers: Radially symmetrical. Sepals 5, united; petals 4–8 (usually 5), separate; stamens 5; all these parts attached at base of ovary.

Leaves: Usually basal, simple; usually covered with sticky, glandular hairs that entrap insects and slowly position them for digestion; entire leaf rarely modified as a rapidly closing trap that ensnares insects.

Fruit: Many-seeded capsule.

There are 4 genera and about 100 species, generally growing in very poor soil. Extra nutrients obtained from digested insects and other small organisms may be devoted mostly to seed production. Some species are cultivated as curiosities.

41 Round-leaved Sundew
Drosera rotundifolia

Description: *White or pinkish flowers* near bent end of a slender stalk growing from a *small basal rosette of leaves.*

Flowers: About ⅜" (9 mm) wide; petals 4–8 (usually 5).

Leaves: 1–4" (2.5–10 cm) long, with long stout stalks, spreading; round blades ¼–½" (6–13 mm) wide, *covered with reddish stalked glands.*

Height: To 10" (25 cm).

Flowering: June–September.
Habitat: Swamps and bogs.
Range: Northwestern California and Sierra
Nevada; also in much of eastern Canada
and United States.
Comments: This plant also occurs across northern
Eurasia. The genus name, derived from
the Greek *droseros* ("dewy"), refers to the
moist, glistening drops on the leaves,
to which small organisms stick. Longer-
stalked glands near the edges of the
leaves slowly bend inward, securing
and placing entrapped organisms in
the digestive areas of stalkless glands.
Narrow-leaved Sundew *(D. anglica)* has
erect leaves with long narrow blades.

HEATH FAMILY
Ericaceae

Usually shrubs or woody, perennial herbs, sometimes trees,
often with showy flowers borne singly or in clusters.

Flowers: Radially or bilaterally symmetrical. Sepals 4–5,
united; petals 4–5, usually united, often in shape of a
miniature lantern; stamens twice as many as petals, each
anther usually opening by a terminal pore; all these parts
attached either at base or top of ovary.
Leaves: Usually alternate, simple, often leathery.
Fruit: Capsule, berry, or drupe.

There are about 125 genera and 3,500 species, mostly in
acidic soil in temperate regions. Numerous handsome ornamentals, including spectacular species of *Rhododendron* and
Azalea, are cultivated as ornamentals. Ericaceae is also the
source of several edible fruits, such as blueberries, huckle-
berries, and cranberries, all members of the genus *Vaccinium.*

480 Kinnikinnick; Bearberry
Arctostaphylos uva-ursi

Description: A low matted plant with smooth, *red-
brown, woody, trailing stems* bearing
leathery, dark green leaves, and small, *pink,
lantern-shaped flowers* in racemes on short
branches.
Flowers: Corolla ¼" (6 mm) long, with 5 lobes
around small opening.

Kinnikinnick

Leaves: ½–1¼" (1.5–3 cm) long, oblong, widest near blunt tip.

Fruit: Bright red berry, ⅜" (9 mm) wide.

Height: Creeper; leaves and flower clusters about 6" (15 cm), stems to 10' (3 m) long.

Flowering: March–June.

Habitat: Open areas near coast or high in mountains.

Range: Alaska south to coastal northern California, east from Washington and Oregon to Rocky Mountains, and then south to New Mexico; also in much of eastern Canada and United States.

Comments: This species also occurs in Eurasia. Kinnikinnick, a Native American word for many tobacco substitutes, is the name most frequently applied to this species in the West. The plant also had many medicinal uses, including the alleged control of several sexually transmitted diseases. In Greek *arctos* means "bear" and *staphyle* "grape," whereas in Latin *uva* means "a bunch of grapes" and *ursus* "bear"; the berries are indeed eaten by bears, as the name redundantly indicates. A similar species found in the Cascade Range and the Sierra Nevada, Pinemat Manzanita *(A. nevadensis),* has a tiny sharp point at the leaf tip. The genus has diversified extensively in California, where there are about 60 species, some as large as small trees, all called Manzanita (Spanish for "little apple"). New species, often highly restricted to peculiar geologic formations, are occasionally discovered.

73 White Heather; Mountain Heather
Cassiope mertensiana

Description: A matted plant with *flowers resembling small white bells* hanging from tips of slender stalks growing from leaf axils near branch ends.

Flowers: Corolla ¼" (6 mm) long, with 5 bluntly pointed lobes.

Leaves: ⅛–¼" (3–6 mm) long, *very narrow, angled upward, opposite, arranged in 4 rows hiding stem.*

Fruit: Capsule, with 4–5 chambers, opening along back of each chamber.

Height: 2–12" (5–30 cm).

Flowering: July–August.

Habitat: Open slopes near and above timberline.

Range: Alaska south to central California, northern Nevada, and western Montana.

Comments: The white flowers, somewhat star-like, may have inspired the genus name of this plant: In Greek mythology Cassiopeia was set among the stars as a constellation. Firemoss Cassiope (*C. tetragona*), found near the Canadian border, has a prominent groove on the lower side of each leaf. Starry Cassiope (*C. stellariana*), which grows in bogs from Washington's Mount Rainier northward, has spreading, alternate leaves.

145 Salal
Gaultheria shallon

Description: A shrub-like plant with spreading or erect, hairy stems, often in large dense patches, and *whitish to pale pink, urn-shaped flowers* hanging along *reddish or salmon racemes* in upper leaf axils.

Flowers:	Corolla ⅜″ (9 mm) long, hairy, with 5 pointed lobes around opening.
Leaves:	2–4″ (5–10 cm) long, ovate, with many minute teeth on edges.
Fruit:	Dark purple berry, ¼–½″ (6–13 mm) wide.
Height:	4–48″ (10–120 cm).
Flowering:	May–July.
Habitat:	Woods and brush.
Range:	British Columbia south to southern California.
Comments:	The berries are a source of food for wildlife and were once also eaten by coastal Native Americans. The leaves are often used in flower arrangements.

---

456 **Alpine Laurel; Bog Laurel**
Kalmia polifolia subsp. *microphylla*

Description:	A low matted plant with several *deep pink, bowl-shaped flowers* facing upward on slender stalks growing near tops of leafy stems.
Flowers:	Corolla ½″ (1.5 cm) wide, with 5 lobes; stamens 10, each held in a little pouch, springing up suddenly as corolla expands or is bent back.
Leaves:	¼–¾″ (6–19 mm) long, rarely to 1¼″ (3 cm) long, opposite, lanceolate,

Alpine Laurel

smooth and *dark green above, gray and
hairy beneath,* edges not or barely curling
downward.

Height: Usually less than 4″ (10 cm).

Flowering: June–September.

Habitat: Bogs and wet mountain meadows.

Range: Alaska south to southern California and
central Colorado; also in eastern United
States.

Comments: In the West there are two subspecies.
The lower-elevation subspecies, *polifolia,*
is usually 8–20″ (20–50 cm) high and
has leaves ¾–1½″ (2–4 cm) long with
edges tightly rolled under. In spite of
the plant's common name, the leaves
are not to be used as a seasoning, as
they are suspected of being poisonous.
The smaller Western Swamp Laurel
(*K. occidentalis*), found from the lowlands
of Alaska south to Oregon, has flowers
½–¾″ (1.5–2 cm) wide.

175 Trapper's Tea
Ledum glandulosum

Description: *A shrub with white flowers in roundish
clusters* at branch ends.

Flowers: About ½″ (1.5 cm) wide; petals 5,
white; stamens 5–12, lower part of
filaments hairy.

Leaves: ½–2½″ (1.5–6.5 cm) long, closely
placed on stem, ovate or elliptical,
with white, felt-like hairs beneath.

Fruit: Roundish, 5-chambered capsule.

Height: 2–7′ (60–210 cm).

Flowering: June–August.

Habitat: Wet places in mountains.

Range: British Columbia south to Sierra
Nevada, northeastern Oregon, central
Idaho, northwestern Wyoming, and
Colorado.

Comments: As with many shrubby species in this
family, Trapper's Tea is poisonous.
Labrador Tea (*L. groenlandicum*) is
found across Canada and occurs in the
West from Alaska south to the coast of
Oregon; it has a rusty hue to the woolly
underside of the leaf.

533 Pink Mountain Heather
Phyllodoce empetriformis

Description:	A low matted shrub *with short, needle-like leaves,* and *deep pink, bell-shaped flowers* hanging at ends of slender stalks in upper leaf axils.
Flowers:	Corolla about ¼″ (6 mm) long, with 5 lobes tightly curled back; stamens 10, shorter than corolla.
Leaves:	⅜–⅝″ (9–16 mm) long, with deep groove on lower side.
Fruit:	5-chambered capsule, splitting open along walls between chambers.
Height:	4–16″ (10–40 cm).
Flowering:	June–August.
Habitat:	Open, rocky slopes and in forests high in mountains.
Range:	Alaska south to northern California, Idaho, and Colorado.
Comments:	Brewer Mountain Heather *(P. breweri),* found in the California mountains, has pink flowers and stamens longer than the corolla. Cream Mountain Heather *(P. glandulifera),* growing in the mountains of Oregon and Wyoming northward, has glandular hairs on a yellowish or greenish-white corolla.

75 White Rhododendron
Rhododendron albiflorum

Description:	A shrub with *1–4 white, bowl-shaped flowers clustered in leaf axils along stem.*
Flowers:	Corolla ½–¾″ (1.5–2 cm) wide, with 5 round lobes; stamens 10, hairy near base.
Leaves:	1½–4″ (4–10 cm) long, broadly lanceolate, with short stalks.
Height:	3–7′ (90–210 cm).
Flowering:	June–August.
Habitat:	Wet places in mountains.
Range:	British Columbia south to Oregon and east to western Montana.
Comments:	This species does not produce the spectacular, brilliant flowers that many of its relatives do, yet its dainty clusters of mildly citrus-scented, white

flowers and bright green leaves are
delightful. The genus name comes
from the Greek *rhodon* ("rose") and
dendron ("tree").

530 Western Azalea
Rhododendron occidentale

Description: A shrub with large, *white to deep pink,*
very fragrant flowers in large clusters at
stem ends.

Flowers: Corolla 1½–2½" (4–6.5 cm) wide,
with a narrow, tubular base and 5 wavy,
pointed lobes, upper lobe with a yellow-
orange patch; stamens 5, with hairy
filaments.

Leaves: 1¼–3½" (3–9 cm) long, thin, bright
green, elliptical.

Height: 4–16½' (1.2–5.1 m).

Flowering: April–August.

Habitat: Moist places; in open areas near coast,
otherwise where partly shaded.

Range: Southwestern Oregon south to southern
California.

Comments: Flower variations include mixtures
of pale pink, deep pink, and yellow-
orange. An evergreen, pink-flowered
relative, California Rosebay *(R.*
macrophyllum), grows from Canada
to California and makes a choice
ornamental; it is the state flower of
Washington, where it is known as
Red Rhododendron.

SPURGE FAMILY
Euphorbiaceae

Commonly herbs with milky sap; also shrubs or trees in
warmer areas and into the tropics.

Flowers: Unisexual, radially symmetrical. Calyx and corolla
each with 5 separate parts, attached at base of ovary in female (pistillate) flowers, or corolla absent, or both calyx
and corolla absent; stamens 1–10 or more.

Leaves: Alternate or opposite, simple or compound.

Fruit: Round capsule, usually 3-lobed; usually divided into
3 sections, each with 1 seed.

There are about 300 genera and 7,500 species, mostly of warm or hot regions. Some plants are grown as ornamentals in tropical areas, including *Croton* species, with their large, multicolored leaves, or as Christmas plants, such as Poinsettia *(Poinsettia pulcherrima)*. Most members of the family are poisonous; their milky sap will irritate the membranes of the eyes and mouth.

27 Rattlesnake Weed
Chamaesyce albomarginata

Description: *Dense thin mats of small, roundish, opposite leaves* and slender stems with *many tiny, white, flower-like cups; sap milky.*

Flowers: Attached to a cup less than ⅛″ (3 mm) wide; 1 at each leaf node; 4–5 small white appendages resembling petals, with a maroon pad at base of each; ovary nearly spherical, smooth, 3-lobed, on stalk in center of cup.

Leaves: ⅛–⅜″ (3–9 mm) long, round or oblong, stalks of 2 leaves on opposite sides of stem connected by 1 white scale on either side.

Fruit: Tiny, plump, triangular capsule; splitting into 3 sections, each containing 1 pale brown seed with a white coat.

Height: Creeper; branches about ½″ (1.5 cm), stems 2–10″ (5–25 cm) long.

Flowering: April–November.

Habitat: Open areas in deserts, arid grasslands, and piñon-juniper woodlands.

Range: Southeastern California and southern Utah east to Oklahoma and south to Mexico.

Comments: One of the showiest of the low spurges, this species was once thought useful for treatment of snakebite, hence its common name. The cup-like structure has many simple flowers: Those producing pollen have only one stamen; those producing seeds consist of just an ovary. Around the edge of the cup are several glands that may or

may not have petal-like appendages.
The entire structure, which resembles a
single flower, is typical of many
Euphorbia species. Most are poisonous,
some dangerously so. The genus
Euphorbia as traditionally circumscribed
is extremely large and cumbersome and
is therefore often subdivided into
smaller genera, with the genus
Chamaesyce containing shorter, often
mat-forming, sometimes weedy plants.
Spurges *(Chamaesyce)* are unwelcome
weeds in lawns. All *Chamaesyce* and
many *Euphorbia* "bleed" with white
milky sap that was once used to help
heal sores.

9 Leafy Spurge
Euphorbia esula

Description: A broad, open, *dome-shaped cluster
of tiny, greenish flowers among broad
paired bracts;* stems with *milky sap.*

Flowers: Attached to inside of a cup about
⅛" (3 mm) wide; 4 tan-green,
crescent-shaped glands perching
at edge of cup; ovary spherical,
smooth or warty, 3-lobed,
protruding on stalk from
center of cup.

Leaves: Those at midstem ¾–2½"
(2–6.5 cm) long, very narrow;
those in flower cluster forming
paired, broadly heart-shaped
bracts, each ½–¾" (1.5–2 cm) long.

Fruit: Spherical capsule, about ⅛" (3 mm)
wide; splitting open explosively.

Height: 8–36" (20–90 cm).

Flowering: May–June.

Habitat: Open areas, especially where disturbed.

Range: Southern Canada and northern half of
United States.

Comments: Introduced from Eurasia, Leafy
Spurge is a noxious weed difficult to
eradicate because of its deeply buried
perennial runners. The milky sap may
irritate the skin. If consumed in
quantity, it is toxic to cattle.

PEA FAMILY
Fabaceae

Trees, shrubs, herbs, or vines with compound or occasionally simple leaves and flowers usually in clusters.

Flowers: 3 distinct types. Pea flower (most commonly described in this book) bilaterally symmetrical; calyx with 5 sepals more or less joined at base and forming a cup or tube; corolla with 1 broad upper petal (banner or standard), 2 lateral petals (wings), and 2 bottom petals (keel) joined by lower edges and shaped like prow of a boat; stamens usually 10, with 9 joined and 1 separate, surrounding ovary and hidden inside keel. Other 2 types: radially symmetrical, with conspicuous stamens (as in acacias); bilaterally symmetrical, without distinct banner and keel (as in sennas).

Leaves: Usually alternate, rarely opposite; pinnately or palmately compound, or sometimes simple.

Fruit: Usually a 1-chambered pod with 1 to many seeds, sometimes 2-chambered with several to many seeds; usually opening along 1–2 seams, sometimes not opening but separating into several 1-seeded segments.

Taken as a single family, there are about 640 genera and 17,000 species. This enormous family, also known as the bean family, includes many economically important genera: Peas belong to *Pisium;* beans to *Phaseolus;* soybeans to *Glycine;* peanuts to *Arachis;* lentils to *Lens;* and chickpeas (garbanzos) to *Cicer.* Alfalfa *(Medicago sativa)* and clover species *(Trifolium)* provide forage for domestic livestock, but many other species are poisonous range weeds. Exotic hardwoods and gum arabic are provided by tropical trees belonging to this family, and numerous members are cultivated as handsome ornamentals. The traditional family name, Leguminosae, reflects some of the family's importance (in Latin it refers to "plants with seedpods," and in French *légume* means "vegetable"). The family is sometimes split into three smaller families, each distinguished by one of the three flower types: the Fabaceae, Mimosaceae, and Caesalpiniaceae. The fruit, an important feature, is similar in all three.

---

553 Field Milkvetch
Astragalus agrestis

Description: A soft green plant tending to grow in patches, with weak stems often leaning on other vegetation, and *pink to lavender or purple pea flowers crowded in short heads.*

Flowers: About ½–¾″ (1.5–2 cm) long; calyx
with short black hairs.

Leaves: *Pinnately compound,* narrow, with 13–21
broadly lanceolate or oval leaflets, each
¼–¾″ (6–20 mm) long.

Fruit: Erect pod, about ½″ (1.5 cm) long,
3-sided, lowest side grooved.

Height: 2–12″ (5–30 cm).

Flowering: May–August.

Habitat: Commonly in moist meadows and
prairies and on cool brushy slopes.

Range: Across much of Canada and south to
northeastern California, southern Utah,
central New Mexico, Kansas, and Iowa.

Comments: This plant is representative of many of
the low *Astragalus* with purplish or pink
flowers; the hundreds of species in the
West are difficult to identify. Poisonous
species of *Astragalus* and *Oxytropis* are
known as locoweeds; apparently this
species is not toxic. It also occurs in Asia.

551 Crescent Milkvetch
Astragalus amphioxys

Description: *A tufted, grayish, hairy plant* with
pinnately compound leaves and *lavender,
pink, or red-violet pea flowers* in short
racemes.

Flowers: ¾–1″ (2–2.5 cm) long.

Leaves: 7–21 ovate leaflets, each ⅛–¾″
(3–20 mm) long.

Fruit: Crescent-shaped or straight pod, ¾–2″
(2–5 cm) long, tapered at both ends,
sharply pointed at tip.

Height: 2–10″ (5–25 cm).

Flowering: March–June.

Habitat: Sandy or gravelly soil in deserts, arid
grasslands, and among piñon and
juniper.

Range: Southern Nevada east to western
Colorado, central New Mexico, and
extreme western Texas.

Comments: Crescent Milkvetch can be distinguished
from many similar species by its pod,
which has only one chamber and a lower
seam that lies in a groove rather than
forming a prominent ridge.

134 Canada Milkvetch
Astragalus canadensis

Description:	*Many whitish to pale yellow or greenish pea flowers* hanging down slightly in dense racemes atop often clustered, leafy stems.
Flowers:	½–¾″ (1.5–2 cm) long.
Leaves:	2½–6″ (6.5–15 cm) long, *pinnately compound,* with 13–29 broadly lanceolate leaflets.
Fruit:	Erect, pointed pod, ½–¾″ (1.5–2 cm) long, commonly grooved on lower (outer) side.
Height:	12–31″ (30–80 cm).
Flowering:	June–September.
Habitat:	Open meadows and clearings in coniferous forests, along roadside ditches, and near creeks and lakeshores.
Range:	Western Canada south to central Sierra Nevada, central Nevada, southern Utah, and central New Mexico.
Comments:	This was the first *Astragalus* from North America to be scientifically described. Representative of many species with white corollas, several notoriously poisonous, Canada Milkvetch has toxic compounds but seems not to be a serious pest.

401 Crimson Woolly Pod; Scarlet Milkvetch
Astragalus coccineus

Description:	Long *red pea flowers* angling upward in loose heads above *tufted, white, woolly, pinnately compound leaves.*
Flowers:	1½″ (4 cm) long.
Leaves:	7–15 broad leaflets, each ⅛–⅝″ (3–16 mm) long.
Fruit:	Plump pod, 1–1½″ (2.5–4 cm) long, covered with woolly white hairs, often bending stem with its weight and lying on ground.
Height:	4–8″ (10–20 cm).
Flowering:	March–June.
Habitat:	Open, gravelly ridges and benches with piñon, juniper, or sagebrush.
Range:	Southeastern California, western Arizona, and northern Baja California.

Comments: Of the several low, tufted, western
Astragalus species with plump woolly
pods, this is the most spectacular. The
position of the unusually long, red
flowers, a rare color in the genus, makes
them easily accessible to hummingbirds.

552 Bent Milkvetch
Astragalus inflexus

Description: A low, *grayish-hairy plant, commonly*
forming small mats, with pinnately
compound leaves and *racemes of rose-pink*
pea flowers on very short stalks.
  Flowers: ¾–1¼" (2–3 cm) long; upper petal
arched upward, hairy on back; calyx with
5 very slender teeth at least half as long
as tubular part; 6–19 flowers per raceme.
  Leaves: 13–29 oval to ovate leaflets, each ¼–¾"
(6–20 mm) long.
  Fruit: Plump, 1-chambered, silky-hairy pod.
  Height: Creeper; flowering branches 1–4"
(2.5–10 cm), prostrate stems to 20"
(50 cm) long.
Flowering: April–July.
  Habitat: Dry hillsides and sagebrush deserts.
  Range: Central Washington south to northern
Oregon and east to western Montana.
Comments: When in full flower, this species forms
conspicuous, bright pink tufts or pads.
There are many similar species
distinguished by technical features.
One, Pursh's Milkvetch *(A. purshii),*
common throughout much of the West,
has densely matted stems rarely longer
than 4" (10 cm) and flowers varying
from cream to deep reddish purple, the
narrowly lanceolate calyx teeth less than
half the length of the tube.

183 Freckled Milkvetch
Astragalus lentiginosus

Description: A more or less succulent plant with
stems varying from erect to prostrate
and *whitish, pinkish, or purplish pea flowers*
in racemes.

Flowers: ⅜–¾″ (9–20 mm) long, spreading
or erect.
Leaves: 11–19 broadly ovate or roundish
leaflets, each ⅜–⅝″ (9–16 mm) long,
smooth or lightly hairy on upper
surface.
Fruit: 2-chambered pod, ½–1½″ (1.5–4 cm)
long, swollen and leathery-walled or
bladdery and thin-walled; end flattened
sideways into a prominent, upcurved
beak.
Height: 4–16″ (10–40 cm) long.
Flowering: May–July.
Habitat: From deserts and salt flats to open slopes
high in mountains.
Range: Western Canada south through most of
West to northwestern Mexico.
Comments: Freckled Milkvetch is one of the most
variable of western plants, with
numerous types differing in height,
flowers, and pods. The common name
refers to the red-mottled pod of many
races.

540 Fairy Duster
Calliandra eriophylla

Description: *Pinkish puffs* made up of *many showy, pale
to deep pink stamens* on a low, densely
branched shrub.
Flowers: Dense heads nearly 2″ (5 cm) wide, on
short stems; calyx tiny, reddish, with
5 teeth; petals 5, each about ¼″ (6 mm)
long, reddish; stamens about ¾″ (2 cm)
long, projecting outward; style red,
slightly longer than stamens.
Leaves: Twice pinnately compound, 2–4 pairs of
main divisions each bearing 5–10 pairs
of oblong leaflets, each ¼″ (5 mm) long.
Height: 8–20″ (20–50 cm).
Flowering: February–May.
Habitat: Sandy washes and slopes in deserts and
arid grasslands.
Range: Southern California east to southwestern
New Mexico and south to Mexico.
Comments: This little shrub is an inconspicuous
part of the arid landscape most of the
year, but in spring the exquisite clusters

of flowers, with their many long
stamens, form delicate, pink balls,
giving the plant a fluffy pink appearance
in full bloom. It belongs to a group of
mostly tropical, woody plants that
includes acacias and mimosas.

284   Twinleaf; Two-leaved Senna
Cassia bauhinioides

Description: A low plant with few stems ending in
open clusters of 1–3 *slightly bilaterally
symmetrical, yellow flowers* on short stalks;
leaves grayish green, with only *2 leaflets*.

Flowers: ½" (1.5 cm) wide; sepals 5, narrow;
petals 5, round, upper petal forward of
others; stamens 10, brown, upper 3 very
small.

Leaves: Leaflets ¾–2" (2–5 cm) long.

Fruit: Hairy pod, ¾–1½" (2–4 cm) long.

Height: 4–16" (10–40 cm).

Flowering: April–August.

Habitat: Hills and flats in arid grasslands and
deserts.

Range: Central Arizona east to western Texas
and south to northern Mexico.

Comments: The large genus *Cassia*, many species
of which are trees or shrubs, is found
primarily throughout the world's
tropics. A recent study of this group
indicates that Twinleaf should be placed
in the genus *Senna*.

286   Blue Palo Verde
Cercidium floridum

Description: A round tree with *smooth, blue-green bark,
leafless most of the year;* when in bloom
covered with *yellow flowers in loose clusters*
hanging from leaf axils.

Flowers: About ¾" (2 cm) wide, slightly
bilaterally symmetrical; petals 5, each
⅜" (9 mm) long, upper petal in front of
others.

Leaves: ½–¾" (1.5–2 cm) long, few, each with
1 pair of ovate leaflets; smaller branches
often spiny.

Fruit:	Pod, 1½–3″ (4–7.5 cm) long.
Height:	To 33′ (10 m).
Flowering:	March–May.
Habitat:	Washes and low sandy places.
Range:	Southern California, southern Arizona, and northwestern Mexico.

Comments: Palo Verde is Spanish for "green tree"; even when leafless, the trees are conspicuously green in the brown desert. Photosynthesis occurs mostly in the bark rather than in the leaves, which conserves water through the reduction of surface area. Little-leaved Palo Verde (*C. microphyllum*), growing in the same area but more frequent on gravelly slopes, has yellow-green bark, 4–8 pairs of leaflets on each leaf, and pale yellow flowers, the uppermost petal often whitish.

426, 549 Western Redbud
Cercis occidentalis

Description: A shrub with many erect stems, leafless when in bloom; *numerous small, rose-pink, bilaterally symmetrical flowers in clusters* along branches and nearly hiding rest of plant.

Flowers: ½″ (1.5 cm) long; petals 5; lower 2 petals cupped, facing each other,

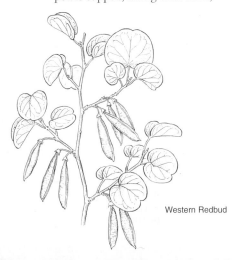

Western Redbud

enclosing 1 pistil and 10 stamens; uppermost petal central, in front of lateral 2 petals.

Leaves: 1¼–3½″ (3–9 cm) wide, roundish, *kidney-shaped or broadly heart-shaped,* smooth, glossy.

Fruit: Flat pod, 1½–3½″ (4–9 cm) long, persisting until late in season.

Height: 6–16½′ (1.8–5.1 m).

Flowering: February–April.

Habitat: Dry brushy slopes.

Range: Most of California east to southern Utah and central Arizona.

Comments: Western Redbud's scientific classification is still slightly unsettled; it is also known as *C. canadensis* var. *orbiculata.* This emphasizes its close similarity to Eastern Redbud, *C. canadensis* var. *canadensis.* The two differ in habit, and the leaves of Eastern Redbud are more pointed. No matter the scientific classification, Western Redbud is one of the handsomest shrubs of the western foothills. It is commonly used as an ornamental, enjoyed for its masses of rose-pink flowers and its dense, dark green foliage that turns reddish in the fall. Native Americans made baskets from the shredded bark, and extracts from the bark were used medicinally.

295 Scotch Broom; Common Broom
Cytisus scoparius

Description: *A shrub with many small, green, strongly angled branches and bright yellow pea flowers* usually borne singly on stalks from leaf axils.

Flowers: About ¾″ (2 cm) long.

Leaves: Those near base of branches with 3 leaflets, each about ½″ (1.5 cm) long; upper leaves with 1 leaflet.

Fruit: Slender pod, 2–3″ (5–7.5 cm) long, hairy only on edges.

Height: To 10′ (3 m).

Flowering: April–June.
Habitat: Road banks, open woods, and fields.
Range: Washington south to California.
Comments: This handsome ornamental, a native of Europe, has proven to be such a pesky shrub that it is classified as a noxious weed; it fills in many areas that were once open prairies and sparse woods. When in full flower the plant is a mass of yellow.

139 White Prairie Clover
Dalea candida

Description: Several branched stems with smooth, bright green leaves, and *dense spikes of white, bilaterally symmetrical flowers.*
Flowers: Spike to 2½" (6.5 cm) long; flowers ¼" (6 mm) long; petals 5, upper ones broader, all with slender stalks; calyx with glands just beneath 5 teeth; stamens 5.
Leaves: Pinnately compound, with 5–9 oblong leaflets, each ½–1½" (1.5–4 cm) long, minutely dotted with glands on lower side.
Fruit: Pod, ⅛" (3 mm) long, with glands on walls.
Height: 1–2' (30–60 cm).
Flowering: May–September.
Habitat: Plains, arroyos, roadsides, and among piñon and juniper.
Range: Central Canada south, mostly along eastern slopes of Rocky Mountains, to Colorado, New Mexico, western Texas, and Mexico; west to Utah and Arizona; and east across Plains states to Illinois and Alabama.
Comments: This species, and others with only five stamens and petals that are all rather similar, were once placed in the genus *Petalostemon.* White Dalea *(D. albiflora),* found from Arizona and southwestern New Mexico south to Mexico, resembles White Prairie Clover but has 10 stamens.

550 Feather Peabush; Feather Plume
Dalea formosa

Description:
: A low scraggly shrub bearing *tiny, pinnately compound leaves* and pea flowers with *yellow and bright purple to pink-purple petals* in short, head-like racemes.

Flowers:
: About ½″ (1.5 cm) wide; petals 5, upper 1 broad and yellow, lower 4 bright purple; calyx with long slender teeth with silky hairs, resembling little feathers.

Leaves:
: To ½″ (1.5 cm) long, divided into 7 or 9 plump folded leaflets.

Height:
: 1–3′ (30–90 cm).

Flowering:
: March–May, often again in September.

Habitat:
: Among scrubby vegetation on high plains and in deserts.

Range:
: Central Arizona east to western Oklahoma and south to northern Mexico.

Comments:
: One of many shrubby species of *Dalea,* this plant—with its dark bark, contorted branches, and small leaves— is an excellent candidate for bonsai.

622 Purple Prairie Clover
Dalea purpurea

Description:
: A fairly slender plant, varying from nearly smooth to grayish-woolly, with *pinnately compound leaves* and *dense hairy spikes of deep reddish-lavender, bilaterally symmetrical flowers.*

Flowers:
: Spike ¾–3″ (2–7.5 cm) long, about ½″ (1.5 cm) thick; flowers about ¼″ (6 mm) long; upper petal broader and protruding less than lower ones; calyx densely hairy; stamens 5, with yellow-orange anthers.

Leaves:
: Usually 5 narrow leaflets, each ½–1″ (1.5–2.5 cm) long.

Fruit:
: Tiny plump pod, usually 1-seeded.

Height:
: 1–3′ (30–90 cm).

Flowering:
: May–August.

Habitat:
: Meadows and coniferous forest openings in dry or moist soil.

Purple Prairie Clover

Range: Central Canada south along eastern base
of Rocky Mountains to eastern New
Mexico and western Texas; also in
central Arizona (perhaps introduced),
and also widespread in eastern United
States.

Comments: The upper petal is probably the only
true petal, the other four modified
stamens. Species with such flowers were
formerly placed in the genus
Petalostemon.

---

402 **Western Coral Bean; Indian Bean;
Chilicote**
Erythrina flabelliformis

Description: *A shrub or small tree with prickly stems and
leafstalks,* and *long, bright red flowers* in
racemes near branch ends.

Flowers: To 3″ (7.5 cm) long, basically a pea
flower but modified so that upper petal
is straight and beak-like, nearly hiding
lower 4 petals; calyx waxy white, nearly
without lobes.

Leaves: Compound, with 3 leaflets, each to 3″
(7.5 cm) long.

Fruit: Pod, with several large, scarlet, bean-
like seeds.

Height: To 15′ (4.5 m), usually much shorter.

Flowering: March–May, occasionally again in September.

Habitat: Rocky hillsides among oaks, juniper, and brush.

Range: Southern Arizona, southwestern New Mexico, and northwestern Mexico.

Comments: This plant is leafless and rather unattractive throughout the winter and early spring. It usually flowers on bare stems in early spring, and the leaves emerge in late spring. The bright seeds, often used in Mexican necklaces, are deadly poisonous.

---

515 Western Sweetvetch
Hedysarum occidentale

Description: Bunched stems with papery brown sheaths at base, *pinnately compound leaves,* and *deep pink or pinkish-purple spires of nodding pea flowers* in dense racemes.

Flowers: About ¾″ (2 cm) long; 2 joined lower petals conspicuously longer than 2 lateral petals; calyx with 5 lobes, upper 2 broader but shorter than lower 3.

Leaves: 9–21 ovate leaflets, each ½–1¼″ (1.5–3 cm) long, with *minute brown dots on upper surface.*

Western Sweetvetch

<table>
<tr><td>Fruit:</td><td>Flat pod, constructed into *1–4 oval segments,* each ¼–½" (6–13 mm) wide, sides with a light network of veins.</td></tr>
<tr><td>Height:</td><td>16–31" (40–80 cm).</td></tr>
<tr><td>Flowering:</td><td>June–September.</td></tr>
<tr><td>Habitat:</td><td>Meadows and open forests at high elevations.</td></tr>
<tr><td>Range:</td><td>Washington east to Montana and south to Colorado.</td></tr>
<tr><td>Comments:</td><td>In the West only four species of *Hedysarum* represent this northern genus of about 100 species.</td></tr>
</table>

311 Hog Potato; Camote de Raton; Pig Nut
Hoffmanseggia glauca

<table>
<tr><td>Description:</td><td>A low plant growing in patches, with *pinnately compound leaves* and *bilaterally symmetrical, yellow-orange flowers* in glandular racemes.</td></tr>
<tr><td>Flowers:</td><td>About ¾" (2 cm) wide; petals with narrow, glandular stalks, upper petal speckled and blotched with orange near base; stamens 10.</td></tr>
<tr><td>Leaves:</td><td>Divided into 5–11 main sections, these again divided into 5–11 pairs of oblong leaflets, each ⅛–⅜" (3–9 mm) long.</td></tr>
<tr><td>Fruit:</td><td>Flat, curved, glandular pod, ¾–1½" (2–4 cm) long.</td></tr>
<tr><td>Height:</td><td>4–12" (10–30 cm).</td></tr>
<tr><td>Flowering:</td><td>March–September.</td></tr>
<tr><td>Habitat:</td><td>In open, alkaline areas; common along roads and as an agricultural weed.</td></tr>
<tr><td>Range:</td><td>Southern California east to southern Colorado and Texas, and south to Mexico.</td></tr>
<tr><td>Comments:</td><td>This plant has small, edible swellings on the roots that provide good nourishment for many animals and were also used as food by Native Americans. The Spanish name, Camote de Raton, means "mouse's sweet potato."</td></tr>
</table>

492 Silky Beach Pea
Lathyrus littoralis

Description: A *silky-haired, gray plant* growing in low patches, with *pink and white pea flowers* in dense racemes among pinnately compound leaves.

Flowers: ¾" (2 cm) long; upper petal usually rose-pink, lower petals white or pale pink.

Leaves: 2–10 broadly lanceolate leaflets, each ¼–¾" (6–20 mm) long.

Fruit: Pod, about 1¼" (3 cm) long.

Height: 8–24" (20–60 cm).

Flowering: April–June.

Habitat: Coastal sand dunes.

Range: Washington south along Pacific Coast to central California.

Comments: This beautifully colored plant forms dense patches among yellow and pink sand verbenas *(Abronia)* and Beach Morning Glory *(Calystegia soldanella),* adding to the spectacular natural garden of coastal dunes. The related Beach Pea *(L. japonicus),* also known as Sand Pea, differs in having smooth stems and leaves and 2–8 flowers, each ¾–1¼" (2–3 cm) long, with reddish-purple petals; it can also be found on sand dunes from northern California to Alaska.

376 Snub Pea
Lathyrus sulphureus

Description: Several sprawling or clambering, angular stems bearing *pinnately compound leaves* and yellowish to orange pea flowers turned to one side in racemes growing from leaf axils.

Flowers: About ½" (1.5 cm) long; corolla at first cream, deepening from *tan-yellow to dull orange;* broad upper petal often with rose veins, its base as broad as or broader than upturned end.

Leaves: 6–12 leaflets, each ¾–2½" (2–6.5 cm) long, tipped with clinging tendrils.

Fruit: Narrow pod, 1½–3" (4–7.5 cm) long.

Height: 2–3′ (60–90 cm).
Flowering: April–June.
Habitat: Slopes in chaparral and open forests.
Range: Southwestern Oregon and northern two-thirds of California.
Comments: The unusually broad base and the barely upturned end of the banner produce a stubby flower, hence the common name. Del Norte Pea *(L. delnorticus),* which grows near the California–Oregon border, has wing-like ridges on the stem.

362 Birdsfoot Trefoil
Lotus corniculatus

Description: Stems trailing on ground and rooting, their tips turning upward, and stalks with *loose heads of yellow pea flowers* in axils of pinnately compound leaves.
Flowers: ⅜–⅝″ (9–16 mm) long; petals 5, bright yellow, becoming increasingly red-tinged with age.
Leaves: Leaflets ¼–¾″ (6–20 mm) long, 3 grouped near tip, 2 placed at junction of leafstalk and stem.
Fruit: Slender pod, ¾–1½″ (2–4 cm) long, projecting mostly horizontally from flower stalk.

Birdsfoot Trefoil

Height:	Creeper; erect stem tips 3–12″ (7.5–30 cm).
Flowering:	May–September.
Habitat:	Meadows, wet low places, and lawns.
Range:	Washington and Idaho south to northern California, central Nevada, and central Utah; frequent in farmlands throughout the northern portion of the West; also nearly throughout eastern Canada and United States.
Comments:	The spreading, slender pods of this Eurasian native collectively resemble a bird's foot, hence the common name.

293 Hill Lotus
Lotus humistratus

Description:	A hairy, matted plant with many *small yellow pea flowers,* each nestled in axil of a *pinnately compound leaf.*
Flowers:	About ¼″ (6 mm) long; petals becoming red with age.
Leaves:	3–5 leaflets, each ¼–½″ (6–13 mm) long.
Fruit:	Hairy pod, ¼–½″ (6–13 mm) long.
Height:	Creeper; flowers and leaves 2″ (5 cm), stems 4–18″ (10–45 cm) long.
Flowering:	March–June.
Habitat:	Disturbed ground, roadsides, riverbanks, gullies, trails, old fields, and vacant lots from low to moderate elevations.
Range:	Most of California east across southern Nevada to southwestern Utah, Arizona, and western New Mexico; also in central Idaho.
Comments:	This common weed in California is attractive when covered with hundreds of deep yellow flowers. The similar Chilean Birdsfoot Trefoil *(L. subpinnatus)* has almost no hairs and grows on California's dry grassy slopes. It is one of nearly 100 plants of various genera also found in Chile and Argentina but not in the intervening thousands of miles. This natural distribution has yet to be satisfactorily explained.

294 Deer Weed; California Broom
Lotus scoparius

Description: *Bunched, erect, tough, green stems* with small, pinnately compound leaves and *1–4 yellow pea flowers in clusters* in upper leaf axils.

Flowers: About ⅜″ (9 mm) long; petals 5, often developing a reddish hue with age.

Leaves: *3 oblong leaflets,* each ¼–½″ (6–13 mm) long.

Fruit: Slender, curved, 2-seeded pod, with a narrow, *knife-like beak.*

Height: 1–3′ (30–90 cm).

Flowering: March–August.

Habitat: Dry brushy slopes.

Range: Most of California south to northern Baja California.

Comments: This is one of the many species of flowering plants that thrive after fire has ravaged chaparral-covered slopes. It persists vigorously for several years, although it is choked out of most areas by the thick brush that eventually returns. By quickly covering exposed slopes, it helps reduce erosion, which would be far greater if the soil depended for cover on the slower-growing brush. Like most other members of the pea family, it has the capacity to enrich the soil with nitrogen.

292 Wright's Deer Vetch
Lotus wrightii

Description: A dark green plant with several erect stems bearing *stalkless, pinnately compound leaves,* and 1 or few *deep yellow pea flowers* on slender stalks in leaf axils.

Flowers: ½″ (1.5 cm) long; petals 5, usually becoming reddish with age.

Leaves: *3–5 crowded leaflets,* each ¼–½″ (6–13 mm) long.

Fruit: Slender pod, about 1″ (2.5 cm) long.

Height: 8–16″ (20–40 cm).

Flowering: April–August.

Habitat: Rocky slopes, mainly among Ponderosa Pine and among piñon and juniper.

Wright's Deer Vetch

Range: Southern Utah and Colorado south to
Arizona and New Mexico.

Comments: Wright's Deer Vetch is a favored browse
for deer and domestic livestock. Like
many species of the pea family, it has an
intricate method of pollination that
generally requires the aid of insects.

306 Tree Lupine; Yellow Bush Lupine
Lupinus arboreus

Description: A large, round, bushy plant with
palmately compound leaves and showy,
dense, sweet-scented, *cone-like racemes of
usually yellow (occasionally violet or blue)
pea flowers* held just above foliage at ends
of short branches.

Flowers: Raceme 4–12″ (10–30 cm) long; flowers
at least ½″ (1.5 cm) long; upper petal
hairless on back.

Leaves: 6–12 leaflets, each to 2½″ (6.5 cm) long,
arranged like wheel spokes.

Height: 2–9′ (60–270 cm).

Flowering: March–June.

Habitat: Sandy areas and canyons near coast.

Range: Washington, Oregon, and northern two-
thirds of California along Pacific Coast.

Comments: Lupines were once believed to be "wolf-
like," devouring soil nutrients (the

genus name comes from the Latin *lupus,* meaning "wolf"). In fact, they prefer poor soil, which they do not further deplete. This species, one of the handsomest in the genus, grows rapidly, and its deep roots make it an effective stabilizer of shifting coastal dunes; it has reclaimed portions of San Francisco that were once unstable sand, and it has been introduced as a sand binder in Oregon and Washington. The truly tree-size lupine *L. jaimehintoniana* grows in the mountains of Oaxaca, Mexico, reaching a height of more than 16½′ (5 m).

654 Miniature Lupine
Lupinus bicolor

Description: A usually small, grayish, hairy, branched plant with *palmately compound leaves* and *blue-violet and white pea flowers arranged in whorls* in short, thick, cone-like racemes.

Flowers: About ⅜″ (9 mm) long; central part of upper petal white, dotted with black; upper edge of lower 2 petals with few hairs near tip; stalks about ⅛″ (3 mm) long.

Leaves: 5–7 leaflets, each ½–1¼″ (1.5–3 cm) long, arranged like wheel spokes.

Fruit: Hairy pod, about ¾″ (2 cm) long, less than ¼″ (6 mm) wide.

Height: 4–16″ (10–40 cm).

Flowering: March–May.

Habitat: Mostly in open, often grassy areas from sea level to moderate elevations.

Range: Southern British Columbia south to southern California.

Comments: Miniature Lupine and California Poppy (*Eschscholzia californica*) are common companions, the blue cast given to fields by the lupine perfectly complementing the fiery orange of the poppy. There are many other annual lupines. The oldest known viable seeds, discovered in 1967 frozen in a lemming burrow, are from an Arctic lupine estimated to be 10,000 years old; when planted the seeds germinated in 48 hours.

620 Stinging Lupine
Lupinus hirsutissimus

Description: An erect, leafy plant with *yellow, stinging bristles* on stems and leaves, and *pinkish-purple to reddish-lavender pea flowers* in racemes.

Flowers: Slightly more than ½" (1.5 cm) long.

Leaves: Palmately compound, with 5–8 leaflets, each ¾–2" (2–5 cm) long, arranged like wheel spokes.

Height: 8–40" (20–100 cm).

Flowering: March–May.

Habitat: Woods, thickets, and open areas at desert edges.

Range: Southern half of California and northern Baja California.

Comments: In a genus of lovely wildflowers, this is an unpleasant exception; its stiff yellow hairs sting like nettles.

310 Butter Lupine
Lupinus luteolus

Description: *Crowded whorls of yellow pea flowers* in long racemes on branched stems.

Flowers: ½" (1.5 cm) long, sometimes pale lilac when young, turning to yellow; lower 2 petals hairy on both edges near base.

Leaves: Palmately compound, with 7–9 leaflets, each ¾–1¼" (2–3 cm) long, arranged like wheel spokes.

Fruit: Harshly hairy pod, ½–¾" (1.5–2 cm) long.

Height: 12–31" (30–80 cm).

Flowering: May–August.

Habitat: Dry slopes and flats in open forests and on grassy slopes.

Range: Southern Oregon south to southern California.

Comments: As a lupine pod matures and dries, its walls become elastic and finally burst open, instantly curling and throwing the seeds some distance. On warm afternoons these opening pods can be heard softly popping, and a person standing in a patch of mature lupines may be hit by flying seeds.

621 Blue-pod Lupine
Lupinus polyphyllus

Description: 1 or several mostly unbranched, stout, hollow stems with *violet or blue-violet pea flowers* in long dense racemes.

Flowers: About ½" (1.5 cm) long.

Leaves: Palmately compound, generally with 9–13 leaflets, each 1½–4" (4–10 cm) long, smooth on upper surface, arranged like wheel spokes.

Height: 2–5′ (60–150 cm).

Flowering: June–August.

Habitat: Moist meadows and forests and along streams from lowlands to mountains.

Range: British Columbia south to Coast Ranges of central California and east to Colorado, Wyoming, Montana, and Alberta.

Comments: This somewhat succulent lupine is one of the tallest and lushest western species. It has been crossed with other lupines, particularly Tree Lupine *(L. arboreus),* for beautiful horticultural hybrids. Along with several other lupine species, it is known to be toxic to livestock.

655 Coulter's Lupine
Lupinus sparsiflorus

Description: Slender, erect, branched stems with *pale blue or blue-lilac pea flowers* in open racemes.

Flowers: ½" (1.5 cm) long; upper petal usually with white or pale yellow center; lower 2 petals usually hairy on lower edge near base, with slender point at tip.

Leaves: Palmately compound, with 5–9 leaflets, each ½–1½" (1.5–4 cm) long, usually about ⅛" (3 mm) wide, arranged like wheel spokes.

Height: 8–16" (20–40 cm).

Flowering: January–May.

Habitat: Open fields, slopes, and deserts.

Range: Southern California east through southern Nevada and Arizona to southwestern Utah and southwestern New Mexico, and south to northern Baja California.

Comments: In a year with ample fall and winter
rains, Coulter's Lupine carpets the
floor of the southern Arizona
desert, combining with *Sphaeralcea*
globemallows and Desert Marigold
(Baileya multiradiata) for mile after
mile of blue-violet, brick red, and
brilliant yellow. Found only in the
Big Bend region of Texas is the similar
Chisos Bluebonnet *(L. havardii),* with
dark blue-violet petals.

516   Harlequin Lupine; Stiver's Lupine
Lupinus stiversii

Description: A freely branched plant with racemes
of *3-colored pea flowers, rose-pink, yellow,
and white.*

Flowers: Slightly more than ½" (1.5 cm) long;
upper petal yellow, lateral petals rose,
lower petals white.

Leaves: Palmately compound, with 6–8 leaflets,
each ½–1½" (1.5–4 cm) long, arranged
like wheel spokes.

Height: 4–18" (10–45 cm).

Flowering: April–July.

Habitat: Open, sandy or gravelly areas in oak and
pine woodlands.

Range: Western slopes of Sierra Nevada south to
southern California mountains.

Comments: The unusual coloration of the flower
immediately distinguishes this species and
accounts for one of its common names.

131   White Sweet Clover
Melilotus alba

Description: A tall, widely branched, leafy plant with
*tiny white pea flowers in numerous slender
racemes.*

Flowers: Raceme 1½–5" (4–12.5 cm) long;
flowers less than ¼" (6 mm) long.

Leaves: 3 lanceolate leaflets, each ¾–1¼"
(2–3 cm) long, with teeth on edges.

Fruit: Usually 1-seeded pod, ¼" (5 mm) long.

Height: 2–10' (60–300 cm).

Flowering: May–October.

White Sweet Clover

Habitat: Roadsides, riverbanks, old fields, in disturbed soil; often forming very dense patches.

Range: Throughout Canada and United States; in West, especially common from Washington south to California.

Comments: The scent of this Eurasian native resembles that of newly mown hay and is especially noticeable on a warm still day. There are two similar species with yellow petals: Yellow Sweet Clover *(M. officinalis),* especially common in the Rocky Mountain region, has flowers about ¼" (6 mm) long and usually grows more than 3' (90 cm) high; the less common Sour Clover *(M. indica)* has flowers ⅛" (3 mm) long and rarely exceeds 3' (90 cm) in height (a true clover, *Trifolium fucatum,* is also called Sour Clover).

---

513 **Purple Locoweed; Lambert's Locoweed; Colorado Locoweed**
Oxytropis lambertii

Description: A tufted plant, usually covered with *silvery hairs,* bearing *dense racemes of purplish-pink to bright reddish-lavender pea flowers* held just above basal leaves on long stalks.

Flowers:	½–1″ (1.5–2.5 cm) long; lower 2 petals with a common slender point projecting forward.
Leaves:	3–12″ (8–30 cm) long, pinnately compound, with leaflets ¼–1½″ (6–38 mm) long.
Fruit:	Erect, plump, pointed pod, ¾–1¼″ (2–3 cm) long, with a groove on side toward stem.
Height:	4–16″ (10–40 cm).
Flowering:	June–September.
Habitat:	Plains and open areas in pine forests.
Range:	Great Plains from Canada south to Texas, west to eastern base of Rocky Mountains in Montana and Wyoming, and farther west through mountains in Colorado and New Mexico to central Utah and Arizona.
Comments:	One of the most dangerously poisonous plants on western ranges, this species is lethally toxic to all kinds of livestock. The single feature that distinguishes this species from other American *Oxytropis* is the hairs attached by their middle to a short stalk forming a miniature teeter-totter, a feature seen only with a lens and even then sometimes escaping notice.

130 White Locoweed; Silky Locoweed; Silverleaf Locoweed
Oxytropis sericea

Description:	A densely tufted, *grayish, hairy plant* with *racemes of white or cream pea flowers* held just above basal leaves on long stalks.
Flowers:	¾–1″ (2–2.5 cm) long; lower 2 petals with a common slender, often purplish point projecting forward.
Leaves:	2–12″ (5–30 cm) long, pinnately compound, with lanceolate leaflets ½–1½″ (1.5–4 cm) long.
Fruit:	Erect plump pod, ½–1″ (1.5–2.5 cm) long, with a groove on side toward stem; thick fleshy walls becoming hard when dry.
Height:	3–16″ (8–40 cm).

Flowering: May–September.
Habitat: Prairies, mountain meadows, and open mountain slopes.
Range: Western Canada south across Montana to southern Idaho, northeastern Nevada, and southern Utah, and on western Great Plains to central New Mexico, central Oklahoma, and northern Texas.
Comments: This species has been implicated in the poisoning of domestic livestock. In some areas it has purple petals, the result of hybridization with Purple Locoweed *(O. lambertii),* but the hairs on the hybrid's leaves are attached by the base rather than by a bisecting stalk.

---

517 Showy Locoweed
Oxytropis splendens

Description: A tufted plant, covered with *silky white hairs,* bearing dense spikes of *deep pink to lavender pea flowers* held just above basal leaves on long stalks.
Flowers: About ½″ (1.5 cm) long; lower 2 petals with a common narrow point projecting forward.
Leaves: Compound, with *clusters of 2–4 leaflets,* each ⅛–¾″ (3–20 mm) long, in 7–15 whorls along main stalk.
Height: 4–16″ (10–40 cm).
Flowering: June–August.
Habitat: Open areas on road banks, riverbanks, and meadows.
Range: Alaska south to northern New Mexico and east to Ontario and Minnesota.
Comments: One of the showiest *Oxytropis,* this plant's bright, deep pink to lavender petals are beautifully set off by the unusual silvery foliage.

---

601 Chaparral Pea
Pickeringia montana

Description: A *spiny, dark green shrub,* often forming impenetrable thickets, with *bright pinkish-purple to reddish-lavender pea flowers* near branch ends.

Flowers:	About ¾″ (2 cm) long.
Leaves:	3 stiff, broadly lanceolate leaflets, each to ½″ (1.5 cm) long.
Fruit:	Flat straight pod, 1¼–2″ (3–5 cm) long.
Height:	To 7′ (2.1 m).
Flowering:	May–August.
Habitat:	Dry hillsides in chaparral.
Range:	Central to southern California.
Comments:	The only species in a genus confined to California, Chaparral Pea contributes to the state's unique flora. Rarely reproducing from seed, it grows new stems from roots that spread, especially after fires.

598   Smoke Tree
Psorothamnus spinosus

Description:	*An intricately branched, ashy gray tree* with spine-tipped branches and *deep blue-purple, bilaterally symmetrical flowers* in numerous short spikes.
Flowers:	About ½″ (1.5 cm) long; calyx dotted with glands.
Leaves:	½–¾″ (1.5–2 cm) long, oblong, notched at tip, soon dropping off.
Fruit:	Tiny pod, barely ¼″ (6 mm) long, dotted with amber-colored glands.
Height:	4–26′ (1.2–8 m).
Flowering:	June–July.
Habitat:	Sandy desert washes.
Range:	Southeastern California, southwestern Arizona, and northwestern Mexico.
Comments:	From a distance, Smoke Tree looks gray and fluffy, like a puff of smoke. Its seeds will not sprout until the hard coat is scratched deeply enough to allow water to enter, usually by tumbling in turbid water and gravel during a heavy flow in the washes. This and other *Psorothamnus* species are hosts of a peculiar flowering parasite, Thurber's Pilostyles *(Pilostyles thurberi),* which remains under the bark most of the year, then produces tiny, inconspicuous, yellowish-brown flowers that break through the bark and bloom early in the summer.

307 Yellow Pea; Golden Pea; Buck Bean
Thermopsis rhombifolia var. *montana*

Description:	1 or several hollow stems, slightly or not at all hairy, and *yellow pea flowers* in long racemes in upper leaf axils.
Flowers:	¾–1″ (2–2.5 cm) long; stamens 10, with separate filaments.
Leaves:	Compound, with 3 *broadly lanceolate leaflets,* each 2–4″ (5–10 cm) long; pair of broadly ovate, leaf-like stipules present where leafstalk joins stem.
Fruit:	Slender, erect, hairy pod, 1½–3″ (4–7.5 cm) long.
Height:	2–4′ (60–120 cm).
Flowering:	May–August.
Habitat:	Meadows and coniferous forest openings in dry or moist soil.
Range:	Western Montana southwest to northeastern Oregon and south through Nevada, Utah, Wyoming, and Colorado to eastern Arizona and western New Mexico.
Comments:	This handsome plant is suspected of being poisonous. This genus resembles *Lupinus,* and this plant is sometimes called False Lupine, but *Thermopsis* has only three leaflets on each leaf, whereas lupines have more. There are several varieties of Yellow Pea in the West, expanding the range from that given to western Washington, south-central Canada, and the western Dakotas. One, called Prairie Thermopsis (variety *rhombifolia*), which grows on the eastern slopes of the Rocky Mountains and on the northwestern Plains, has pods that either coil or spread outward in an arc.

539 Sour Clover; Bull Clover; Puff Clover
Trifolium fucatum

Description:	A clover with several stout hollow stems often leaning or lying on ground and *usually swollen pea flowers* clustered in heads.
Flowers:	Head 1–2″ (2.5–5 cm) wide; petals 5, at first *white, pink,* or *yellow,* becoming very

large, swollen, and deeper pink or
purplish with age; papery involucre
with 5–9 lobes beneath head.

Leaves: Compound, with 3 broad leaflets, each
¼–1¼″ (6–31 mm) long, with small
teeth on edges.

Height: 4–31″ (10–80 cm).

Flowering: April–June.

Habitat: Grassy slopes, roadsides, moist fields,
and somewhat brackish areas.

Range: Southern Oregon and most of California.

Comments: The enlargement of the banner into a
bladder is unusual; this also occurs in
another species with smaller flowers,
Bladder Clover *(T. depauperatum),* also
called Balloon Clover.

---

537 Bighead Clover
Trifolium macrocephalum

Description: An unusual, low clover with large round
heads of *pink to red pea flowers.*

Flowers: Head 1¼–2″ (3–5 cm) wide; calyx with
feathery teeth; involucre absent beneath
head.

Leaves: Palmately compound, with 6–9
(occasionally as few as 3) leaflets, each
¼–1″ (6–25 mm) long, thick, leathery,
with teeth on edges.

Height: 4–12″ (10–30 cm).

Bighead Clover

Flowering: April–June.
Habitat: Sagebrush deserts and pinewoods.
Range: Eastern Washington south to east-central California and western Nevada, and east to Idaho.
Comments: The large red heads of two-tone flowers make this one of the prettiest clovers. The genus name, *Trifolium,* referring to a trio of leaflets, is contradicted in this species, which usually has 6–9 leaflets.

538 Red Clover
Trifolium pratense

Description: A softly but sparsely haired, fairly tall clover with several stems in a clump and *deep pink pea flowers in round or egg-shaped heads.*
Flowers: Head 1–1½″ (2.5–4 cm) wide; involucre absent beneath head.
Leaves: Compound, with 3 broad leaflets, each ¾–2½″ (2–6.5 cm) long; upper 2 leaves usually close to head.
Height: 1–3′ (30–90 cm).
Flowering: June–August.
Habitat: Fields, roadsides, riverbanks, vacant lots, and in disturbed soil.
Range: Throughout Canada and United States.
Comments: Red Clover is native to Europe. Like many clovers, it does not make good hay. If cut late in the season and fed in quantity to livestock, it is debilitating, for reasons not entirely known.

184 White Clover
Trifolium repens

Description: Creeping stems, and *white or very pale pink, round heads of tiny pea flowers* held just above leaves on long leafless stalks.
Flowers: Head about ½″ (1.5 cm) wide; calyx hairless; involucre absent beneath head.
Leaves: Compound, with 3 broad leaflets, each ½–¾″ (1.5–2 cm) long, with tiny teeth on edges.
Height: Creeper; flower stalks 4–24″ (10–60 cm).
Flowering: April–September.

Habitat: Pastures, meadows, vacant lots, lawns, and roadsides.

Range: Throughout Canada and United States.

Comments: A native of Eurasia, this is the common clover in lawn-seed mixes. It is also an important agricultural forage. The similar Alsike Clover *(T. hybridum)* is distinguished by its pinker corollas and tufts of hair at the base of calyx lobes; animals pastured on it are likely to develop extreme skin sensitivity to sunlight.

---

554 Cow Clover
Trifolium wormskioldii

Description: Several stems, erect or leaning on ground, bearing *round heads of deep pink to reddish-lavender pea flowers.*

Flowers: Head ¾–1¼" (2–3 cm) wide; petals usually with very pale or white tip; involucre with jagged edges beneath head.

Leaves: Compound, with 3 leaflets, each ½–1¼" (1.5–3 cm) long, hairless, rather narrow, with tiny teeth on edges.

Height: 4–31" (10–80 cm).

Flowering: May–September.

Habitat: Coastal dunes, mountain meadows, and streambanks.

Range: British Columbia south along Pacific Coast to northern Mexico and east to New Mexico, Colorado, western Wyoming, and Idaho.

Comments: This clover is one of the most common wild *Trifolium.* The relatively large flowers with white-tipped petals and the jagged-edged involucre are distinctive features.

---

514 American Vetch
Vicia americana

Description: A slender, climbing plant clinging to other vegetation or structures by slender, *coiling tendrils* at end of each leaf; loose racemes of 3–10 *deep pinkish-purple to reddish-lavender pea flowers* on stalks from leaf axils.

Flowers:	½–1¼″ (1.5–3 cm) long; petals becoming bluish with age.
Leaves:	Pinnately compound, with 8–12 leaflets, each ½–1½″ (1.5–4 cm) long.
Height:	2–4′ (60–120 cm).
Flowering:	May–July.
Habitat:	Open places in woods, road banks, and fencerows.
Range:	Throughout West; also in eastern Canada and northeastern United States.
Comments:	With showy flowers unusually large for the genus, this plant resembles many species of *Lathyrus* but is distinguished by the distribution of the hairs at the tip of the style. In *Vicia* the hairs usually surround the tip, resembling a shaving brush; in *Lathyrus* they are generally on the upperside, like a little hairbrush. The seeds of some *Vicia* contain compounds producing toxic levels of cyanide when ingested.

619 Bird Vetch; Tufted Vetch; Cat Peas
Vicia cracca

Description:	*A climbing plant* clinging to structures, other vegetation, or its own stems by *coiling tendrils* at end of each leaf; racemes of 20–70 closely packed, *reddish-lavender to bluish-purple pea flowers* on stalks in leaf axils.
Flowers:	½–¾″ (1.5–2 cm) long; calyx slightly swollen and pouch-like beyond attachment to flower stalk.
Leaves:	Pinnately compound, with 19–29 leaflets, each ¾–1½″ (2–4 cm) long.
Fruit:	Pod, about ¾″ (2 cm) long.
Height:	4–7′ (1.2–2.1 m).
Flowering:	May–July.
Habitat:	Road banks, fencerows, and fields.
Range:	Throughout Canada and United States; in West, especially frequent from western Washington south to northern California.
Comments:	As are most vetches, this is a native of Europe. It is also known as Tinegrass. A similar species with racemes of many lavender to purple flowers is Hairy Vetch

(*V. villosa*), which has a conspicuous, swollen, pouch-like base beyond the attachment to the flower stalk.

OCOTILLO FAMILY
Fouquieriaceae

Unusual shrubs and trees covered with spines, with red or white flowers in clusters at branch ends.

Flowers: Radially symmetrical. Sepals 5, separate; petals 5, united into a tube; stamens 10–15; all these parts attached at base of ovary.
Leaves: Simple, mostly in little clusters in axils of spines.
Fruit: Capsule.

There is only 1 genus with about 11 species, all found in North America and all but one restricted to Mexico. Ocotillo (*Fouquieria splendens*) is the northernmost species; the most unusual is Boojum Tree (*Fouquieria columnaris*) of Baja California, with its conical trunk and radiating spiky branches. Leaves appear very quickly after rain and wither when the soil dries, a cycle commonly repeated several times during the warm season.

408 Ocotillo
Fouquieria splendens

Description: A funnel-shaped shrub with several woody, almost unbranched, *spiny, commonly straight stems,* leafless most of year, and a tight *cluster of red flowers* at each branch tip.

Flowers: Corolla ½–1″ (1.5–2.5 cm) long, tubular, with 5 short, curled-back lobes; cluster to 10″ (25 cm) long.

Leaves: To 2″ (5 cm) long, narrowly ovate, broader above middle, nearly stalkless, in bunches above spines.

Height: To 30′ (9 m).

Flowering: March–June, sometimes later.

Habitat: Open, stony, desert slopes.

Range: Southeastern California east to western Texas and south to northern Mexico.

Comments: The common name (pronounced *o-ko-tee-yo*) refers to a pitchy Mexican pine and calls attention to the resinous nature of the stems.

FUMITORY FAMILY
Fumariaceae

Leafy herbs with succulent stems and flowers in racemes.

Flowers: Bilaterally symmetrical. Calyx with 2 small sepals that drop off; corolla with 2 pairs of petals, 1 pair often spurred or sac-like at base; stamens 4 and separate, or 6 and united into 2 groups of 3; all these parts attached at base of ovary.

Leaves: Alternate or in rosettes, several times compound or divided.

Fruit: Long, 1-chambered capsule; rarely hard, nut-like.

There are about 19 genera and 400 species, chiefly distributed in the northern temperate region of Eurasia. These plants are sometimes included in the poppy family (Papaveraceae).

309 Golden Smoke; Scrambled Eggs
Corydalis aurea

Description: A soft plant, with stems weakly erect or supported by vegetation or rocks, bearing *yellow flowers in racemes* shorter than leaves.

Flowers: ½–¾" (1.5–2 cm) long; sepals 2, tiny, dropping off; petals 4, very different; upper petal as long as flower, forming a hollow spur behind and an arched hood in front; lowest petal forming a scoop in front; inner 2 petals facing each other, enclosing 6 stamens and 1 pistil.

Leaves: 3–6" (7.5–15 cm) long, each pinnately divided into 5–7 main divisions again divided, those divisions lobed, soft, succulent but thin.

Fruit: Narrow curved pod, ¾–1" (2–2.5 cm) long.

Height: 4–24" (10–60 cm).

Flowering: February–September.

Habitat: Gravelly hillsides among rocks or brush and flats along creek bottoms under trees.

Range: Throughout West east of Cascade Range and Sierra Nevada, and across Plains states to Pennsylvania, Illinois, and Arkansas.

Comments: This plant is believed to be poisonous to livestock if consumed in quantity.

129 Case's Fitweed
Corydalis caseana

Description: A rather *soft, almost succulent, tall plant*
with leafy, hollow stems, *large, fern-like
leaves,* and *dense racemes of 50–200
pinkish-white flowers.*

Flowers: ¾–1″ (2–2.5 cm) long; sepals 2, tiny,
dropping off; petals 4, purplish at tip,
very different; upper petal as long as
flower, curving upward at front, forming
a straight spur behind; lowest petal
forming a scoop in front; inner 2 petals
facing each other, enclosing 6 stamens
and 1 pistil.

Leaves: 12–20″ (30–50 cm) long, triangular in
outline, pinnately divided 3 times, with
leaflets ½–2″ (1.5–5 cm) long, ovate.

Fruit: Plump hanging pod, ½″ (1.5 cm) long.

Height: 2–7′ (60–210 cm).

Flowering: June–August.

Habitat: Shady moist areas in mountains.

Range: Northeastern Oregon south to central
Sierra Nevada and east to Idaho and
Colorado.

Comments: This plant contains alkaloids poisonous
to livestock, particularly sheep. The
pods of this and other species have
elastic walls that instantly curl back and
explosively eject seeds when touched.
Scouler Corydalis *(C. scouleri),* found
from British Columbia south to
northern Oregon, is similar but has only
15–35 flowers in the largest racemes; its
petals are pink, usually with purple at
the tips.

---

315 Golden Ear-drops
Dicentra chrysantha

Description: Peculiar, *yellow flowers,* with *outer petals
bent at midlength and sticking out sideways,*
in open branched clusters atop several
stems bearing *fern-like leaves.*

Flowers: About ½″ (1.5 cm) long; sepals 2, small,
at base, dropping off; petals 4, in 2
pairs; outer pair of petals with pouch at
base, tips bent outward; inner pair of

petals facing each other, with a
crinkled crest on back, enclosing
6 stamens and 1 pistil.

Leaves: 6–12″ (15–30 cm) long, pinnately
compound, with leaflets sharply
divided into narrow lobes, smooth,
bluish green.

Fruit: Pod, ¾–1″ (2–2.5 cm) long.

Height: 1½–5′ (45–150 cm).

Flowering: April–September.

Habitat: Dry, often brushy slopes.

Range: Southern two-thirds of California
and northern Baja California.

Comments: This species is most common in
disturbed areas; it is frequently
found in chaparral after burns.

491 Western Bleeding Heart
Dicentra formosa

Description: *Pink, heart-shaped flowers hanging
in small branched clusters above soft,
fern-like, bluish-green leaves at base.*

Flowers: About ¾″ (2 cm) long; sepals 2,
small, at base, dropping off; petals 4,
pale pink or rose, in 2 pairs; outer
pair of petals with pouch at base,
forming a heart-shaped outline,
tips spreading; inner pair of petals
facing each other, with a wavy
crest on back, enclosing 6 stamens
and 1 pistil.

Leaves: 9–20″ (22.5–50 cm) long, long-stalked,
elaborately pinnately compound, leaflets
¾–2″ (2–5 cm) long, oblong, cut into
divisions about ⅛″ (3 mm) wide, soft.

Fruit: Plump pod, ½–¾″ (1.5–2 cm) long.

Height: 8–18″ (20–45 cm).

Flowering: March–July.

Habitat: Damp shaded places and open woods in
wetter climates.

Range: Southern British Columbia south to
central California.

Comments: This is one of the nursery-trade
species. Bleeding Heart *(D. spectabilis),*
introduced from Japan, has larger,
rosy red or white flowers about 1″
(2.5 cm) long.

488 Steer's Head
Dicentra uniflora

Description: A tiny plant with leaves and flower stalks growing separately, each attached to root cluster deep beneath ground; each stalk ending in *1 pink or white flower resembling a steer's skull with horns.*

Flowers: About ½" (1.5 cm) long; sepals 2, small, at base; petals 4, in 2 pairs; outer pair of petals with pouch at base, narrow tips curving backward; inner pair of petals facing and joining each other, enclosing 6 stamens and 1 pistil.

Leaves: ¾–4" (2–10 cm) long, about as tall as flower stalk, divided into 3 main segments, each divided into narrow lobes.

Height: 1–4" (2.5–10 cm).

Flowering: February–June.

Habitat: Open, well-drained ground from sagebrush in foothills to open woods at high elevations in mountains.

Range: Washington south to northern California and east to Idaho, western Wyoming, and northern Utah.

Comments: Though common, this low plant blooms early and is usually obscured by the surrounding sagebrush.

GENTIAN FAMILY
Gentianaceae

Leafy herbs, commonly with showy, bell- or trumpet-shaped flowers in a branched cluster.

Flowers: Radially symmetrical. Sepals usually 4–5, separate or united; petals usually 4–5, united; stamens as many as petals; all these parts attached at base of ovary.
Leaves: Alternate, opposite, or whorled; simple.
Fruit: Usually a capsule, rarely a berry.

There are about 75 genera and 1,000 species, found in many different habitats in temperate and subtropical regions. Some species are cultivated as ornamentals.

452 Centaury; Rosita
Centaurium calycosum

Description: An erect, sparsely leaved plant with *pink, trumpet-shaped flowers* in small clusters at ends or in forks of many branches.

Flowers: ⅜–½" (9–13 mm) wide; calyx with 5 very slender lobes pressed against corolla tube; corolla with 5 abruptly flared, ovate lobes as long as its tube; stamens 5, with spirally twisted anthers.

Leaves: ½–2½" (1.5–6.5 cm) long, opposite.

Height: 5–24" (12.5–60 cm).

Flowering: April–June.

Habitat: Moist open areas along streams, in prairies and meadows, and on hillsides.

Range: Southeastern California northeast to southern Utah, east to central Texas, and south to northern Mexico.

Comments: The brilliant pink corolla resembles that of *Phlox* species, which have three branches on the style; the style on *Centaurium* species ends with a small knob or two short branches.

---

558 Prairie Gentian; Tulip Gentian; Bluebell
Eustoma grandiflorum

Description: Small clumps of erect stems bearing *evenly spaced, opposite leaves* and topped with small clusters of *large, erect, bell-shaped, usually bluish to purplish flowers.*

Flowers: 1¼–1½" (3–4 cm) long; calyx to 1¼" (3 cm) long, with 5 needle-like lobes; corolla bluish purple, pinkish, white, or white and purplish- or yellowish-tinged, with a short broad tube and 5 broad lobes 1¼–1½" (3–4 cm) long.

Leaves: To 3" (7.5 cm) long, ovate, with 3 conspicuous veins.

Height: 10–28" (25–70 cm).

Flowering: June–September.

Habitat: Moist places in prairies and fields.

Range: Eastern Colorado and Nebraska south to eastern New Mexico and Texas.

Prairie Gentian

Comments: This species is one of the handsomest prairie wildflowers. *Eustoma,* from the Greek *eu* ("good") and *stoma* ("mouth"), refers to the large opening into the flower's "throat" where the corolla lobes join. A closely related species, Catchfly Gentian *(E. exaltatum),* has corolla lobes to 1″ (2.5 cm) long; it is found from southern California east to Florida and southward.

640 Explorer's Gentian
Gentiana calycosa

Description: Several leafy stems in a clump, topped by *1–3 blue, broadly funnel-shaped flowers.*
Flowers: 1–1½″ (2.5–4 cm) long; calyx bell-shaped, 5-lobed, with a membranous lining; corolla varying from blue to yellowish green (often with greenish streaks), with 5 pointed and nearly erect lobes; pleats cut into fine segments at end between corolla lobes.
Leaves: ½–1¼″ (1.5–3 cm) long, opposite, broadly ovate, bases of lower leaves joined, forming a sheath around stem.
Height: 2–12″ (5–30 cm).
Flowering: July–October.
Habitat: Mountain meadows and streambanks.
Range: British Columbia south to Sierra Nevada and east to Rocky Mountains of Wyoming, Montana, and Canada.

Comments: Gentians are among the loveliest of
mountain wildflowers and are rock-
garden favorites. The genus name honors
King Gentius of Illyria, ruler of an
ancient country on the east side of the
Adriatic Sea, who is reputed to have
discovered medicinal virtues in gentians.

451 Northern Gentian
Gentianella amarella

Description: A leafy plant with angled, erect stems,
commonly with erect branches, and
*small, trumpet-shaped, purplish, bluish,
or pinkish flowers from near base to top.*
Flowers: Sepals joined at base; corolla ½–¾"
(1.5–2 cm) wide, varying from pale
yellowish and lightly blue-tinged to
clear blue, lavender, pinkish, purplish,
or dark bluish purple, with 5 lobes
flaring only slightly from tube and a
fringe of hairs inside at base of lobes.
Leaves: ¼–1½" (6–38 mm) long, oblong,
opposite, without stalks.
Height: 2–16" (5–40 cm).
Flowering: June–September.
Habitat: Meadows and moist areas, mostly in
mountains.
Range: Alaska south and east across much of
Canada to Atlantic Coast and
northeastern United States, and south to
California, Arizona, New Mexico, and
North Dakota.
Comments: This native of Eurasia is one of the
smaller, less showy gentians, but it often
grows in dense, colorful patches. The
genus name means "little gentian,"
reflecting its relationship to *Gentiana,* a
genus within which it was once
included.

579 Fringed Gentian
Gentianopsis detonsa

Description: Several clumped stems with few leaves
at base, 2–4 pairs of leaves on stem, and
few *bell-shaped, deep blue or blue-violet*

flowers at stem ends or in upper leaf
axils on leafless stalks.

Flowers: 1¼–2" (3–5 cm) long; calyx ½–1"
(1.5–2.5 cm) long, with bell-shaped
base and 4 pointed lobes; corolla
with 4 lobes fringed on broad end;
stamens 4.

Leaves: ½–2" (1.5–5 cm) long, opposite,
narrowly lanceolate.

Height: 4–16" (10–40 cm).

Flowering: July–August.

Habitat: Meadows, bogs, and moist ground.

Range: Across Canada, and south throughout
most of the western mountains to
eastern Nevada, Utah, and northern
New Mexico.

Comments: Differing from *Gentiana* by the
absence of pleats between the
corolla lobes, many races of this
wide-ranging species are fairly
different. The Rocky Mountain
race has been called *G. thermalis,*
after the hot springs in Yellowstone
National Park where it is the
park flower, but most botanists
consider this a synonym of *G. detonsa.*
In the Sierra Nevada, the mountains
of southern California, and in extreme
western Nevada is the race known
as Tufted Gentian *(G. holopetala);*
its petals are not fringed or only
fringed slightly at the tips.

562 Felwort; Star Swertia
Swertia perennis

Description: Several erect stems, with most
leaves at base, topped by *star-like,
pale bluish-purple flowers* with greenish
or white spots in an open, narrowly
branched cluster.

Flowers: About ¾" (2 cm) wide; corolla
with 5 pointed lobes joined
at base; 2 fringed glands at base
of each corolla lobe; style very
short, thick.

Leaves: Those at base 2–8" (5–20 cm)
long, lanceolate blades tapered

to a slender stalk; those on stem in
1–2 pairs, smaller.

Height: 2–20″ (5–50 cm).

Flowering: July–September.

Habitat: Meadows and moist areas at high
elevations in mountains.

Range: Alaska south to southern Sierra
Nevada, east to New Mexico, and
north through Rocky Mountains
to Canada.

Comments: The genus is named for E. Sweert, a
16th-century Dutch gardener,
herbalist, and author.

---

12 Monument Plant; Deer's Ears
Swertia radiata

Description: A narrowly cone-shaped plant
with 1 stout, tall, erect stem
bearing *large leaves in evenly spaced
whorls* and clusters of *yellowish-green
flowers* in axils of upper leaves
and leaf-like bracts.

Flowers: 1–1½″ (2.5–4 cm) wide; corolla
with 4 pointed lobes joined at
base, spotted with purple; 2 oblong
glands in lower central part of each
corolla lobe; stamens 4.

Leaves: Parallel-veined; those at base 10–20″
(25–50 cm) long, lanceolate, 3–4 in a
whorl; those on stem equally spaced,
progressively smaller.

Height: 4–7′ (1.2–2.1 m).

Flowering: May–August.

Habitat: Rich soil in woodland openings from
moderate to high elevations.

Range: Eastern Washington south to central
California and east to western Texas,
eastern Wyoming, and Montana;
also in northern Mexico.

Comments: The broad leaves are shaped like
the ears of a deer, giving this plant
one of its common names, and are
also a good browse for deer. This
species was previously known as
Frasera speciosa. Swertia and *Frasera*
are so similar that they are no longer
considered separate genera.

GERANIUM FAMILY
Geraniaceae

Leafy herbs with white, pink, or purple, showy flowers in clusters.

Flowers: Usually radially symmetrical. Sepals 5, separate or slightly united at base; petals 5, separate; stamens 5, 10, or 15, with filaments sometimes united at base; all these parts attached at base of ovary.

Leaves: Alternate or opposite; simple, pinnately or palmately lobed, or compound.

Fruit: Developing from 1 long-beaked pistil with 5 united chambers at base, each chamber 1-seeded, with a long style attached to central core and coiling away from it at maturity, thus lifting chambers of ovary upward and aiding in seed dispersal.

There are about 11 genera and 700 species, many frequent in the northern temperate region. Cultivated geraniums belong to *Pelargonium,* a tropical genus especially well developed in South Africa.

---

428 Filaree; Clocks; Storksbill
Erodium cicutarium

Description:	Usually reddish branched stems leaning or lying on ground with small, fern-like leaves, *2–10 small, deep reddish-lavender to purplish-pink flowers* in loose clusters, and long, slender, pin-like fruit sticking straight up.
Flowers:	About ½" (1.5 cm) wide; petals 5.
Leaves:	1¼–4" (3–10 cm) long, pinnately divided, each segment further divided; stalk less than one-fourth as long as blade.
Fruit:	¾–2" (2–5 cm) long, including slender center, with 5 lobes at base.
Height:	Sometimes tightly tufted, barely 1" (2.5 cm); or more open and branched, 1' (30 cm), with sprawling branches to 20" (50 cm) long.
Flowering:	February–June.
Habitat:	Open areas, often in disturbed soil.
Range:	Throughout West; also in much of East.
Comments:	This native of Eurasia, sometimes also called Afilaria, is one of the earliest flowers to bloom in the spring. Texas

Storksbill *(E. texanum),* a native U.S. plant, has flowers nearly 1″ (2.5 cm) wide and leaves ovate and deeply lobed; it is found on prairies and deserts from southeastern California east to central Texas and southwestern Oklahoma, and south to northern Mexico.

54 Richardson's Geranium; Crane's Bill
Geranium richardsonii

Description: Several stems with *palmately cleft leaves on long stalks,* most near base, and few *white or pale pink flowers* in a branched cluster.

Flowers: About 1″ (2.5 cm) wide; petals 5, each ½–¾″ (1.5–2 cm) long, with purplish veins, hairy on upperside at least on lower half and sometimes on upper portion; stamens 10; branches of cluster with purplish-tipped, glandular hairs.

Leaves: 1½–6″ (4–15 cm) wide, blades nearly round, cleft into 5–7 main segments, each with few pointed lobes.

Fruit: About 1″ (2.5 cm) long, including slender, pointed center, with 5 lobes at base.

Height: 8–31″ (20–80 cm).

Flowering: June–August.

Habitat: Partial shade in woods from lowlands to mountains.

Richardson's Geranium

Range: Southeastern British Columbia south
          through eastern Washington and
          Oregon to southern California, and
          east to New Mexico, South Dakota,
          and Saskatchewan.

Comments: One of the most widespread western
          geraniums, this species frequently
          hybridizes with other species, often
          making identification difficult. The
          genus name, from the Greek *geranos*
          ("crane"), refers to the fruit's beak; more
          than one *Geranium* species is called
          Crane's Bill.

---

427   **Sticky Geranium; Crane's Bill**
      Geranium viscosissimum

Description: A lightly hairy plant with several stems,
             leaves on long stalks, most near base, and
             few *pink-lavender to purplish flowers* in an
             open cluster near top.

Flowers: About 1" (2.5 cm) wide; petals 5, each
           ½–¾" (1.5–2 cm) long, broad, hairy on
           upperside only on lower third; stamens
           10; branches of cluster with glandular
           hairs.

Leaves: 1½–5" (4–12.5 cm) wide, palmately
           cleft, deeply divided into 5–7 segments
           with sharp teeth on ends and edges.

Sticky Geranium

Fruit: 1–2″ (2.5–5 cm) long, including slender, pointed center, with 5 lobes at base.

Height: 1–3′ (30–90 cm).

Flowering: May–August.

Habitat: Open woods and meadows from lowlands to well into mountains.

Range: Southern British Columbia south through eastern Washington and Oregon to northern California, and east to western Colorado, western South Dakota, and Saskatchewan.

Comments: This is one of several western geraniums with pinkish-purple flowers; all are similar, distinguished only by technical features. Dove's Foot Geranium *(G. molle),* with small pink flowers, is a common weed on lawns and in vacant lots.

BUCKEYE FAMILY
Hippocastanaceae

Trees or shrubs with large hanging leaves and flowers in showy clusters.

Flowers: Slightly bilaterally symmetrical. Calyx with 5 unequal, joined sepals; petals 4–5, unequal, each with slender stalk at base; stamens 5–8, long, slender; all these parts attached at base of ovary.

Leaves: Opposite, palmately compound.

Fruit: Leathery, round capsule, usually with 1 large, brown, shiny seed.

There are 2 genera and 15 species in this small family. Some are grown as handsome ornamentals.

112 California Buckeye; California Horse Chestnut
Aesculus californica

Description: A large round bush or small tree with large leaves and many *cone-shaped clusters of whitish flowers.*

Flowers: Cluster 4–8″ (10–20 cm) long; petals 5, each ½″ (1.5 cm) long, crinkled, white or blushed with pale rose; stamens 5–7; style 1, sweeping downward, projecting from front.

Leaves: Palmately compound, with 5–7 leaflets, each 2–6″ (5–15 cm) long, lanceolate, with teeth on edges.

Fruit: About 1½″ (4 cm) wide, pear-shaped, with thick rind and 1 large, glossy, brown seed.

Height: To 40′ (12 m).

Flowering: May–June.

Habitat: Dry slopes and canyons.

Range: California.

Comments: This is a unique western tree, a remnant of ancient times when wetter summers prevailed in western North America. The poisonous seeds were pulverized by Native Americans and thrown into dammed streams to stupefy fish, making them easier to catch.

HYDRANGEA FAMILY
Hydrangeaceae

Usually small trees or shrubs, sometimes herbs, with flowers often in roundish or flattish clusters sometimes arranged in heads.

Flowers: Radially symmetrical. Sepals 4–10; petals 4–10; stamens at least 4; all these parts attached at top of ovary.
Leaves: Opposite, usually simple.
Fruit: Capsule, with 2–5 chambers.

There are about 17 genera and 170 species, found in the northern temperate and subtropical regions and in South America. *Hydrangea* species are popular ornamental shrubs. Members of this family are sometimes included in the saxifrage family (Saxifragaceae).

39 Mock Orange; Lewis's Syringa; Indian Arrowhead
Philadelphus lewisii

Description: *A loosely branched shrub,* covered in spring with many *white flowers* in clusters at ends of short branches.

Flowers: ¾–1¼″ (2–3 cm) wide; petals 4–5; stamens many.

Leaves: 1¼–3″ (3–7.5 cm) long, opposite, on short stalks, ovate, smooth or minutely toothed on edges.

Fruit:	Woody capsule.
Height:	4–10′ (1.2–3 m).
Flowering:	May–July.
Habitat:	Rocky slopes and open banks in open pinewoods and mixed woodlands.
Range:	British Columbia south to central California and east to western Montana.
Comments:	This is Idaho's state flower. When in full bloom the flowers scent the air with a delightfully sweet fragrance reminiscent of orange blossoms. The genus is named for the Egyptian king Ptolemy Philadelphus; the species name (and one of the common names) honors the scientist-explorer Meriwether Lewis, who was the first European to discover and collect the plant during his exploration of the Louisiana Purchase. Native Americans used its straight stems in making arrows.

180 Yerba de Selva; Modesty
Whipplea modesta

Description:	Many erect, leafy branches, each tipped with a *small head of white flowers,* growing from long, trailing, rooting stems.
Flowers:	Petals 4–6, each about ⅛″ (3 mm) long, spatula-shaped; stamens 8–12.
Leaves:	½–1″ (1.5–2.5 cm) long, opposite, elliptical.
Height:	Creeper; branches 4–8″ (10–20 cm).
Flowering:	April–June.
Habitat:	In open or light woods, usually in dry rocky areas.
Range:	Western Washington south to central California near Pacific Coast.
Comments:	This plant often forms low dense patches on rocky banks or in open mixed woods of broadleaf trees and conifers. The Spanish name, Yerba de Selva, means "herb of the forest."

WATERLEAF FAMILY
Hydrophyllaceae

Usually herbs, rarely shrubs, often bristly or glandular, with flowers often arranged along one side of branches or at stem tips in coils resembling fiddlenecks.

Flowers: Radially symmetrical. Calyx with 5 united sepals; corolla with 5 united petals, varying from nearly flat to bell- or funnel-shaped; stamens 5, often protruding; all these parts attached at base of ovary.
Leaves: Alternate or opposite, often in basal rosettes; simple or pinnately compound.
Fruit: Capsule, with 1 to many seeds.

There are about 20 genera and 250 species, nearly world-wide; the western United States is the main center of diversity. A few species are grown as ornamentals.

---

234 Whispering Bells
Emmenanthe penduliflora

Description: *Pale yellow, bell-shaped flowers hanging from very slender stalks in a branched cluster; delicate, erect, branched stems covered with sticky hairs exuding a somewhat medicinal but pleasant odor.*
Flowers: About ½″ (1.5 cm) long; corolla with 5 round lobes; stamens 5, hidden within.
Leaves: 1–4″ (2.5–10 cm) long, narrowly oblong, pinnately lobed.
Fruit: Many-seeded capsule.
Height: 6–20″ (15–50 cm).
Flowering: March–July.
Habitat: Brushy hills and desert washes.
Range: Central California south to Baja California and east to central Arizona.
Comments: The dried-up corolla remains on the plant as a tissue-paper-like bell that rustles in gentle breezes. In the hills of southern California plants may have pink corollas.

---

33 Dwarf Hesperochiron
Hesperochiron pumilus

Description: A low plant with *1 slender stalk* growing from *leaves in a basal rosette* and topped by *1–5 white, saucer-shaped flowers.*

Flowers:	Corolla ½–1¼" (1.5–3 cm) wide, with 5 ovate lobes with fine purplish lines; corolla tube short, with dense hairs inside; stamens 5; style with 2 branches.
Leaves:	1–3" (2.5–7.5 cm) long, lanceolate.
Height:	1–2" (2.5–5 cm).
Flowering:	April–June.
Habitat:	Moist meadows, flats, and slopes.
Range:	Eastern Washington south to southern California and northern Arizona, and east to western Montana.
Comments:	California Hesperochiron *(H. californicus),* the one other species that grows in the same region, has a funnel- or bell-shaped corolla with oblong lobes.

624 Dwarf Waterleaf; Woolen Breeches
Hydrophyllum capitatum

Description:	A low plant with *round heads of small, white or pale purple flowers* on short stalks among *pinnately divided leaves.*
Flowers:	Head about 1¼" (3 cm) wide; each flower ¼–⅜" (6–9 mm) long; corolla with 5 round lobes at end; stamens 5, projecting.
Leaves:	To 4" (10 cm) wide, 6" (15 cm) long, triangular, divided into 7–11 segments often with 2–3 large *teeth on ends but none on edges;* some leaves with long stalks attached below ground.
Height:	4–16" (10–40 cm).
Flowering:	March–July.
Habitat:	Brushy areas and open woods.
Range:	Southern British Columbia and southwestern Alberta south through eastern Washington, Idaho, and Oregon to central California, and east through northern Nevada and northern Utah to western Colorado.
Comments:	In the northeastern United States plants of this genus were cooked for greens by Native Americans and settlers. A form of Dwarf Waterleaf in south-central Washington and northern Oregon has flower heads on long stalks above the leaves.

623 Fendler's Waterleaf
Hydrophyllum fendleri

Description: A fairly coarse plant with 1 stem bearing downward-projecting hairs, *few large, pinnately divided leaves,* and *white or lavender, bell-shaped flowers* in a loose branched cluster at top or on stalks growing from leaf axils.

Flowers: ¼–⅜″ (6–9 mm) wide; corolla with 5 round lobes at end; stamens 5, projecting.

Leaves: To 10″ (25 cm) long, with 7–15 lanceolate segments bearing 4–8 sharp teeth on each edge; stalks long or short.

Height: 8–31″ (20–80 cm).

Flowering: May–August.

Habitat: Moist places in brush and open areas from low to high elevations.

Range: Cascade Range from British Columbia south to northern California; southeastern Washington south to northeastern Oregon and east to west-central Idaho; and southern Wyoming south to southern New Mexico and southeastern Utah.

Comments: This is a common, rather plain-looking woodland plant. Pacific Waterleaf *(H. tenuipes),* which grows west of the Cascade Range and the Sierra Nevada from British Columbia south to northern California, has leaves barely longer than wide, divided into 5–9 segments. California Waterleaf *(H. occidentale)* has blunt points on the leaf segments, unlike the long tapered points of Fendler's Waterleaf, and only 2–4 teeth on each edge.

476 Purple Mat
Nama demissum

Description: Mats of slender, hairy *stems, leafy toward ends and lying on ground,* with several *bell-shaped, deep pink to reddish-lavender flowers* growing from leaf axils.

Flowers: ⅜″ (9 mm) wide; corolla with 5 round lobes at end; stamens 5, hidden within.

Leaves: 1½″ (4 cm) long, sticky, narrowly
spatula-shaped or ovate.

Height: Creeper; flower clusters 1–3″ (2.5–7.5
cm), stems to 8″ (20 cm) long.

Flowering: March–May.

Habitat: Desert flats and washes.

Range: Southwestern Utah south to central
Arizona, southeastern California, and
northwestern Mexico.

Comments: *Nama* in Greek means "a water spring."
There are many species in the genus, both
perennials and showy annuals, that carpet
the desert floor with purple after adequate
rainfall. Hispid Nama (*N. hispidum*),
with erect, bushy-branched stems and
very narrow leaves, is another low
species common in deserts from
southern California to western Texas
and northern Mexico.

563 Baby Blue Eyes
Nemophila menziesii

Description: A low plant with *pale or bright blue to
purplish-blue, bowl-shaped flowers* borne
singly on slender stalks near ends of
slender, leaning, branched stems.

Flowers: ½–1½″ (1.5–4 cm) wide; corolla with
5 broad lobes, often paler near base,
generally with small black dots; stamens
5; style with 2 branches at tip.

Leaves: ¾–2″ (2–5 cm) long, opposite, oblong,
pinnately divided into segments with
teeth along edges.

Height: 4–12″ (10–30 cm).

Flowering: March–June.

Habitat: Grassy hillsides and among brush.

Range: Central Oregon south to southern
California.

Comments: One of the most charming and best-known
spring wildflowers in California, Baby Blue
Eyes is often included in commercial
wildflower seed mixtures; it has been
cultivated in England for more than a
century. Closely related is the equally
delightful Five Spot (*N. maculata*) of
central California, which has white petal
lobes, each with a large, blue-violet spot.

638 Desert Bell
Phacelia campanularia

Description: A stiff, erect, leafy, glandular-hairy plant with *dark blue, bell-like flowers in loose coils* at end of a branched open cluster.

Flowers: Corolla ¾–1½" (2–4 cm) long, with 5 round lobes, tube not constricted at base; stamens with expanded, hairless bases.

Leaves: ¾–3" (2–7.5 cm) long, ovate, edges shallowly lobed and sharply toothed.

Height: 8–30" (20–75 cm).

Flowering: February–April.

Habitat: Dry, sandy or gravelly places in deserts.

Range: Southern California; introduced along roadsides in western Arizona.

Comments: In a spring following a wet winter, thousands of these plants will bloom, forming masses of deep rich blue. The similar California Bell *(P. minor),* found in southern California and northern Baja California, has a violet corolla with a cream spot on each lobe, the opening slightly constricted, and hair on the expanded stamen bases.

556 Wild Heliotrope; Common Phacelia
Phacelia distans

Description: A finely hairy, branched plant, glandular in upper parts, with *fern-like leaves and coils of broadly bell-shaped, blue to bluish-purple flowers.*

Flowers: ¼" (6 mm) wide; calyx with 5 unequal lobes; corolla with 5 round lobes; stamens 5, barely projecting.

Leaves: ¾–4" (2–10 cm) long, 1–2 times pinnately divided into pinnately lobed segments.

Height: 8–31" (20–80 cm).

Flowering: March–June.

Habitat: Fields, brushy slopes, and washes.

Range: Northern California south to Baja California and east to southern Nevada and eastern Arizona.

Comments: This plant matures rapidly as the soil dries in the late spring. Despite one of its common names, it is not related to garden heliotropes.

657 Silverleaf Phacelia
Phacelia hastata

Description: Many tight *coils of small white, pale blue, or pale purple flowers with harsh hairs on calyx lobes* on short branches at ends of leafy stems.

Flowers: Corolla ¼″ (6 mm) long, bell-shaped, with 5 round lobes at end; stamens 5, protruding.

Leaves: 1¼–2½″ (3–6.5 cm) long, lanceolate, *prominently and nearly parallel-veined,* with dense, silvery hairs lying flat, 2 small lobes occasionally on edges at base.

Height: 8–20″ (20–50 cm).

Flowering: May–July.

Habitat: Dry rocky places in sagebrush and in coniferous forests.

Range: Southern British Columbia south to northern California and east to Colorado, western Nebraska, and Alberta.

Comments: This species belongs to a complex group of closely related plants of dry rocky mountain habitat, all with whitish flowers. They are distinguished from other phacelias by their leaf veins.

557 Scalloped Phacelia
Phacelia integrifolia

Description: Glandular, malodorous, sticky, commonly stout, leafy stems with *purplish-lavender or bluish-purple flowers in coils* at ends of upper branches.

Flowers: Corolla about ¼″ (6 mm) wide, funnel-shaped, with 5 round lobes at end; stamens 5, protruding.

Leaves: To 3″ (7.5 cm) long, narrowly ovate, scalloped or shallowly lobed.

Fruit: Capsule, with 4 dark seeds, each with 2 grooves on inner side, no wrinkles in grooves.

Height: 6–30″ (15–75 cm).

Flowering: March–September.
Habitat: Rocky or sandy places in deserts and among piñon and juniper.
Range: Southern Utah south to Arizona and northern Mexico, and east to New Mexico, western Texas, and western Oklahoma.
Comments: *Phacelia* is a large, mostly western American genus distinguished by bluish or purplish flowers in coils usually with protruding stamens. Identification of individual species is determined by technical features, such as seed details.

555 Threadleaf Phacelia
Phacelia linearis

Description: Slender, commonly branched, erect stems topped with *pinkish- to reddish-lavender flowers in loose coils.*
Flowers: Corolla ⅜–¾″ (9–20 mm) wide, broadly bell-shaped, with 5 round lobes; stamens 5, barely protruding.
Leaves: ½–4″ (1.5–10 cm) long, narrowly lanceolate, hairy, sometimes with 1–4 pairs of small lobes in lower half.
Fruit: Small capsule, with 6–15 seeds with pitted surfaces.
Height: 4–20″ (10–50 cm).
Flowering: April–June.
Habitat: Brush and open, grassy areas in foothills and on plains.
Range: Southern British Columbia south to northern California and east across much of Utah and Idaho to western Wyoming.
Comments: A common, showy species, this plant is distinguished from other phacelias by its comparatively large broad corolla and narrow leaves.

610 Purple Fringe; Alpine Phacelia
Phacelia sericea

Description: A cluster of several erect stems bearing most leaves near base, covered with dense hairs with a silvery-gray hue; *purple or dark blue-violet flowers in many*

	short dense coils in a tight, cylindrical cluster, fringed with protruding stamens.
Flowers:	Corolla about ¼″ (6 mm) long, bell-shaped, with 5 round lobes.
Leaves:	1–4″ (2.5–10 cm) long, broadly lanceolate, pinnately cleft into many narrow lobes.
Height:	To 16″ (40 cm).
Flowering:	June–August.
Habitat:	Open or wooded, rocky places in mountains, often at high elevations.
Range:	Southern British Columbia south to northeastern California, east to Alberta, and south in mountains to Colorado.
Comments:	This common mountain wildflower is easily distinguished from other phacelias by its cylindrical inflorescence.

ST. JOHN'S WORT FAMILY
Hypericaceae

Leafy herbs or shrubs with yellow to orange (sometimes pink) flowers in branched clusters and leaves covered with numerous often black or translucent dots.

Flowers: Bisexual, radially symmetrical. Sepals 4–5, separate; petals 4–5, separate; stamens numerous, usually united into several bunches by bases of filaments; all these parts attached at base of ovary.
Leaves: Opposite or whorled, simple.
Fruit: Usually a many-seeded capsule.

There are 8 genera and about 400 species, found in temperate and tropical regions. Some are grown as ornamentals. Many species have leaves with translucent dots; when held up to the light; these appear as tiny pinholes. This family is sometimes combined with the Clusiaceae (also known as Guttiferae), a tropical family of mostly trees and shrubs.

200 Tinker's Penny
Hypericum anagalloides

Description:	Prostrate stems forming leafy mats, with *small, golden yellow or salmon-yellow flowers* at ends of short erect branches.
Flowers:	About ¼″ (6 mm) wide; sepals 5, slightly shorter or slightly longer than petals; petals 5; stamens 15–25, about as long as petals; styles 3, atop ovary.

Leaves: ¼–⅝″ (5–16 mm) long, opposite, ovate.

Height: Creeper; branches to 3″ (7.5 cm), stems to 8″ (20 cm) long.

Flowering: June–August.

Habitat: Wet places from sea level to high elevations.

Range: British Columbia south to Baja California and east to Montana.

Comments: Some *Hypericum* species are given the name St. John's Wort. Their flowers bloom around June 24, the feast day of Saint John the Baptist. For centuries the plants had the reputation of warding off evil; when hung about the house or kept in pockets, they were thought to guard against thunder and witches.

199 Klamath Weed; Common St. John's Wort
Hypericum perforatum

Description: Several erect stems, especially leafy and branched near top, with *bright yellow, star-like flowers* in an open, round-topped, terminal cluster.

Flowers: About 1″ (2.5 cm) wide; petals 5, longer than sepals, sometimes with black dots near tips; stamens many, in 3–5 bunches.

Leaves: ½–1½″ (1.5–4 cm) long, opposite, elliptical, with *translucent dots.*

Height: 1–3′ (30–90 cm).

Flowering: June–September.

Habitat: Roadsides and pastures.

Range: Throughout much of United States and Canada; in West, especially common from western Washington south to California.

Comments: This highly branched perennial is the most common St. John's wort and is easily recognized by the tiny, translucent dots that can be seen when the leaves are held up to the light. Native to Europe and first discovered in the eastern United States in 1793, this noxious weed appeared in California near the Klamath River around 1900; by 1940 this aggressive perennial had made

250,000 acres of California rangeland nearly worthless by crowding out vegetation valuable for domestic livestock. In addition, the livestock that consumed the plant became photosensitive, particularly if they were light-skinned or had patches of light skin, suffering the equivalent of serious, debilitating sunburn; in a few instances ingestion of the weed proved lethally toxic. After 1945 it was quickly controlled by two European beetles that feed only on this plant. This is the species commonly sold as an herbal remedy.

IRIS FAMILY
Iridaceae

Herbs growing from rhizomes, bulbs, or swollen, under-ground stems, with narrow, basal leaves, sometimes arranged edge to edge in fan-shaped clusters, and showy flower clusters at tips of long stalks.

Flowers: Usually radially symmetrical. Sepals 3, petal-like; petals 3; stamens 3; all these parts attached at top of ovary.

Leaves: Simple, folded and overlapping one another at base, aligned in 2 rows.

Fruit: Many-seeded capsule.

There are about 80 genera and 1,500 species, found in temperate and tropical regions. Irises *(Iris),* freesias *(Freesia),* gladiolus *(Gladiolus),* and montbretias *(Tritonia)* are popular ornamentals. Saffron dye is obtained from Saffron Crocus *(Crocus sativus),* and "essence of violets," used in perfumes, is extracted from the rhizomes of irises.

572 Douglas's Iris
Iris douglasiana

Description: *Large, reddish-purple, pinkish, white, or cream flowers,* with lilac veins, on stout branched stalks rising from *clumps of sword-shaped leaves.*

Flowers: 3–4" (7.5–10 cm) wide; sepals 3, long, petal-like, curved downward; petals 3, erect, about as long as sepals, slightly

Douglas's Iris

narrower; sepals and petals joined to
form a tube at base ½–1″ (1.5–2.5 cm)
long; pair of bracts beneath flower
nearly opposite each other, bases not
separated by space on stem.

Leaves: To 3′ (90 cm) long (usually shorter),
¾″ (2 cm) wide, flexible, tough.

Height: 6–31″ (15–80 cm).

Flowering: March–May.

Habitat: Grassy slopes and open brush.

Range: Coast Ranges from southern Oregon
south to central California.

Comments: This is a common iris in the Redwood
region. The genus name, Greek for
"rainbow," refers to the variegated
coloration of the flower. In Greek
mythology, Iris, a member of Hera's
court and goddess of the rainbow, so
impressed Hera with her purity that
she was commemorated with a flower
that blooms in the rainbow colors of
her robe.

574 Ground Iris; Bowl-tube Iris
Iris macrosiphon

Description: *Large, deep golden yellow, cream, pale
lavender, or deep blue-purple flowers,* usually
with distinct veins, on short stalks
among *sword-shaped leaves.*

Flowers: 2½–4" (6.5–10 cm) wide; sepals 3, petal-like, curved downward; petals 3, erect, slightly narrower and shorter than sepals; sepals and petals joined to form a *tube at base 1½–3" (4–7.5 cm) long.*

Leaves: To 10" (25 cm) long, about ¼" (6 mm) wide, flexible, tough.

Height: 6–8" (15–20 cm).

Flowering: April–May.

Habitat: Grassy or open, wooded slopes.

Range: California in northern Coast Ranges and foothills of Sierra Nevada.

Comments: The range in coloration may be partly due to hybridization with other native species, which is common among western irises.

573 Rocky Mountain Iris; Western Blue Flag
Iris missouriensis

Description: Large, delicate, *pale blue or blue-violet flowers,* often with purple veins, atop *stout leafless stalks* growing from dense clumps of *flexible, tough, sword-shaped leaves.*

Flowers: 3–4" (7.5–10 cm) wide; sepals 3, petal-like, curved downward; petals 3, erect.

Leaves: 8–20" (20–50 cm) long, ¼–½" (6–13 mm) wide; sometimes 1 short leaf present on flower stalk.

Height: 8–20" (20–50 cm).

Flowering: May–July.

Habitat: Meadows and streambanks with abundant moisture until flowering time.

Range: British Columbia south to southern California and east to Montana, western South Dakota, Colorado, and New Mexico.

Comments: The only native species east of the Cascade Range and the Sierra Nevada, this iris often forms large dense patches in low spots in pastures, where the tough leaves are avoided by cattle. It is suspected of being poisonous.

571 **Tough-leaved Iris**
Iris tenax

Description: *Large, delicate, lavender to deep purple,*
(sometimes white, rarely yellow)
flowers, usually with dark violet
veins, atop short stalks in *dense*
clumps of narrow tough leaves about
as tall as stalks.

Flowers: 3–4″ (7.5–10 cm) wide; sepals 3, petal-
like, curved downward; petals 3, erect,
slightly shorter than sepals; sepals and
petals joined to form a tube at base
¼–½″ (6–13 mm) long; bracts beneath
flower joined to stem at distinctly
different levels.

Leaves: To 16″ (40 cm) long.

Height: To 16″ (40 cm).

Flowering: April–June.

Habitat: Pastures, fields, and woodland openings.

Range: Southwestern Washington south to
northwestern California west of Cascade
Range.

Comments: In Oregon's Willamette Valley these
handsome flowers provide brilliant color
displays along highways. The species
name, Latin for "tenacious," refers to the
tough leaves. Native Americans used
fibers from the edges of the leaves of
some western species to make strong,
pliable rope and cord.

561 **Grass Widow**
Olsynium douglasii var. *inflatum*

Description: Few *reddish-lavender or purple, bowl-shaped*
flowers atop stems rising from clumps of
narrow, sword-like leaves.

Flowers: 1¼–2″ (3–5 cm) wide; petal-like
segments 6, pointed, broadest in upper
half; stamens 3, joined to form a globe
at base.

Leaves: Usually about 4″ (10 cm) long, with
lower half sheathing stem.

Height: 4–12″ (10–30 cm).

Flowering: March–June.

Habitat: Grassy areas in sagebrush and
open woods.

Range: Southern British Columbia south
to northern Oregon and east to
central Idaho, northern Nevada,
and northern Utah.

Comments: Once considered a member of the
genus *Sisyrinchium,* Grass Widow,
with its inflated stamen base, is now
placed in the closely related genus
Olsynium. There is only one species in
the West, with two varieties. The
variety *inflatum,* from mostly east of the
Cascade Range, has a distinctly flared
stamen base. The variety *douglasii* has an
indistinctly flared stamen base; it occurs
mostly west of the Cascade Range, from
British Columbia south to northern
California.

635 Blue-eyed Grass
Sisyrinchium angustifolium

Description: Several *delicate, blue or deep blue-violet
flowers* in 2 broad bracts atop a *flat stem,*
generally with 1 flower in bloom at a
time; stems taller than clusters of
narrow, sword-shaped leaves near base.

Flowers: ½–1½″ (1.5–4 cm) wide; petal-like
segments 6, each with a fine point on
otherwise blunt or notched tip.

Leaves: 2–10″ (5–25 cm) long, ⅛–¼″ (3–6 mm)
wide.

Height: 4–20″ (10–50 cm).

Flowering: April–September.

Habitat: Moist, generally open places (at least
early in season) from lowlands to well
into mountains.

Range: Throughout Canada and United States,
except Prairie Provinces and northern
Plains states.

Comments: This genus is one of the most perplexing
groups of plants, with many, often
intergrading variants named as
species. The common names of
western *Sisyrinchium* species identify
them as grasses because of the rather
grass-like appearance of their narrow
leaves, but they are not closely related
to true grasses (Poaceae).

331   Golden-eyed Grass
Sisyrinchium californicum

Description: 1 or few delicate, *bright yellow flowers, resembling 6-pointed stars,* held above leaves atop a flat stem in 2 broad bracts, generally with 1 flower in bloom at a time; 1 cluster of *narrow, sword-shaped leaves near base.*

Flowers: About ½–¾" (1.5–2 cm) wide; petal-like segments 6, each broadly lance-shaped or rounded at tip; veins brownish, especially noticeable on back.

Leaves: From about half as tall as stems to equal in height, ⅛–¼" (2–6 mm) wide.

Height: 8–24" (20–60 cm).

Flowering: May–June.

Habitat: Moist places near coast.

Range: British Columbia south to central California.

Comments: There are only a few yellow-flowered *Sisyrinchium* in the West. Two species from Arizona resemble *S. californicum,* both called Yellow-eyed or Golden-eyed Grass: *S. cernuum,* found in southeastern Arizona and Mexico, has petal-like segments less than ¼" (6 mm) long, with flowers on slender bent stalks; *S. longipes,* found from northern Arizona to Mexico, has petal-like segments ⅜–½" (8–13 mm) long, with flowers on erect stalks. Elmer's Golden-eyed Grass *(S. elmeri),* which has stems generally less than ⅛" (2 mm) wide, is found in much of California. Arizona Golden-eyed Grass *(S. arizonicum)* is a robust plant with branched stems bearing yellow-orange flowers more than 1" (2.5 cm) wide; it grows in the mountains of eastern Arizona and western New Mexico.

RATANY FAMILY
Krameriaceae

Small, intricately branched shrubs or perennial herbs, usually with reddish-purple flowers in leaf axils or in racemes.

Flowers: Bilaterally symmetrical. Sepals 4–5, unequal, often petal-like; corolla with 5 petals, upper 3 with stalks at base, lower 2 thick and short; stamens 3–4; all these parts attached at base of ovary.
Leaves: Simple, or rarely divided into 3 leaflets.
Fruit: 1-chambered, bristly globe, with 1 large seed.

There is only 1 genus with 17 species, found in warm parts of the Americas. Native Americans used various species medicinally, for tanning leather, and as a source of dye.

591	**Pima Ratany; Purple Heather** *Krameria erecta*
Description:	A low, grayish, *intricately branched, very twiggy shrub* with *1 reddish-lavender to reddish-purple flower* on each *slender stalk bearing many gland-tipped hairs.*
Flowers:	About ¾″ (2 cm) wide; sepals 5, reddish lavender inside; upper 3 petals much smaller than sepals, reddish lavender, joined at base; lower 2 petals resembling small greenish pads.
Leaves:	¼–½″ (6–13 mm) long, very narrow, grayish, hairy.
Fruit:	Roundish pod, about ¼″ (6 mm) wide, with long reddish prickles, each with scattered barbs near tip.
Height:	6–24″ (15–60 cm).
Flowering:	March–October.
Habitat:	Desert slopes, flats, and dry plains.
Range:	Southeastern California and southern Nevada east to western Texas and south to northern Mexico.
Comments:	This species is commonly found with Creosote Bush. Similar species lack glands beneath the flowers and have different barb arrangements on the fruit prickles.

MINT FAMILY
Lamiaceae

Aromatic herbs or shrubs, rarely trees or vines, usually with stems square in cross section, and flowers in long clusters, heads, or interrupted whorls on stem.

Flowers: Bilaterally symmetrical. Calyx with usually 5 united sepals, often each evident as a point on calyx, or sometimes calyx 2-lipped (or occasionally without points or lips); corolla with 5 united petals, usually forming an upper and lower lip, occasionally with 2 petals so well united corolla appears 4-lobed; stamens 2 or 4; all these parts attached at base of 4-lobed ovary.

Leaves: Opposite or whorled, usually simple.

Fruit: Nestled in persistent calyx, with 4 lobes, each lobe forming a hard, 1-seeded nutlet; rarely a drupe.

There are about 200 genera and 3,200 species, nearly worldwide. The Mediterranean region, the chief area of diversity, produces many spices and flavorings, such as oregano and marjoram *(Origanum),* thyme *(Thymus),* sage *(Salvia),* basil *(Ocimum),* and mints *(Mentha).* Catnip *(Nepeta cataria)* and Lavender *(Lavandula officinalis)* also belong to the family. Members of several genera, including *Coleus* and *Salvia,* are popular ornamentals. The family's traditional name, Labiatae, refers to the lip-like parts of the united petals.

509 Nettleleaf Horsemint
Agastache urticifolia

Description:	Numerous leafy, *4-sided stems with opposite leaves* and, near top, *pale pink to lavender, bilaterally symmetrical flowers* in dense circles crowded into *tight spikes.*
Flowers:	Spike 1¼–6″ (3–15 cm) long; corolla about ½″ (1.5 cm) long, upper and lower lips bent back from tube opening; stamens 4, protruding, upper 2 longer than and bent down between lower 2.
Leaves:	1¼–3″ (3–7.5 cm) long, ovate, toothed, smooth on underside.
Height:	1–5′ (30–150 cm).
Flowering:	June–August.
Habitat:	Open slopes in woods.
Range:	Southeastern British Columbia south through eastern Washington and eastern Oregon to southern California, and east to western Colorado and western Montana.
Comments:	*Agastache,* from the Greek *agan* ("much") and *stachys* ("ear of grain"), refers to the flower clusters. The spikes, short corolla lobes, and protruding stamens are distinctive.

594 **Creeping Charlie; Ground Ivy;**
Gill-over-the-ground
Glechoma hederacea

Description: Weak, creeping, *4-sided stems with opposite*
leaves and *few bilaterally symmetrical,*
lavender to blue-violet flowers in clusters in
each leaf axil.

Flowers: ½–1″ (1.5–2.5 cm) long; corolla spotted
with purple; lower corolla lip 3-lobed,
central lobe broad; upper corolla lip
arching outward like a hood, notched at
tip, hiding 2 stamens; other 2 stamens
inside corolla tube.

Leaves: ½–1¼″ (1.5–3 cm) long, round or
kidney-shaped, with scalloped edges, on
long stalks.

Height: Creeper; stem tips 4–16″ (10–40 cm).

Flowering: March–June.

Habitat: Moist woods and thickets.

Range: Throughout much of Canada and
United States.

Comments: In many areas this aggressive European
native is now considered a lawn weed. If
consumed in large amounts, it is toxic to
horses.

536 **Common Henbit;**
Common Dead Nettle
Lamium amplexicaule

Description: A small plant bearing several
4-sided stems and few *purplish-pink*
to reddish-lavender, bilaterally
symmetrical flowers in clusters in
opposite bracts.

Flowers: Corolla ½–¾″ (1.5–2 cm) long, with a
long narrow tube; lower corolla lip
notched at tip, strongly constricted at
base; upper corolla lip ¼″ (6 mm) long,
like a hood, hiding 4 stamens, upper
side with deep purple hairs.

Leaves: ¾–1¼″ (2–3 cm) long, roundish,
scalloped on edges, without stalks.

Height: 3–6″ (7.5–15 cm).

Flowering: February–October.

Habitat: Fields and gardens.

Range: Throughout much of North America.

Comments: Two other species, also introduced from
Eurasia, occur in the West; both have
stalked leaves. Spotted Henbit (*L.
maculatum*) has an upper corolla lobe
¼–½" (6–13 mm) long. Red Henbit
(*L. purpureum*) has flowers about the
same size as Common Henbit.

544 Field Mint; Wild Mint
Mentha arvensis

Description: A branched, minty-smelling plant with
stems in patches and *dense whorls of small,
pale pink or lavender flowers* in leaf axils,
nearly hidden by opposite leaves.

Flowers: Corolla barely ¼" (6 mm) long, nearly
radially symmetrical, upper lobe broader
and notched at tip.

Leaves: ¾–3" (2–7.5 cm) long, broadly
lanceolate, sharply toothed.

Height: 8–31" (20–80 cm).

Flowering: July–September.

Habitat: Moist places, especially along streams.

Range: Throughout much of Canada and
United States, except from Louisiana to
Florida.

Comments: This species also occurs across northern
Eurasia. The clusters of flowers along
the stem distinguish it from many other
Mentha that have flowers in slender
spikes at the stem tips or in upper leaf
axils. The genus name comes from
Mintho, mistress of Pluto, ruler of
Hades. Pluto's jealous queen,
Proserpine, upon learning of Mintho,
trampled her, transforming her into a
lowly plant forever to be walked upon.
Pluto made this horrible fate more
tolerable by willing that the more the
plant was trampled, the sweeter it
would smell.

418 Red Monardella
Monardella macrantha

Description: A generally low plant with *aromatic
leaves* lining several stems topped by

tight clusters of *bright red, slightly
bilaterally symmetrical, tubular flowers.*

Flowers: 1¼–2″ (3–5 cm) long; corolla pointed,
with 5 lobes, 2 closer together than
other 3; stamens 4.
Leaves: ½–1¼″ (1.5–3 cm) long, opposite, ovate.
Height: 4–20″ (10–50 cm).
Flowering: June–August.
Habitat: Dry slopes in chaparral and pine forests.
Range: Southern California and Baja California.
Comments: The bright red flowers attract
hummingbirds, which carry pollen from
flower to flower while they seek nectar.
Most monardellas have much smaller,
whitish or lavender corollas.

545 Coyote Mint
Monardella odoratissima

Description: A grayish, aromatic plant with erect,
bunched, leafy stems bearing *opposite
leaves* and topped by *small, whitish to pale
purple or pink flowers in a dense head.*
Flowers: Corolla ½″ (1.5 cm) long, bilaterally
symmetrical, with 5 lobes, 2 closer
together than other 3; stamens 4,
protruding; bracts beneath head broadly
ovate, purplish, membrane-like.
Leaves: To 1¼″ (3 cm) long, lanceolate.
Height: 6–14″ (15–35 cm).
Flowering: June–September.
Habitat: Dry slopes and rocky banks from low
elevations to well into mountains.
Range: Eastern Washington south through
eastern Oregon to California, and east to
northern Idaho, western Wyoming, and
central New Mexico.
Comments: Coyote Mint has many races in the
West, varying in density of foliage hairs,
breadth of heads, and relative length of
bracts and calyx.

602 Bladder Sage
Salazaria mexicana

Description: A grayish-green shrub with spine-
tipped twigs bearing *papery bladders.*

Flowers:	¾" (2 cm) long, in loose racemes; *calyx bladder-like, pale orange or greenish,* swelling to ¾" (2 cm) wide; corolla bilaterally symmetrical, with a deep blue-violet upper lip and a pale blue tube and lower lip.
Leaves:	About ½" (1.5 cm) long, opposite, broadly lanceolate.
Height:	2–3' (60–90 cm).
Flowering:	March–June.
Habitat:	In deserts, commonly in washes.
Range:	Southern Utah south through western Arizona and southern California to northern Mexico, and east through Mexico to southwestern Texas.
Comments:	The bladder-like calyx may be blown by the wind, thus dispersing seeds to new areas.

604 Thistle Sage
Salvia carduacea

Description:	A handsome, *whitish-woolly plant* with *vivid lavender, bilaterally symmetrical flowers in a stacked series of prickly round clusters* near top of leafless stems.
Flowers:	¾–1" (2–2.5 cm) long; corolla with fringed upper and lower lips; stamens 2, each with 2 slender stalks joined near base and resembling a teeter-totter, each stalk with 1 anther, longer stalk with anther projecting beyond corolla, shorter stalk with smaller anther held within tube.
Leaves:	1–6" (2.5–15 cm) long, in a basal rosette, lanceolate, irregularly indented, prickly.
Height:	4–20" (10–50 cm).
Flowering:	March–June.
Habitat:	Sandy or gravelly, open places.
Range:	Central California south to Baja California.
Comments:	This is one of the most beautiful native sages; the brilliant lavender flowers are strikingly contrasted against the pale foliage, and the vermilion anthers provide color accent.

628 **Chia**
Salvia columbariae

Description: Small, *very deep blue to purple, bilaterally symmetrical flowers* in few *dense round clusters* in intervals near top of *4-sided stems*.

Flowers: Corolla about ½″ (1.5 cm) long, with prominent upper and lower lips; stamens 2; reddish-purple, spine-tipped bracts beneath cluster.

Leaves: To 4″ (10 cm) long, mostly at base, oblong, irregularly divided.

Height: 4–20″ (10–50 cm).

Flowering: March–June.

Habitat: Open places in chaparral and deserts.

Range: Southern half of California south to Baja California and east to southwestern Utah, Arizona, and southwestern New Mexico.

Comments: Chia (pronounced ***chee**-ah*) is the common name of several *Salvia* species from which Native Americans made pinole, a meal ground from parched seeds. The seeds were also steeped in water to produce a thick sticky drink.

627 **Gray-ball Sage; Desert Sage**
Salvia dorrii

Description: *A broad bush* with many rigid, spine-tipped branches, *silvery leaves, and bright blue to violet-blue, bilaterally symmetrical flowers.*

Flowers: Corolla about ½″ (1.5 cm) long; lower corolla lip with a very broad, spreading middle lobe bent downward and 2 small outer lobes at side of opening to tube; upper corolla lip with 2 short, ear-like lobes; 2 stamens and 1 style arching out in front; reddish-purple bracts among flowers.

Leaves: ½–1½″ (1.5–4 cm) long, broadly lanceolate, broadest near tip, tapering to a stalk-like base, opposite, often clustered along stem.

Height: 8–31″ (20–80 cm).

Flowering: May–July.

Habitat:	Dry flats and slopes, often in sagebrush.
Range:	Washington south to southern California east of Cascade Range and Sierra Nevada, and east to central Arizona, Utah, and southwestern Idaho.
Comments:	It is this sage, not sagebrush, that is referred to in Zane Grey's classic western *Riders of the Purple Sage.* It is a handsome plant, pretty in leaf as well as in flower.

658 Death Valley Sage
Salvia funerea

Description:	A compact, densely branched, *ghostly white-woolly shrub with deep bluish-violet to violet, bilaterally symmetrical flowers.*
Flowers:	About ½″ (1.5 cm) long; corolla protruding from densely woolly calyx.
Leaves:	½–¾″ (1.5–2 cm) long, ovate, thick, leathery, spine-tipped, covered with white wool.
Height:	1½–4′ (45–120 cm).
Flowering:	March–May.
Habitat:	Hot rocky washes and canyon walls.
Range:	Mountains around Death Valley, California, and adjacent regions of Nevada.
Comments:	This plant's conspicuous white wool probably serves to reflect heat and reduce the effect of the strong drying winds that sweep through the hot canyons much of the year. It is protected by law and should not be picked.

511 Autumn Sage
Salvia greggii

Description:	A *minty-smelling shrub* with many branches and few *deep pink to reddish-lavender, bilaterally symmetrical flowers* in each leafless raceme.
Flowers:	Corolla 1–1¼″ (2.5–3 cm) long, tube swollen but abruptly narrowed near opening, with lower lip about as long as lightly glandular-hairy upper lip.
Leaves:	½–1″ (1.5–2.5 cm) long, elliptical, leathery, on short stalks.

Height:	To 3' (90 cm).
Flowering:	March–May.
Habitat:	Rocky soil on brushy slopes.
Range:	Western and central Texas to Mexico.
Comments:	The bright, vibrant, nearly red flowers make this species a favorite of all who visit the Big Bend region in western Texas. The species is popular in cultivation in the Southwest, as its nectar-laden flowers attract hummingbirds into yards to feed.

411 Crimson Sage
Salvia henryi

Description:	A slender plant covered with soft gray hairs and bearing *bright red, bilaterally symmetrical flowers* in pairs at intervals near top of *4-sided stems.*
Flowers:	Corolla 1½" (4 cm) long, 3-lobed lower lip bent downward, upper lip projecting forward, tube expanding abruptly just past tip of calyx; stamens 2.
Leaves:	1–2½" (2.5–6.5 cm) long, opposite, pinnately divided, end segment largest.
Height:	To 20" (50 cm).
Flowering:	April–September.
Habitat:	Rocky slopes and canyons, often among piñon and juniper.
Range:	Southern Arizona east to western Texas and south to northern Mexico.
Comments:	The gray foliage complements the brilliant flowers, making this plant particularly attractive in its arid, sometimes barren habitat.

510 Lemmon's Sage
Salvia lemmonii

Description:	An *aromatic,* leafy, branched plant, somewhat woody near base, with *upward-angled, bilaterally symmetrical, deep pink to crimson flowers* in raceme-like clusters at stem ends.
Flowers:	Corolla 1–1½" (2.5–4 cm) long, upper lip projecting forward like a visor, very

broad lower lip bent downward;
usually 2 flowers opposite each
other in a long cluster.

Leaves: 1–2″ (2.5–5 cm) long, ovate, with stalks.
Height: 1–3′ (30–90 cm).
Flowering: July–October.
Habitat: In dry woods on rocky slopes and in
canyons.
Range: Southern Arizona and northern Mexico.
Comments: This handsome plant has the long,
tubular, reddish flowers typical of many
plants visited by hummingbirds.

181 Yerba Buena
Satureja douglasii

Description: Long, slender, trailing stems with
*1 white or pale purplish, bilaterally
symmetrical flower* in each upper
leaf axil.
Flowers: Corolla about ¼″ (6 mm) long;
upper corolla lip short, projecting
forward, with a shallow notch at
tip; lower corolla lip longer,
3-lobed, bent downward; stamens 4.
Leaves: ½–1″ (1.5–2.5 cm) long, opposite,
roundish.
Height: Creeper; erect stems to 1′ (30 cm),
trailing stems to 2′ (60 cm) long.
Flowering: April–October.
Habitat: Shaded woods.
Range: Southern British Columbia,
northern Idaho, and south on
western side of Cascade Range
and Sierra Nevada to Baja California.
Comments: The common name Yerba
Buena, Spanish for "good herb,"
has been applied to several
species of mint, especially Spearmint
(Mentha spicata), but in the West
it generally refers to *S. douglasii.*
The mild and delightful tea made
from the leaves of this delicately
fragrant plant has been used to
treat many ailments and to
alleviate the pain of childbirth.

599 Marsh Skullcap
Scutellaria galericulata

Description: A plant growing in patches, with *1 blue to purple, bilaterally symmetrical flower in each upper leaf axil.*

Flowers: Corolla ½–¾" (1.5–2 cm) long, upper lip helmet-shaped, lower lip bent downward; upper and lower edges of calyx without teeth, with a raised crest across top.

Leaves: ¾–2" (2–5 cm) long, opposite, lanceolate, faintly scalloped on edges.

Height: 4–31" (10–80 cm).

Flowering: June–September.

Habitat: Wet meadows, swamps, and along streams at moderate elevations.

Range: Throughout much of the Northern Hemisphere; in West, south to central California, southern Idaho, northern Arizona, northern New Mexico, and Nebraska; also in eastern United States.

Comments: This species also occurs in Eurasia. In the West, where many species of *Scutellaria* prefer dry sites, this is one that prefers a moist habitat.

Marsh Skullcap

600   Austin's Skullcap
Scutellaria siphocampyloides

Description:	A low plant with pairs of *deep blue-violet, bilaterally symmetrical flowers angling upward* atop erect stems.
Flowers:	Corolla 1–1½″ (2.5–4 cm) long, upper lip arching forward like a small helmet, lower lip bent down, slender tube curving upward at base; calyx broad, bell-shaped, 2-lipped, with a crescent-shaped ridge or crest across top.
Leaves:	½–1″ (1.5–2.5 cm) long, nearly erect, lanceolate, broadest well above middle, without stalks.
Height:	4–12″ (10–30 cm).
Flowering:	May–July.
Habitat:	In gravelly or rocky places among pines and brush.
Range:	Most of California.
Comments:	The species is representative of several skullcaps with dark blue-violet flowers. Narrowleaf Skullcap *(S. angustifolia),* which grows from eastern Washington south to southeastern Oregon and east to northern and central Idaho, has leaves with definite stalks and a corolla ¾–1¼″ (2–3 cm) long. Snapdragon Skullcap *(S. antirrhinoides),* found from southern Idaho to southern Oregon, northern California, central Nevada, and Utah, has flowers only ½–¾″ (1.5–2 cm) long.

407   Texas Betony; Scarlet Hedge Nettle
Stachys coccinea

Description:	A stout, erect, leafy plant covered with soft hairs and bearing *scarlet, bilaterally symmetrical flowers in whorls at intervals in a spike* atop 4-sided stems.
Flowers:	¾–1″ (2–2.5 cm) long; corolla with a faint but abrupt constriction in tube near base, upper lip bent upward, 3-lobed lower lip bent downward.
Leaves:	To 3″ (7.5 cm) long, opposite, nearly triangular, with teeth on edges.
Height:	To 3′ (90 cm).
Flowering:	March–October.

Habitat: Moist rich soil in rock crevices of steep stony slopes.

Range: Central Arizona east to western Texas and south to northern Mexico.

Comments: *Stachys* species have no stinging hairs, as do true nettles, but some have rather stiff hairs and resemble nettles in other ways, especially before flowering. In the Old World some grow near hedges, hence the latter part of the common name. Its scarlet color distinguishes this species from other western *Stachys*, which are pink or purplish.

512 Great Hedge Nettle
Stachys cooleyae

Description: Stout, *4-sided, leafy stems* growing in patches and topped by *deep purplish-pink to reddish-lavender, bilaterally symmetrical flowers in whorls at intervals* in a spike.

Flowers: Corolla ½–1″ (1.5–2.5 cm) long; upper corolla lip projecting like a short hood; lower corolla lip 3-lobed, much longer, bent downward.

Leaves: 2½–6″ (6.5–15 cm) long, opposite, with stalks, broadly lanceolate, with blunt teeth on edges.

Height: 2–5′ (60–150 cm).

Flowering: June–August.

Habitat: Swamps and moist low ground from sea level to moderate elevations.

Range: Southern British Columbia south to southern Oregon from eastern slopes of Cascade Range to Pacific Coast.

Comments: The moist habitat is typical of hedge nettles. Other western species may have smaller, paler flowers and middle and upper leaves without stalks.

609 Vinegar Weed; Common Blue Curls
Trichostema lanceolatum

Description: A tall, leafy, *malodorous plant* with *pale blue to purple, bilaterally symmetrical flowers* in long clusters in leaf axils.

Flowers: About ½" (1.5 cm) long; corolla with a narrow tube strongly bent upward near base of 5 narrow lobes; stamens 4, long, with style projecting from between upper 2 corolla lobes, bent toward back of flower, then arching up and forward.

Leaves: ¾–3" (2–7.5 cm) long, narrowly lanceolate, opposite, usually much longer than section of stem between pairs of leaves.

Height: 2–5′ (60–150 cm).

Flowering: July–October.

Habitat: Dry slopes and fields.

Range: Northwestern Oregon south to Baja California.

Comments: The genus name comes from the Greek *trichos* ("hair") and *stemon* ("stamen"), referring to the long slender stamens, which are characteristic of the genus. Among the several other species is the handsome, pleasantly aromatic shrub Woolly Blue Curls *(T. lanatum),* also known as Romero, which grows in southern California and has blue flowers in dense, terminal clusters covered with violet wool.

BLADDERWORT FAMILY
Lentibulariaceae

Herbs of moist or aquatic habitats, usually carnivorous, with flowers borne singly or in racemes.

Flowers: Bilaterally symmetrical. Sepals 2–5, united; petals 5, united, forming an upper and lower lip, lower lip with a backward-projecting spur; stamens 2; all these parts attached at base of ovary.

Leaves: Alternate or in rosettes, simple or highly divided.

Fruit: 1-chambered, several-seeded capsule, with a central column to which seeds attach.

This small family has about 5 genera and 200 species, distributed throughout the world.

---

592 Common Butterwort
Pinguicula vulgaris

Description: A small plant with stalkless, *broadly lanceolate leaves in a basal rosette* and 1 bilaterally symmetrical, lavender or purple flower (rarely white) on a leafless stalk.

Flowers: About ½″ (1.5 cm) wide; corolla with 2-lobed upper lip, 3-lobed lower lip, backward-projecting spur about ¼–⅜″ (5–9 mm) long.

Leaves: ¾–2″ (2–5 cm) long, fleshy, densely studded with microscopic glands giving a greasy feel to upper surface.

Height: 2–6″ (5–15 cm).

Flowering: April–August.

Habitat: Bogs and wet soil, rocks, and banks.

Range: Alaska south to northwestern California and east across Canada and northern United States.

Comments: This species also occurs in Eurasia. The genus name means "greasy little one," referring to the slimy upper surface and fatty texture of the soft fleshy leaves. Small organisms that stick to the leaves are digested by the plant.

296 Common Bladderwort; Horned Bladderwort
Utricularia vulgaris

Description: A small floating plant with 6–20 bilaterally symmetrical, yellow flowers in each rather stout, erect raceme.

Flowers: Corolla about ½–¾″ (1.5–2 cm) long, with a spur curving forward and downward from near base.

Leaves: ½–2″ (1.5–5 cm) long, repeatedly and finely divided into almost hair-like segments, with bladders to ⅛″ (3 mm) wide.

Height: Aquatic; flower stalks 2½–8″ (6.5–20 cm) above water.

Flowering: June–August.

Habitat: Ponds and slow-moving water.

Range: Throughout much of North America.

Comments: This species also occurs in Eurasia. Of possibly five *Utricularia* species in the West, several difficult to distinguish, this has the largest flowers. Another species easy to identify is Mountain Bladderwort *(U. intermedia)*, with bladders on special branches distinct from the leaves. In all species of *Utricularia* the bladders are elaborate traps. When a small organism brushes hairs near a bladder pore, the pore's tiny door opens inward and water rushes inside, carrying the organism with it. The door quickly closes, the trapping process taking $\frac{1}{460}$ second. Enzymes digest the victim. Comparatively large organisms, such as mosquito larvae, may be caught in the door; if the door is repeatedly triggered, they are then digested little by little.

LILY FAMILY
Liliaceae

Mostly perennial herbs (some rather woody and tree-like) growing from rhizomes, bulbs, or swollen, underground stems, often with showy flowers borne singly or in some-times branched clusters.

Flowers: Usually bisexual, radially symmetrical. Calyx with 3 (rarely 2) separate sepals, green or colored like petals; corolla with 3 (rarely 2) separate petals; or 6 (rarely 4) petal-like segments united below into a tube; stamens usually 6; all these parts attached at base of ovary.
Leaves: Alternate, whorled, or basal; simple, usually narrow.
Fruit: 3-chambered capsule, with at least 3 seeds; or a berry, with at least 1 seed.

This extremely complex family has about 280 genera and 4,000 species. Many botanists subdivide this family, but it has not yet been agreed how many families there are, or which species belong to certain families. Many species, including tulips *(Tulipa)* and day lilies *(Hemerocallis),* are handsome ornamentals. Species of asparagus *(Asparagus)* and onion *(Allium),* as well as of the medicinally useful genus *Aloe,* are members of this family. A few species are poisonous.

548 Hooker's Onion
Allium acuminatum

Description: An *oniony-smelling* plant with *1 umbel of pink or deep pink flowers* atop a leafless stalk.
Flowers: About ½″ (1.5 cm) long; petal-like segments 6, each with a long point,

inner 3 slightly longer than outer 3, edges with almost microscopic teeth; bracts beneath umbel 2, papery, pointed.

Leaves: 4–6″ (10–15 cm) long, 2–3, at base, very narrow.

Height: 4–12″ (10–30 cm).

Flowering: May–July.

Habitat: Open, often rocky slopes among brush and pines.

Range: British Columbia south to central California and southern Arizona, and east to western New Mexico, western Colorado, and southern Wyoming.

Comments: This is one of the most common of the many western wild onions; all have edible bulbs, but some are extremely potent or unpalatable. Native Americans saved at least one exploration party from scurvy by alerting the ill explorers to the curative properties of wild onions. One must exercise caution, however, for there are several quite poisonous plants that appear similar to *Allium* species.

547 Nodding Onion
Allium cernuum

Description: A long *erect stalk, bent like a shepherd's crook, with 1 umbel of many pink or white flowers hanging at tip,* growing from a basal cluster of several long narrow leaves.

Nodding Onion

Flowers:	About ¼" (6 mm) long; petal-like segments 6, ovate; bracts beneath umbel 2, papery, dropping off by flowering time.
Leaves:	2–10" (5–25 cm) long.
Height:	4–20" (10–50 cm).
Flowering:	June–October.
Habitat:	Moist soil in sagebrush and woods.
Range:	Across northern North America; in West, south to southern Oregon, Arizona, New Mexico, western Texas, and adjacent regions of Mexico; also throughout much of East.
Comments:	The nodding umbel distinguishes this from all other species of *Allium* in the West.

351 Golden Stars
Bloomeria crocea

Description:	*1 umbel of yellow to orange, star-like flowers atop a stem with 1 narrow, grass-like leaf at base.*
Flowers:	½–1" (1.5–2.5 cm) wide; petal-like segments 6, separate, with dark lines down middle; stamens 6, each with a cup-like flap at base of filament, notched at tip.
Leaves:	4–12" (10–30 cm) long, ¼–½" (5–13 mm) wide.
Height:	6–24" (15–60 cm).
Flowering:	April–June.
Habitat:	Dry flats and on hillsides in grass, brush, and oak woodlands.
Range:	Southern third of California to Baja California.
Comments:	The golden, star-like flowers with separate petal-like parts distinguish this genus. The similar San Diego Golden Stars *(Muilla clevelandii)* is threatened by urbanization; it has several leaves, each less than ⅛" (3 mm) wide, and the flap at the base of each stamen is not notched.

576 Elegant Brodiaea; Harvest Brodiaea
Brodiaea elegans

Description: *1 umbel of several violet or blue-violet,*
funnel-shaped flowers atop a leafless stalk
bearing few long, very narrow, basal
leaves usually withered by flowering
time.

Flowers: 1–1½″ (2.5–4 cm) long; petal-like
segments 6, narrow; stamens 3, inside,
alternating with flat white scales
separated from and shorter than stamens.

Leaves: 4–16″ (10–40 cm) long.

Height: 4–20″ (10–50 cm).

Flowering: April–July.

Habitat: Dry plains and grassy hillsides.

Range: Northern Oregon south to southern
California.

Comments: This plant begins to flower as fields dry
out in the early summer. Several species
of *Brodiaea* (pronounced *bro-dee-ah*) are
similar. In *B. coronaria,* so similar it is
also commonly known as Harvest
Brodiaea, found from British Columbia
south to southern California, the scales
between the stamens are concave on
their inner side, longer than the
stamens, and lean toward them. One of
the handsomest near relatives to this
group is *Triteleia laxa,* known variously
as Wally Basket, Grass Nut, or Ithuriel's
Spear, which grows in heavy soil in
grasslands or brush from southern
Oregon to southern California; it reaches
a height of up to 28″ (70 cm) and has
many flowers in a large umbel, each
flower with six stamens and beneath the
ovary a stalk two or three times its length.

74 White Globe Lily; Fairy Lantern
Calochortus albus

Description: *Egg-shaped, white flowers hanging* in an
open branched cluster.

Flowers: About 1″ (2.5 cm) long; sepals 3,
greenish white, often purplish-tinged,
lanceolate; petals 3, broad, satiny, white.

Leaves:	Those on branched stems 2–6″ (5–15 cm) long; single leaf at base 8–20″ (20–50 cm) long.
Height:	1–2′ (30–60 cm).
Flowering:	April–June.
Habitat:	Shaded, often rocky places in open woods and brush.
Range:	Southern two-thirds of California.
Comments:	The several *Calochortus* species with egg-shaped flowers are generally called globe lilies, whereas those with more open flowers are known as mariposa lilies and star tulips. Other common names of this species include White Fairy Lantern, Snowdrops, Indian Bells, and Satin Bells. Rose Globe Lily (*C. amoenus*), with deep pink flowers, grows on the western slopes of the Sierra Nevada in California's San Joaquin Valley.

240 Yellow Globe Lily; Golden Fairy Lantern; Diogenes's Lantern
Calochortus amabilis

Description:	*Deep, clear yellow, egg-shaped flowers* hanging in an open branched cluster.
Flowers:	About 1″ (2.5 cm) long; sepals 3, each about ¾″ (2 cm) long, lanceolate; petals 3, broad, slightly longer than sepals, finely fringed on edges, bearing on inner surface a crescent-shaped gland covered by yellow hairs.
Leaves:	Those on branched stems ¾–8″ (2–20 cm) long; single leaf at base to 20″ (50 cm) long, narrow.
Height:	8–20″ (20–50 cm).
Flowering:	April–June.
Habitat:	Dry slopes in brush and open woods.
Range:	Northern California.
Comments:	The nodding, yellow flowers are a delight to behold, as indicated by the plant's scientific name, which translates as "lovable, beautiful grass."

55 Elegant Cat's Ears; Star Tulip
Calochortus elegans

Description: A small plant with slender bent stems with *few white flowers* in a branched cluster shorter than *1 grass-like leaf.*

Flowers: About 1″ (2.5 cm) wide; sepals 3, lanceolate; petals 3, broad, slightly longer than sepals, densely hairy on surface, each often with a purple crescent near base above a gland bearing a fringed membrane on lower side.

Leaves: 4–8″ (10–20 cm) long.

Height: 2–8″ (5–20 cm).

Flowering: May–June.

Habitat: Grassy hillsides and open coniferous woods.

Range: Southeastern Washington and northeastern Oregon east to western Montana; also in southwestern Oregon and northwestern California.

Comments: The common name Elegant Cat's Ears refers to each petal's resemblance to a kitten's ear, and Star Tulip refers to the overall flower shape. Similar species are distinguished by characteristics of the gland and pod.

372 Desert Mariposa Lily
Calochortus kennedyi var. *kennedyi*

Description: Short stems topped by umbel-like clusters of 1–6 handsome, *bell-shaped, vermilion or orange flowers.*

Flowers: 1–2″ (2.5–4 cm) wide; sepals 3, lanceolate; petals 3, broad, fan-shaped, each with a dark maroon blotch near base and a round depressed gland surrounded by a fringed membrane; few hairs with enlarged tips present near gland.

Leaves: 4–8″ (10–20 cm) long, few, narrowly lanceolate.

Height: 4–20″ (10–50 cm).

Flowering: March–June.

Habitat: Heavy soil in open or brushy areas from Creosote Bush deserts to piñon-juniper rangelands.

Range: Southern California and southern
Nevada east to central Arizona and
south to northwestern Mexico.

Comments: This is one of the most brilliant of
the mariposa lilies; all color phases
are spectacular. The vermilion phase
is more common in California, and
the orange is more common to the
east. There is also a yellow phase
(known as *C. kennedyi* var. *munzii*),
which is occasionally found
throughout the range, especially
at higher elevations.

220 Yellow Mariposa Lily
Calochortus luteus

Description: Slender stems with few narrow leaves
topped by *1–4 large, deep yellow, bell-
shaped flowers* in an umbel-like cluster.

Flowers: 1–1½" (2.5–4 cm) wide; sepals 3,
lanceolate; petals 3, broad, fan-shaped,
long, each usually with fine, red-brown
lines on lower portion and red-brown
blotch at center; gland near petal base
broadly crescent-shaped, covered with
short matted hairs.

Leaves: 4–8" (10–20 cm) long.

Height: 8–24" (20–60 cm).

Flowering: April–June.

Habitat: Heavy soil in grasslands and open forests
at low elevations.

Range: California's Channel Islands, Coast
Ranges, and western foothills of Sierra
Nevada.

Comments: This species and some others in the
genus frequently reproduce asexually by
means of small bulblets in the leaf axils
that drop to the ground and grow into
new plants.

454 Sagebrush Mariposa Lily
Calochortus macrocarpus

Description: Stout, erect, generally unbranched stems
topped by *1–3 handsome, bell-shaped, lilac
flowers* in a loose, umbel-like cluster.

Flowers: 1½–2½″ (4–6.5 cm) wide; sepals 3,
narrowly lanceolate, slightly longer than
petals; petals 3, broad, fan-shaped, each
with a greenish stripe down middle;
oblong gland near petal base surrounded
by a fringed membrane, often marked
above by a deep lilac, crescent-shaped
patch.

Leaves: 2–4″ (5–10 cm) long, several on stem,
very narrow, usually curled at tip.

Height: 8–20″ (20–50 cm).

Flowering: May–August.

Habitat: Loose dry soil on plains, in sagebrush,
and in Ponderosa Pine forests.

Range: Southern British Columbia south to
northern California and northern
Nevada on eastern side of Cascade
Range, and east across central and
northern Idaho to western Montana.

Comments: This is one of the most frequent
mariposa lilies in the arid Northwest.
A white phase with a reddish stripe on
each petal occurs in southeastern
Washington and adjacent regions of
west-central Idaho.

---

58 Sego Lily
Calochortus nuttallii

Description: Erect, unbranched stems with few leaves
topped by *1–4 showy, white, bell-shaped
flowers* in an umbel-like cluster.

Flowers: 1–2″ (2.5–5 cm) wide; sepals 3,
lanceolate, slightly shorter than petals;
petals 3, broad, fan-shaped, each yellow
around gland at base and marked with
reddish brown or purple above; gland
circular, surrounded by a fringed
membrane.

Leaves: 2–4″ (5–10 cm) long, narrow edges
rolled upward.

Height: 6–18″ (15–45 cm).

Flowering: May–July.

Habitat: Dry soil on plains, in sagebrush, and in
open pine forests.

Range: Eastern Idaho east through southern
Wyoming to northwestern Nebraska
and southwestern North Dakota, and

south to southern Nevada, northern
Arizona, and northwestern New Mexico.

Comments: Occasionally petals are magenta or
tinged with lilac. This is Utah's state
flower; the Utes called it *sago,* and
taught Mormon settlers to eat the bulbs
when food was scarce.

645 Camas
Camassia quamash

Description: A raceme of *light to deep violet-blue, star-
shaped flowers,* and several narrow, grass-
like leaves mostly near base.

Flowers: 1½–2½″ (4–6.5 cm) wide, *slightly
bilaterally symmetrical;* petal-like
segments 6, narrow, lower segments
tending to curve out from stem more
strongly than upper ones.

Leaves: To 2′ (60 cm) long.

Height: 8–28″ (20–70 cm).

Flowering: April–June.

Habitat: Moist meadows.

Range: Southern British Columbia south to
northern California and east to northern
Utah, Wyoming, and Montana.

Comments: This species is sometimes so abundant it
colors entire meadows with blue-violet.
Native Americans pit-roasted the bland
bulbs with other leaves, and also boiled
them to yield a syrup. A phase growing
west of the Cascade Range and the Sierra
Nevada has radially symmetrical
flowers; it has been classified *C.
leichtlinii* but now is usually included
within *C. quamash.*

64 Wavy-leaved Soap Plant; Amole
Chlorogalum pomeridianum

Description: Delicate, *star-like, white flowers* in a *large,
freely and openly branched cluster.*

Flowers: 1–1½″ (2.5–4 cm) wide; petal-like
segments 6, narrow, curving back.

Leaves: To 2′ (60 cm) long, several, narrow, grass-
like, mostly at base, with wavy edges.

Height: 2–10′ (60–300 cm).

Wavy-leaved Soap Plant

Flowering: May–August.

Habitat: Dry open hills and plains, often in open brush or woods.

Range: Southwestern Oregon south to southern California.

Comments: By day this plant appears ungainly, the branches stark and unattractive, but toward evening, or on cloudy days, the delicate flowers open, resembling thistledown caught among the twigs. Native Americans crushed the plant's bulbs and added water to produce a lather for cleaning clothing and baskets. They also roasted bulbs to produce a substance used to glue feathers to arrow shafts and to treat rashes caused by Poison Oak.

420 Red Clintonia; Andrew's Clintonia
Clintonia andrewsiana

Description: *1 umbel-like cluster of red or reddish-lavender, narrowly bell-shaped flowers* atop a nearly leafless stalk growing from a basal rosette; smaller, few-flowered clusters occasionally beneath main flower cluster.

Flowers: Petal-like segments 6, each about ½" (1.5 cm) long, narrow.

Leaves:	6–10″ (15–25 cm) long, usually 5–6, broadly elliptical.
Fruit:	Deep blue berry, to ½″ (1.5 cm) long.
Height:	10–20″ (25–50 cm).
Flowering:	May–July.
Habitat:	Shaded damp forests near coast.
Range:	Southwestern Oregon south to central California.
Comments:	This is one of the few wildflowers that grow in the dim light of the Pacific Coast Redwood forests. The genus name honors DeWitt Clinton, a naturalist and governor of New York in the early 19th century.

63   Queen's Cup; Bride's Bonnet
Clintonia uniflora

Description:	*1 (rarely 2) white, star-like flower* on each short leafless stalk growing from a basal cluster of *2–3 oblong or elliptical, shiny leaves.*
Flowers:	1–1½″ (2.5–4 cm) wide; petal-like segments 6, lanceolate, forming a broad bell.
Leaves:	2½–6″ (6.5–15 cm) long.
Fruit:	Lustrous, deep blue berry, ¼–½″ (6–13 mm) long.
Height:	2½–6″ (6.5–15 cm).
Flowering:	May–July.
Habitat:	Coniferous forests, often where moist.
Range:	Alaska south along Pacific Coast to northern California and inland to southern Sierra Nevada, and east to eastern Oregon and western Montana.
Comments:	There are generally several clusters of leaves in a patch, for the plant produces an extensive system of underground stems.

625   Ookow
Dichelostemma congestum

Description:	*1 head of blue-violet flowers* atop a long stalk with few grass-like leaves at base.
Flowers:	½–¾″ (1.5–2 cm) long; petal-like segments 6, joined to form a broad tube

not or only barely constricted just below opening; stamens 3, each with a forked scale; between stamens is a tiny stub.

Leaves: 1–3' (30–90 cm) long, ¼–½" (6–13 mm) wide.

Height: 1–3' (30–90 cm).

Flowering: April–June.

Habitat: Open, grassy hillsides.

Range: Western Washington south to central California.

Comments: This wildflower blooms as grasses mature and begin to brown, signaling the onset of summer. Roundtooth Ookow *(D. multiflorum),* found from southern Oregon south to central California, has round ends on the three scales projecting from the center of the flower. Blue Dicks *(D. capitatum),* found from southern Oregon south to northwestern Mexico and east to southern Utah and southern New Mexico, has six stamens hidden within the flower tube and no projecting scales.

419 Firecracker Flower
Dichelostemma ida-maia

Description: *Tubular, red flowers hanging in an umbel atop a leafless stalk commonly with 3 long, narrow, grass-like leaves at base.*

Flowers: 1–1½" (2.5–4 cm) long; petal-like segments 6, joined into a red tube; *separate tip of each segment yellow-green,* short, curling back around tube opening; 3 cream stamens and 3 short, pale yellow scales projecting from center of tube.

Leaves: 12–20" (30–50 cm) long.

Height: 1–3' (30–90 cm).

Flowering: May–July.

Habitat: Grassy slopes in woodland openings at low or moderate elevations.

Range: Southwestern Oregon to northwestern California.

Comments: The brilliant red flowers resemble loose clusters of firecrackers tied together by the ends of their fuses. It is one of the

most charming and unusual of
California wildflowers. The species
name is said to have been suggested by a
stagecoach driver who showed the plant
to an early collector; it honors the
driver's niece, Ida May.

65 Wartberry Fairybell
Disporum trachycarpum

Description: A beautiful woodland plant with 1–2
small, *creamy white, narrowly bell-shaped
flowers hanging beneath leaves* at ends of
forking branches.

Flowers: ⅜–⅝" (9–16 mm) long; petal-like
segments 6; style without hairs.

Leaves: 1½–5" (4–12.5 cm) long, many along
stem, ovate, round or indented at base,
smooth on upper surface, with hairs on
edges sticking straight out.

Fruit: Round berry, about ⅜" (9 mm) wide, at
first yellow, becoming red.

Height: 1–2' (30–60 cm).

Flowering: May–July.

Habitat: Wooded areas, often near streams.

Range: British Columbia south to northeastern
Oregon, east to eastern North Dakota,
and south through Rocky Mountain
region to western New Mexico and
southern Arizona.

Comments: The regularly forked branches of this
attractive and orderly plant bear leaves
that are mostly oriented horizontally.
There are two other western species.
Smith's Fairybell *(D. smithii),* which
grows in moist woods on the western
side of the Cascade Range and the Sierra
Nevada from British Columbia south to
central California, has the largest
flowers, ½–1" (1.5–2.5 cm) long.
Hooker's Fairybell *(D. hookeri),* which
occurs from British Columbia south to
northwestern Oregon and east to
Alberta and western Montana, is very
similar to Wartberry Fairybell, but the
style is usually hairy, as are the upper
surfaces of the leaves, and the hairs on
the leaf edges point forward.

111 Lonely Lily
Eremocrinum albomarginatum

Description: Few *white, star-like flowers* in a dense
raceme atop a stalk growing from a
basal cluster of long narrow leaves.

Flowers: ¾–1″ (2–2.5 cm) wide; petal-like
segments 6, broadly lanceolate.

Leaves: To 1′ (30 cm) long.

Height: 6–12″ (15–30 cm).

Flowering: June.

Habitat: Sandy soil.

Range: Southern Utah and northern Arizona.

Comments: The genus name is from the Greek
eremos ("lonely, solitary, desolate") and
krinon ("lily"). It is the only species in
its genus, and it occurs in one of the
most sparsely populated parts of
the continent.

238 Yellow Fawn Lily
Erythronium grandiflorum

Description: *1–5 pale to golden yellow flowers hanging* at
end of a stalk growing between *2 broadly
lanceolate basal leaves.*

Flowers: Petal-like segments 6, each 1–2″
(2.5–5 cm) long, lanceolate, curving
back behind base; stamens 6,
protruding from center.

Leaves: 4–8″ (10–20 cm) long, gradually
tapering to a broad stalk.

Fruit: Swollen, 3-sided capsule.

Height: 6–12″ (15–30 cm).

Flowering: March–August.

Habitat: Sagebrush slopes and mountain
woodland openings, often near
melting snow.

Range: Southern British Columbia south to
northern California and east to western
Colorado, Wyoming, and western
Montana.

Comments: This species often blooms as snow
recedes. A form with white or cream
petal-like segments with a band of
golden yellow at the base grows in
southeastern Washington and adjacent
regions of Idaho. Another species with

bright yellow flowers, Mother Lode
Fawn Lily *(E. tuolumnense),* grows in
low-elevation woodlands on the western
slopes of the Sierra Nevada.

66 Avalanche Lily; Glacier Lily
Erythronium montanum

Description:	*1–5 showy white flowers nodding at end of a stalk* growing between *2 broadly lanceolate basal leaves.*
Flowers:	About 2½″ (6.5 cm) wide; petal-like segments 6, curving back, white except for yellow band at base, becoming pink with age; stamens 6, protruding from center.
Leaves:	4–8″ (10–20 cm) long, abruptly tapering to a distinct stalk.
Height:	6–10″ (15–25 cm).
Flowering:	June–September.
Habitat:	Alpine or subalpine meadows and forests.
Range:	British Columbia south to northern Oregon.
Comments:	This mountain species blooms just after the snow melts, often carpeting meadows with its white flowers. There are a number of similar western species, some with cream or yellow flowers, others with pinkish ones.

379 Mission Bells; Checker Lily
Fritillaria affinis

Description:	Several *nodding, greenish-brown, deeply bowl-shaped flowers* on an erect stem, leafy in upper part, leafless below.
Flowers:	¾–1½″ (2–4 cm) long; petal-like segments 6, lanceolate, brownish, mottled green or yellow.
Leaves:	1¼–6″ (3–15 cm) long, lanceolate, generally less than 10 times as long as wide, in several whorls on stem.
Height:	1–4′ (30–120 cm).
Flowering:	February–June.
Habitat:	Grassy or brushy flats and slopes and in open woods.

Range: Southern British Columbia south to southern California and east to northern Idaho.

Comments: The genus name comes from the Latin *fritillus* (meaning "dice box") and refers to the short broad fruit capsule, which is characteristic of the genus. There are several similar species. Spotted Mountain Bells *(F. atropurpurea)*, also called Checker Lily throughout much of the West, has flowers ½–¾" (1.5–2 cm) long and leaves at least 15 times as long as wide. Black Lily or Kamchatka Fritillary *(F. camschatcensis)*, found from Alaska south to northwestern Washington, has dark purplish-brown flowers. Chocolate Lily *(F. biflora)*, found in the Coast Ranges of California, has dark brownish, unmottled flowers, and all its leaves are on the lower part of the stem.

453 Adobe Lily
Fritillaria pluriflora

Description: *1–7 nodding, pinkish-lavender, bell-shaped flowers in an open raceme above leaves.*

Flowers: 1–1½" (2.5–4 cm) long; petal-like segments 6; stamens 6, hidden inside; style longer than stamens.

Leaves: To 5" (12.5 cm) long, narrowly lanceolate, clustered near base.

Height: 1–18" (2.5–45 cm).

Flowering: February–April.

Habitat: Heavy soil in grasslands and in brush.

Range: Oregon south to interior hills of Coast Ranges of northern California.

Comments: This is one of the prettiest species of *Fritillaria.* Generally only a few scattered plants are seen. Candy Bells *(F. striata)*, found in the hills at the southern end of California's San Joaquin Valley, has white or pink flowers, often with red stripes, and a style not longer than the stamens. Fragrant Fritillary *(F. liliacea)*, which grows near the central California coast in brush or forest, has white flowers with pale green stripes.

235 Yellow Bell; Yellow Fritillary
Fritillaria pudica

Description: A dainty plant with *1 yellow, narrowly bell-shaped, hanging flower.*

Flowers: ½–1″ (1.5–2.5 cm) long; petal-like segments 6.

Leaves: 2–8″ (5–20 cm) long, 2 or several borne near mid-stem.

Height: 4–12″ (10–30 cm).

Flowering: March–June.

Habitat: Grasslands, in sagebrush, and open coniferous forests.

Range: British Columbia south on eastern side of Cascade Range to northern California, and east to Alberta, western North Dakota, central Wyoming, and northwestern Colorado.

Comments: This charming, modest fritillary is unmistakable; the narrow, yellow bell becomes rusty red or purplish as the flower ages.

392 Scarlet Fritillary
Fritillaria recurva

Description: A smooth, gray-green plant with most leaves near mid-stem and *1–9 scarlet, narrowly bell-shaped flowers* hanging in an open raceme at top.

Flowers: ¾–1¼″ (2–3 cm) long, outside tinged with purple, inside checkered with yellow; petal-like segments 6, tip of each curving back.

Leaves: 1–4″ (2.5–10 cm) long, narrow.

Height: 1–3′ (30–90 cm).

Flowering: March–July.

Habitat: Dry, brushy or wooded hillsides.

Range: Southern Oregon south to central California and western Nevada.

Comments: This is the only red fritillary. The species name refers to the recurved tips of the petal-like segments. However, in the inner parts of the Coast Ranges of northern California grows a brilliant red-flowered form whose petal-like segment tips are not recurved.

69 Desert Lily
Hesperocallis undulata

Description:	*Large, white, funnel-shaped flowers* in a stout raceme above long, narrow, *basal leaves with wavy edges.*
Flowers:	To 2½″ (6.5 cm) long; petal-like segments 6, each with a bluish-green band on back.
Leaves:	8–20″ (20–50 cm) long.
Height:	1–6′ (30–180 cm).
Flowering:	March–May.
Habitat:	Sandy, desert flats and gentle slopes.
Range:	Southeastern California, western Arizona, and northwestern Mexico.
Comments:	The genus name means "western beauty," an apt name for this plant that resembles a small commercial Easter Lily *(Lilium longiflorum)* and grows in the harsh arid environment of the Southwest. Plants are conspicuous and easily seen as one drives along desert roads. The bulbs of this species, the only one in its genus, were once used by Native Americans for food.

67 Star Lily; Sand Lily; Mountain Lily
Leucocrinum montanum

Description:	A low plant with several *star-like, white flowers in a basal rosette of narrow, grass-like leaves.*
Flowers:	About 1¼″ (3 cm) wide; petal-like segments 6, lanceolate, joined at base to form a long slender tube attached to underground flower base.
Leaves:	To 8″ (20 cm) long.
Fruit:	Underground capsule.
Height:	To 8″ (20 cm).
Flowering:	April–June.
Habitat:	Among sagebrush and in open coniferous forests.
Range:	Central Oregon south to northern California and east to northern New

Mexico, Colorado, and western North
and South Dakota.

Comments: With its flowers nestled among the
leaves, this little lily is unmistakable.
The only species in the genus, it is also
known as Star of Bethlehem.

---

237   Tiger Lily; Columbia Lily; Oregon Lily
Lilium columbianum

Description: *Large, showy, orange to yellow-orange,*
nodding flowers atop a leafy stem.
Flowers: 2–3″ (5–7.5 cm) wide; petal-like
segments 6, each long, strongly curved
back behind base, yellow- to red-orange,
spotted with deep red or purple; stamens
6, with anthers less than ¼″ (6 mm) long.
Leaves: 2–4″ (5–10 cm) long, narrowly
lanceolate, in several whorls, or not in
whorls but evenly scattered along stem.
Fruit: Plump, 3-sided capsule.
Height: 2–4′ (60–120 cm).
Flowering: May–August.
Habitat: Prairies, thickets, and open forests.
Range: Southern British Columbia south to
northwestern California and east to
northern Nevada and Idaho.
Comments: This popular western wildflower is now
in serious decline because of habitat
destruction and from being dug up
for gardens, where it usually does
not do well. The similar Leopard
Lily *(L. pardalinum),* also called
Panther Lily, which grows along
forest streams or near springs
throughout most of California,
has bright orange-red flowers with
anthers ⅜–⅝″ (9–15 mm) long.

---

394   Rocky Mountain Lily; Wood Lily; Red Lily
Lilium philadelphicum

Description: *1–3 mostly red, funnel-shaped flowers*
atop an erect, leafy stem.
Flowers: 2–2½″ (5–6.5 cm) wide; petal-like

Rocky Mountain Lily

segments 6, lanceolate, each red or red-orange near gently outwardly curved tip, yellowish and with purple spots at base.

Leaves:	2–4″ (5–10 cm) long, narrowly lanceolate, lower ones scattered on stem, upper ones in 1–2 whorls.
Height:	12–28″ (30–70 cm).
Flowering:	June–August.
Habitat:	Meadows and forests, commonly in aspen groves.
Range:	British Columbia east to Saskatchewan, south along eastern edge of Rocky Mountains to southern New Mexico, and east to Michigan and Ohio.
Comments:	Formerly much more common, this species is too often picked by visitors to the mountains. It also may disappear rapidly from intensively grazed meadowland.

62 Cascade Lily; Washington Lily
Lilium washingtonianum

Description:	A stout leafy stem topped by several *large, fragrant, trumpet-shaped flowers, delicate, waxy white or pale pink, often dotted with minute, purple spots.*
Flowers:	3–4″ (7.5–10 cm) wide; petal-like segments 6.

Leaves:	2–4″ (5–10 cm) long, lanceolate, scattered on lower portion of stem, in several whorls on upper part.
Height:	2–7′ (60–210 cm).
Flowering:	June–July.
Habitat:	Brush and open forests.
Range:	Northern Oregon south to northern California mountains and southern Sierra Nevada.
Comments:	Northern races tend to be more deeply colored. Near Mount Shasta, in northern California, there is a race of this species called Shasta Lily that has narrower spaces between the petal-like segments. The species known variously as Chaparral Lily, Lilac Lily, Redwood Lily, or Chamise Lily *(L. rubescens),* which grows in brush or woods in the Coast Ranges of central and northern California, has smaller flowers, 1½–2½″ (4–6 cm) long, at first white with purple spots but aging to a rich wine color.

68 Alpine Lily
Lloydia serotina

Description:	Usually *1 broadly funnel-shaped, whitish flower* atop a stem about as tall as *very narrow basal leaves.*
Flowers:	About ¾″ (2 cm) wide; petal-like segments 6, oblong, each mostly white, yellowish at base, purplish on outside, with pale green or purple veins.
Leaves:	2–8″ (5–20 cm) long, mostly at base, several, very narrow.
Height:	2–6″ (5–15 cm).
Flowering:	June–July.
Habitat:	Gravelly ridges and in rock crevices high in mountains.
Range:	Alaska south to northwestern Oregon, northern Nevada, and northern Utah, and throughout Rocky Mountains to northern New Mexico.
Comments:	This is the only native species in the genus. It is also found in Eurasia, whereas the other 10–12 *Lloydia* species are found only in Eurasia.

141 False Lily-of-the-valley
Maianthemum dilatatum

Description: A plant growing in low patches with *slender racemes of tiny white flowers* held stiffly erect just above *heart-shaped leaves.*

Flowers: Petal-like segments 4, each about ⅛" (3 mm) long; stamens 4.

Leaves: 2–4½" (5–11.5 cm) long, usually 2 per stem.

Fruit: Red berry, ¼" (6 mm) wide.

Height: 6–14" (15–35 cm).

Flowering: May–June.

Habitat: Moist or shaded places in woods.

Range: Alaska south to Coast Ranges of northern California.

Comments: The genus name, from the Greek *maios* ("May") and *anthemon* ("flower"), refers to the time of flowering. Members of this genus have four petal-like segments, rather than the more common six among Liliaceae. This plant, which spreads by rhizomes, makes an attractive groundcover in woodland gardens. It vaguely resembles Lily-of-the-valley *(Convallaria majalis),* a European plant that is a popular ornamental in the United States, hence its common name.

382 Fetid Adder's Tongue; Slink Pod; Slink Lily
Scoliopus bigelovii

Description: A peculiar little plant with 3–12 leafless, *3-sided stalks,* each topped by 1 *dull reddish-brown and green flower,* growing between *2 basal leaves mottled with maroon patches.*

Flowers: About 1" (2.5 cm) wide; sepals 3, lanceolate, spreading, greenish with maroon veins; petals 3, erect, horn-like, maroon; stamens 3.

Leaves: 2½–8" (6.5–20 cm) long, broadly lanceolate.

Fruit: 3-angled capsule.

Height: To 8" (20 cm).

Flowering: February–March.
Habitat: Moist woods.
Range: Coast Ranges of northern California.
Comments: The genus name, from the Greek *skolios* ("crooked") and *pous* ("foot"), as well as the common names Slink Lily and Slink Pod, refer to the way the flower stalk bends and sprawls on the ground as the pod matures. The flowers have an unpleasant odor (hence the common name Fetid Adder's Tongue), which is what probably attracts flies as pollinators. The smaller Hall's Fetid Adder's Tongue *(S. hallii)* grows in western Oregon. Another common name for *S. bigelovii* is Brownies.

142 False Solomon's Seal
Smilacina racemosa

Description: Commonly with several leaning, leafy stems, each tipped with a *branched dense cluster of many tiny white flowers*.
Flowers: Petal-like segments 6, ovate, each about ⅛″ (2 mm) long; stamens 6, slightly longer.
Leaves: 2½–8″ (6.5–20 cm) long, ovate, clasping stem at base.
Fruit: Reddish berry, ¼″ (6 mm) long.

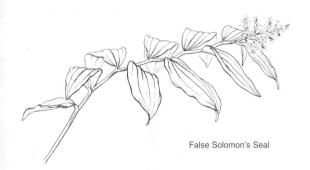

False Solomon's Seal

Height: 1–3' (30–90 cm).
Flowering: March–July.
Habitat: Moist woods from near sea level to moderate mountain elevations.
Range: Alaska south to California and east across much of West; also widespread in eastern North America, and in Mexico.
Comments: True solomon's seals (*Polygonatum*), found in the eastern United States, are similar in leaf arrangements but differ by having flowers in the leaf axils. Another western species, Star Solomon's Seal or Star Flower *(S. stellata),* has up to 20 flowers loosely assembled in a zigzag raceme, each appearing as a dainty, white, 6-pointed star about ¼" (6 mm) wide.

378 Western Stenanthium
Stenanthium occidentale

Description: *Pale greenish-bronze or purplish-green flowers resembling dainty bells* hanging in open racemes above several narrow, grass-like, basal leaves.
Flowers: ½–¾" (1.5–2 cm) long; petal-like segments 6, narrow, tip of each curving back.
Leaves: 4–12" (10–30 cm) long.

Western Stenanthium

Height: 4–20″ (10–50 cm).
Flowering: June–August.
Habitat: Wet cliffs and banks and moist mountain meadows and forests.
Range: British Columbia south to northern California and western Montana.
Comments: Flowers tend to turn to one side of the inflorescence and resemble miniature strings of bells, reminiscent of those once decorating horse-drawn sleighs.

393 Rosy Twisted-stalk
Streptopus roseus

Description: *Small, bell-shaped, pinkish- to reddish-brown flowers hanging on twisted stalks* along leafy stems.
Flowers: ¼–½″ (6–13 mm) long; petal-like segments 6, pale greenish brown and spotted or streaked with deep pink, often appearing reddish.
Leaves: 1¼–4″ (3–10 cm) long, broadly lanceolate.
Height: 6–16″ (15–40 cm).
Flowering: June–July.
Habitat: Moist woods and streambanks.
Range: Alaska south to Oregon; also in eastern Canada and northeastern United States.
Comments: The arching stems and orderly arrangement of leaves resemble those of fairybells *(Disporum)* and False Solomon's Seal *(Smilacina racemosa).* However, *Streptopus* (meaning "twisted foot," in reference to the contorted flower stalk) seems to break a botanical rule: The flowers appear not to grow from leaf axils as usual; they actually do, but the base of the flower stalk is fused to the stem up to the level of the next leaf so that it appears to grow from there.

104 Western False Asphodel
Tofieldia occidentalis

Description: A plant leafy in lower part and glandular in upper part, with many *tiny white flowers in a dense, often interrupted cluster* at top.

Flowers: Petal-like segments 6, each ⅛–¼″
(3–6 mm) long, spreading; stamens 6,
lying against segments.

Leaves: 2–8″ (5–20 cm) long, erect, narrow,
sheathing stem at base.

Height: 4–20″ (10–50 cm), sometimes to 31″
(80 cm).

Flowering: June–August.

Habitat: Wet places, meadows, and alpine ridges.

Range: Alaska south to central California and
east to Wyoming.

Comments: A satisfactory classification of the North
American races of *Tofieldia* has eluded
botanists; the western species are often
considered a western race of the more
widespread Sticky False Asphodel *(T.
glutinosa),* which also occurs in eastern
North America.

57 Western Wake Robin; Trillium
Trillium ovatum

Description: A low plant with *1 white flower on a short
stalk* growing from center of a *whorl of 3
broad ovate leaves* atop an otherwise
leafless stem.

Flowers: 1½–3″ (4–7.5 cm) wide; petals 3, ovate,
becoming pink or reddish with age.

Leaves: 2–8″ (5–20 cm) long, stalkless.

Height: 4–16″ (10–40 cm).

Flowering: February–June.

Habitat: Along streambanks and in open or deep
woods from low to high elevations.

Range: British Columbia south to central
California and east to northwestern
Colorado, Montana, and Alberta.

Comments: The common name Wake Robin indicates
that the flowers bloom in early spring,
about the time the robin arrives. Only
one other *Trillium* species in the West
has a stalk between the flower and the
leaves: Klamath Trillium *(T. rivale),*
found in southwestern Oregon and
northwestern California. Giant Wake
Robin *(T. chloropetolum),* which grows in
dense patches west of the Cascade Range
and in the Sierra Nevada, has no stalks
at the base of the mottled leaves. Its

petals vary from white to maroon; if maroon, they usually have a white base. Roundleaf Trillium *(T. petiolatum),* found in eastern Washington and Oregon, has long-stalked leaves and dark red-brown petals.

---

659   Douglas's Triteleia
Triteleia douglasii

Description: *Pale or deep blue, narrowly bell-shaped flowers in an umbel* atop a leafless stem with 1–2 grass-like, basal leaves.

Flowers: About ¾″ (2 cm) wide; petal-like segments 6, joined at base to form a broad tube about ½″ (1.5 cm) long, inner 3 segments strongly ruffled and nearly closing tube opening; stamens 6, attached to tube at different levels by filaments about as thick as broad.

Leaves: To 20″ (50 cm) long.

Height: 8–28″ (20–70 cm).

Flowering: April–July.

Habitat: In grassy areas, sagebrush, and pine forests.

Range: Southern British Columbia south on eastern side of Cascade Range to southeastern Oregon, and east to western Montana, western Wyoming, and northern Utah.

Comments: The ruffled, petal-like segments make this flower unusual. Howell's Triteleia *(T. howellii),* found from southern British Columbia south to northern Oregon near the Cascade Range, has much shorter flower stalks and only slightly ruffled petal-like segments varying from white to blue.

---

164   White Brodiaea
Triteleia hyacinthina

Description: *White, rarely pale blue, bowl-shaped flowers in an umbel* atop a stem with long, narrow, grass-like leaves at base.

Flowers: About ½″ (1.5 cm) wide; petal-like segments 6, joined at base, each with a greenish midvein.

Leaves:	4–16″ (10–40 cm) long.
Height:	10–28″ (25–70 cm).
Flowering:	May–August.
Habitat:	Grassy flats, especially low spots moist in spring, and in open areas in brush and forests.
Range:	Southern British Columbia south to northern two-thirds of California and east to northern Nevada and Idaho.
Comments:	The delicate, white, bowl-shaped flowers are unusual among the members of *Triteleia* and serve to distinguish this species, which perhaps appeared hyacinth-like to the naming botanist. At one time this species was included in the genus *Brodiaea,* hence its common name.

352 Pretty Face
Triteleia ixioides

Description:	*Yellow, funnel-shaped flowers in an umbel* atop a leafless stalk with few long, narrow, grass-like leaves at base.
Flowers:	About ¾″ (2 cm) wide; petal-like segments 6, lanceolate, joined at broad base; stamens 6, all attached at same level to cup-like flower base; scale tipped with 2 teeth on back of each stamen.
Leaves:	6–16″ (15–40 cm) long.
Height:	4–18″ (10–45 cm).
Flowering:	March–August.
Habitat:	Grassy, open areas and in open woods from low to high elevations.
Range:	Southern Oregon south to southern California.
Comments:	Some plants have cream, straw-colored, or dull yellow flowers, and in some others flowers become purplish with age.

126 California Corn Lily; False Hellebore
Veratrum californicum

Description:	A tall plant with a *long, branched, dense cluster of relatively small, whitish or greenish flowers* atop a stout leafy stem.

Flowers:	Petal-like segments 6, each ½–¾″ (1.5–2 cm) long, with a V-shaped, green gland at base.
Leaves:	8–12″ (20–30 cm) long, numerous, *broad, ovate, pleated,* without stalks, angled upward.
Height:	4–8′ (1.2–2.4 m).
Flowering:	June–August.
Habitat:	Swamps, creek bottoms, wet meadows, and moist forests.
Range:	Western Washington south to southern California and east to New Mexico, Colorado, Wyoming, and Montana.
Comments:	This species is extremely poisonous. Sheep that eat the plant in the early weeks of gestation produce lambs with deformed heads. The flowers are toxic even to insects and may cause serious losses in honeybee populations.

8 Green False Hellebore; Indian Poke
Veratrum viride

Description:	A stout plant with *large, somewhat hairy leaves* clasping a stem bearing a branching cluster *of greenish-white, star-shaped, hairy flowers.*
Flowers:	½–¾″ (1.5–2 cm) wide; petal-like segments 6, sometimes finely toothed on edges; stamens 6, curved.
Leaves:	6–14″ (15–35 cm) long, 3–6″ (7.5–15 cm) wide, *pleated, parallel-veined.*
Height:	2–7′ (60–210 cm).
Flowering:	July–August.
Habitat:	Wet mountain meadows and brushy areas.
Range:	Alaska south to northern California, Idaho, and Montana; also in East.
Comments:	Along with other species of *Veratrum,* this plant is distinguished by its size and large pleated leaves. Although used medicinally by Native Americans, the roots and leaves are poisonous to humans and livestock and should be avoided. The foliage has a burning taste and is ordinarily avoided by animals.

140 Bear Grass; Indian Basket Grass
Xerophyllum tenax

Description: Many tiny flowers in a *dense, broad, white raceme* atop a stout stalk growing from a *massive bunch of basal leaves.*

Flowers: Petal-like segments 6, each about ⅜" (9 mm) long, flat.

Leaves: About 1–2½' (30–75 cm) long, very narrow, basal.

Height: To 5' (1.5 m).

Flowering: May–August.

Habitat: Open woods and clearings, often above timberline.

Range: British Columbia south to central California and east to Idaho and Montana.

Comments: Native Americans used the leaves to weave garments and baskets and ate the roasted rootstock. This species is also called Elk Grass, Turkey Beard, Bear Lily, and Pine Lily.

103 Elegant Camas; Alkali Grass
Zigadenus elegans

Description: Long, grass-like, basal leaves, and *cream or greenish-white, bowl-shaped flowers* in a raceme or branched cluster.

Flowers: About ¾" (2 cm) wide; petal-like segments 6, broad, each with a greenish, heart-shaped gland at base; all parts attached around sides of ovary rather than at base.

Leaves: 6–12" (15–30 cm) long.

Height: 6–28" (15–70 cm).

Flowering: June–August.

Habitat: Mountain meadows, rocky slopes, and forests.

Range: Alaska southeast to Manitoba and south through western Washington, eastern Oregon, and Nevada to Arizona; in Rocky Mountain region south to New Mexico; and on Plains south to Nebraska, Iowa, and Missouri.

Comments: Species of *Zigadenus* are among the most infamous western plants, poisoning many livestock, especially sheep. Native Americans and early settlers were also poisoned whenever they mistook the bulbs for those of edible plants, such as camas species *(Camassia)*. The highly poisonous Death Camas *(Z. venenosus)* grows throughout most of the western United States; it has petal-like segments about ¼″ (6 mm) long, the inner three slightly longer and with a short stalk at the base, and stamens about as long as the segments.

FALSE MERMAID FAMILY
Limnanthaceae

Delicate, leafy herbs of moist places with usually white or yellow flowers on long slender stalks growing from leaf axils.

Flowers: Radially symmetrical. Sepals 3 or 5, separate; petals 3 or 5, separate; stamens 6 or 10, forming 2 circles; all these parts attached at base of ovary.
Leaves: Pinnately divided.
Fruit: 3 or 5 hard, 1-seeded nutlets.

There are 2 genera and about 12 species in this small family, all restricted to North America, primarily California.

218   Douglas's Meadow Foam
Limnanthes douglasii

Description: A delicate, branched plant bearing broadly bell-shaped flowers, usually with a *yellow center with a white rim* (sometimes all yellow or all white), on slender stalks in upper leaf axils.
Flowers: About ¾″ (2 cm) wide; petals 5, broad, notched at tip; stamens 10, each about ¼″ (6 mm) long.
Leaves: 2–5″ (5–12.5 cm) long, divided into jagged segments.
Fruit: Dividing into 5 smooth or slightly warty, seed-like nutlets.
Height: 4–16″ (10–40 cm).
Flowering: March–May.
Habitat: Low moist places in grasslands and open woods.
Range: Southern Oregon south to southern California.

Douglas's Meadow Foam

Comments: A form with all-yellow petals
grows on Point Reyes in northern
California; in the Coast Ranges
the flower may have white petals,
often with dark purple veins,
whereas in and around the Central
Valley the petals may be white
with rose veins, becoming all pink
with age.

FLAX FAMILY
Linaceae

Herbs, rarely shrubs or trees, with flowers in a forked
cluster.

Flowers: Radially symmetrical. Sepals 5, separate; petals 5,
separate, each with a narrow base, readily dropping off;
stamens 10, joined by bases of filaments; all these parts
attached at base of ovary.
Leaves: Alternate or opposite, simple.
Fruit: 5-chambered, several-seeded capsule; rarely a drupe.

There are about 6 genera and 220 species, found nearly
throughout the world. Linseed oil and the fibers from which
linen is woven are obtained from Common Flax *(Linum
usitatissimum)*.

631 **Wild Blue Flax; Western Blue Flax**
Linum perenne subsp. *lewisii*

Description:	An open plant with mostly *unbranched, leafy stems* and *delicate, blue flowers* on slender stalks near top.
Flowers:	¾–1½" (2–4 cm) wide; petals 5, broad; stamens 5; styles 5, longer than stamens.
Leaves:	½–1¼" (1.5–3 cm) long, narrow, with 1 vein.
Height:	6–31" (15–80 cm).
Flowering:	March–September.
Habitat:	Well-drained soil in prairies, meadows, open mountain slopes, and ledges.
Range:	Alaska and central Canada south to California, Arizona, New Mexico, and along western Great Plains to western Texas; also in northern Mexico.
Comments:	Several Native American tribes used this plant for making rope. Common Flax *(L. usitatissimum)* often escapes from cultivation and grows in the wild; it has blue petals about ½" (1.5 cm) long and 3-veined leaves. Narrow-leaved Flax *(L. angustifolium),* found from western Oregon south to central coastal California, also has 3-veined leaves, but its petals are about ⅜" (9 mm) long.

221 **Chihuahua Flax**
Linum vernale

Description:	A very slender, erect plant with *yellow-orange, bowl-shaped flowers, each with a maroon center.*
Flowers:	About ¾" (2 cm) wide; sepals lanceolate, with gland-tipped teeth on edges; petals 5, fan-shaped; style with 5 branches at tip.
Leaves:	About ½" (1.5 cm) long, very narrow.
Fruit:	5-chambered capsule, walls between chambers open at top, fringed at opening.
Height:	4–20" (10–50 cm).
Flowering:	March–October.
Habitat:	Rocky, limestone soil in deserts.
Range:	Southern New Mexico, western Texas, and northern Mexico.
Comments:	This is a common species in parts of the Chihuahuan Desert. Only the very bases

of the petals are joined, and when the corolla falls from the flower, breezes may blow it across the ground like a fragile saucer. It is representative of a number of western yellow-flowered species, most slender and wiry and many without maroon centers in the flowers.

STICKLEAF FAMILY
Loasaceae

Mostly herbs with barbed, bristly, or stinging hairs, pale stems, and showy, orange-yellow or cream flowers usually in branched clusters.

Flowers: Radially symmetrical. Sepals 5, separate; petals 5; stamens 5, or many often bunched in 5 clusters, outer stamens often broad, flat, and sterile, resembling additional petals; all these parts attached at base of ovary.
Leaves: Alternate or opposite, simple or deeply pinnately lobed.
Fruit: 1-chambered capsule.

There are about 15 genera and 250 species, mostly in the warm and dry regions of the Americas.

206   Desert Rock Nettle
Eucnide urens

Description: A rounded, bushy plant, generally much broader than tall, with *stinging, bristly hairs* and *large, cream or pale yellow flowers* in branched clusters nearly obscuring foliage.

Flowers: 1–2″ (2.5–5 cm) wide; petals 5, broad, translucent; stamens in 5 clusters, joined to base of petals.

Leaves: ¾–2½″ (2–6.5 cm) long, ovate, coarsely toothed, covered with harsh hairs.

Height: 1–2′ (30–60 cm).

Flowering: April–June.

Habitat: Dry rocky places in deserts, often on cliffs.

Range: Southwestern Utah south to western Arizona, southeastern California, and Baja California.

Comments: The lovely flowers invite picking, but the hairs sting viciously.

205   **White-bracted Stickleaf**
Mentzelia involucrata

Description:	A low leafy plant with *satiny white stems* and narrow, *translucent, pale yellow flowers* at branch ends.
Flowers:	1–1¼" (2.5–3 cm) long; petals 5, erect; stamens many; style with 3 lobes; bracts beneath flowers white, with green toothed edges.
Leaves:	1–3" (2.5–7.5 cm) long, lanceolate, sharply and irregularly toothed, rough to the touch.
Height:	6–12" (15–30 cm).
Flowering:	March–May.
Habitat:	Dry desert hillsides, flats, and washes.
Range:	Southeastern California, western Arizona, and northwestern Mexico.
Comments:	This spring wildflower has distinctive showy, whitish bracts.

217   **Blazing Star**
Mentzelia laevicaulis

Description:	*Many large, star-like, lemon yellow flowers* on branches atop a stout, *satiny, white stem.*
Flowers:	2–5" (2.5–12.5 cm) wide; petals 5, lanceolate; stamens many, long, 1 between each pair of petals with a broad, petal-like filament.
Leaves:	4–12" (10–30 cm) long, narrowly lanceolate, very rough, edges with large, irregular teeth.
Height:	1–3' (30–90 cm).
Flowering:	June–September.
Habitat:	Gravelly or sandy slopes and plains, mostly in arid regions.
Range:	Southeastern British Columbia south to southern California and east to Utah, Wyoming, and Montana.
Comments:	There are many species of *Mentzelia* in the West, some of which are given the name Stickleaf because of the barbed hairs on the leaves that readily cling to fabric.

LOOSESTRIFE FAMILY
Lythraceae

Herbs, shrubs, or trees with flowers in racemes or branched clusters.

Flowers: Radially or bilaterally symmetrical. Sepals 4–6, joined at base to form a tube to which petals and stamens attach; petals as many as sepals, separate, often crumpled like crepe paper, or absent; stamens usually twice as many as sepals, in 2 series of different lengths; all these parts joined to tube attached at base of ovary.
Leaves: Usually opposite or whorled, simple.
Fruit: Many-seeded capsule, with 1–6 chambers.

There are about 24 genera and 550 species, distributed throughout the world except for very cold regions. A few species yield dyes, such as henna, derived from the leaves of Henna *(Lawsonia inermis);* some, including Crape Myrtle *(Lagerstroemia indica),* are grown as ornamentals.

502 Purple Loosestrife
Lythrum salicaria

Description:	Dense patches of leafy, angular stems topped with *crowded spikes of brilliant pinkish-lavender flowers.*
Flowers:	Petals 5, each nearly ½″ (1.5 cm) long, attached to a purplish, calyx-like tube with several pointed teeth.
Leaves:	1¼–4″ (3–10 cm) long, narrow, opposite, notched at base.
Height:	2–7′ (60–210 cm).
Flowering:	August–September.
Habitat:	Marshes.
Range:	In West, most common from western Washington to northern California, but spreading and occasionally encountered in interior West; also throughout much of East.
Comments:	Purple Loosestrife illustrates the danger of introducing new plants to an area. This lovely plant was introduced from Europe as an ornamental in the 1880s, but since then has made itself so much at home that it crowds out native species and reduces habitat for native wildlife. Continuously spreading, it is now

common along the Pacific Coast and has come to be classified as a noxious weed. The plants sometimes form a spectacular display around freshwater lakes, marshes, and along streams, signaling the destruction of a native ecosystem.

MALLOW FAMILY
Malvaceae

Herbs, shrubs, or rarely small trees, often velvety, with star-like or branched hairs; flowers borne singly or in branched clusters.

Flowers: Usually bisexual, radially symmetrical. Sepals 3–5, partly united; petals 5, separate, bases often joined to base of stamen tube; stamens many, joined by filaments into a tube; all these parts attached at base of ovary.

Leaves: Simple, often palmately veined and lobed or deeply divided, with stipules.

Fruit: At least 5 chambers, each with 1 to few seeds, separating from one another or forming a many-seeded capsule; rarely a berry.

There are about 75 genera and 1,500 species, many in tropical America. Many species, such as Rose-of-Sharon (*Hibiscus syriacus*) and Hollyhock (*Althaea rosea*), are grown as ornamentals. The vegetable okra is the edible fruit of Okra (*Hibiscus esculentus*). The hairs of seeds of *Gossypium* provide the fiber cotton.

472   **Desert Five Spot**
       Eremalche rotundifolia

Description: *Flowers forming purplish-pink or lilac globes,* each open at top and with a deep *reddish center,* on short branches near top of an erect, sparsely leaved plant.

Flowers: ¾–1¼" (2–3 cm) wide; petals 5; stamens many, joined at base, forming a tube around style.

Leaves: ¾–2" (2–5 cm) wide, few, round, toothed.

Height: 4–24" (10–60 cm).

Flowering: March–May.

Habitat: Desert washes and flats.

Range: Southeastern California, southern Nevada, and western Arizona.

Comments: The pinkish, spherical corollas are
distinctive; when light passes through
them, they resemble glowing lanterns.
This species was once placed in the
genus *Malvastrum,* but three western
North American species have recently
been recognized as belonging in their
own genus, *Eremalche,* which means
"lonely mallow" and refers to the
desert habitat.

219 Desert Rosemallow
Hibiscus coulteri

Description: A shrubby plant with rough hairs,
undivided lower leaves, *divided upper
leaves,* and *large, cup-shaped, whitish to
yellow flowers* often tinged with red.
Flowers: 1–2" (2.5–5 cm) wide; petals 5, broad;
stamens many, joined at base, forming
a tube around style.
Leaves: Lower ones about 1" (2.5 cm) wide,
ovate; upper ones divided into 3 narrow,
coarsely toothed lobes.
Height: To 4' (1.2 m).
Flowering: April–August; throughout year in
warm areas.
Habitat: Brushy, desert hills and canyons.
Range: Southern Arizona east to western Texas
and south to northern Mexico.
Comments: This is a humble relative of the brilliant
tropical hibiscus plants. The genus
contains almost 300 species.

470 Pale Face; Rock Hibiscus
Hibiscus denudatus

Description: A scraggly *pale plant* covered with
whitish hairs and bearing *bowl-shaped,
white to pinkish-lavender flowers,* more
deeply colored in center, in upper leaf
axils and along ends of *leafless, erect
branches.*
Flowers: 1–1½" (2.5–4 cm) wide; petals 5;
stamens many, joined at base, forming
a tube around style.
Leaves: ½–1" (1.5–2.5 cm) long, very few, ovate.

Height: 1–3′ (30–90 cm).
Flowering: February–October.
Habitat: Rocky, desert slopes.
Range: Southern California east to western Texas and south to northern Mexico.
Comments: Characteristic of many desert-adapted species, this plant has few leaves compared to some of its tropical cousins. The delicate flowers are small for the genus and lack the flamboyance of ornamental species.

222 Flower-of-an-hour
Hibiscus trionum

Description: A hairy, leafy plant with some stems lying on ground, others more upright, with *1 pale yellow flower, blackish maroon in center,* on a stalk from each leaf axil.
Flowers: About 1½″ (4 cm) wide; sepals 5, papery, bristly, with many dark veins; petals 5; stamens many, joined at base, forming a tube around style.
Leaves: ¾–1¼″ (2–3 cm) wide, pinnately divided into 3 or 5 divisions.
Fruit: Sepals form a bladder around a capsule dividing into 5 sections.
Height: 1–2′ (30–60 cm).
Flowering: August–September.
Habitat: Open places, commonly in disturbed ground.
Range: Southern half of West; also in southern part of East.
Comments: The flowers close in the shade, hence the common name. Sometimes grown as an ornamental, this central African plant is now rapidly spreading and becoming a garden nuisance.

497 Mountain Globemallow; Streambank Globemallow
Iliamna rivularis

Description: A stout plant with *large, maple-like leaves* and *showy, pink or pinkish-lavender flowers* in long loose racemes atop stems and in shorter racemes in upper leaf axils.

Flowers: 1–2″ (2.5–5 cm) wide; petals 5; stamens many, joined at base, forming a tube around branched style, each branch ending in a tiny knob.

Leaves: 2–8″ (5–20 cm) wide, nearly round, with 5 or 7 triangular lobes.

Fruit: Many chambers in a ring, each containing 3–4 seeds.

Height: 3–7′ (90–210 cm).

Flowering: June–August.

Habitat: Springs and along mountain streams.

Range: British Columbia, eastern Washington, and eastern Oregon east to Montana and south to Utah and Colorado.

Comments: The several western *Iliamna* globemallows are commonly found in wet places. They are recognizable by their maple-like leaves and pink or rose petals, and are distinguished from other members of the mallow family by having more than one seed in each ovary segment.

---

498 Checkermallow
Sidalcea neomexicana

Description: Many *deep pink flowers crowded in long narrow clusters* atop leafy stems.

Flowers: 1–1½″ (2.5–4 cm) wide; petals 5; stamens many, joined at base, forming a tube around branched style, each slender branch lacking knob at tip.

Leaves: Lower ones to 4″ (10 cm) wide, nearly round, with 5–7 shallow lobes with coarse teeth; upper ones smaller, palmately divided into usually 7 lobes.

Height: 1–3′ (30–90 cm).

Flowering: June–September.

Habitat: Moist, often heavy soil in mountain valleys and along streams and ponds at lower elevations.

Range: Eastern Oregon south to southern California and northern Mexico, and east to New Mexico, Colorado, and Wyoming.

Comments: The many checkermallows with pink flowers, found from coastal marshes to moderate elevations, are difficult to

distinguish and differentiated only by
technical characteristics.

---

366 Scarlet Globemallow; Red False Mallow
Sphaeralcea coccinea

Description: *Red-orange or brick red flowers* in narrow
clusters in upper leaf axils on a leafy,
branched, velvety-haired plant.

Flowers: 1–1¼″ (2.5–3 cm) wide; petals 5;
stamens many, joined at base, forming
a tube around style.

Leaves: ¾–2″ (2–5 cm) wide, nearly round,
divided into 3 broad or narrow,
variously divided or toothed lobes.

Height: To 20″ (50 cm); stems often leaning
at base.

Flowering: April–August.

Habitat: Open ground in arid grasslands and
among piñon and juniper.

Range: Central Canada south through western
Montana, eastern Idaho, most of Utah,
northeastern Arizona, and most of New
Mexico, and east to Texas and Iowa.

Comments: The approximately 60 species of
Sphaeralcea globemallows are common
plants on western ranges; as a group
they are easy to identify because of
their five commonly bright orange-red
petals. In that respect they are nearly
unique in the region. Identification
of particular species is another matter;
this requires very careful attention to
the fine details on the sides of the
wedge-like sections of the mature
fruit. One of the easiest species to
recognize is Scaly Globemallow
(*S. leptophylla*), which is covered
with gray, scale-like hairs and has
very narrow upper leaves that are not
divided or toothed; it grows from
southern Utah, southwestern Colorado,
and northeastern Arizona east to western
Texas and south to northern Mexico. At
least two species have populations that
vary from the usual red-orange flower
color: Desert Globemallow (*S. ambigua*)

has red-orange flowers in southwestern Utah, Arizona, and westward, but there are lavender- to white-flowered populations between Phoenix and Tucson and in northern California; Polychrome Globemallow *(S. polychroma)* has white, lavender, and red-orange plants all mixed together in populations in southern New Mexico and southward.

367 Coulter's Globemallow
Sphaeralcea coulteri

Description: Erect, slender stems with thin, grayish-velvety leaves and *orange or red-orange flowers in long narrow clusters.*
Flowers: ¾–1″ (2–2.5 cm) wide; petals 5; stamens many, joined into a tube.
Leaves: ½–1¼″ (1.5–3 cm) long, ovate or nearly round, not lobed or with 3 or 5 deep or shallow lobes, edges scalloped.
Height: 8–60″ (20–150 cm).
Flowering: January–May.
Habitat: Sandy, desert flats.
Range: Southeastern California, southern Arizona, and northwestern Mexico.
Comments: In years of ample winter rain, this species carpets the desert floor with red-orange.

UNICORN PLANT FAMILY
Martyniaceae

Herbs covered with sticky, glandular hairs, and with large flowers in showy, terminal racemes.

Flowers: Bilaterally symmetrical. Sepals 5, united; petals 5, united, forming an upper and lower lip; stamens 5, the fifth rudimentary and sterile, or 2 fertile and 3 sterile and smaller; all these parts attached at base of ovary.
Leaves: Alternate or opposite, often palmately veined and lobed.
Fruit: Capsule, with a curved horn or hook on end.

There are about 5 genera and 20 species, found in warm regions of the Western Hemisphere. These plants are sometimes included in the Eastern Hemisphere family Pedaliaceae.

289 Devil's Claw; Unicorn Plant
Proboscidea althaeifolia

Description: A coarse plant with stems lying on ground and few yellow, *bilaterally symmetrical flowers* in racemes.

Flowers: Corolla 1–1½" (2.5–4 cm) long, commonly flecked with maroon or rust-brown, with 5 lobes spreading from a broad opening.

Leaves: Blades ¾–3" (2–7.5 cm) long, fleshy, roundish; edges plain, scalloped, or deeply lobed.

Fruit: Pod, about 2½" (6.5 cm) long, with a *curved horn* nearly 5" (12.5 cm) long.

Height: Creeper; flower stalks to about 1' (30 cm), spreading to nearly 3' (90 cm) wide.

Flowering: June–September.

Habitat: Sandy soil in deserts and arid grasslands.

Range: Southern California east to western Texas.

Comments: As the plump fruit matures, it divides into halves and its outer, fleshy layer peels off, revealing the hard inner portion of the fruit, the single horn of which splits into two "devil's claws." There are several species in the Southwest, some with pink or magenta flowers. The dark fibers in the pods are used with fibers of other plants in weaving fine baskets.

BUCKBEAN FAMILY
Menyanthaceae

Perennial herbs of freshwater ponds or marshes with flowers in showy clusters.

Flowers: Radially symmetrical. Calyx with usually 5 united sepals; corolla with usually 5 united petals; stamens usually 5; all these parts attached at base of ovary.
Leaves: Simple or with 3 leaflets.
Fruit: 1-celled, many-seeded capsule.

There are 5 genera and 30 species, found in temperate regions and tropical Asia. Indigenous peoples have made use of the leaves of some species for medicinal purposes. Menyanthaceae is sometimes included in the gentian family (Gentianaceae).

159 Buckbean; Bogbean
Menyanthes trifoliata

Description:	Large, long-stalked leaves and racemes or narrow clusters of *white or purple-tinged, star-like flowers* atop stout stalks, about as high as leaves.
Flowers:	Corolla about ½″ (1.5 cm) wide, forming a tube ¼–⅜″ (6–9 mm) long (about twice as long as calyx), with 5–6 pointed lobes covered with short hairs.
Leaves:	4–12″ (10–30 cm) long; leaflets 3, each 1½–5″ (4–12.5 cm) long, broadly lanceolate.
Height:	Aquatic; leaves and flower stalks 4–12″ (10–30 cm) above water.
Flowering:	May–August.
Habitat:	Bogs and shallow lakes.
Range:	Canada south to southern Sierra Nevada and central Colorado; also in East.
Comments:	This species also occurs in northern Eurasia. Its leaves were sometimes used as a hops substitute in beer brewing. Deer Cabbage *(Fauria crista-galli),* a species traditionally placed in the genus *Nephrophyllidium,* has similar flowers but undivided, kidney-shaped leaves; it grows in wet places on the Olympic Peninsula and around the northern Pacific Coast.

INDIAN PIPE FAMILY
Monotropaceae

Saprophytic, perennial herbs, usually somewhat fleshy and white, yellow, brown, pink, or red, lacking chlorophyll.

Flowers: Radially symmetrical; borne singly or in racemes or heads. Sepals usually 4–5, occasionally joined at base, or absent, when sepals absent bracts on upper stem may be sepal-like; petals usually 4–5, separate or united; stamens usually twice as many as petals, with anthers opening by slits or terminal pores; all these parts attached at base of ovary.
Leaves: Simple, reduced to scales.
Fruit: Usually a 5-chambered capsule, sometimes a berry.

There are about 10 genera and 12 species, mostly in the temperate regions of the Northern Hemisphere. The roots of these plants grow in a close association with fungi, from which they receive all their nutrition and water; the fungi also form an association with the roots of trees, making Monotropaceae indirect parasites. Classification is equivocal: Some botanists place the species in a family of their own, as is done here; other botanists include them in the heath family (Ericaceae) or in the wintergreen family (Pyrolaceae).

404 Candystick; Sugarstick
Allotropa virgata

Description: Lustrous, erect, *leafless, scaly stems resembling peppermint sticks* with flowers hanging in a raceme along top.

Flowers: Petals 5, each about ¼" (6 mm) long, white, sometimes pink, forming an inverted bowl; stamens conspicuous, projecting beyond petals, with *bright maroon-red anthers.*

Leaves: Reduced to scales.

Height: 4–12" (10–30 cm).

Flowering: May–August.

Habitat: In humus of coniferous forests.

Range: British Columbia south to southern Sierra Nevada.

Comments: Lacking chlorophyll, this plant absorbs nutrients from the rich thick humus in which it grows.

82 Indian Pipe
Monotropa uniflora

Description: *A waxy white plant* (blackening with age) with several clustered stems, each bent like a shepherd's hook with *1 flower hanging at end* like a narrow bell.

Flowers: About ¾" (2 cm) long; petals 4–6 (usually 5), separate; stamens 10.

Leaves: Reduced to scales, pressed against stem.

Height: 2–10" (5–25 cm).

Flowering: June–August.

Habitat: In humus of deep shaded woods.

Range: Alaska south to northwestern California and east across northern North America; also in northern Mexico south into South America.

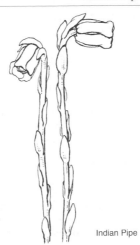

Indian Pipe

Comments: Indian Pipe also occurs in eastern Asia. The genus name refers to the one-sided inflorescence.

317 Pinedrops; Albany Beechdrops
Pterospora andromedea

Description: *A reddish-brown plant* with stiffly erect, leafless stems often growing in clusters and covered with glandular hairs; *pale yellowish-brown, egg-shaped flowers hanging in a long raceme.*

Flowers: Corolla about ¼″ (6 mm) long, with 5 tiny lobes around opening.

Leaves: Reduced to scales.

Height: 1–3′ (30–90 cm).

Flowering: June–August.

Habitat: In humus of coniferous forests; especially common in West under Ponderosa Pines.

Range: Alaska south throughout West to northern Mexico; also from southeastern Canada to northeastern United States.

Comments: Stems grow for only one year but remain as dried stalks for several years. The genus name, from the Greek words for "winged seeds," refers to the net-like wing at one end of each minute seed that carries it to a new site as it is sprinkled from the capsule.

406 Snow Plant
Sarcodes sanguinea

Description: An unusual, stout, fleshy, *entirely bright red plant* with bracts overlapping on lower stem and curled among racemes of flowers above.

Flowers: Corolla ½–¾" (1.5–2 cm) long, bell-shaped, with 5 round lobes.

Leaves: Reduced to scales.

Height: 8–24" (20–60 cm).

Flowering: April–July.

Habitat: In humus of coniferous woods.

Range: Southern Oregon south to southern California.

Comments: Once seen, this plant is never forgotten; the brilliant red is startling in the filtered sunlight against the dark background of the forest. Plants poke through the forest floor as snow recedes, drawing their nutrition from the rich humus.

FOUR O'CLOCK FAMILY
Nyctaginaceae

Mostly herbs, shrubs, or vines, also small trees in the tropics, with flowers borne in leaf axils, in umbels, heads, racemes, or openly branched clusters.

Flowers: Usually bisexual, radially or slightly bilaterally symmetrical. Sepals 4–5, petal-like, usually united into a trumpet-shaped structure; petals absent; stamens 1–30; ovary tightly enclosed by lower part of calyx, which becomes part of fruit, so that all parts appear to be attached at top of ovary.

Leaves: Opposite, simple; those of a pair often unequal in size.

Fruit: 1-seeded, fleshy or dry; smooth, glandular, or winged.

There are 30 genera and 300 species, best represented in North and South America; the warm deserts of North America are areas of high diversity. Beneath the flowers is often a ring of bracts (involucre), which may be mistaken for a calyx. Sometimes these bracts are joined together into a cup- or saucer-shaped structure. In species of *Bougainvillea* the bracts are brightly colored. Four o'clocks (*Mirabilis*), sand verbenas (*Abronia*), and bougainvilleas are grown as ornamentals.

151 Snowball; Sweet Sand Verbena
Abronia elliptica

Description: *Many fragrant, white, trumpet-shaped flowers in heads* at ends of long stalks in upper leaf axils.

Flowers: Head 1–3″ (2.5–7.5 cm) wide; 5 lobes on end of "trumpet."

Leaves: Blades ½–2½″ (1.5–6.5 cm) long, opposite, ovate to diamond-shaped, long-stalked.

Fruit: 1-seeded, usually with 5 papery wings, each with a flat, diamond-shaped pad at top.

Height: 4–20″ (10–50 cm); stems often leaning on ground.

Flowering: April–September.

Habitat: Sandy, arid grasslands and among piñon and juniper.

Range: Central and southern Nevada east to northern Arizona, northwestern New Mexico, Utah, and western Colorado, and northeast to northern Wyoming.

Comments: Throughout most of its range, this is the only sand verbena with white flowers. *A. fragrans,* also called Snowball or Sweet Sand Verbena, has sweet-smelling flowers but lacks pads atop the wings of the fruit and is often taller, with stems to 3′ (90 cm); it grows from eastern Montana and western North and South Dakota south to eastern Utah, northwestern Arizona, southern New Mexico, and western and central Texas. White Sand Verbena *(A. mellifera),* found from eastern Washington and eastern Oregon to southern Idaho, has nearly scentless flowers.

358 Yellow Sand Verbena
Abronia latifolia

Description: *Many yellow, trumpet-shaped flowers in heads* atop long stalks in leaf axils of trailing stems.

Flowers: Head 1–2″ (2.5–5 cm) wide; 5 lobes on end of "trumpet."

Leaves:	½–2½″ (1.5–6.5 cm) long, opposite, fleshy, roundish.
Fruit:	With 3–5 wings.
Height:	Creeper; flower stalks to 6″ (15 cm), stems to 3′ (90 cm) long.
Flowering:	May–August.
Habitat:	Coastal dunes.
Range:	British Columbia south along Pacific Coast to southern California.
Comments:	This is the only yellow-flowered sand verbena. Two similar species, each differing primarily by flower color, grow along the Pacific Coast: Beach Pancake *(A. maritima),* found from southern California to Mexico, has wine red flowers; Beach Sand Verbena *(A. umbellata),* found from British Columbia south to Baja California, has flowers varying from deep pink to white.

630 Desert Sand Verbena
Abronia villosa

Description:	A soft-haired, sticky plant with *bright pinkish purple, trumpet-shaped flowers in heads* on stalks growing from leaf axils.
Flowers:	Head 2–3″ (5–7.5 cm) wide; 5 lobes on end of "trumpet."
Leaves:	½–1½″ (1.5–4 cm) long, opposite, ovate, with slightly wavy, scalloped edges.
Fruit:	With 3–5 wings.
Height:	Creeper; flower stalks to about 10″ (25 cm), trailing stems to 3′ (90 cm) long.
Flowering:	March–October.
Habitat:	Sandy, desert soil.
Range:	Southeastern California, southern Nevada, southwestern Utah, western Arizona, and northwestern Mexico.
Comments:	Following ample winter rains, Desert Sand Verbena may carpet miles of desert with pink. There are several pink- or rose-flowered *Abronia* sand verbenas in the West, some erect with succulent leaves.

80 Angel Trumpets
Acleisanthes longiflora

Description: Highly branched stems spreading on ground or sprawling over shrubs and bearing *erect white flowers standing like miniature trumpets* in leaf axils.

Flowers: 3½–6½" (9–16 cm) long, ½–¾" (1.5–2 cm) wide.

Leaves: About 1" (2.5 cm) long, opposite, triangular.

Fruit: About ¼" (6 mm) long, with 5 rounded ribs on sides.

Height: Creeper; branches to 8" (20 cm), reclining stems to 3' (90 cm) long.

Flowering: May–September.

Habitat: Rocky slopes in deserts or on plains.

Range: Southeastern California east to central New Mexico and western Texas, and south to Mexico.

Comments: During the day, flowers that bloomed the night before are bent like melted candles, and those yet to bloom are held rigidly erect as brownish-green tubes that blend with the foliage. In the cool of evening, new flowers open and flare their white funnel tops, which attract night-flying moths that drink the nectar and pollinate the flowers.

446 Trailing Four O'Clock; Trailing Windmills
Allionia incarnata

Description: A trailing plant with brilliant, *deep pink flowers* near ground, *3 in each crowded cluster and resembling 1 radially symmetrical flower.*

Flowers: Individual flowers bilaterally symmetrical; cluster ¼–1" (6–25 mm) wide, short-stalked, in leaf axil; calyx-like involucre of 3 bracts, each partly enclosing a fruit, beneath cluster.

Leaves: ½–1½" (1.5–4 cm) long, opposite, ovate.

Fruit: Less than ¼" (6 mm) wide, convex on one side, with 2 rows of 3 or 5 curved teeth on concave side.

Height: Creeper; flower stalks to 4″ (10 cm), stems to 3′ (90 cm) long.

Flowering: April–September.

Habitat: Dry, gravelly or sandy soil in sun.

Range: Southern Utah and southern Colorado south to southeastern California, Arizona, New Mexico, Texas, Mexico, and South America.

Comments: The flowers remain open most of the day, not just in the evening as suggested by the name. Smooth Trailing Four O'Clock *(A. choisyi),* found from Arizona to Texas and southward, has a perianth ¼″ (5 mm) long or less, and the curved edges of the fruit each bear 5–8 slender, gland-tipped teeth.

98 Southwestern Ringstem
Anulocaulis leiosolenus

Description: An ungainly, spindly plant with large *fleshy leaves* near base and *pale pink or pink and white, trumpet-shaped flowers* scattered about widely branched top.

Flowers: 1¼–1½″ (3–4 cm) long, slightly bilaterally symmetrical; stamens 3, projecting about 1½″ (4 cm) beyond perianth; slender style projecting beyond stamens.

Leaves: To 10″ (25 cm) wide, opposite, nearly round, rough, with small, wart-like hairs.

Fruit: Resembling a wrinkled little pot with a cone-shaped lid.

Height: To 4′ (1.2 m).

Flowering: June–November.

Habitat: On rocky soil containing gypsum.

Range: Southern Nevada, central Arizona, southern New Mexico, and western Texas.

Comments: In the heat of the day, the tubes of spent flowers hang bedraggled. At sundown, as new flowers open, the long stamens and style unravel and align in a graceful sweep from the narrow opening. The common name ringstem derives from the sticky, glandular rings encircling the stem.

397 Red Four O'Clock
Mirabilis coccinea

Description: A spindly plant with *very narrow leaves* and *small clusters of trumpet-shaped, red to deep pink flowers.*

Flowers: ½–¾" (1.5–2 cm) long; calyx petal-like, 5-lobed; petals absent; calyx-like ring of joined bracts beneath each cluster, becoming larger and papery as fruits mature.

Leaves: ¾–5" (2–12.5 cm) long, opposite.

Fruit: ¼" (5 mm) long, seed-like, club-shaped, with 5 broad rounded ribs on sides.

Height: 1–3' (30–90 cm).

Flowering: May–September.

Habitat: Dry, rocky, brushy hillsides.

Range: Southeastern California east across southern Arizona and New Mexico to western Texas, and south to northern Mexico.

Comments: This night-flowering plant has the deepest pink flowers of all the small-flowered four o'clocks. Flowers remain open until late in the morning.

79 Sweet Four O'Clock; Maravilla
Mirabilis longiflora

Description: A leafy plant with stout forking stems and *slender, white or pale pink, trumpet-shaped flowers,* rarely darker, in cups in axils of upper leaves.

Flowers: 3–7" (7.5–17.5 cm) long; stamens and style purple, projecting as much as 2" (5 cm) beyond flower.

Leaves: To 5" (12.5 cm) long, opposite, broadly ovate or heart-shaped.

Fruit: About ¼" (6 mm) long, hard, seed-like, roundish, dark gray or black.

Height: 1½–5' (45–150 cm).

Flowering: July–September.

Habitat: Brushy canyons and banks.

Range: Southern Arizona east to western Texas and south to Mexico.

Comments: *Mirabilis,* in Latin, and Maravilla, in Spanish, both mean "marvelous," which the flowers certainly are. They open in

the shade of the late afternoon. This
lovely native species is a close relative
of Common Four O'Clock *(M. jalapa),*
a plant originally from Mexico, popular
in gardens since the Aztecs, and now
commonly escaping into the wild; it has
purple, yellow, or sometimes white or
variegated flowers generally not longer
than 2½″ (6.5 cm).

---

445 Mountain Four O'Clock
Mirabilis melanotricha

Description: A leafy plant with erect or leaning stems
and *3 lavender-pink flowers in a little cup*
with black hairs at branch ends.

Flowers: About ½″ (1.5 cm) wide, broadly
funnel-shaped; calyx petal-like, 5-lobed;
each cup expanding into a 5-lobed,
papery saucer as fruits mature.

Leaves: 1¼–4″ (3–10 cm) long, opposite,
broadly lanceolate, hairless.

Fruit: Barely more than ⅛″ (3 mm) long, seed-
like, club-shaped, with 5 ribs, minutely
hairy.

Height: To 3′ (90 cm).

Flowering: June–October.

Habitat: Open woods or brush in mountains.

Range: Southern Colorado south to Arizona,
New Mexico, extreme western Texas,
and Mexico.

Comments: All small-flowered four o'clocks in the
West, whether white- or pink-flowered,
have flowers that open in the evening and
remain open through the cool part of the
next day. They are visited by many insects
and seem to be a favorite morning flower
of hummingbirds. There are numerous
forms, varying particularly in the shape
and thickness of the leaves. Establishing
correct scientific species names remains
an unsolved problem. Mountain Four
O'Clock intergrades with another four
o'clock, *M. oblongifolia,* often a species
of lower elevations that commonly has
sticky-hairy leaves in this region and
fewer or no black hairs on the cups
beneath the flowers.

531 Desert Four O'Clock; Colorado Four O'Clock; Maravilla
Mirabilis multiflora

Description: A bushy plant with *vibrant, deep pink, broadly tubular flowers in 5-lobed cups* growing in leaf axils.

Flowers: About 1" (2.5 cm) wide; calyx petal-like, 5-lobed; stamens 5.

Leaves: 1–4" (2.5–10 cm) long, opposite, broadly ovate or heart-shaped, short-stalked.

Fruit: ½" (1.5 cm) long, seed-like, roundish, nearly brown or black.

Height: To 1½' (45 cm).

Flowering: April–September.

Habitat: Open, sandy areas among juniper and piñon, extending into deserts and grasslands.

Range: Southern California east across southern Nevada and southern Utah to southern Colorado, and south through Arizona, New Mexico, and western Texas to northern Mexico.

Comments: Flowers open in the evening. Native Americans chewed or powdered the large root and applied it as a poultice for various ailments. An infusion in water was used to appease the appetite. Two similar species occur in totally separate areas: Green's Four O'Clock *(M. greenei),* found on dry slopes in northern California, and MacFarlane's Four O'Clock *(M. macfarlanei),* found in canyons in northeastern Oregon and adjacent regions of Idaho.

WATER LILY FAMILY
Nymphaeaceae

Perennial, aquatic herbs, usually with round or heart-shaped, often floating leaves and large flowers either floating or held above water on long stalks.

Flowers: Radially symmetrical. Sepals 3–14, often intergrading into many petals; stamens many; pistil 1, narrowing beneath a broad stigma.

Leaves: Simple, with very long stalks.

Fruit: Each pistil opening on one side or forming a nutlet, or all pistils growing together as a leathery berry.

There are about 5 genera and 50 species, found in aquatic habitats throughout temperate and tropical regions. Several are cultivated as pond ornamentals.

232   Indian Pond Lily; Yellow Water Lily; Spatterdock
Nuphar lutea

Description: An aquatic with floating, *heart-shaped, leathery leaves* with roundish tips and *cup-shaped, bright yellow flowers* either floating on surface or held just above water; leaves and flowers both attached by long stalks to stout stems buried in mud.

Flowers: 2½–4″ (6.5–10 cm) wide; sepals usually 9, each 1¼–2½″ (3–6.5 cm) long, bluntly fan-shaped, outer ones greenish, inner ones bright yellow or tinged with red; petals narrow, inconspicuous, about same length as numerous stamens.

Leaves: 4–18″ (10–45 cm) long.

Height: Aquatic; leaves and flowers floating or 1–3″ (2.5–7.5 cm) above water, submerged leafstalks and flower stalks to about 3′ (90 cm) long.

Flowering: April–September.

Habitat: Ponds and slow streams.

Range: Alaska south to southern California and east to Colorado.

Comments: Native Americans ground the seeds for flour and also roasted them as popcorn. This aquatic (and some others, including rice) gives off alcohol instead of carbon dioxide as it takes in oxygen. This species is also known as Wakas.

216   Fragrant Water Lily
Nymphaea odorata

Description: An aquatic with *floating round leaves and large, white, floating flowers;* leaves and flowers both attached to long stems buried in mud.

Flowers:	3–6″ (7.5–15 cm) wide; petals 20–30; stamens 50–100.
Leaves:	Blades to 10″ (25 cm) wide, attached at base of deep notch to a long submerged stalk.
Height:	Aquatic; leaves and flowers floating or about 1″ (2.5 cm) above water, submerged leafstalks and flower stalks 2–4′ (60–120 cm) long.
Flowering:	July–October.
Habitat:	Quiet fresh water.
Range:	Throughout much of Canada and United States.
Comments:	This native of the eastern United States is now found in ponds in many places in the West. The fragrant flowers open in the morning and close in the afternoon. Yellow Water Lily or Banana Water Lily *(N. mexicana),* with bright yellow flowers, has been introduced into California's San Joaquin Valley; it is considered a noxious weed. Pygmy Water Lily *(N. tetragona),* with flowers about 2½″ (6.5 cm) wide and only 7–15 petals, is found across northern North America, but in the West it occurs only in a few places in Washington and Idaho.

OLIVE FAMILY
Oleaceae

Small or large shrubs, trees, or woody vines, with flowers borne in racemes or branched clusters.

Flowers: Radially symmetrical. Sepals usually 4, united; petals usually 4, united, or occasionally absent; stamens 2; all these parts attached at base of ovary.

Leaves: Alternate or opposite, simple or pinnately compound.

Fruit: Berry, drupe, or capsule.

There are 29 genera and 600 species, especially frequent in temperate and tropical Asia. Ornamentals include lilacs *(Syringa),* privets *(Ligustrum),* jasmines *(Jasminum),* and golden bells *(Forsythia).* Species of ash *(Fraxinus)* are used as ornamentals and are important lumber trees. Olives and olive oil are obtained from a tree, Olive *(Olea europea).*

191 Rough Menodora
Menodora scabra

Description:	Numerous erect, rough, leafy stems with *pale yellow flowers* in loose clusters.
Flowers:	½–¾" (1.5–2 cm) wide; corolla with a short narrow tube and 5 spreading lobes; *stamens 2, hidden within.*
Leaves:	½–1½" (1.5–4 cm) long, broadly lanceolate, usually erect; upper leaves alternate, lower leaves opposite.
Fruit:	Capsule of 2 translucent spheres side by side, each nearly ¼" (6 mm) wide.
Height:	5–14" (12.5–35 cm).
Flowering:	March–September.
Habitat:	Grassy slopes and brushy deserts.
Range:	Southeastern California and southern Utah east to western Texas and south to northern Mexico.
Comments:	*Menodora* is a small but widespread genus with species in southern North America, southern South America, and southern Africa.

EVENING PRIMROSE FAMILY
Onagraceae

Usually herbs, rarely shrubs or trees, with often showy flowers borne singly or in racemes, spikes, or branched clusters.

Flowers: Usually radially symmetrical. Sepals usually 4, mostly separate; petals 4, mostly separate; sepals and petals united into a long, short, or barely discernible tube at base; stamens usually 4 or 8; all these parts attached at top of ovary.

Leaves: Alternate or opposite, simple.

Fruit: Usually a 4-chambered, many-seeded capsule; sometimes a berry or a hard, nut-like structure.

There are about 17 genera and 675 species, found worldwide but especially abundant in temperate regions of western North and South America. Evening primroses (*Oenothera*), fuchsias (*Fuchsia*), and lopezias (*Lopezia*) are popular ornamentals. The name primrose is derived from a Latin word meaning "first"; true primroses (Primulaceae), unrelated to this family, are among the first flowers to bloom in the spring. Apparently, in the early 1600s when an eastern U.S. species of *Oenothera* was being described, its sweet scent reminded the botanist of the wild primroses of Europe; he named these plants accordingly, and the name stuck. The name Onagraceae refers to *Oenothera,* the flowers of which open late in the afternoon or evening; other genera have flowers that bloom early in the morning. In some, flowers last only one day, but in others they may last several days.

354 Desert Primrose
Camissonia brevipes

Description: A nearly leafless, reddish stem growing from a basal rosette of leaves and bearing a *broad raceme of bright yellow flowers* just below the drooping top.

Flowers: ¼–1½" (6–38 mm) wide; petals 4, nearly round; stamens 8, with filaments about ¼" (6 mm) long; style at least ½" (1.5 cm) long, tipped with a large round knob.

Leaves: 1–5" (2.5–12.5 cm) long, pinnately lobed, end lobe largest.

Fruit: Slender pod, ¾–3½" (2–9 cm) long.

Height: 1–30" (2.5–75 cm).

Flowering: March–May.

Habitat: Desert slopes and washes.

Range: Southwestern Utah south to western Arizona and southeastern California.

Comments: This species blooms at sunrise rather than sunset. All *Camissonia* have a knob on the style, a feature that separates these species from the genus *Oenothera,* in which they once were placed.

195 Beach Primrose
Camissonia cheiranthifolia

Description: *Leafy stems lying on sand,* radiating from a central rosette of grayish leaves, with *bright yellow flowers* facing upward near ends.

Flowers: ½–1¼" (1.5–3 cm) wide; petals 4, nearly round; stamens 8; style tipped with a large knob.

Leaves: ½–2" (1.5–5 cm) long, ovate, covered with grayish hairs.

Fruit: Slender, 4-sided pod.

Height: Creeper; branches to about 6" (15 cm), stems 2–4' (60–120 cm) long.

Flowering: April–August.
Habitat: Beach sands.
Range: Southern Oregon south along Pacific Coast to Baja California.
Comments: The large knob on the end of the style, as well as several technical characteristics, shows that this is a fairly close relative of Desert Primrose (*C. brevipes*).

231 Tansy-leaved Evening Primrose
Camissonia tanacetifolia

Description: A dandelion-like *rosette of jagged-edged leaves* and *bright yellow flowers* with 4 broad petals.
Flowers: About 1″ (2.5 cm) wide; tube between petals and ovary 1–3½″ (2.5–9 cm) long; stamens 8; style tipped with a knob.
Leaves: 2–8″ (5–20 cm) long, in a rosette, lanceolate, edges deeply cut and lobed.
Fruit: Hard pod, about ¾″ (2 cm) long, 4-sided, corners narrow and wing-like, sitting in center of rosette of leaves.
Height: 1–4″ (2.5–10 cm).
Flowering: June–August.
Habitat: Soil moist in spring but drying by summer, from sagebrush plains to pine forests.
Range: Eastern Washington south through Sierra Nevada and east to Idaho and Montana.
Comments: This is representative of several low, yellow-flowered evening primroses without stems. The root of this plant branches beneath the ground, and the plants form patches on the surface. It was previously placed in the big genus *Oenothera*, but the knob at the end of the style indicates it belongs in *Camissonia*.

499 Fireweed
Chamerion angustifolium

Description: *Pink-purple spires of flowers* atop tall, erect, leafy stems.

Flowers:	Sepals 4; petals 4, each ½–¾″ (1.5–2 cm) long, usually deep pink, occasionally white.
Leaves:	4–6″ (10–15 cm) long, with veins joined in loops near edge.
Fruit:	Slender pod, 2–3″ (5–7.5 cm) long, standing out rigidly from stem.
Height:	2–7′ (60–210 cm).
Flowering:	June–September.
Habitat:	Disturbed soil in cool areas, from lowlands well into mountains; frequent along highways and in burned areas.
Range:	Throughout West and much of East.
Comments:	This plant is also found in Eurasia. It often grows in spectacular, dense patches, especially after fires, hence its common name. Though attractive, it is aggressive in a moist garden, spreading from persistent underground stems. The close-up photo shows a common behavior in plants that serves to increase the potential for cross-pollination: The younger flowers higher on the stalk are shedding their pollen, to be picked up by insects, but stigmas are not yet receptive; the lower flowers have receptive stigmas, increasing the chance for pollen to be brought by insects from adjacent plants. Recent work at the genetic level has shown that *Chamerion,* recognized by its alternate leaves, is distinct from *Epilobium* (with leaves opposite, at least near the base), the genus in which this species was formerly placed.

110 Enchanter's Nightshade
Circaea alpina

Description:	Slender stems with several pairs of heart-shaped leaves and *tiny white flowers in racemes.*
Flowers:	About ⅛″ (3 mm) wide; sepals 2; petals 2, each notched and 2-lobed; stamens 2.
Leaves:	To 2½″ (6.5 cm) long.
Height:	4–20″ (10–50 cm).
Flowering:	May–July.
Habitat:	Cool damp woods.

Range: Across northern North America; in
         West, south mostly in mountains to
         southern California, Arizona, and New
         Mexico; in East, south to Georgia.

Comments: Circe, the Greek enchantress for whom the
            genus is named, possessed magical powers
            and a knowledge of poisonous herbs; she
            could change men into swine. A Eurasian
            species of Enchanter's Nightshade, with
            races in eastern North America, was one
            of Circe's magical plants.

471   Farewell to Spring
Clarkia amoena

Description: An open plant with *showy, pink, cup-
              shaped flowers* in a loose inflorescence.

Flowers: Sepals 4, reddish, twisted to one side,
           remaining attached by tips; petals 4,
           each ¾–1½" (2–4 cm) wide, fan-shaped,
           often with a red-purple blotch in center;
           stamens 8.

Leaves: ¾–3" (2–7.5 cm) long, lanceolate.

Height: 6–36" (15–90 cm).

Flowering: June–August.

Habitat: Dry grassy slopes and openings in brush
           and woods.

Range: Southern British Columbia south to
         central California.

Comments: As the lush grass watered by spring
            rains begins to turn gold in the dry
            heat of summer, the aptly named
            Farewell to Spring begins to flower.
            The flowers close at night and reopen in
            the morning. It is often sold in nurseries
            as Godetia. The genus name honors
            Captain William Clark of the Lewis
            and Clark expedition to the Northwest
            in 1806. There are about 30 species,
            most in California, some very rare.

528   Red Ribbons
Clarkia concinna

Description: A low, many-branched plant with
              elaborate, bright pink flowers crowded in
              leaf axils.

<table>
<tr><td align="right">*Flowers:*</td><td>1½–2″ (4–5 cm) wide; sepals 4; petals 4, slender at base, with 3 lobes at end, middle lobe at least as wide as 2 side lobes.</td></tr>
<tr><td align="right">*Leaves:*</td><td>½–2″ (1.5–5 cm) long, broadly lanceolate.</td></tr>
<tr><td align="right">Height:</td><td>To 1′ (30 cm), rarely taller.</td></tr>
<tr><td align="right">Flowering:</td><td>May–June.</td></tr>
<tr><td align="right">Habitat:</td><td>Loose, partly shaded slopes.</td></tr>
<tr><td align="right">Range:</td><td>California's Coast Ranges.</td></tr>
<tr><td align="right">Comments:</td><td>In the very similar Beautiful Clarkia *(C. pulchella),* sometimes also called Deerhorn Clarkia or Ragged-robin Clarkia, the middle lobe of each petal is twice as wide as the side lobes; it is found from southern British Columbia to southeastern Oregon and east to western Montana. Brewer's Clarkia *(C. breweri),* growing in central California, has a central petal lobe about half as wide as the side lobes. Gunsight Clarkia *(C. xantiana),* found in southern California, has a needle-like middle petal lobe.</td></tr>
</table>

501 Elegant Clarkia
Clarkia unguiculata

<table>
<tr><td align="right">Description:</td><td>A slender plant with few lanceolate leaves and *buds nodding along an erect raceme of few pink flowers.*</td></tr>
<tr><td align="right">*Flowers:*</td><td>1–1½″ (2.5–4 cm) wide; sepals 4, reddish, joined by ends, turning to one side after flower opens; petals 4, with circular, diamond-shaped, or broadly triangular ends, each with a reddish blotch and narrowly stalked base.</td></tr>
<tr><td align="right">*Leaves:*</td><td>¾–3″ (2–7.5 cm) long.</td></tr>
<tr><td align="right">Height:</td><td>6–36″ (15–90 cm).</td></tr>
<tr><td align="right">Flowering:</td><td>June–July.</td></tr>
<tr><td align="right">Habitat:</td><td>Dry slopes, often in disturbed soil.</td></tr>
<tr><td align="right">Range:</td><td>Southern two-thirds of California.</td></tr>
<tr><td align="right">Comments:</td><td>The long slender petal stalks help distinguish this from several similar species in the West, most of which are limited to California.</td></tr>
</table>

400 California Fuchsia; Hummingbird's Trumpet; California Fire Chalice
Epilobium canum

Description: A somewhat shrubby, green or grayish, often many-branched plant with a profusion of *brilliant red, trumpet-shaped flowers* near ends, commonly all oriented in same direction.

Flowers: 1½–2½″ (4–6.5 cm) long; sepals and petals 4 each, red, growing from a red, tubular base; stamens 8, red, protruding.

Leaves: ½–1½″ (1.5–4 cm) long, very narrow and gray with hair, or broader, lanceolate, and greener.

Height: 1–3′ (30–90 cm).

Flowering: August–October.

Habitat: Dry slopes and ridges from sea level to high in mountains; damp canyons in Southwest.

Range: Southwestern Oregon south to Baja California and east to southwestern New Mexico.

Comments: This species is related to the popular ornamental fuchsias, most of which are originally from Central and South America. In California it blooms late in the season, after the summer heat has turned grasses brown and driven most wildflowers to seed. The bright scarlet flowers produce nectar, supplying hummingbirds with food for the start of their southward migration. On the basis of the distinctive flower, this species was formerly placed in the genus *Zauschneria*.

---

227 Yellow Willow Herb
Epilobium luteum

Description: Erect, leafy stems, growing in patches, with *yellow flowers* in upper leaf axils.

Flowers: 1–1½″ (2.5–4 cm) wide; petals 4, each notched at tip; stamens 8.

Leaves: ¾–3″ (2–7.5 cm) long, opposite, lanceolate.

Fruit: Slender pod, containing seeds with long hairs.

Height:	8–28″ (20–70 cm).
Flowering:	July–September.
Habitat:	Moist places in mountains.
Range:	Alaska south to northwestern California.
Comments:	Yellow *Epilobium* are unusual in the West. Shrubby Willow Herb *(E. suffruticosum),* with smaller flowers, is found in the mountains of central Idaho, western Montana, and Wyoming.

462 Rock Fringe; Rose Epilobium
Epilobium obcordatum

Description:	*A matted plant* with a short creeping stem and, in upper leaf axils, *deep pink flowers* seemingly too large for plant and often hiding foliage.
Flowers:	¾–1¼″ (2–3 cm) wide; petals 4, perfectly heart-shaped.
Leaves:	¼–½″ (6–13 mm) long, opposite, crowded, ovate.
Height:	Creeper; flower stalks about 2″ (5 cm), stems to 6″ (15 cm) long.
Flowering:	July–September.
Habitat:	High mountain meadows, rocky slopes, and ledges.
Range:	Oregon south in Sierra Nevada and east to Nevada and central Idaho.
Comments:	Most *Epilobium* species are tall, but this, like many other alpine plants, is low and compact, which protects it from the drying mountain winds and freezing temperatures.

500 Scarlet Gaura
Gaura coccinea

Description:	A grayish plant with leafy branched stems growing in clumps and topped by *reddish-pink flowers in nodding racemes.*
Flowers:	About ½″ (1.5 cm) wide, bilaterally symmetrical; petals 4, narrow, spreading upward, *white in the evening, deep pink by midmorning;* stamens 8.
Leaves:	½–2½″ (1.5–6.5 cm) long, crowded, narrowly lanceolate.

Fruit:	Hard pod, less than ½″ (1.5 cm) long, shaped somewhat like an old-fashioned toy top.
Height:	Usually 6–24″ (15–60 cm).
Flowering:	May–September.
Habitat:	Sandy soil in grasslands and among piñon and juniper.
Range:	Central Canada south in West mostly east of Rocky Mountains to Missouri and Texas, and west from Colorado and New Mexico across southern Utah and Arizona to southeastern California; sporadically introduced elsewhere in West.
Comments:	The whiteness of the newly opened flowers attracts night-flying moths, the primary pollinators of this plant. By early the next day, the flowers are pink, the color intensifying throughout the morning. The flower remains open less than a day.

46 Birdcage Evening Primrose; Devil's Lantern; Lion-in-a-cage
Oenothera deltoides

Description:	A grayish plant with *large, white, tissue-like flowers* on a short central stalk or at leafy ends of otherwise nearly leafless, reclining stems growing from a *dense basal rosette;* buds at stem tips droop.
Flowers:	1½–3″ (4–7.5 cm) wide; petals 4, broad, tube between sepals and ovary ¾–1½″ (2–4 cm) long.
Leaves:	¾–3″ (2–7.5 cm) long, broadly ovate or diamond-shaped.
Height:	Branches 2–12″ (5–30 cm); reclining stems 4–40″ (10–100 cm) long.
Flowering:	March–May.
Habitat:	Sandy deserts.
Range:	Eastern Oregon south to southern California and east to Arizona and Utah.
Comments:	In years with ample rain, this plant grows profusely. Each evening flowers quickly pop open. In the early morning light, before the large flowers close, the desert may appear as if strewn with tissue paper. When a plant dies, its

stems curve upward, forming a
"birdcage"; alternate common names,
including Basket Evening Primrose,
also refer to this peculiar characteristic.
Studies of *Oenothera* have shown that
many of the species in the once much
larger genus would be better placed in
smaller, closely related genera. Some
species were placed in *Camissonia.* Those
with four style branches forming a cross
remain within *Oenothera.*

196 Hooker's Evening Primrose
Oenothera elata

Description: A tall, erect, usually unbranched
stem with *large yellow flowers* in
a raceme.

Flowers: 2–3″ (5–7.5 cm) wide; sepals 4,
reddish; petals 4, broad, yellow in
the evening, becoming rather orange
the following day; stamens 8.

Leaves: 6–12″ (15–30 cm) long, lanceolate,
numerous, progressively smaller
up stem.

Fruit: Slender, rigid pod, 1–2″
(2.5–5 cm) long.

Height: 2–3′ (60–90 cm).

Flowering: June–September.

Habitat: Open slopes, road banks, and
grassy areas from lowlands well
into mountains.

Range: Throughout much of western
United States from Pacific Coast
to western Plains states; also
central Canada.

Comments: Common Evening Primrose
(*O. villosa*), found throughout most
of the United States, has similar
erect stems, but its petals are less
than 1″ (2.5 cm) long. Both are
closely related to the garden Evening
Primrose (*O. glazioviana*), a taller
plant with redder sepals, paler
petals about 1½″ (4 cm) long, and
crinkled leaves; it is found scattered
in the wild from western Washington
south to California.

ORCHID FAMILY
Orchidaceae

Perennial herbs with complicated, unusual, often beautiful flowers borne singly or in spikes, racemes, or branched clusters.

Flowers: Usually bisexual, bilaterally symmetrical; usually twisting one-half turn during development, the bottom of flower becoming the top. Sepals 3, separate, often petal-like; petals 3, separate, lower petal usually different from upper 2 and modified into an elaborate lip, often bearing a backward-projecting spur or sac; stamens 1–2, united with style and stigma, forming a complex structure (column); all these parts attached at top of ovary.
Leaves: Usually alternate, simple.
Fruit: Usually a 1-chambered, rarely 3-chambered, many-seeded capsule.

There are 1,000 genera and about 20,000 species, most abundant in the tropics, where they frequently grow on other plants (elsewhere they are usually terrestrial), but some species grow even in the Arctic. This is possibly the largest family of flowering plants in number of species, but it is rarely, if ever, dominant. Vanilla is obtained from the fruit of the tropical genus *Vanilla.* Many species are grown as beautiful greenhouse novelties. Certain species and hybrids, once very rare and difficult to acquire, are now reproduced in great numbers by cloning. Others are being driven to extinction by habitat destruction. The elaborate flower has highly specialized relationships with pollinators. Pollen is usually held together in masses and in many cases must be properly positioned on the insect for pollination of another flower to occur. Natural pollination is so precise that these plants have not evolved other ways of preventing hybridization, making possible the production of many hybrids, even between unrelated species, by artificial pollination.

---

490 **Calypso; Fairy Slipper**
Calypso bulbosa

Description: 1 mostly *pink, bilaterally symmetrical flower* hanging at tip of an erect, reddish stalk growing above *1 basal leaf.*
Flowers: About 1¼″ (3 cm) long; 3 sepals and upper 2 petals rose-pink, narrowly lanceolate, spreading sideways or upward and forward; lip petal divided

Calypso

into a white, spoon-like tip with
reddish-purple spots and a 2-lobed,
sac-like base with reddish-purple stripes.

Leaves: 1¼–2½" (3–6.5 cm) long, shallowly
pleated, tapering to a purplish stalk.

Height: To 8" (20 cm).

Flowering: March–July.

Habitat: Thick humus and mossy ground in
woods.

Range: Much of northern North America; in
West, south to northern California,
northeastern Arizona, and southern
New Mexico; in East, south to Vermont,
Michigan, and South Dakota.

Comments: This species also grows in Eurasia. It
was named for the sea nymph Calypso
of Homer's *Odyssey,* who detained the
willing Odysseus on his return from
Troy; like Calypso, the plant is beautiful
and prefers secluded haunts.

122 Phantom Orchid; Snow Orchid
Cephalanthera austiniae

Description: *A waxy, white, nearly leafless plant* with
stems in clusters and racemes of 5–20
bilaterally symmetrical, white flowers.

Flowers: 3 sepals and upper 2 petals each ½–¾"
(1.5–2 cm) long, lanceolate, gently
curving inward and surrounding lip

petal; lip petal divided into 2 parts, constricted in middle, tipped with a yellow fleck.

Leaves: Reduced to sheaths on lower stem.
Height: 9–20″ (22.5–50 cm).
Flowering: June–August.
Habitat: Dense, moist, usually coniferous woods.
Range: Northern Washington south to northern California mountains and southern Sierra Nevada, and east to Idaho.
Comments: This aptly named plant appears ghostly in the dim light of the forest floor. Since it is not green and is therefore incapable of photosynthesis, it absorbs all its nutrition from the humus of the forest floor, aided by a fungus in its roots. This species was once considered the sole member of the genus *Eburophyton;* it is now recognized as belonging to *Cephalanthera,* a genus of about 12 species throughout the Northern Hemisphere.

385   Spotted Coral Root
Corallorhiza maculata

Description: 1 to many *yellowish-, reddish-, or purplish-brown, nearly leafless stems* with loose racemes of several or many bilaterally symmetrical flowers the same color as stems.
Flowers: About ¾″ (2 cm) wide; 3 sepals and upper 2 petals lanceolate, spreading sideways and upward; lip petal about ½″ (1.5 cm) long, nearly as wide, white, usually purple-spotted, bent downward, with 2 lobes near base.
Leaves: Reduced to few tubular sheaths on stem.
Height: 8–31″ (20–80 cm).
Flowering: April–September.
Habitat: Shady woods.
Range: Throughout West south to Central America; also in much of East.
Comments: This is the most common coral root in the United States. Clumps of stems often occur in extensive colonies.

412 Striped Coral Root
Corallorhiza striata

Description: A nearly leafless plant with several or
many erect, *reddish-purple stems* bearing
several or many *reddish-striped, pale
pinkish, bilaterally symmetrical flowers* in a
raceme.

Flowers: About 1″ (2.5 cm) wide; sepals 3, with 3
veins; upper 2 petals similar to sepals,
with 5 veins; lip petal ⅜–½″ (9–13 mm)
long, ovate, bent downward at base, spoon-
like near tip, with deep purplish-brown
stripes at base tending to merge at tip.

Leaves: Reduced to sheaths on lower stem.

Height: 6–20″ (15–50 cm).

Flowering: May–August.

Habitat: Deep woods.

Range: Throughout West south to Mexico; in
East, much of Canada south to New
York and west to Nebraska.

Comments: *Corallorhiza* means "coral root," though
the "root" is actually a hard mass of
rhizomes associated with a fungus that
aids in absorbing nutrients from the
humus on the forest floor. After
producing flower stalks, the rhizomes
may remain dormant for several years.

5 Early Coral Root; Pale Coral Root
Corallorhiza trifida

Description: Several or many erect, *pale yellowish or
greenish, nearly leafless stems* in a clump,
each stem with a raceme of small,
bilaterally symmetrical flowers the same
color as stem except for *white lower lip.*

Flowers: About ¼″ (6 mm) long; 3 sepals and
upper 2 petals arching upward and
forward; lip petal bent downward,
sometimes with few purple spots at
base, irregularly and minutely scalloped
around end.

Leaves: Reduced to sheaths on lower stem.

Height: 3–12″ (7.5–30 cm).

Flowering: May–August.

Habitat: Moist woods from moderate to high
elevations.

Range: Alaska south and east to Labrador,
            and south in West to Washington,
            northeastern Oregon, northern
            Sierra Nevada, central Utah, and
            Colorado; also in northern portion
            of eastern United States.

Comments: Of all the coral roots, this small
            pale species is perhaps the least showy.
            It is also found in Eurasia.

117   California Lady's Slipper
Cypripedium californicum

Description: 1 bilaterally symmetrical, *yellow-
              green flower with a white pouch* in each
              upper leaf axil of unbranched,
              clumped stems; 3–10 flowers
              per plant.

Flowers: Sepals 3, each ½–¾″ (1.5–2 cm) long,
              lanceolate, yellow-green, upper sepal
              pointing upward, lower 2 almost
              completely joined and pointing
              downward; upper 2 petals similar to
              upper sepal; lip petal about ¾″ (2 cm)
              long, a bulbous white pouch sometimes
              blushed with pink or spotted with
              purple, with a small opening on top
              near base.

Leaves: 2–6″ (5–15 cm) long, broadly
              lanceolate.

Height: 1–4′ (30–120 cm).

Flowering: May–July.

Habitat: Along streams and seeps in open shade.

Range: Southwestern Oregon and northern
              California.

Comments: This is one of the most charming
              lady's slippers, often having many
              flowers all turned in the same
              direction and seeming to peer from
              cool hideaways among maidenhair
              ferns, Salal *(Gaultheria shallon)*,
              Western Azalea *(Rhododendron
              occidentale)*, and Crimson Columbine
              (Aquilegia formosa). The genus name
              derives from the Greek *Kypris* ("Venus")
              and *pes* ("foot"), referring to the flower's
              moccasin-like lip petal.

384 Clustered Lady's Slipper
Cypripedium fasciculatum

Description: Several short stems in a cluster, each
stem with *2 broad leaves and 2–4
drooping, brownish to greenish, bilaterally
symmetrical flowers.*

Flowers: About 1½" (4 cm) wide; sepals 3, lower
2 joined but with 2 tips; upper 2 petals
similar to upper sepal; lip petal about
½" (1.5 cm) long, a greenish pouch
streaked or mottled with purple.

Leaves: 2–6" (5–15 cm) long, ovate.

Height: 2–8" (5–20 cm).

Flowering: April–July.

Habitat: Moderately high-elevation forests.

Range: British Columbia south to central
California and northern Colorado.

Comments: Each lady's slipper species attracts
insects into its pouch, from which there
is only one exit, past the stigma, where
pollen from a previously visited flower is
brushed off. Then the insect must go
under one of the anthers, where new
pollen is picked up. This procedure
helps maintain genetic diversity, thus
increasing the ability of the species to
adapt to its environment.

100 Mountain Lady's Slipper
Cypripedium montanum

Description: A leafy plant with few stems in a clump,
each stem with 1–3 *white and dull purple,
bilaterally symmetrical flowers* near top, 1
in each upper leaf axil.

Flowers: Sepals 3, each 1¼–3" (3–7.5 cm) long,
lanceolate, dull purple, upper sepal
pointing upward, lower 2 almost
completely joined and pointing
downward; upper 2 petals similar to
upper sepal, twisted; lip petal ¾–1¼"
(2–3 cm) long, a bulbous white pouch
blushed with pink or purple, with
opening on top near base.

Leaves: 2–6" (5–15 cm) long, ovate.

Height: 8–28" (20–70 cm).

Flowering:	May–July.
Habitat:	Dry or moist, open or lightly shaded, brushy or wooded valleys and slopes.
Range:	Alaska south to northern California, northern Idaho, and northwestern Wyoming.
Comments:	Most lady's slippers are handsome plants, all the more charming because of the mystique and romance surrounding orchids. So many species have been dug up that most are now rare in the wild. Although many enthusiasts try to cultivate these plants as ornamentals, lady's slippers generally die in the garden.

383 Stream Orchid; Chatterbox; Giant Helleborine
Epipactis gigantea

Description:	Leafy stems, usually in dense patches, with 1 *bilaterally symmetrical, greenish-brown and pinkish flower* in each upper leaf axil.
Flowers:	1–1½″ (2.5–4 cm) wide; sepals 3, coppery green, lanceolate; upper petals 2, pinkish rose or purplish, lanceolate, with purple veins, pointing forward, about as long as sepals; lip petal ½–¾″ (1.5–2 cm) long, 2 parts separated by deep constriction in middle, spoon-like half at base with purple veins; triangular tip or "tongue" of lip petal waxy, pink or salmon.
Leaves:	2–8″ (5–20 cm) long, broadly lanceolate, with prominent veins.
Height:	1–3′ (30–90 cm).
Flowering:	March–August.
Habitat:	Springs or seeps, near ponds, and along streams from deserts to mountains.
Range:	British Columbia south to Mexico, and from Pacific Coast east to Rocky Mountains and beyond to southwestern South Dakota.
Comments:	The petal lip and "tongue" move when the flower is touched or shaken, hence the common name Chatterbox.

489 Texas Purple Spike
Hexalectris warnockii

Description: Slender, *nearly leafless, reddish-brown stems* with up to 10 mostly *reddish-brown, bilaterally symmetrical flowers in a loose raceme.*

Flowers: 1–1¼" (2.5–3 cm) wide; 3 sepals and upper 2 petals similar, narrow; lip petal broad, curving upward, widest and with pinkish edges near base; center of lip petal white or yellowish, with 3 fringed ridges; tip of lip petal fringed, blunt, often maroon.

Leaves: Reduced to few bracts.

Height: To 1′ (30 cm).

Flowering: June–August.

Habitat: Open, brushy woods.

Range: Southeastern Arizona, central Texas, and Big Bend region of western Texas.

Comments: This is the most common *Hexalectris* in Big Bend National Park. There are four other species in the Southwest, all also found in the park; all have yellowish or reddish stems. Crested Coral Root *(H. spicata),* found from southeastern Arizona to the eastern United States, has yellowish-brown sepals, petals with darker veins, and a yellowish or white lip petal with purple veins.

7 Broad-leaved Twayblade
Listera convallarioides

Description: A little plant with a *pair of leaves* at midstem below a slender raceme of about 20 *small, green, bilaterally symmetrical flowers.*

Flowers: 3 sepals and upper 2 petals similar, narrowly lanceolate, short, sharply bent backward; lip petal ⅜–½" (9–13 mm) long, with 2 round lobes at end, widest near tip, evenly tapered and then abruptly narrowed to a stalk-like base.

Leaves: ¾–3" (2–7.5 cm) long, elliptical.

Height: 2–14" (5–35 cm).

Flowering: June–August.

Habitat: Moist woods.
Range: Alaska south and east to Newfoundland,
          and south in West to southern
          California, Idaho, northeastern Nevada,
          northern Utah, and central Colorado;
          also in southern Arizona, and in
          northern portion of eastern United
          States.
Comments: Broad-leaved Twayblade also occurs in
          Asia. The small green flowers attract
          little insects. When the insect enters the
          flower, it trips a mechanism that fires a
          spot of pollen that sticks to the insect
          and is carried by it to another flower,
          thus facilitating pollination. There are
          three other species in the West with the
          characteristic pair of leaves at midstem,
          but none with sepals and upper petals
          sharply bent backward.

118 Elegant Rein Orchid
Piperia elegans

Description: Many *white, fragrant, bilaterally
              symmetrical flowers* in a raceme at tip of a
              stout stem with leaves near base.
Flowers: 3 sepals and upper 2 petals each about
              ¼" (6 mm) long, bluntly lanceolate,
              with a pale green central stripe; upper 2
              petals barely joined to upper sepal; base
              of lip petal constricted slightly, bearing
              a slender, almost straight spur about ½"
              (1.5 cm) long, extending behind flower.
Leaves: To 5" (12.5 cm) long, oblong, withering
              before end of flowering.
Height: 8–16" (20–40 cm).
Flowering: July–September.
Habitat: Open sites in shrublands and coniferous
              forests.
Range: British Columbia south to central
              California and east to Montana.
Comments: The photograph and description above is
              of this species' coastal phase, which
              occurs south from northern Washington
              to central California. Near the coast the
              northern populations were once called
              Coastal Rein Orchid *(Habenaria greenei)*.
              The more stout and more densely

flowered coastal plants intergrade with
the more slender inland plants, which
are sometimes called Slender Rein
Orchid. The name *Habenaria elegans* was
formerly restricted to inland plants,
which inhabit rather dry, open woods.
Because the inland and coastal plants
intergrade, they are presently considered
the same species, now in the genus
Piperia, and may be all included under
the common name Elegant Rein Orchid.
The inland Slender Rein Orchid has an
open inflorescence and pale greenish-
yellow flowers, each with a spur more
than ¼″ (6 mm) long. Careful study has
revealed two new species among these
similar-appearing plants. Two species,
both with greenish stripes on the petals
and found from central California
northward, have recently been named.
Monterey Rein Orchid *(P. yadonii)* has
white petals with green outer borders
and usually more than six bracts on the
stem; it is rare, occurring only in
Monterey County, California. White-lip
Rein Orchid *(P. candida)* has white
petals with a green midvein, less than
six bracts on the stem, and flowers
turned mostly to one side; it occurs near
the Pacific Coast from Washington to
central California.

6 Alaska Rein Orchid
Piperia unalascensis

Description: 1 or few stems, leafy near base, with *pale green, bilaterally symmetrical flowers* in long, slender, open racemes.

Flowers: Sepals 3, each about ⅛″ (3 mm) long, broadly lanceolate, with 1 vein; lower 2 sepals spreading to sides and downward; upper 2 petals about as long as sepals, joined to upper sepal, forming a hood; lip petal fleshy, lanceolate, projecting forward, with a backward- or downward-projecting spur at base only ¹⁄₁₆–¼″ (1–5 mm) long.

Leaves: To 10″ (25 cm) long, lanceolate.

Height: 8–31″ (20–80 cm).
Flowering: June–August.
Habitat: Dry woods, gravelly streambanks, and open slopes.
Range: Alaska south and east to Quebec, and south to Baja California, northern Nevada, Utah, Colorado, western South Dakota, and Minnesota; also near Great Lakes.
Comments: The species name comes from Unalaska, an island in the Aleutians. A number of small northern orchids were formerly put in the inclusive genus *Habenaria,* which has been divided into several smaller genera, including *Piperia.*

---

120 Bog Rein Orchid; Bog Candles
Platanthera leucostachys

Description: Erect, leafy stems with many *fragrant, white, bilaterally symmetrical flowers in a spike.*
Flowers: Upper sepal joined to upper 2 petals, forming a hood about ¼″ (6 mm) long; lower 2 sepals each ¼–⅜″ (5–9 mm) long, lanceolate, spreading horizontally; lip petal about as long as sepals, hanging down, base almost 3 times as wide as slender tip; slender or stout spur extending from back of lip petal downward and forward beneath flower.
Leaves: Those at midstem largest, each 2–12″ (5–30 cm) long, narrowly or broadly lanceolate, clasping.
Height: 6–52″ (15–130 cm).
Flowering: June–September.
Habitat: Wet or boggy ground.
Range: British Columbia south to southern California, northern Nevada, northwestern Arizona, southwestern Utah, Idaho, and northwestern Wyoming.
Comments: Plants in the Rocky Mountain region often have more stout, shorter spurs. Study has shown that this plant, once called *Habenaria dilatata,* is better

placed in the genus *Platanthera,*
where it has been given a different
scientific name for technical reasons;
Platanthera refers to the wide anther.

119 Round-leaved Rein Orchid
Platanthera orbiculata

Description: 1 stalk rising between *2 broadly
elliptical or round basal leaves lying
on ground,* bearing up to 25 *white or
greenish-white, bilaterally symmetrical
flowers in a raceme.*

Flowers: Upper sepal and upper 2 petals
arching forward; lower 2 sepals
bent backward; lip petal ½–¾"
(1.5–2 cm) long, narrow, hanging
down; spur ½–1" (1.5–2.5 cm)
long, slender, extending backward
and often slightly upward from
beneath base of lip petal.

Leaves: 2½–6" (6.5–15 cm) long.

Height: 8–24" (20–60 cm).

Flowering: June–August.

Habitat: Moist forest floors.

Range: British Columbia east to Labrador
and south to northern Oregon,
northern Idaho, and northwestern
Montana; also in northern regions
of eastern United States.

Comments: This species has the largest flowers
of all western rein orchids. Several
kinds of moths feed on nectar in the
spur and probably pollinate the flower.

121 Hooded Ladies' Tresses
Spiranthes romanzoffiana

Description: 1 stem, or several in a clump, with
3–6 leaves near base and a dense
spike of *up to 60 creamy white,
bilaterally symmetrical flowers* in
1–4 gently spiraled rows.

Flowers: ⅜–½" (9–13 mm) long; sepals 3,
lanceolate, projecting forward, tips
of lower 2 often curling back; upper
2 petals forming a hood; lip petal

bent downward at middle, projecting from beneath hood, constricted behind a finely fringed tip.

Leaves: 2–10″ (5–25 cm) long, to about ½″ (1.5 cm) wide, lanceolate.

Height: 4–24″ (10–60 cm).

Flowering: July–October.

Habitat: Generally moist open places from coastal bluffs to high in mountains.

Range: Most of northern North America; in West, south to southern California, Arizona, and New Mexico; also in northern regions of eastern United States.

Comments: Western Ladies' Tresses (S. porrifolia), which grows in similar habitats from southern Washington to southern California and also in northern Utah, has a triangular lip petal barely constricted behind the tip, and the sepals are only about ⅜″ (9 mm) long.

BROOMRAPE FAMILY
Orobanchaceae

Herbaceous root parasites, annual or perennial, usually somewhat fleshy and some shade of yellow, brown, violet, or red, lacking chlorophyll.

Flowers: Bilaterally symmetrical; in racemes, spikes, or borne singly atop a slender stem. Sepals 2–5, united; petals 5, united, forming an upper and lower lip; stamens 4; all these parts attached at base of ovary.

Leaves: Simple, reduced to scales.

Fruit: 1-chambered capsule.

There are about 17 genera and 150 species, primarily in the northern temperate region, especially the warmer parts of Europe. The common name of the family alludes to the parasitism of various species of Orobanche on shrubs in the pea family (Fabaceae) known as brooms (Cytisus). Other Orobanchaceae may parasitize various families of plants, some becoming serious agricultural pests. This family is very closely related to the figwort family (Scrophulariaceae).

386 California Ground Cone
Boschniakia strobilacea

Description: An unusual plant, resembling a slender, *dark purplish-brown pinecone,* standing erect on ground with cupped, spoon-like bracts widest near blunt tip.

Flowers: About ½" (1.5 cm) long, bilaterally symmetrical, in axils of bracts; corolla bent at middle of tube; upper lip hood-like, lower lip 3-lobed.

Leaves: Reduced to bracts, among flowers.

Height: 4–10" (10–25 cm).

Flowering: May–July.

Habitat: In forests or brush associated with manzanita shrubs or madrone trees.

Range: Southern Oregon south to southern California.

Comments: This perennial parasite flowers each season and causes large knobs to form on the roots of manzanita shrubs *(Arctostaphylos)* and madrone trees *(Arbutus).* Small Ground Cone *(B. hookeri),* which grows near the Pacific Coast from Canada to northern California, is half the size of California Ground Cone, with pointed bracts widest at about the middle.

618 Cooper's Spike Broomrape
Orobanche cooperi

Description: *A fleshy plant with dense spikes,* singly or in clusters, of *bilaterally symmetrical, dark purple flowers.*

Flowers: ¾–1¼" (2–3 cm) long, with long-stalked, glandular hairs; upper corolla lobes ¼–⅜" (6–10 mm) long, slightly longer than lower lobes, all bluntly pointed; spike 1¾–2" (4–5 cm) wide.

Leaves: Reduced to more or less triangular scales, pressed against stem.

Height: 4–16" (10–40 cm).

Flowering: January–May.

Habitat: Sandy, desert soil.

Range: Southwestern Utah south to southeastern California, southern Arizona, and northwestern Mexico.

Comments: The proper classification of this plant
remains unclear. It is often considered a
subspecies of Prairie Broomrape (*O.
ludoviciana*), a species widespread in the
West, and its distinction from Spike
Broomrape (*O. multiflora*) is also
debated. All *Orobanche* are parasites on
the roots of other plants; this species is
particularly common on White Bur Sage
(*Ambrosia dumosa*), a shrubby member of
the aster family (Asteraceae). It has also
become a parasite on tomato crops in
southeastern California's Coachella
Valley.

99 Naked Broomrape
Orobanche uniflora

Description: *1 purple, lavender, yellowish, or whitish,
bilaterally symmetrical flower at tip of each
slender, yellowish-brown, leafless stalk.*

Flowers: About 1″ (2.5 cm) long; corolla slightly
bent downward in middle of tube, with
2 yellow stripes on lower side, lobes
fringed with fine hairs.

Leaves: Reduced to tiny scales.

Height: Stalks 1¼–4″ (3–10 cm); main stem
mostly underground.

Flowering: April–August.

Habitat: Open places from lowlands to moderate
elevations in mountains.

Range: Southwestern Canada south throughout
West; also from southeastern Canada
south throughout eastern United States,
except most of Great Plains north of
Kansas.

Comments: This species is parasitic on several kinds
of plants, often stonecrops (*Sedum*).

WOOD SORREL FAMILY
Oxalidaceae

Herbs, shrubs, rarely trees, with alternate or basal, usually
compound leaves and flowers usually borne singly or in an
umbel; sap often sour.

Flowers: Radially symmetrical. Sepals 5, separate; petals 5,

separate or united at base; stamens 10, joined by filaments; all these parts attached at base of ovary with 5
styles.
Leaves: Usually palmately compound and clover-like, with
usually 3 leaflets; or pinnately compound.
Fruit: 5-chambered capsule, rarely a berry.

There are about 8 genera and 900 species, primarily in
tropical and subtropical regions. Several are cultivated as ornamentals, and the greens of a few are used in salads or as
potherbs. The tree-like, tropical species Carambola *(Aver-
rhoa carambola)* produces the 5-angled starfruit increasingly
seen in grocery stores and fresh-food markets.

---

460 **Redwood Sorrel**
Oxalis oregana

Description: A low plant growing in patches,
with *3 heart-shaped leaflets* on each
leaf and *1 funnel-shaped, white or
rose-pink flower* at end of each stalk;
leafstalks and flower stalks of equal
length and attached to plant at
ground level.
Flowers: ½–¾" (1.5–2 cm) wide; petals 5,
often with purple veins.
Leaves: Leaflets 3, each ½–1½" (1.5–4 cm)
long, heart-shaped, often with a pale
blotch in center, attached by points
to tip of erect stalk.
Height: 2–7" (5–17.5 cm).
Flowering: April–September.
Habitat: Shady forests.
Range: Washington south to coastal central
California and east to eastern side
of Cascade Range.
Comments: This species forms lush, solid,
inviting carpets on the cool floor
of coastal redwood forests. The sour
sap is characteristic of the genus; the
genus name is from the Greek *oxys*
("sour"). A similar species in the
same general region and habitat,
Great Oxalis *(O. trilliifolia),* has at
least two flowers per stalk. There are
also several yellow-flowered species
of *Oxalis* in the West, some of which
are aggressively weedy.

459   Violet Wood Sorrel
Oxalis violacea

Description:	A delicate plant with *clover-like foliage and several rose-violet flowers* on each stalk rising above leaves.
Flowers:	¾–1″ (2–2.5 cm) wide; petals 5, flaring, joined at base and forming a yellowish-green or whitish tube; usually 2–8 flowers in a loose umbel.
Leaves:	Leaflets 3, each ¼–¾″ (6–20 mm) long, heart-shaped, with an orange spot in notch, attached by points.
Fruit:	Several-seeded capsule, ⅛–¼″ (3–5 mm) long.
Height:	3–6″ (7.5–15 cm).
Flowering:	March–October.
Habitat:	Open woods and grassy areas, among rocks, and on banks.
Range:	Arizona and New Mexico; also in much of eastern United States.
Comments:	Some plants have flowers with long styles and short stamens, and others have flowers with short stamens and long styles, which ensure cross-pollination. Mountain Wood Sorrel *(O. alpina)* is similar but has flowers with styles of three different lengths, leaves with several orange spots scattered on the surface or near the edges (or sometimes none), and capsules often more than ¼″ (6 mm) long; it occurs from northern New Mexico and central Arizona south to Guatemala. Ten-leaved Wood Sorrel *(O. decaphylla),* found in the Southwest and Mexico, has 4–11 leaflets.

PEONY FAMILY
Paeoniaceae

Somewhat succulent, occasionally rather shrubby herbs with large flowers.

Flowers: Radially symmetrical. Sepals 5, separate; petals 5 or 10, separate; stamens many; pistils 2–5, separate; ovary partially surrounded by a conspicuous, fleshy disk.
Leaves: Compound.
Fruit: Many-seeded, leathery pod.

There are 2 genera and about 34 species, found in the northern temperate region. Several species and many hybrids and horticultural forms of *Paeonia* are cultivated, most with doubled flowers.

380 Western Peony
Paeonia brownii

Description: A rather *fleshy, bluish-green, leafy plant,* usually with several clustered stems, divided leaves, and 1 *greenish and reddish-brown, round flower* hanging at end of each stalk.

Flowers: 1–1½" (2.5–4 cm) wide; sepals 5–6, greenish, spoon-shaped; petals 5, maroon or bronze in center, green on edges, about as long as sepals.

Leaves: Blades to 2½" (6.5 cm) long, divided into 3 main segments on short stalks, segments again divided into 3 parts, each with lobes at end.

Height: 8–24" (20–60 cm).

Flowering: April–June.

Habitat: Chaparral, sagebrush, and pine forests.

Range: Eastern Washington south through northern two-thirds of California and east to Utah, western Wyoming, and Idaho.

Comments: The genus name comes from Paeon, the physician of the Greek gods. Northwestern Native Americans made tea from the roots to treat lung ailments. California Peony *(P. californica),* the only other species in the West, occurs only in southern California; its leaf segments have gently tapering, long-pointed tips.

POPPY FAMILY
Papaveraceae

Annual or perennial herbs, occasionally shrubs, rarely small trees, often with clear, white, or colored sap.

Flowers: Radially symmetrical; mostly borne singly. Sepals 2–3, separate or united into a cone (calyptra), quickly dropping off; petals 4–6, separate, showy, often crumpled in bud; stamens numerous; all these parts attached at base of ovary.

Leaves: Usually alternate, sometimes opposite or basal; simple or deeply divided.

Fruit: Usually a capsule, varying from long and slender to more or less urn-shaped, sometimes with a cap-like structure at top, opening by slits or well-defined pores near top (when cap present pores are just beneath rim).

There are about 25 genera and 200 species, mostly in temperate and subtropical regions. Several genera are well developed in western North America. Several species are grown as ornamentals. Poppy seeds used in baking are obtained from species of *Papaver.* Opium is extracted from the sap of Opium Poppy *(Papaver somniferum).* The seeds of some Papaveraceae have a white, oily appendage attractive to ants as food; the insects carry the seeds about, aiding in dispersal.

---

44 Great Desert Poppy; Great Bear Poppy; White Bear Poppy
Arctomecon merriamii

Description: *1 large white flower* atop each of several stalks with *hairy leaves, most near base.*

Flowers: 2–3″ (5–7.5 cm) wide; sepals 3, hairy, dropping off as flower opens; petals 6, widest near tip; stamens many, yellow.

Leaves: 1–3″ (2.5–7.5 cm) long, pale blue-green, narrowly fan-shaped, toothed across blunt end, covered with long straight hairs.

Height: 8–20″ (20–50 cm).

Flowering: April–May.

Habitat: Loose rocky slopes and deserts.

Range: Southeastern California and southern Nevada.

Comments: Little Desert Poppy *(A. humilis),* found in southwestern Utah and northwestern Arizona, has four white petals; it is generally less than 10″ (25 cm) high. Yellow Desert Poppy *(A. californica),* found in southern Nevada and northwestern Arizona, has six yellow petals.

45 Prickly Poppy
Argemone polyanthemos

Description: A branched, pale blue-green, leafy plant with *white flowers, yellow sap, and slender, yellow prickles all over.*

Flowers: About 3″ (7.5 cm) wide; buds with 2–3 sepals bearing erect prickles and at tip a stout horn ¼–⅝″ (6–16 mm) long, sepals dropping off as flower opens; petals 4–6, broad, crumpled; stamens many, yellow.

Leaves: To 8″ (20 cm) long, deeply lobed, prickly on veins and edges but not (or very lightly) on surfaces between.

Fruit: Spiny capsule; largest spines without small prickles at base.

Height: To 4′ (1.2 m).

Flowering: April–July.

Habitat: Sandy or gravelly soil on plains and brushy slopes.

Range: Eastern Wyoming and South Dakota south to south-central New Mexico and northern half of Texas.

Comments: The Greek word *argema* means "cataract of the eye," for which species of this genus were supposedly a remedy. There are several species in the West, all

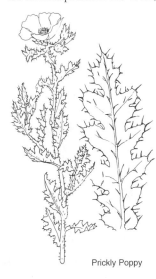

Prickly Poppy

similar, a few with yellow, pinkish, or lavender petals. All parts of the plants are poisonous (including the seeds), but fortunately the foliage is prickly and distasteful to animals.

209 Tree Poppy
Dendromecon rigida

Description: A stiff roundish *shrub with brilliant yellow, cup-shaped flowers* at ends of short branches or on long stalks in leaf axils.
Flowers: 1–2½" (2.5–6.5 cm) wide; sepals 2, dropping off as flower opens; petals 4, broad; stamens many, short.
Leaves: 1–4" (2.5–10 cm) long, leathery, lanceolate, bluish green, stalk twisted so that flat sides of blade face sideways.
Height: 4–20' (1.2–6 m).
Flowering: April–June.
Habitat: Dry slopes in chaparral.
Range: Northern California south to Mexico.
Comments: Tree Poppy may be very common several years after a fire in chaparral. There is only one other species in the genus, Island Tree Poppy *(D. harfordii),* found on islands off the coast of southern California.

Tree Poppy

370 California Poppy
Eschscholzia californica subsp. *californica*

Description: A *smooth, bluish-green plant with fern-like leaves,* usually several stems, and often *orange flowers* borne singly on a long stalk; often perennial.

Flowers: 1–2" (2.5–5 cm) wide; sepals joined into a calyptra ⅜–1½" (1–4 cm) long; petals 4, fan-shaped, evenly deep orange to yellow-orange, or sometimes yellow near tips and orange near base; stamens many; flat, conspicuous, pinkish rim at base of ovary ⅟₁₆–¼" (2–6 mm) wide.

Leaves: Blades ¾–2½" (2–6.5 cm) long, divided into narrow segments, on long stalks.

Fruit: Slender capsule, 1¼–4" (3–10 cm) long, slightly curved.

Height: 8–24" (20–60 cm).

Flowering: February–September.

Habitat: Open areas; common on grassy slopes.

Range: Southern Washington south to southern California.

Comments: On sunny days in spring, California Poppy, the state flower, often turns hillsides orange. It is a popular ornamental. Responsive to sunlight, the flowers close at night and on cloudy days. The spicy fragrance attracts mainly beetles, which serve as pollinators. Flowers produced early in the season tend to be larger than those later on. There are other species in California, but none has the conspicuous pink rim at the base of the ovary.

---

369 Mexican Gold Poppy;
Amapola del Campo
Eschscholzia californica subsp. *mexicana*

Description: A *smooth, bluish-green plant with fern-like leaves* mostly near base, often 1 or few stems, and usually *orange-yellow flowers* borne singly on a long stalk; always annual.

Flowers: ¾–1½" (2–4 cm) wide; sepals joined into a calyptra ⅜–½" (8–13 mm) long; petals 4, fan-shaped, yellow-orange,

orange, or yellow near tips and orange near base, occasionally cream; stamens many; flat, pinkish rim at base of ovary about 1/16″ (1 mm) wide.

Leaves: Blades 1/2–2″ (1.5–5 cm) long, divided into narrow segments, on long stalks.

Height: To 16″ (40 cm).

Flowering: March–May.

Habitat: Open, gravelly, desert slopes.

Range: Southeastern California east to western tip of Texas and south to northern Mexico.

Comments: The Spanish name means "poppy of the countryside." This is appropriate, for when there are ample winter rains in the desert, this poppy grows in profusion, covering gravelly outwash fans and arid flats with a golden carpet. Once considered a separate species, Mexican Gold Poppy is now recognized as a desert-inhabiting subspecies of California Poppy (*E. californica*). The two subspecies are exceedingly similar, one consistent difference being that the first leaves on seedlings of Mexican Gold Poppy are linear and undivided, whereas on seedlings of California Poppy they are divided in a Y-shape (a difference learned by careful greenhouse study).

368 Fire Poppy; Western Poppy
Papaver californicum

Description: 1 bowl-shaped flower atop each stem, with *4 fan-shaped, reddish-orange petals* with a greenish spot at each base; *bud drooping* before flower opens.

Flowers: About 1″ (2.5 cm) wide; sepals 2, hairy, dropping off as flower opens; stamens many, yellow; cap-shaped stigma with lines radiating from center atop nearly cylindrical ovary.

Leaves: 1 1/4–3 1/2″ (3–9 cm) long, pinnately divided into few segments with teeth or lobes.

Height: 1–2′ (30–60 cm).

Flowering: April–May.

Habitat: Open brush and woods, especially
           after fires.
Range: Coast Ranges from San Francisco Bay
           south to southern California; not
           common in northern half of range.
Comments: Opium is extracted from the sap
           of Opium Poppy *(P. somniferum),*
           which probably originated in the
           western Mediterranean, or from a
           variant of *P. setigerum* in southwestern
           Asia. Early in history it was spread
           through much of the civilized
           world, and its origin is obscure.
           Opium Poppy was once commonly
           (and innocently) grown in gardens
           and is still found scattered in the
           United States.

---

208 Alpine Poppy
Papaver radicatum

Description: A low, tufted, brownish-hairy
              plant bearing *1 bowl-shaped flower
              with 4 pale yellow or white petals*
              atop each stalk.
Flowers: ¾–1½" (2–4 cm) wide; sepals 2,
              covered with brown hairs, dropping
              off as flower opens; stamens many.
Leaves: ¾–4" (2–10 cm) long (including stalk),
              pinnately lobed, lobes generally with
              few teeth.
Height: 2–6" (5–15 cm).
Flowering: June–August.
Habitat: Tundra and rocky, alpine slopes.
Range: Throughout much of Arctic
              North America and south in
              Rocky Mountains to northeastern
              Utah and northern New Mexico.
Comments: Alpine Poppy was only recently
              named, after completion of a study
              of all poppies from northern Canada
              and high in the Rocky Mountains.
              The smaller Pygmy Poppy *(P.
              pygmaeum),* 1¼–2½" (3–6.5 cm)
              tall, with pale salmon petals ½"
              (1.5 cm) long, grows at high
              elevations in southern Alberta
              and northwestern Montana.

210 Cream Cup
Platystemon californicus

Description: A soft-haired plant with several stems, each topped with 1 small, bowl-shaped flower *resembling a pale yellow or cream buttercup.*

Flowers: ½–1″ (1.5–2.5 cm) wide; sepals 3, dropping off as flower opens; petals 6; stamens many, with flat filaments; stigmas 6–25, on ovary separating into as many sections when fruit forms.

Leaves: ¾–3″ (2–7.5 cm) long, opposite, narrowly lanceolate, mostly on lower half of plant.

Height: 4–12″ (10–30 cm).

Flowering: March–May.

Habitat: Open, grassy areas.

Range: Most of California east to southwestern Utah and central Arizona, and south to northern Baja California.

Comments: This genus consists of only one species, within which there are some races with nearly white petals, others with yellow petals, and still others with cream petals that are yellow at the base.

43 Matilija Poppy
Romneya coulteri

Description: Tall, heavy, leaning, leafy, branched stems growing in patches, with 5–8 *large, fragrant, white flowers* near ends.

Flowers: 4–7″ (10–17.5 cm) wide; sepals 3, smooth, dropping off as flower opens; petals 6, fan-shaped; stamens many, yellow, forming ball in center; ovary bristly-hairy.

Leaves: 2–8″ (5–20 cm) long, gray-green, pinnately divided into 3 or 5 main divisions with few teeth or again divided.

Fruit: Capsule, with bristly hairs.

Height: 3–8′ (90–240 cm).

Flowering: May–July.

Matilija Poppy

Habitat: Brush in coastal mountains.
Range: Southern California.
Comments: The large white flowers are conspicuous from a distance. A second species, Bristly Matilija Poppy *(R. trichocalyx),* has bristly hairs on the sepals and on the stalk beneath the flower. Hybrids of the two are grown as ornamentals.

PASSIONFLOWER FAMILY
Passifloraceae

Herbaceous or woody vines, climbing by tendrils borne in leaf axils, less often shrubs or trees, with bizarre, elaborate flowers usually in pairs in leaf axils.

Flowers: Radially symmetrical. Sepals usually 5, often petal-like, usually separate, sometimes united at base; petals 5, separate, or sometimes absent; numerous thread-like structures forming a crown (corona) at base of corolla; stamens 3–5, or 10; ovary with 3–5 styles, often raised on a stalk also bearing stamens.
Leaves: Simple, often deeply lobed.
Fruit: Capsule or berry.

There are about 16 genera and 650 species in this mostly tropical American family. Several species are cultivated for their unusual and often gaudy flowers; a few *Passiflora* produce edible fruit, known as passion fruit.

1 Green Passionflower
Passiflora tenuiloba

Description: A vine with *tendrils in leaf axils* and *bizarre, greenish flowers.*

Flowers: About ¾″ (2 cm) wide; sepals 5; petals absent; fringed corona between stamens and sepals, with 2 circles of many hair-like segments; stamens 5, bent downward; styles 3, arching outward; stamens and ovary borne on stalk in center of flower.

Leaves: To 6″ (15 cm) wide, broader than long, divided into 3 main narrow lobes; stalk with large glands.

Height: Vine; stems to 7′ (2.1 m) long.

Flowering: April–October.

Habitat: Climbing over shrubs and grasses on hillsides.

Range: Southern New Mexico, southwestern Texas, and northern Mexico.

Comments: Unlike this species, which has evolutionarily lost its petals, most *Passiflora* have 10 petal-like parts; the common name passionflower relates to the resemblance of these flower parts to aspects of the Crucifixion story. The 10 petal-like parts represent the disciples, excluding Peter and Judas; the five stamens, the wounds Jesus received; the knob-like stigmas, the nails; and the fringed corona, the crown of thorns. There are several *Passiflora* species in the Southwest.

PLANTAIN FAMILY
Plantaginaceae

Herbs mostly with basal leaves and inconspicuous flowers in spikes or heads.

Flowers: Radially symmetrical. Calyx with 4 united, membranous sepals; corolla with 4 united, papery petals; stamens 4, protruding; all these parts attached at base of ovary.

Leaves: Often basal, simple, with major veins mostly parallel or curved from base to tip.

Fruit: Seeded capsule, with top lifting free; or a small nut.

There are 3 genera and about 250 species, found nearly throughout the world. Some are unwelcome weeds. The seeds of certain species become sticky when wet; those of Psyllium *(Plantago afra)* and related species are used in making natural laxatives.

---

136 English Plantain
Plantago lanceolata

Description: *A narrow, cylindrical spike* of tiny, crowded, *brownish-white flowers* atop a long, slender, leafless stalk growing from a basal rosette of leaves.

Flowers: Petals 4, each about ⅛″ (3 mm) long, parchment-like; stamens 4, projecting on hair-like filaments and ending in large, cream-colored anthers; spike ¾–3″ (2–7.5 cm) long.

Leaves: 2–16″ (5–40 cm) long, lanceolate, dark green, parallel-veined.

Height: 6–24″ (15–60 cm).

Flowering: April–August.

Habitat: Lawns, roadsides, and pastures.

Range: Throughout much of Canada and United States.

Comments: This native of Europe is a common companion of Common Dandelion *(Taraxacum officinale)*. The common name plantain (from the Latin *planta,* meaning "sole of the foot") refers to the broad, flat, low-lying leaves of some species.

LEADWORT FAMILY
Plumbaginaceae

Herbs or shrubs with leaves often in basal rosettes and small flowers in heads, modified racemes, or branched clusters.

Flowers: Radially symmetrical. Sepals 5, united, often pleated, showy, stiff and membranous; petals 5, united, corolla often deeply lobed and seeming to have separate petals; stamens 5, each opposite a corolla lobe; all these parts attached at base of ovary.
Leaves: Alternate or in a basal rosette.
Fruit: 1-chambered, 1-seeded, often leathery; not opening, or opening very late.

There are about 12 genera and 400 species, found predominantly in dry parts of the Mediterranean region and in central Asia. A few species are cultivated as ornamentals.

526 California Thrift
Armeria maritima

Description:	A low plant with a *basal cluster of many narrow leaves,* and a slender, leafless stalk topped by a *round head of pale lilac flowers* above several broad, purplish, papery bracts.
Flowers:	Calyx funnel-shaped, pinkish, parchment-like; corolla with 5 lobes, joined at base; head ¾–1″ (2–2.5 cm) wide.
Leaves:	2–4″ (5–10 cm) long.
Height:	2–16″ (5–40 cm).
Flowering:	March–August.
Habitat:	Beaches, coastal bluffs, and slightly inland prairies.
Range:	Pacific Coast from British Columbia south to southern California; also in Arctic North America.
Comments:	This plant also occurs in Eurasia. It resembles a small onion plant, but the similarity is superficial, for onions are in a very distantly related family, the Liliaceae.

PHLOX FAMILY
Polemoniaceae

Usually leafy herbs, rarely small shrubs, commonly with showy flowers in open or dense clusters branched in a forked manner.

Flowers: Radially symmetrical or slightly bilaterally symmetrical. Calyx with 5 united sepals; corolla with 5 united petals, sometimes dish-like, more often forming a slender tube with an abruptly expanded top; stamens 5; style 3-branched; all these parts attached at base of ovary.
Leaves: Alternate or opposite, simple or pinnately compound.
Fruit: 3-chambered capsule.

There are about 18 genera and 300 species in this chiefly North American family. It is especially well developed in the western United States. Some species are grown as ornamentals.

431 Alpine Collomia
Collomia debilis

Description: *Numerous sprawling stems forming a loose mat,* with leaves and cream, white, pink, lavender, or blue flowers crowded at ends.

Flowers: About ¾″ (2 cm) wide; corolla ½–1″ (1.5–2.5 cm) long, 5-lobed, trumpet-shaped.

Leaves: ½–1¼″ (1.5–3 cm) long, varying from lanceolate to deeply divided into 3–5 lobes.

Height: Creeper; flower stalks about 2″ (5 cm), mats 6–18″ (15–45 cm) wide.

Flowering: June–August.

Habitat: Shifting, rocky, high-mountain slopes.

Range: Cascade Range of Washington east to western Montana and western Wyoming, and southeast to northeastern Oregon, northeastern Nevada, and central Utah.

Comments: The species name, meaning "weak," refers to the sprawling stems, which actually might be considered a strength, for the plant's low compact habit helps protect it from cold mountain winds. A similar species, Talus Collomia *(C. larsenii),* has highly divided leaves (with 3–7 lobes, some or all cleft again) and a corolla only to ½″ (1.5 cm) long; it grows from the Cascade Range and Olympic Mountains of Washington to northern California.

430 Bridge's Gilia
Gilia leptalea

Description: A bushy, airy plant with *many slender branches,* small leaves, and *small, deep pink, funnel-shaped flowers* on thread-like stalks in leaf axils.

Flowers: ⅜–¾″ (9–20 mm) long; corolla with 5 lobes, each about ¼″ (5 mm) long; stamens 5, attached at different levels to inside of corolla.

Leaves: ½–2″ (1.5–5 cm) long, very narrow, with glandular hairs, often pinnately divided into few lobes.

Height:	2–14″ (5–35 cm).
Flowering:	June–September.
Habitat:	Openings in brush and dry woods.
Range:	Southern Oregon south to southern California.
Comments:	The pink color of the flowers is among the richest in the genus; the flowers of many other species are nearly white, pale pink, or lavender. The species of this large western genus are difficult to distinguish from one another but usually can be recognized as *Gilia* by the fairly small, trumpet- or funnel-shaped flowers, the three branches on the style, and the alternate, often pinnately divided leaves.

566 Blue Gilia
Gilia rigidula

Description:	A low, often tufted plant with *violet-blue flowers* borne singly or few in a loose cluster near *dense, rigid, prickly, divided leaves* often hidden by flowers.
Flowers:	Corolla nearly ¾″ (2 cm) wide, with 5 round lobes spreading from a narrow tube with a yellow ring (the "eye") around opening.
Leaves:	½–1½″ (1.5–4 cm) long.
Height:	To 10″ (25 cm).
Flowering:	April–September.
Habitat:	Sandy or rocky slopes on prairies and among piñon and juniper.
Range:	Eastern Arizona east to western Texas and north to southeastern Colorado and western Kansas; also in northern Mexico.
Comments:	The violet-blue flower with the bright yellow center is unique. The "eye" serves to guide insects to the nectar.

410 Skyrocket; Desert Trumpets; Skunk Flower
Ipomopsis aggregata

Description:	Clusters of showy, *bright red or deep pink, trumpet-shaped flowers* in upper leaf axils and atop sparsely leaved stems.

Flowers:	Corolla ¾–1¼″ (2–3 cm) long, with 5 pointed lobes.
Leaves:	1–2″ (2.5–5 cm) long, densest near base, pinnately divided into narrow segments.
Height:	6–84″ (15–210 cm).
Flowering:	May–September.
Habitat:	Dry slopes from sagebrush to forests.
Range:	British Columbia southeast to Montana and south to southern California, Arizona, New Mexico, Texas, and northern Mexico.
Comments:	Skyrocket is one of the most common western wildflowers. It grows readily from seed, and the brilliant red trumpets are handsome in wildflower gardens. Its beauty compensates for the faint skunky smell of its glandular foliage, for which it bears the less complimentary common name Skunk Flower. *Ipomopsis* was once considered part of *Gilia,* hence another alternate common name, Scarlet Gilia.

155 Ballhead Gilia
Ipomopsis congesta

Description:	Branched and woody near base, with *roundish heads of small, trumpet-shaped, dingy white flowers* at ends of stems and branches.
Flowers:	About ¼″ (6 mm) long; corolla 5-lobed, with a short tube at base; head about ¾–1″ (2–2.5 cm) wide.
Leaves:	Usually less than 1″ (2.5 cm) long, divided into 3–5 very narrow lobes, sometimes again divided.
Height:	8–12″ (20–30 cm).
Flowering:	June–September.
Habitat:	Dry open slopes from lowlands to high-mountain elevations.
Range:	Eastern Oregon and eastern California east to northwestern New Mexico, western Nebraska, and western North Dakota.
Comments:	Some forms may at first be mistaken for sandworts *(Arenaria),* but the latter have simple leaves and five separate petals.

577 **Pale Trumpets**
Ipomopsis longiflora

Description: Slender, *pale blue-violet, pale blue,*
or white, trumpet-shaped flowers,
borne singly or in pairs, spreading
from axils of upper bracts on a
spindly, openly branched, sparsely
leaved plant.

Flowers: Corolla 1–1½″ (2.5–4 cm) long,
with a very narrow tube and a
flared end resembling a 5-pointed star.

Leaves: Those near base to 1½″ (4 cm) long,
pinnately divided into few narrow lobes;
those on stem shorter, less divided.

Height: To 2′ (60 cm).

Flowering: March–October.

Habitat: Sandy deserts and arid grasslands.

Range: Southern Utah northeast to western
Nebraska and south to western Texas,
New Mexico, Arizona, and northern
Mexico.

Comments: The flowers look almost too delicate for
the intense heat of the desert and plains,
but this rather ungainly plant is
vigorous and often grows in profusion.
At night moths attracted to the pale
flowers feed on the nectar.

559 **Spotted Langloisia; Lilac Sunbonnet**
Langloisia setosissima subsp. *punctata*

Description: *Low bristly tufts with pale violet or lilac,*
purple-dotted, radially symmetrical flowers
peering from among leaves.

Flowers: Corolla about ½″ (1.5 cm) wide, 5-
lobed, each lobe with *many fine purple*
spots and 2 yellow dots near base.

Leaves: ¾–1¼″ (2–3 cm) long, broadest near
top, with 3–5 bristle-tipped teeth;
bristles on stalk-like base often with
2–3 branches.

Height: 1½–6″ (4–15 cm); forming tufts to 10″
(25 cm) wide.

Flowering: April–June.

Habitat: Dry, gravelly places in deserts, in
Creosote Bush, and among piñon
and juniper.

Range: Southwestern Idaho, extreme eastern Oregon, western Nevada, and southeastern California.

Comments: *Langloisia* was once considered to have four species. Recent studies have shown that two are better placed in a new genus, *Loeseliastrum.* The remaining two are now considered to be subspecies of *L. setosissima,* the only species in *Langloisia.* Bristly Langloisia (subspecies *setosissima*) has bluish corollas that may be unmarked or streaked; it grows from southeastern Oregon and southwestern Idaho south to western Nevada, southeastern California, and western Arizona.

433 Prickly Phlox
Leptodactylon californicum

Description: Slightly woody stems covered with *small prickly leaves* and forming a loose clump with *pink flowers in small clusters* near top.

Flowers: Corolla about 1″ (2.5 cm) wide, with a narrow tube abruptly flaring into 5 broad, round, usually pink (often white, cream, or lilac) lobes, brownish on back.

Leaves: About ½″ (1.5 cm) long, palmately cleft into 5–9 narrow, rigid, prickly lobes; in clusters along stem.

Height: 1–3′ (30–90 cm).

Prickly Phlox

Flowering: March–June.
Habitat: Dry places and rocky ridges in brush.
Range: Southern California.
Comments: The genus name refers to the finger-like division of the leaves. Granite Gilia *(L. pungens),* a more widespread species found from southern British Columbia to Baja California and east to New Mexico, western Nebraska, and Montana, is 4–16″ (10–40 cm) high.

---

434   **False Baby Stars**
Linanthus androsaceus

Description: *A knob-like cluster of prickly leaves and deep pink, lilac, white, or yellow, trumpet-shaped flowers* atop a small spindly plant.
Flowers: Corolla ½–¾″ (1.5–2 cm) wide, 5-lobed, with a slender tube; calyx with 5 needle-pointed lobes joined by a short, inconspicuous membrane.
Leaves: ½–1¼″ (1.5–3 cm) long, divided into 5–9 narrow, pointed lobes; most in cluster at top, fewer in widely spaced pairs resembling rings of needles around slender stem.
Height: 2–12″ (5–30 cm).
Flowering: April–June.
Habitat: Grassy slopes and open places.
Range: Most of California west of Sierra Nevada south to edge of southern desert.
Comments: The many *Linanthus* species are mostly slender, perky little annuals, commonly forked, with opposite, palmately divided, prickly leaves, often clustered near the top, and colorful flowers that seem almost too big for the plant. Nearly 40 species occur in California alone, but there are few elsewhere.

---

223   **Desert Gold**
Linanthus aureus

Description: A tiny, spindly plant, usually with 3 branches at a fork, with *pale to deep yellow, funnel-shaped flowers* on very slender stalks.

Flowers:	Corolla ¼–½″ (6–13 mm) wide, 5-lobed, with a narrow tube, often with maroon at opening.
Leaves:	Opposite, divided into 3 narrow, pointed lobes, each about ¼″ (6 mm) long, forming a ring of needles around stem.
Height:	2–4″ (5–10 cm).
Flowering:	April–June.
Habitat:	Desert floors and sandy slopes.
Range:	Southern California east to southern Nevada and through southern Arizona to southwestern New Mexico, and south to northern Mexico.
Comments:	Northern Linanthus *(L. septentrionalis)*, found from Alberta south to Colorado and west to the Sierra Nevada and Cascade Range, has a similar manner of branching but grows to 10″ (25 cm) high and has flowers with a white, pale blue, or lavender corolla about ⅛–¼″ (3–6 mm) long.

436 Mustang Linanthus; Mustang Clover
Linanthus montanus

Description:	Erect stems with a *dense cluster of prickly bracts* near top and long, *pink, trumpet-shaped flowers* projecting from bracts.
Flowers:	Corolla about ¾″ (2 cm) wide, 1–2″ (2.5–5 cm) long, paler in center, 5-lobed, with a purple spot at base of each lobe, outside of tube minutely glandular-hairy.
Leaves:	¾–1¼″ (2–3 cm) long, opposite, pinnately divided into 5–11 lobes, each pair resembling a ring of needles around stem.
Height:	4–24″ (10–60 cm).
Flowering:	May–August.
Habitat:	Dry, gravelly places in open woods.
Range:	Western slopes of Sierra Nevada.
Comments:	The unusually long flowers of Mustang Linanthus make it one of the showiest of this California-based genus.

18 Nuttall's Linanthus
Linanthus nuttallii

Description: *White or cream flowers in clusters* atop many leafy stems.

Flowers: Corolla about ½" (1.5 cm) wide, with a narrow tube and 5 broad, widely flared lobes.

Leaves: ¾" (2 cm) long, opposite, each cleft into 5–9 narrow lobes, resembling *rings of many narrow leaves.*

Height: About 1′ (30 cm).

Flowering: June–September.

Habitat: Open or sparsely wooded, often rocky slopes in mountains.

Range: British Columbia southeast to Montana and south to southern California, Arizona, New Mexico, and Mexico.

Comments: This attractive plant is sweetly aromatic. Recent studies have removed this species from the tiny genus *Linanthastrum* and placed it in the more inclusive *Linanthus.*

593 Desert Calico
Loeseliastrum matthewsii

Description: *Small bristly tufts or mats* with colorful *white to pink or lavender-dotted, bilaterally symmetrical flowers* nestled among leaves.

Flowers: Corolla about ½" (1.5 cm) wide, 5-lobed, *upper 3 lobes marked with red and white,* lower 2 lobes generally unmarked.

Leaves: ½–1½" (1.5–4 cm) long, with bristles at tips of sharp teeth.

Height: 1–2" (2.5–5 cm); 1–12" (2.5–30 cm) wide.

Flowering: March–June.

Habitat: Open, gravelly or sandy deserts.

Range: Southern California northeast to northwestern Arizona and south to Mexico.

Comments: All species in this genus are tufted and rather bristly. Schott's Calico *(L. schottii),* also bilaterally symmetrical, has a pale lavender corolla with purple spots or a purple, arch-shaped patch. Species of *Loeseliastrum* were once considered to

be part of the larger genus *Langloisia*.
Flower shape and other features
distinguish the two genera.

---

17 Tufted Phlox
Phlox caespitosa

Description:	A low, tufted, slightly woody plant with *prickly, needle-like leaves and pale purple, pink, or white flowers.*
Flowers:	Corolla with narrowly tubular base ¼–½" (6–13 mm) long, flaring into 5-lobed end ½–¾" (1.5–2 cm) wide; calyx with 5 narrow, pointed lobes joined by a flat, translucent membrane.
Leaves:	¼–½" (6–13 mm) long, simple, opposite.
Height:	2–6" (5–15 cm).
Flowering:	April–June.
Habitat:	Dry open pinewoods, sometimes in sagebrush.
Range:	Southern British Columbia south to central Washington, northeastern Oregon, northern Idaho, and northwestern Montana.
Comments:	Tufted Phlox resembles the smaller Granite Gilia *(Leptodactylon pungens),* which has leaves divided into needle-like segments. Cushion Phlox *(P. pulvinata),* found from eastern Oregon to southwestern Montana, in the Sierra Nevada, and throughout the Rocky Mountain region south to New Mexico, has been mistakenly called *P. caespitosa;* unlike Tufted Phlox, it forms tight mats, and its stems are not at all woody.

---

435 Long-leaved Phlox
Phlox longifolia

Description:	Slender stems often growing in dense clumps and bearing *bright pink, pale lilac, or chalky-white flowers* in loose clusters.
Flowers:	Corolla about 1" (2.5 cm) wide, with a slender tube about ½–¾"

(1.5–2 cm) long and 5 round lobes; calyx with 5 pointed lobes joined by an outward-folding membrane; style several times as long as 3 branches at tip.

Leaves: To 3″ (7.5 cm) long, very narrow, opposite.

Height: 4–16″ (10–40 cm).

Flowering: April–July.

Habitat: Dry, open, rocky places from low to moderate elevations.

Range: Southern British Columbia south to southern California and east to Rocky Mountain region from New Mexico to western Montana.

Comments: Phloxes are beautiful and popular wildflowers found in nearly all western habitats. The most spectacular have densely clumped stems that, when the plant is in bloom, are completely hidden under a hemisphere of pink, white, or pale lilac flowers. Long-leaved Phlox consists of many intergrading geographic races, a number of which are recognized as species by some botanists.

---

607 Western Polemonium
Polemonium occidentale

Description: Many *broadly funnel-shaped, sky blue flowers* crowded in a branched cluster near top of a leafy plant.

Flowers: Corolla ½–¾″ (1.5–2 cm) wide, with 5 round lobes.

Leaves: Narrow, pinnately compound, bearing 19–27 lanceolate leaflets, each ½–1½″ (1.5–4 cm) long.

Height: 1–3′ (30–90 cm).

Flowering: June–August.

Habitat: Wet places at moderate elevations.

Range: Alaska and Yukon south to southern California, Nevada, Utah, and Colorado.

Comments: The leaves resemble long ladders; the genus is known by the common name Jacob's Ladder. Leafy Polemonium *(P. foliosissimum),* which grows from Idaho and Wyoming south to Arizona and

Western Polemonium

New Mexico, is somewhat leafier
than Western Polemonium, the
upper leaves not much smaller
than those at the base.

578 Sky Pilot
Polemonium viscosum

Description:	A leafy plant with stems in clumps and topped by *funnel-shaped, blue-violet flowers* in loose heads; *sticky, glandular hairs* covering leaves and stems exude skunk-like odor.
Flowers:	Corolla ½–¾″ (1.5–2 cm) wide, with 5 round lobes.
Leaves:	To 6″ (15 cm) long, narrow, pinnately compound, each leaflet divided to its base into 3–7 tiny lobes.
Height:	4–16″ (10–40 cm).
Flowering:	June–August.
Habitat:	Open, rocky ridges in high mountains.
Range:	Eastern Washington, northern Oregon, and central Nevada east to Rocky Mountain region from New Mexico to Alberta.
Comments:	The name Sky Pilot comes from this plant's preferred high habitat. Elegant Polemonium *(P. elegans),* found high in the Cascade Range of Washington and British Columbia, has undivided leaflets.

MILKWORT FAMILY
Polygalaceae

Herbs, shrubs, or small trees with oddly shaped flowers in spikes, racemes, or branched clusters.

Flowers: Bilaterally symmetrical. Sepals usually 5, separate, inner 2 larger and petal-like; petals 3, often fringed; stamens usually 8, united; all these parts attached at base of ovary.
Leaves: Simple.
Fruit: Usually a 2-chambered capsule.

There are about 12 genera and 750 species, found nearly throughout the world. A few species are grown as ornamentals. The flower superficially resembles the pea flower of the pea family (Fabaceae) and is often confused with it by those unfamiliar with milkworts.

128 White Milkwort
Polygala alba

Description: Numerous slender, erect stems, each topped by *tiny, white, bilaterally symmetrical flowers in a narrowly cone-shaped raceme.*

Flowers: Sepals 5, inner 2 white, extending to side like wings, each ⅛" (3 mm) long, larger than other 3; petals 3, white, often greenish at base, lowest petal like a keel, often tipped with purple; raceme ¾–3" (2–7.5 cm) long.

Leaves: ¼–1" (6–25 mm) long, *very narrow,* many scattered on stem, lowest in 1–2 whorls.

Height: 8–14" (20–35 cm).

Flowering: March–October.

Habitat: Sandy flats and rocky hills.

Range: Eastern Montana south to eastern Colorado, New Mexico, and central Arizona, east to Texas, and north through much of the Great Plains to Minnesota; also in Mexico.

Comments: *Polygala* comes from a Greek word meaning "much milk"; some species were thought to stimulate the flow of milk in cattle and nursing mothers.

BUCKWHEAT FAMILY
Polygonaceae

Mostly herbs, sometimes shrubs or vines, rarely trees, with small flowers in racemes, spike-like clusters, or heads and stems commonly with swollen nodes.

Flowers: Usually bisexual, radially symmetrical. Sepals 3–6, separate, petal-like, sometimes in 2 series of 3, outer series differing somewhat from inner; petals absent; stamens 3–9; all these parts attached at base of ovary.
Leaves: Usually alternate, simple; stipules commonly fused into a papery sheath around stem at each node.
Fruit: Small, hard, seed-like, generally 3-sided or lens-shaped.

There are about 30 genera and 1,000 species, primarily in the northern temperate region. Rhubarb *(Rheum rhabarbarum)* and Buckwheat *(Fagopyrum esculentum)* are sources of food, and a few species are cultivated as ornamentals. The name Polygonaceae, derived from Greek words meaning "many knees," refers to the stems' swollen nodes. This family has also been known as the knotweed family.

359 Northern Buckwheat
Eriogonum compositum

Description: Matted clumps of basal leaves with *leafless stems and roundish clusters of tiny, whitish to deep yellow flowers.*
Flowers: Cluster 1–4″ (2.5–10 cm) wide; each flower about ⅛″ (3 mm) long, with 6 petal-like segments not hairy on outside, tapering to a slender base about as thick as slender stalk joined to flower, clustered in cups with several teeth.
Leaves: 1–10″ (2.5–25 cm) long, blades heart-shaped, triangular, or ovate, whitish beneath, lightly hairy on top; stalks about as long as blades.
Height: 4–20″ (10–50 cm).
Flowering: May–July.
Habitat: Rocky, open ground from lower elevations well into mountains.
Range: Eastern Washington south to northern California and east to Idaho.
Comments: This is a highly variable species in a genus of many species, most of which are difficult to distinguish from one

another. The seeds are an important food for small wildlife, including ants. *Eriogonum,* from the Greek *erion* ("wool") and *gony* ("knee" or "joint"), refers to the hairy stems of many species.

361 Desert Trumpet; Bladder Stem; Indianpipe Weed
Eriogonum inflatum

Description: A *spindly plant* with 1 or few leafless, erect *stems swollen just below branches.*
Flowers: Tiny, yellow, on very slender stalks, growing at branch ends in woolly cups with 6 teeth.
Leaves: ½–2″ (1.5–5 cm) long, oval, long-stalked, in a basal rosette.
Height: 8–40″ (10–100 cm).
Flowering: March–July.
Habitat: Sandy or rocky ground in deserts.
Range: Southern Utah south to much of Arizona, southern California, and Baja California.
Comments: This is a common desert plant, conspicuous because of the stark, swollen, gray-green stems, which have a pleasant sour taste. Dried stems were used by Native Americans as tobacco pipes, hence one of its common names.

534 Cushion Buckwheat
Eriogonum ovalifolium

Description: A matted plant, often grayish-haired, with basal leaves and *round heads of tiny, reddish or purplish to cream flowers* on long, erect, leafless stems.
Flowers: Head about 1″ (2.5 cm) wide; each flower about ⅛″ (3 mm) long, with 6 petal-like segments, on a slender stalk growing from a cylindrical, 5-toothed cup.
Leaves: ½–5″ (1.5–12.5 cm) long, varying from short, spatula-shaped, and without stalks to long-stalked with roundish blades.
Height: 1–12″ (2.5–30 cm).

Flowering:	May–August.
Habitat:	In open areas from sagebrush plains to open coniferous woodlands, alpine ridges, and rocky mountain slopes.
Range:	British Columbia south to northern California and east to Rocky Mountains from New Mexico to Alberta.
Comments:	There is much variation, as is to be expected in a widespread species such as this, occurring over a broad elevational range. Alpine plants are generally dwarf; plants growing in sagebrush are usually taller. Flowers vary from cream to yellow when young; as they age, they may become reddish or purple.

328 Sulfur Flower
Eriogonum umbellatum

Description:	Long erect stalks with *tiny, yellow or cream flowers in ball-like clusters* at ends of branches of an umbel-like cluster.
Flowers:	Ball-like cluster 2–4″ (5–10 cm) wide, composed of numerous little cups from which grow several flowers on very slender stalks; each flower about ¼″ (6 mm) long, with 6 petal-like segments hairy on outside; circle of bract-like leaves immediately beneath umbel-like cluster.
Leaves:	½–1½″ (1.5–4 cm) long, on slender stalks, ovate, 2–3 times as long as wide, very hairy on lower side; clustered at ends of short woody branches.
Height:	4–12″ (10–30 cm).
Flowering:	June–August.
Habitat:	Dry areas from sagebrush deserts to foothills and alpine ridges.
Range:	British Columbia south to southern California and east to eastern slopes of Rocky Mountains from Colorado to Montana.
Comments:	Tiny flowers growing from small cups is a feature of *Eriogonum,* the large genus of wild buckwheats. The highly variable Sulphur Flower adds to the difficulties of identification in a complex group of similar western species.

518 Water Smartweed;
Water Lady's Thumb
Polygonum amphibium

Description: Freely rooting, long, prostrate
stems *growing across mud or in
water* and topped with erect,
dense, *narrowly egg-shaped,
pink flower clusters.*

Flowers: Cluster ½–7" (1.5–17.5 cm)
long; each flower with 5 petal-like
segments about ⅛" (4 mm) long.

Leaves: Those of terrestrial plants to 8"
(20 cm) long, lanceolate, tapering at
both ends; those of aquatic plants to 6"
(14.5 cm) long, lanceolate-ovate, tip
rounded or pointed, base rounded
or heart-shaped.

Fruit: Seed-like, dark brown or black,
lens-shaped.

Height: Terrestrial plants 2–3' (60–90 cm);
aquatic plants with stems to 7'
(2.1 m) long, flower clusters 1–6"
(2.5–15 cm) above water.

Flowering: June–September.

Habitat: In mud or floating on still
fresh water.

Range: Throughout much of Canada and
United States.

Comments: This species also occurs in Eurasia.
Its seeds provide food for waterfowl.
Some authorities recognize two
intergrading, environmentally
variable varieties in the West.
The variety *stipulaceum* (shown in
the photograph) has short oval
flower clusters and is not especially
aggressive; the pink flower masses
of this variety are very attractive,
but since the plants grow quickly,
they can become an unwelcome weed
in decorative ponds. The variety
emersum has lanceolate leaves with
narrowly tapering tips and slender
flower clusters at least 1½" (4 cm)
long; once called *P. coccineum,* a
separate species, this variety is
aggressive to the point of being
classified as a noxious weed.

137 Western Bistort; Smokeweed
Polygonum bistortoides

Description: *Dense, white or pale pink flower clusters* atop slender, erect, reddish stems.

Flowers: Cluster 1–2″ (2.5–5 cm) long; each flower less than ¼″ (6 mm) long, with 5 petal-like segments.

Leaves: 4–8″ (10–20 cm) long, lanceolate, mostly near base of stem, each with a brownish, papery sheath at node.

Height: 8–28″ (20–70 cm).

Flowering: May–August.

Habitat: Moist mountain meadows and streamsides.

Range: Western Canada south to southern California, Arizona, and New Mexico; also in East.

Comments: One of the most frequent mountain wildflowers, this species sometimes covers meadows. The stout roots were prepared by Native Americans for food. Young leaves may be cooked as greens.

363 Winged Dock; Wild Begonia
Rumex venosus

Description: Stout, erect, leafy, reddish stems with conspicuous white sheaths at nodes and *reddish-orange flowers in thick clusters.*

Flowers: At first inconspicuous, with 6 sepal-like segments, inner 3 greatly enlarging to broadly heart-shaped bracts, each ½–1½″ (1.5–4 cm) long, surrounding a tiny fruit.

Leaves: To 6″ (15 cm) long, numerous, ovate or lanceolate.

Height: 6–20″ (15–50 cm).

Flowering: April–June.

Habitat: Open banks, ravines, grasslands, and sagebrush deserts, often where sandy.

Range: Southern British Columbia south to northeastern California and east to central Canada; also throughout Great Plains.

Comments: The reddish-orange flower clusters are conspicuous in the late spring. Although their pale translucence and shape are reminiscent of clusters of begonias (hence one of the common names), this plant is not closely related to begonias. After flowering, the broad, sepal-like segments catch the wind and tumble the seed to new places. The similar Canaigre (pronounced *can-i-gray*) Desert Rhubarb *(R. hymenosepalus),* found in sandy areas from Wyoming south to southern California and western Texas, has sepal-like segments rarely more than ¾″ (2 cm) wide and stout stems growing from a cluster of thick roots; tannin extracted from its roots was used by early Spanish settlers to tan hides. A common name for many of the more weedy *Rumex* species is Sour Dock; the sour flavor comes from oxalic acid.

PURSLANE FAMILY
Portulacaceae

Herbs, often succulent, with delicate flowers borne singly or in branched clusters.

Flowers: Radially symmetrical. Sepals usually 2, united or separate; petals at least 4–6, separate or united at base; stamens many, or 1 opposite each petal; all these parts attached at base of ovary.
Leaves: Alternate, opposite, or in a dense basal rosette; simple.
Fruit: Usually a capsule, opening lengthwise or top coming off like a lid.

There are about 20 genera and 500 species, found throughout the world, many in the Americas. A few are grown as ornamentals, and some are used as potherbs.

560 Red Maids
Calandrinia ciliata

Description: Small, *brilliant, bright reddish-pink, shallowly bowl-shaped flowers* on short stalks growing from axils of upper leaves on a *succulent plant* with spreading or erect stems.

Flowers: About ½″ (1.5 cm) wide; sepals 2, with coarse hairs; petals 5.

Leaves:	½–3″ (1.5–7.5 cm) long, narrow, upper ones much smaller.
Height:	2–16″ (5–40 cm).
Flowering:	April–May.
Habitat:	Open places or among weeds in moist soil.
Range:	Washington south to California and east to southwestern New Mexico.
Comments:	This species is a member of a large genus of the western Americas and Australia, named for the 18th-century Swiss botanist J. L. Calandrini.

535 Pussy Paws
Calyptridium umbellatum

Description:	*Flowers in dense pink clusters* at ends of ascending or prostrate stems *resembling upturned pads of cats' feet.*
Flowers:	Sepals 2, pale pink, papery, translucent, becoming larger as flower matures, each ultimately to ½″ (1.5 cm) long; petals 4, each ¼″ (6 mm) long, quickly withering, pinkish; stamens 3.
Leaves:	¾–3″ (2–7.5 cm) long, narrow, in a dense rosette.
Height:	Creeper; branching stalks 2–10″ (5–25 cm).
Flowering:	May–August.
Habitat:	Loose soil in coniferous forests.
Range:	British Columbia south to Baja California and east to Utah, Wyoming, and Montana.
Comments:	Stems often lie on the ground, with the relatively heavy "pussy paws" forming a perfect ring around the leaf rosette.

24 Broad-leaved Claytonia
Claytonia cordifolia

Description:	A succulent plant with most leaves at base and a *pair of broadly ovate or heart-shaped leaves on stem below 3–10 white flowers in a very open raceme* without bracts.
Flowers:	About ½″ (1.5 cm) long; sepals 2; petals 5; stamens 5.

Leaves:	¾–2½″ (2–6.5 cm) wide, opposite, those at base long-stalked.
Height:	4–16″ (10–40 cm).
Flowering:	May–September.
Habitat:	Wet soil near springs and streams; more common in mountains.
Range:	Southern British Columbia south to northern California and western Montana, and east to northern Utah.
Comments:	Claytonias such as this, with broad, succulent leaves, have edible, sweet-tasting foliage. The very similar Candy Flower *(C. sibirica),* growing in shaded places from Alaska south to southern California and east to Montana and Utah, has smaller, pink-tinged flowers, with a bract at the base of each individual flower stalk in the raceme. Once placed in the genus *Montia,* the western species in this group are now considered part of *Claytonia.*

77 Western Spring Beauty
Claytonia lanceolata

Description:	A small, slender, delicate plant with a *pair of succulent leaves at midstem* and a *loose raceme of white, pink, or rose, bowl-shaped flowers.*
Flowers:	¼–¾″ (6–20 mm) wide; sepals 2; petals 5, if pale then often with darker veins; stamens 5.
Leaves:	½–3½″ (1.5–9 cm) long, narrow, lanceolate; commonly also 1–2 narrow leaves near base of stem, often withering before flowers bloom.
Height:	2–10″ (5–25 cm).
Flowering:	April–July.
Habitat:	Moist ground, especially near snowbanks, from foothills to high mountains.
Range:	British Columbia south to southern California and east to Rocky Mountains from New Mexico to Alberta.
Comments:	As the name suggests, Western Spring Beauty blooms in the spring, barely waiting for the snow to melt. This

perennial grows from a deeply buried, spherical, underground stem; when cooked, the stem tastes like a potato.

76 Miner's Lettuce; Indian Lettuce
Claytonia perfoliata

Description: *A succulent plant* with slender stems seeming to grow through middle of *1 circular leaf* and topped by a *raceme of tiny white flowers.*

Flowers: ⅛–¼″ (3–6 mm) wide; sepals 2; petals 5, from slightly longer to nearly twice as long as sepals.

Leaves: Circular leaf to 2″ (5 cm) wide; those at base several, from half to fully the height of flowering stems, almost uniformly narrow or with lanceolate blade and slender stalk.

Height: 1–14″ (2.5–35 cm).

Flowering: March–July.

Habitat: Loose moist soil in shady places.

Range: British Columbia south to Baja California and east to Arizona, Utah, Wyoming, and the Dakotas.

Comments: The circular stem leaf is actually two, paired side by side and grown together. Sometimes they are not grown together at all, or grown together on only one side. As the common names indicate, the leaves are edible. This species was once included in the genus *Montia.*

442 Cliff Maids; Siskiyou Lewisia
Lewisia cotyledon

Description: Leafless branched stalks growing from a dense basal rosette of succulent leaves and topped by flowers with *8–10 pale to deep pink or white-and-red-striped petals.*

Flowers: 1–1¼″ (2.5–3 cm) wide; sepals 2, with glandular teeth; stamens 5–8; bracts on flower stalk.

Leaves: To 5″ (12.5 cm) long, spatula-shaped.

Height: 4–12″ (10–30 cm).

Flowering: April–May.

Habitat: Rock crevices, often on cliffs.

Range: Southwestern Oregon and northern California.

Comments: This plant forms beautiful bouquets on precipitous cliffs, to which it clings by a massive root tightly wedged in a tiny cleft. Because of its precise adaptation to its rugged habitat, it finds the gentle environment of the garden inhospitable; though it may persist for a number of years, it ultimately perishes.

441 Bitterroot
Lewisia rediviva

Description: A low little plant with comparatively big, *deep pink to nearly white flowers* on short stalks nearly within a *rosette of narrow, succulent leaves.*

Flowers: 1½–2½″ (4–6.5 cm) wide; sepals 6–8; petals 12–18; stamens 30–50; narrow bracts in ring of 5–8 at middle of each flower stalk.

Leaves: ½–2″ (1.5–5 cm) long.

Height: ½–2″ (1.5–5 cm).

Flowering: May–July.

Habitat: Open places in sagebrush and pinewoods.

Range: British Columbia south to southern California and east to Colorado, Wyoming, and Montana.

Comments: Of the several pretty, ground-hugging *Lewisia* species, this one is perhaps the showiest. It is Montana's state flower. It was first collected by Meriwether Lewis of the Lewis and Clark expedition, who is honored by the genus name.

201 Common Purslane; Pusley; Verdolaga
Portulaca oleracea

Description: *A very succulent, fleshy, matted weed* with *small yellow flowers* borne singly or in small clusters in leaf axils or at ends of commonly smooth, lustrous, prostrate, bronze-green stems.

Flowers: About ¼″ (6 mm) wide; sepals 2; petals 5.

Leaves:	½–1½″ (1.5–4 cm) long, fleshy, spatula-shaped, commonly broadest in upper half.
Height:	Usually a low creeper, with stems to 2′ (60 cm) long; sometimes erect and to 6″ (15 cm).
Flowering:	June–September.
Habitat:	Open places, especially in disturbed soil; frequent as a garden weed.
Range:	Throughout much of southern Canada and United States.
Comments:	This annual species is a variable worldwide weed found in tropical and warm, temperate regions. Its leaves and stems were used as a source of food in India and Persia more than 2,000 years ago, and the plant has a long history of use in the Americas as a potherb and a medicinal plant, probably even prior to the first arrival of Europeans. Spanish-Americans now call it Verdolaga and use it with tomatoes, onions, and various seasonings. The genus name may be derived from *portula* ("little gate"), referring to the lid on the fruit capsule. Noted not for its beauty but for its ubiquity, this plant grows rapidly and produces thousands of tiny black seeds. If pulled and left as mulch, it will live on stored water and food and, even with roots turned upward, will continue to mature seeds.

365 Flame Flower
Talinum aurantiacum

Description:	Rather stout, erect stems with *evenly distributed, narrow, succulent leaves* and *1 orange or reddish-orange flower* in each upper leaf axil.
Flowers:	About 1″ (2.5 cm) wide; sepals 2, dropping off as flower matures; petals 5, broad; stamens at least 20.
Leaves:	¾–2″ (2–5 cm) long, ⅟₁₆–⅛″ (2–3 mm) wide.
Height:	6–14″ (15–35 cm).
Flowering:	June–October.
Habitat:	Rocky slopes in desert canyons.

Range: Southern Arizona east to western Texas.
Comments: Native Americans once cooked the fleshy
roots. A very similar species found in the
same region is Narrow-leaved Flame
Flower *(T. angustissimum);* its petals are
paler, generally yellow-orange, and its
leaves are less than ¹⁄₁₆″ (2 mm) wide.

443 Pygmy Talinum
Talinum brevifolium

Description: A low plant with *crowded, narrow,
succulent leaves* and comparatively large,
deep pink flowers in upper leaf axils.
Flowers: About ¾″ (2 cm) wide; sepals 2, oval;
petals 5, broad; stamens about 20.
Leaves: ⅛–½″ (3–13 mm) long, almost
cylindrical.
Height: 1–3″ (2.5–7.5 cm).
Flowering: May–September.
Habitat: On rocky slopes, especially limestone
sites.
Range: Southern Utah and northern Arizona
east to western Texas.
Comments: The bright pink flowers seem to sit on
the ground, often obscuring the short
erect stems. This species is
representative of several others, most
more open and spindly but all with
white to rose flowers. In one, Spiny
Talinum *(T. spinescens),* found in central
Washington, the midribs persist as
spines as the leaves wither and dry.

PRIMROSE FAMILY
Primulaceae

Leafy herbs, usually with showy flowers borne singly or in
clusters.

Flowers: Radially symmetrical. Calyx with 5 sepals often
united at base; corolla with usually 5 united or separate
petals, or absent; stamens usually 5, each opposite a petal
or corolla lobe, or alternate with sepals if corolla absent;
all these parts usually attached at base of ovary.
Leaves: Alternate, opposite, whorled, or basal; usually simple.
Fruit: 1-chambered capsule, with few to many seeds.

There are about 30 genera and 1,000 species, mostly in the northern temperate region. In the United States the family is most diverse in the eastern region. Primroses (*Primula*), cyclamens (*Cyclamen*), and several others are grown as ornamentals.

364 Scarlet Pimpernel; Poor Man's Weatherglass
Anagallis arvensis

Description: A matted plant with *creeping, 4-sided stems,* shiny, bright green leaves, and *small, flat, bright pinkish-orange flowers* at ends of very slender stalks.

Flowers: Corolla about ¼" (6 mm) wide, with 5 round lobes united only at base.

Leaves: To ¾" (2 cm) long, opposite or in whorls of 3 along stem.

Height: Creeper; stems 4–10" (10–25 cm) long.

Flowering: March–July.

Habitat: Open, disturbed ground at low elevations; frequent as a lawn and garden weed.

Range: Nearly throughout southern Canada and United States; in West, most frequent in California and Oregon.

Comments: This species is native to Eurasia. The common name Scarlet Pimpernel is not entirely apt, for the flowers are pinkish orange; there is also a blue phase (rare in the West). Flowers close in cloudy or humid weather, giving the name Poor Man's Weatherglass, and open again when the sun shines, probably inspiring the genus name, which is derived from the Greek *ana* ("again") and *agallein* ("to delight in"). However charming, this plant is poisonous.

171 Northern Fairy Candelabra
Androsace septentrionalis

Description: A small plant with a *basal rosette of leaves* and several erect stalks ending in an *open umbel of small white flowers.*

Flowers: Corolla slightly more than ⅛" (3 mm) wide, with a broad tube and 5 roundish

Northern Fairy Candelabra

lobes; calyx lobes shorter than tubular
part, broadly pointed.

Leaves: ½–1¼" (1.5–3 cm) long, lanceolate,
sometimes with low, irregular teeth near
tip.

Height: 1–10" (2.5–25 cm).

Flowering: May–August.

Habitat: Moist mountain soil.

Range: Throughout western mountains and east
across Great Plains to Mississippi Valley.

Comments: This small, very slender plant is often
overlooked. Its umbels of white flowers
resemble miniature star bursts.

---

580 Alpine Shooting Star
Dodecatheon alpinum

Description: A smooth stalk growing from a basal
rosette of leaves and topped by an umbel
of *1–9 pinkish-purple flowers, each
resembling a small rocket.*

Flowers: ¾–1" (2–2.5 cm) long; corolla with *4
reddish-lavender, narrow lobes sharply bent
back* at yellow base; stamens dark purple,
forming nose of "rocket"; *stigma a
conspicuous knob at least as thick as style.*

Leaves: 1¼–4" (3–10 cm) long, usually less than
½" (1.5 cm) wide.

Height: 4–12" (10–30 cm).

Flowering: June–July.

Habitat:	Mountain meadows and along mountain streams.
Range:	Eastern Oregon south to southern California and east to Arizona and Utah.
Comments:	There are about 10 western species of *Dodecatheon* with reddish-lavender corollas, two also with a large knob at the end of the style. Tall Mountain Shooting Star *(D. jefferyi)*, found from the Alaskan mountains south to the southern Sierra Nevada and east to Idaho and Montana, has 4–5 corolla lobes and minute, glandular hairs on the leaves and flower cluster. Sticky Shooting Star *(D. redolens)*, found from the mountains of southern California east to Nevada and Utah, is densely covered with glandular hairs, and its corolla has five lobes; the tubular portion covers the base of the anthers.

78 White Shooting Star; Dentate Shooting Star
Dodecatheon dentatum

Description:	*Small, dart-like flowers* pointing in all directions from ends of branches of an umbel on a stalk growing from a basal rosette of leaves.
Flowers:	About 1″ (2.5 cm) long; corolla with 5 narrow, usually *white or cream* (occasionally pink or pale violet) lobes, yellow at base above purple ring in center; stamens dark maroon to black, or yellow, forming point of dart.
Leaves:	1¼–4″ (3–10 cm) long, edges toothed, base tapering to a narrow stalk.
Height:	6–16″ (15–40 cm).
Flowering:	May–July.
Habitat:	Moist soil near waterfalls and streams and in shady damp places.
Range:	Southern British Columbia south to northern Oregon and east to central Idaho and northern Utah; also in Arizona and New Mexico.
Comments:	This species has toothed (dentate) leaves, hence one of its common names. It is the

only shooting star to have populations with consistently white flowers. In Utah, petals may be pink or pale violet; elsewhere petals are white or cream. Plants in Arizona and New Mexico have stamens with yellow filaments; in the Northwest filaments are dark maroon or black.

432 Few-flowered Shooting Star
Dodecatheon pulchellum

Description: Few *deep pink, dart-like flowers* pointing in all directions from an umbel atop a long erect stalk growing from a basal cluster of leaves.

Flowers: ¾–1″ (2–2.5 cm) long; corolla with 4–5 narrow lobes sharply bent back from yellowish ring usually with dark purplish lines; stamens yellowish to purplish, forming point of dart; tube beneath anthers not wrinkled, or slightly wrinkled lengthwise; stigma barely broader than stalk.

Leaves: 2–16″ (5–40 cm) long, broadly lanceolate, gradually tapering to long stalks, edges smooth or with small teeth.

Height: 4–24″ (10–60 cm).

Flowering: April–August.

Habitat: Coastal prairies to mountain meadows and streamsides.

Range: Throughout West from Alaska to Mexico; also in much of East.

Comments: This common species varies in the color of the tube below the anthers, the presence or absence of glandular hair on the foliage, and the shape of the leaves.

449 Smooth Douglasia
Douglasia laevigata

Description: Stems spreading on ground and forming rather *extensive mats* below 2–10 *deep reddish-pink flowers* (aging to lavender) in tight umbels on short leafless stalks.

Flowers:	About ⅜″ (9 mm) wide; corolla with 5 round lobes flaring from a narrow tube.
Leaves:	¼–¾″ (6–20 mm) long, smooth, lanceolate, gathered in dense rosettes at ends of stems.
Height:	Creeper; flower stalks ¾–2½″ (2–6.5 cm), stems to 1′ (30 cm) long.
Flowering:	March–August.
Habitat:	Moist coastal bluffs to rocky, alpine slopes and ledges.
Range:	Western Washington and northwestern Oregon.
Comments:	*Douglasia,* named for David Douglas, an early-19th-century explorer of western North American plants, are prized rock-garden subjects. The plants need not be dug up, as they grow well from cuttings or seed. The genus superficially resembles *Phlox,* in which each stamen in the corolla tube is attached in line with the notch between corolla lobes; in *Douglasia* each stamen is attached in line with the middle of a corolla lobe.

197 Fringed Loosestrife
Lysimachia ciliata

Description:	Stems forming open patches and *yellow flowers on slender arched stalks in leaf axils.*
Flowers:	About ¾″ (2 cm) wide; corolla with 5 round lobes, each generally with a tiny point at middle of broad end, base granular with minute hairs.
Leaves:	1–2½″ (2.5–6.5 cm) long, opposite, ovate, evenly distributed on stem, blade and stalk fringed with stiff hairs.
Height:	1–4′ (30–120 cm).
Flowering:	June–August.
Habitat:	Shallow ponds, streamsides, and wet meadows.
Range:	Eastern Washington south to Arizona and east across most of United States and southern Canada.
Comments:	This species is distinguished by having five sterile stamens, which appear as small points of tissue between the bases of the fertile stamens. Much less

frequent in the West is Lance-leaved
Loosestrife *(L. lanceolata),* which also
has flowers on slender stalks in the leaf
axils, but its yellow corollas are about
½" (1.5 cm) wide.

300   Bog Loosestrife; Swamp Candles
Lysimachia terrestris

Description:	Erect stems with opposite leaves and *racemes of star-like, yellow flowers.*
Flowers:	Corolla ½–¾" (1.5–2 cm) wide, flat, with 5 pointed lobes streaked with purplish black.
Leaves:	2–6" (5–15 cm) long.
Height:	8–31" (20–80 cm).
Flowering:	June–August.
Habitat:	Swampy or boggy areas.
Range:	Western Washington; widespread in East.
Comments:	This handsome species was inadvertently introduced into the Northwest's cranberry bogs from eastern North America.

360   Tufted Loosestrife
Lysimachia thyrsiflora

Description:	Erect stems with evenly distributed leaves and *yellow flowers in dense slender racemes in leaf axils near midstem;* entire plant finely dotted with black or dark purple.
Flowers:	Corolla with 5 narrow lobes, each about ¼" (6 mm) long, with narrow stalks leading to a united base.
Leaves:	To 6" (15 cm) long, opposite, lanceolate.
Height:	8–31" (20–80 cm).
Flowering:	May–July.
Habitat:	Swamps, lakes, and ditches.
Range:	Much of North America south to northern California and east to northern Colorado.
Comments:	This plant also occurs in Eurasia. The tight racemes of yellow flowers immediately distinguish this species, with the erect stamens giving the racemes a fuzzy appearance.

522 Parry's Primrose
Primula parryi

Description: A rather stout, leafless stalk growing from a basal rosette of somewhat fleshy, oblong leaves and topped by *3–12 deep pink flowers in a loose umbel.*

Flowers: Corolla ½–1¼" (1.5–3 cm) wide, with 5 round lobes flaring from a slender tube; calyx and flower stalks covered with minute, glandular hairs.

Leaves: 2–12" (5–30 cm) long.

Height: 3–16" (7.5–40 cm).

Flowering: June–August.

Habitat: Wet ground, often along streams, at high elevations.

Range: Idaho and Montana south to Nevada, northern Arizona, and northern New Mexico.

Comments: In spite of the plant's carrion odor, its brilliant color makes it a favorite with mountain hikers. The species is heterostylous (half of the plants have long styles and anthers attached low in the tube, and half have short styles and anthers attached high in the tube), which helps ensure genetic variation.

521 Sierra Primrose
Primula suffrutescens

Description: Leafless stalks growing above mats of basal leaf rosettes and topped by *2–9 deep pink to reddish-lavender flowers in an umbel.*

Flowers: Corolla about ¾" (2 cm) wide, with 5 lobes, each notched at end, flaring abruptly from a narrow tube with yellow around opening.

Leaves: ¾–1¼" (2–3 cm) long, thick, wedge-shaped, ends with even teeth (as if cut by pinking shears); clustered in rosettes at ends of creeping, woody branches.

Height: Creeper; flower stalks 3–6" (7.5–15 cm).

Flowering: July–August.

Habitat: Rocky areas at high elevations.

Range: Mountains of northern California south through Sierra Nevada.

Comments: This plant is extremely small and often
overlooked, but it is one of our
handsomest native species.

450 Western Starflower; Indian Potato
Trientalis latifolia

Description: A delicate stem topped by a *whorl of
3–8 ovate leaves* with 1 or several *pink,
star-shaped flowers* in the center, each
on a thread-like stalk.

Flowers: Corolla about ½″ (1.5 cm) wide, with
5–9 (usually 6) pointed lobes.

Leaves: 1¼–4″ (3–10 cm) long.

Height: 4–10″ (10–25 cm).

Flowering: April–June.

Habitat: Open woods and prairies.

Range: British Columbia south through
northern two-thirds of California and
east to northern Idaho.

Comments: The genus name derives from the Latin
word for "one-third foot," referring to
the height of this charming plant.
Although it is commonly called Indian
Potato, modern references do not
mention edibility, so caution is advised.
The similar Northern Starflower *(T.
arctica),* which grows in wet places from
Alaska south to northwestern California,
has white flowers and obovate leaves.

WINTERGREEN FAMILY
Pyrolaceae

Perennial herbs, with or without leaves; flowers often dish-
shaped, borne singly, in racemes, or in branched clusters.

Flowers: Radially symmetrical. Sepals 4–5, separate or
slightly united; petals 4–5, separate; stamens usually 10,
with anthers opening by terminal pores; all these parts
attached at base of ovary.
Leaves: Alternate, opposite, nearly whorled, or basal; simple.
Fruit: More or less spherical capsule, with 4–5 chambers.

There are 4 genera and about 40 species, mostly in the
northern temperate region. Pyrolaceae has also been known
as the shinleaf family; these species are sometimes considered part of the heath family (Ericaceae).

60 Little Pipsissewa; Little Prince's Pine
Chimaphila menziesii

Description: A low plant with 1–3 shallowly *bowl-shaped, pink, pinkish-white, or pinkish-green flowers* hanging at ends of branches above leathery, dark green leaves.

Flowers: About ½" (1.5 cm) wide; petals 5, roundish; stamens 10, swollen and hairy at base.

Leaves: ¾–2½" (2–6.5 cm) long, lanceolate, commonly with small sharp teeth on edges.

Height: 2–6" (5–15 cm).

Flowering: June–August.

Habitat: Coniferous woods.

Range: British Columbia south to southern California; also possibly in Idaho and Montana.

Comments: The genus name, from the Greek *cheima* ("winter") and *philos* ("loving"), refers to the evergreen nature of the plant. The common name Little Pipsissewa is believed to be derived from the Cree Indian word *pipisisikweu,* meaning "it breaks it into small pieces"; the plant was once used in preparations for breaking up kidney stones or gallstones. The similar Prince's Pine or Common Pipsissewa *(C. umbellata),* common throughout the West, usually has more than three flowers, and the swollen bases of its stamens have a few stiff hairs. Spotted Wintergreen *(C. maculata),* found in Arizona, Mexico, and the eastern United States, has whitish mottling along the leaf veins.

47 Wood Nymph; Single Delight; Waxflower
Moneses uniflora

Description: A little plant topped with *1 nodding, white or pale pink, saucer-shaped flower.*

Flowers: ¾" (2 cm) wide; petals 5, roundish; stamens 10, swollen at base; ovary greenish, 5-lobed.

Leaves:	½–1″ (1.5–2.5 cm) long, opposite or in whorls of 3–4 toward base of stem, nearly round, with tiny round teeth above middle.
Height:	2–6″ (5–15 cm).
Flowering:	May–August.
Habitat:	Coniferous forests.
Range:	Alaska south and east to eastern Canada, and south throughout western mountains to northern California, Arizona, and New Mexico; also in northeastern United States.
Comments:	This species also occurs in Eurasia. *Moneses,* from the Greek words *monos* ("single") and *hesis* ("delight"), refers to the single pretty flower.

146 One-sided Wintergreen; Side Bells
Orthilia secunda

Description:	Low patches of shiny, bright green leaves below *racemes of 6–20 whitish-green or white flowers all turned to one side.*
Flowers:	Corolla ¼″ (6 mm) long; petals 5, white or whitish green; stamens 10.
Leaves:	½–2½″ (1.5–6.5 cm) long, ovate, with minutely scalloped or toothed edges.
Height:	2–8″ (5–20 cm).
Flowering:	June–August.
Habitat:	Moist coniferous woods.
Range:	Alaska south and east to Labrador, and south to southern California, Nevada, Utah, New Mexico, and Nebraska; also in eastern United States and northern Mexico.
Comments:	This species is also found south to Central America and in Eurasia. It is the only species in the genus *Orthilia;* it was once included in *Pyrola,* a larger genus of species that inhabit damp woods. Both common names refer to the straight, one-sided flower cluster. Leaves remain green throughout the winter, hence the common name wintergreen.

503 Bog Wintergreen
Pyrola asarifolia

Description:	A little woodland plant with *shiny, leathery leaves* near base and *5–25 pink to reddish-pink flowers hanging in racemes* at top.
Flowers:	Corolla about ½" (1.5 cm) wide; petals 5, roundish, forming a bowl; style curved outward.
Leaves:	To 3" (7.5 cm) long, broadly elliptical or heart-shaped, long-stalked.
Height:	6–16" (15–40 cm).
Flowering:	June–September.
Habitat:	Moist ground, generally in woods.
Range:	Alaska south and east to Labrador, and south in West to southern California, Nevada, Utah, New Mexico, and South Dakota; also in northern regions of eastern United States.
Comments:	This plant also grows in Asia. *Pyrola* species are common woodland wildflowers. Sometimes they are leafless, in which case they are saprophytes, absorbing their nutrition from the rich humus. All such, regardless of their biological species, were once classified as Leafless Pyrola *(P. aphylla),* but leafless phases with pink flowers are probably Bog Wintergreen.

BUTTERCUP FAMILY
Ranunculaceae

Usually leafy herbs, sometimes woody vines or shrub-like, with flowers borne singly, in racemes, or in branched clusters.

Flowers: Usually bisexual, radially or sometimes bilaterally symmetrical. Sepals and petals variable in number, separate, or petals absent and sepals petal-like; stamens usually many; pistils 1 to many.

Leaves: Alternate or rarely opposite; commonly shallowly to deeply palmately lobed, sometimes palmately compound, or pinnately lobed or compound, or simple and not lobed.

Fruit: Small, hard, seed-like; or a small pod or a berry.

There are about 50 genera and 2,000 species, primarily in cool regions of the Northern Hemisphere. Several are grown as ornamentals. Some species are used medicinally, and some are poisonous. The family is most likely to be confused with the rose family (Rosaceae), from which it is distinguished by the absence of a cup-like flower base (hypanthium) and by the absence of stipules.

---

651 Western Monkshood; Aconite
Aconitum columbianum

Description: A usually tall, leafy plant with *bilaterally symmetrical, hood-like, blue or blue-violet flowers in a showy raceme.*

Flowers: Sepals 5, petal-like, uppermost forming a large arched hood ½–1¼″ (1.5–3 cm) long, side 2 broadly oval, lower 2 narrow; petals 5, hidden under hood, 3 generally undeveloped.

Leaves: 2–8″ (5–20 cm) wide, palmately lobed, with jagged teeth.

Height: 1–7′ (30–210 cm).

Flowering: June–August.

Habitat: Moist woods and subalpine meadows.

Range: Alaska south to southern Sierra Nevada and east to New Mexico, Colorado, South Dakota, and western Montana.

Comments: Some *Aconitum* have been used medicinally, and most are poisonous to humans and livestock. *A. lycotonum,* a European monkshood, is the celebrated Wolfbane of werewolf lore.

Western Monkshood

182, 425 Baneberry
Actaea rubra

Description:	A usually branched plant with *racemes of many small white flowers* in leaf axils or at stem ends.
Flowers:	Sepals 3–5, dropping off as flower opens; petals 4–5, each ⅛″ (3 mm) long, spatula-shaped, also dropping off; stamens many.
Leaves:	Few, very large, pinnately and repeatedly divided into sharply toothed leaflets, each ¾–3½″ (2–9 cm) long.
Fruit:	Glistening red or pearly white berry, ¼–½″ (6–13 mm) wide.
Height:	1–3′ (30–90 cm).
Flowering:	May–July.
Habitat:	Moist woods and streambanks.
Range:	Across northern North America and south throughout West; also south on Great Plains to Nebraska and throughout northern portion of eastern United States.
Comments:	The attractive berries are poisonous but are not reported to have caused death to humans or livestock in the United States. European species have fatally poisoned children.

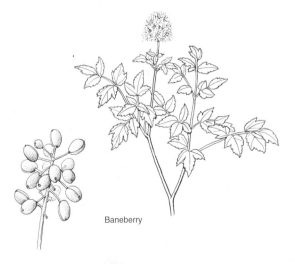

Baneberry

636   Blue Anemone
Anemone oregana

Description:	A plant forming open patches with an erect stem topped by *1 usually bluish-lavender flower.*
Flowers:	1–1½" (2.5–4 cm) wide; sepals 5–8, long, petal-like, generally bluish lavender, varying to reddish lavender or pale pink (rarely white); petals absent; stamens 35–100.
Leaves:	1 at base, 3 in a whorl on stem, divided into *3 leaflets,* each to 3" (7.5 cm) long, often deeply divided and toothed.
Fruit:	Seed-like, finely hairy, with a minute, hairless beak at tip; many in a tight round head.
Height:	4–12" (10–30 cm).
Flowering:	March–June.
Habitat:	Open woods and brushy hillsides.
Range:	Northern Washington south to northern California.
Comments:	This anemone spreads by its stout, underground stems. It intergrades with the white-flowered Western Wood Anemone *(A. lyallii).* There are more than 100 *Anemone* species distributed in cool places throughout much of the world. Within its immediate region, each species blooms early, often at Eastertime.

51   Desert Anemone
Anemone tuberosa

Description:	Several stems in a cluster with *1 pinkish-purple or white flower* at end of each erect branch.
Flowers:	1–1½" (2.5–4 cm) wide; sepals 5–8, petal-like, generally darker and hairy on back; petals absent; stamens many.
Leaves:	1¼–2" (3–5 cm) wide, several at base, 3 in a whorl at about midstem, repeatedly divided into narrow short segments.
Fruit:	Seed-like, bearing a short woolly beak about ¹⁄₁₆" (2 mm) long; many in a dense, woolly, cylindrical head.
Height:	4–16" (10–40 cm).
Flowering:	March–April.

Habitat: Among rocks on desert slopes.
Range: Southeastern California northeast to southern Utah and east to southern New Mexico and western Texas; also in Mexico.
Comments: There are several similar anemones in the western mountains. They differ from pasque flowers *(Pulsatilla)* by the absence of hairs on the style.

239 Golden Columbine
Aquilegia chrysantha

Description: Several stems and highly divided leaves forming a bushy plant with handsome, *bright yellow flowers* on long stalks.
Flowers: 1½–3″ (4–7.5 cm) wide; sepals 5, long, spreading, lanceolate, petal-like; petals 5, *scoop-shaped, each with a backward-projecting spur* 1½–3″ (4–7.5 cm) long; many stamens and 5 styles protruding from center of flower.
Leaves: Large, repeatedly divided into leaflets, each to 1½″ (4 cm) long, about as wide, deeply cleft and lobed on end.
Height: 1–4′ (30–120 cm).
Flowering: July–August.
Habitat: Moist sheltered places.
Range: Southwestern Utah and Arizona east to central Colorado, New Mexico, and western Texas; also in northern Mexico.
Comments: The name columbine comes from the Latin *columbinus* ("dove"), referring to

Golden Columbine

the flower's resemblance to a cluster of five doves. The spurs represent the birds' heads and shoulders; the spreading sepals, the wings; the petals, the bodies. The genus name, from the Latin *aquila* ("eagle"), alludes to the spurs of the petals, which resemble talons. There are several yellow-flowered species in the West, some rare and now considered endangered. Yellow Columbine *(A. flavescens),* a mountain species growing from southern British Columbia south to northern Oregon and east to Colorado, western Wyoming, and Alberta, has bent tips on the spurs, which form hooks.

---

637   Blue Columbine
Aquilegia coerulea

Description: Several stems and many divided leaves forming a bushy plant with beautiful *white and blue flowers tipped upward* at stem ends.

Flowers: 2–3" (5–7.5 cm) wide; sepals 5, spreading, lanceolate, petal-like, pale to sky blue; petals 5, scoop-shaped, generally paler than sepals or white, each extending into a backward-projecting spur 1¼–2" (3–5 cm) long; many stamens and 5 styles protruding from center of flower.

Leaves: Repeatedly divided into leaflets, each ½–1¼" (1.5–3 cm) long, about as wide, deeply cleft and lobed.

Height: To 3′ (90 cm).

Flowering: June–August.

Habitat: Mountains, commonly in aspen groves.

Range: Western Montana south to northern Arizona and northern New Mexico.

Comments: Blue Columbine is Colorado's state flower. Popular in cultivation, it has several color phases and doubled flowers. Hybridization with other species has produced further cultivated variants. Phases in the wild with pale or white sepals are frequent. Alpine Blue Columbine *(A. saximontana),* a species with blue sepals and white petal tips but only 2–8″ (5–20 cm) tall, has blue spurs hooked at the tips; it grows high in the Colorado mountains.

---

391 Crimson Columbine; Red Columbine; Sitka Columbine
Aquilegia formosa

Description: Handsome *red and yellow flowers* nodding at branch ends above a bushy plant with several stems and many divided leaves.

Flowers: About 2″ (5 cm) wide; sepals 5, petal-like, red, lanceolate, spreading; petals 5, yellow, scoop-shaped, each extending into a backward-projecting spur; many yellow stamens and 5 styles protruding from center of flower.

Leaves: Repeatedly divided into leaflets, each ¾–1½″ (2–4 cm) long, about as wide, lobed and cleft across end.

Height: 6–36″ (15–90 cm).

Flowering: May–August.

Habitat: On banks and near seeps in open woods.

Range: Southern Alaska south to Baja California and east to Utah, Idaho, northwestern Wyoming, and western Montana.

Comments: The species name, Latin for "beautiful," aptly describes this plant, especially when it bears dozens of lovely, nodding flowers. This and other species with mostly red flowers attract hummingbirds as pollinators.

---

570 Limestone Columbine
Aquilegia jonesii

Description: *Deep blue or violet-blue flowers tipped upward* and held barely above low, densely tufted, divided leaves.

Flowers: 1½–2″ (4–5 cm) wide; sepals 5, sometimes darker than petals; petals 5, each with a slender straight spur ¼–⅝″ (6–16 mm) long.

Leaves: Leaflets crowded, leathery, forming compact blades about ½″ (1.5 cm) wide, barely longer.

Height: 2–5″ (5–12.5 cm).
Flowering: June–August.
Habitat: Rocky, limestone slopes and crevices high in mountains.
Range: Southern Alberta south to northwestern Wyoming.
Comments: As is characteristic of plants growing in limestone, this columbine does not transplant successfully. It is also rare; those fortunate enough to find it must leave it for others to enjoy.

---

84 Coville's Columbine
Aquilegia pubescens

Description: A tufted plant with highly divided leaves and *large cream flowers tinted with pastel blue, pink, or yellow and tipped upward.*
Flowers: About 1½″ (4 cm) wide; sepals 5, broadly lanceolate, spreading; petals 5, scoop-shaped, each extending into a backward-projecting spur 1–1½″ (2.5–4 cm) long; many stamens and 5 styles protruding from center of flower.
Leaves: Repeatedly divided into leaflets, each ½–1¼″ (1.5–3 cm) wide, about as long, deeply cleft and scalloped.
Height: 8–14″ (20–35 cm).
Flowering: June–August.
Habitat: Rocky places high in mountains.
Range: Southern Sierra Nevada.
Comments: The pale flowers and long, straight, nectar-filled spurs attract moths as pollinators. Where this species and Crimson Columbine *(A. formosa)* grow in the same region, cross-pollination between the two may result in hybrid plants.

---

49 Marsh Marigold; Elk's Lip
Caltha leptosepala

Description: An erect, leafless stem with several leaves at base and usually topped by *1 white, bowl-shaped flower.*

Flowers: ½–1¼" (1.5–3 cm) wide; sepals 5–12, petal-like; petals absent; stamens many; pistils several.

Leaves: To 3" (7.5 cm) long, oblong, with minutely scalloped edges, on stalks either shorter than blade or much longer.

Height: 1–8" (2.5–20 cm).

Flowering: May–August.

Habitat: Wet places high in mountains.

Range: Alaska south throughout western mountains to southern Sierra Nevada, eastern Arizona, and northern New Mexico.

Comments: This species often blooms very close to receding snowbanks. The name Elk's Lip refers to the shape of the long leaf. Twin-flowered Marsh Marigold *(C. biflora),* found from Alaska south to California and east to Colorado, is very similar but has leaves about as wide as long and nearly always two flowers on each stem. Some botanists consider *C. biflora* and *C. leptosepala* the same species.

581 Vase Flower; Sugar Bowls; Leather Flower
Clematis hirsutissima

Description: A hairy plant generally with several stems in a dense clump, each stem with *1 purplish-brown, dull reddish-lavender, or dull violet flower hanging like a small, inverted urn* at end.

Flowers: About 1" (2.5 cm) long; sepals 4, leathery, lanceolate, petal-like, hairy on outside, joined at base, tips flaring outward; petals absent; stamens many, inside urn.

Leaves: To 5" (12.5 cm) long, opposite, finely divided, carrot-like.

Fruit: Base seed-like, bearing a silvery plume to 2½" (6 cm) long; many in a shaggy round head.

Height: 8–24" (20–60 cm).

Flowering: April–July.

Habitat: Grasslands, open pine forests, and in sagebrush.

Range: British Columbia south to eastern
        Washington, east to Montana and
        Wyoming, and south through Utah and
        Colorado to northern Arizona and New
        Mexico; also in western South Dakota,
        western Nebraska, and western
        Oklahoma.

Comments: Unlike most other *Clematis* species, this
           is not a vine. Another of its common
           names, Lion's Beard, refers to the shaggy
           fruit cluster.

173 White Virgin's Bower; Pipestems; Traveler's Joy
Clematis ligusticifolia

Description: *A woody vine* climbing over other
              vegetation and covered with *hundreds of
              cream flowers.*

Flowers: About ¾″ (2 cm) wide; sepals usually 5,
          petal-like; petals absent; some plants
          bearing flowers with pistils and no
          stamens, some bearing flowers with
          stamens and no pistils.

Leaves: Opposite, pinnately compound, with
         5–7 leaflets, each to 3″ (7.5 cm) long,
         broadly lanceolate, toothed.

Fruit: Base seed-like, bearing a silvery plume
        1–2″ (2.5–5 cm) long; many in a shaggy
        round head.

Height: Vine; to 10′ (3 m) long.

Flowering: May–September.

Habitat: Along creek or gully bottoms from
          deserts to pine forests.

Range: British Columbia east to Manitoba and
        south throughout West to southern
        California, Arizona, New Mexico, and
        Oklahoma; introduced in Pennsylvania.

Comments: This species' traditional name, Pepper
           Vine, referred to the acrid, peppery taste
           of the stems and leaves, which Native
           Americans chewed as a remedy for colds
           and sore throats. It is said that the
           crushed roots were placed in the nostrils
           of tired horses to revive them. Caution is
           advised: The genus is known to have
           poisonous species.

455 Western Clematis; Bell Rue; Virgin's Bower
Clematis occidentalis var. *grosseserrata*

Description: A vine, creeping on ground or climbing over other vegetation, with *1 pale purplish-pink to blue-violet, bell-shaped flower* at end of each leafless stalk growing from leaf axils.

Flowers: Sepals 4, each 1¼–2½" (3–6.5 cm) long, lanceolate, petal-like; petals absent; stamens many, yellow, inside bell.

Leaves: Opposite, with 3 leaflets, each 1–2½" (2.5–6.5 cm) long, broadly lanceolate, toothed or deeply lobed.

Fruit: Base seed-like, bearing a silvery plume 1¼–2½" (3–6 cm) long; many in a shaggy round head.

Height: Vine; to 10′ (3 m) long.

Flowering: May–July.

Habitat: Wooded or brushy areas in mountains, often on steep rocky slopes.

Range: British Columbia south to northeastern Oregon and east to Wyoming and Montana.

Comments: The hanging, bell-like flowers and the silvery puffs of feathery fruit make this plant a delight to find in the woods. It is part of a complex of rather similar western plants. Cutleaf Clematis *(C. occidentalis* var. *dissecta),* restricted to north-central Washington, is more of a tufted plant; the leaflets are often dissected, with prominently toothed edges. Rocky Mountain Clematis (*C. columbiana* var. *columbiana,* once called *C. pseudoalpina*), found from Montana south to New Mexico and northeastern Arizona, is similar, but each of the three leaflets is divided into three smaller, jaggedly toothed leaflets. Matted Purple Virgin's Bower *(C. columbiana* var. *tenuiloba),* found in Montana, Wyoming, and western South Dakota and south to northeastern Utah and central Colorado, has similar flowers, but plants form low mats rather than vines, and the leaves are even more finely divided.

390   Scarlet Larkspur; Cardinal Larkspur
Delphinium cardinale

Description: *A loose spire of brilliant red, bilaterally
symmetrical flowers atop a tall stem with
palmately lobed leaves near base.*

Flowers: ¾–1¼" (2–3 cm) wide; sepals 5, broadly
lanceolate, more or less forward-
pointing, scarlet, uppermost with a
backward-projecting spur ½–1"
(1.5–2.5 cm) long; petals 4, yellow,
often with scarlet tips.

Leaves: 2–8" (5–20 cm) wide, nearly round,
divided into 5 or 7 main lobes, each
deeply cut and toothed.

Height: 1–9' (30–270 cm).

Flowering: May–July.

Habitat: Openings in brush and woods, often in
rocky areas.

Range: Coast Ranges from central to southern
California, and in northern Baja
California.

Comments: The species name refers to the vibrant
red of the flower, like the red of a
cardinal's robe. Masses on a slope have
been likened to a hill on fire. The red
flower attracts hummingbirds as the
primary pollinators. Red Larkspur *(D.
nudicaule),* also known as Orange
Larkspur, is a smaller plant, rarely more
than 4' (1.2 m) tall, with not quite as
brilliant flowers; its sepals are noticeably
forward-pointing, much like a half-
opened bud of Scarlet Larkspur. This
flower shape gave *D. nudicaule* another
common name used long ago, Christmas
Horns; it grows from central California
to southern Oregon.

115   Plains Larkspur; White Larkspur;
Prairie Larkspur
Delphinium carolinianum subsp. *virescens*

Description: Stiffly erect, felt-covered stems bearing
pinnately divided leaves and topped by a
*spike-like raceme of white, very pale blue, or
occasionally dark blue, bilaterally
symmetrical flowers.*

Flowers:	About 1″ (2.5 cm) wide; sepals 5, petal-like, crinkled, uppermost with a backward-projecting spur about ½″ (1.5 cm) long; petals 4, in center of flower.
Leaves:	About 3″ (7.5 cm) wide, about as long, main leaf divisions again divided into very narrow segments.
Height:	To about 5′ (1.5 m).
Flowering:	May–July.
Habitat:	Open hills, prairies, and fields.
Range:	Southern Manitoba, North Dakota, Minnesota, and Wisconsin south to eastern Colorado, central Texas, and northeastern Missouri.
Comments:	Plains Larkspur was once considered to be a separate species, *D. virescens,* but studies of variation in larkspurs have now classified it as a subspecies of the widespread *D. carolinianum.* The species, with three subspecies, ranges from the eastern edge of the West to the southeastern United States. Some phases may be blue. Larkspurs intergrade among species, and flower color varies from white to pale or dark blue in some species, making them difficult to classify and identify. Most blue-flowered species have white-flowered variants, and a few are consistently white or very pale blue. The geographic range of the white-flowered Wooton's Larkspur *(D. wootoni)* overlaps with that of Plains Larkspur on the plains of eastern Colorado and southwestern Nebraska, but most of its range is to the south and west, to southeastern Arizona and western Texas. Wooton's Larkspur usually has leaves mostly at the base and reflexed sepals, whereas Plains Larkspur has leafy stems and spreading sepals. Also white-flowered are Alkali Larkspur *(D. gypsophilum),* found in the San Joaquin Valley and the southern Coast Ranges of California; Peacock Larkspur, a hybrid between *D. menziesii* subsp. *pallidum* and Cow Poison *(D. trolliifolium),* with brightly glandular-hairy petals, found in western Oregon; and Pale Larkspur *(D. leucophaeum),* without glandular petals, found in the vicinity of Portland, Oregon.

652 Nuttall's Larkspur
Delphinium nuttallianum

Description: Generally 1 stem with few leaves, mostly at base, and *blue or blue-violet, bilaterally symmetrical flowers* in 1 or several open racemes.

Flowers: About 1″ (2.5 cm) wide; sepals 5, blue, ovate, flaring outward from a slender, stalk-like base; uppermost sepal with a backward-projecting spur ½–1″ (1.5–2.5 cm) long; petals 4, each about ¼″ (5 mm) long; lower 2 petals deep blue or white with blue marks, deeply notched on lower edge; upper 2 petals white or pale blue, angling upward from center of flower.

Leaves: To 3″ (7.5 cm) wide, nearly round, pinnately divided into narrow forked lobes.

Height: 4–16″ (10–40 cm).

Flowering: March–July.

Habitat: Well-drained soil in sagebrush deserts and open pine forests.

Range: British Columbia south to northern California and east to Colorado, Nebraska, Wyoming, and Montana.

Comments: Nuttall's Larkspur is representative of a host of low larkspurs with blue or blue-violet flowers occurring in many

Nuttall's Larkspur

habitats, from dry California grasslands
and chaparral to southwestern deserts
and high mountaintops. These plants are
difficult to distinguish from one another.
In the West they are second only to
locoweeds (*Astragalus* and *Oxytropis*) as a
livestock poison, especially of cattle.

608 Parry's Larkspur; Parry's Delphinium
Delphinium parryi

Description: Stiffly erect, hairy stems bearing *deeply pinnately divided leaves* and topped by dense, *spike-like racemes of bright bluish-purple, bilaterally symmetrical flowers.*

Flowers: About 1″ (2.5 cm) wide; sepals 5, each about ½″ (1.5 cm) long, petal-like, cupped forward, uppermost extending into a backward-projecting spur about ½″ (1.5 cm) long; petals 4, with whitish hairs.

Leaves: Those at midstem 2–3″ (5–7.5 cm) wide, about as long, divided into very narrow, lobed segments; those at base usually withering before flowers bloom.

Height: 1–3′ (30–90 cm).

Flowering: April–May.

Habitat: Grassy slopes in chaparral, pine forests, and bluffs near coast.

Range: Southern California and Baja California.

Comments: This common but variable larkspur frequents grassy areas and is recognizable by its very narrow leaf divisions.

653 Cow Poison
Delphinium trolliifolium

Description: A stately plant with stout, hollow, leafy, generally tall stems and *bilaterally symmetrical, deep purplish-blue flowers in long loose racemes;* upper stems and flower stalks commonly covered with minute, yellowish hairs.

Flowers: 1–1½″ (2.5–4 cm) wide; sepals 5, broadly lanceolate, blue, uppermost with a backward-projecting spur about

¾" (2 cm) long; petals 4, broad lower
pair blue and notched on lower edge,
smaller upper pair white.

Leaves: 4–8" (10–20 cm) wide, nearly round,
divided into 3 or 5 main lobes, deeply
cut and toothed.

Height: 2–6' (60–180 cm).

Flowering: April–June.

Habitat: Moist shady woods and wet banks.

Range: Southern Washington south to northern
California.

Comments: This handsome native species is
common in wet parts of the Northwest.
Members of the genus *Delphinium* are
known as both delphinium and larkspur.
Gardeners generally call the tall,
perennial species delphinium and the
smaller, annual species larkspur.
Botanists usually call all species
delphinium. Cattle ranchers, who despise
the plants because of their toxicity to
livestock, call all species larkspur.

53   **Western Pasque Flower; Mountain
Pasque Flower**
Pulsatilla occidentalis

Description: A hairy plant with *finely divided leaves*
and each of several stems topped by *1
white or cream flower.*

Flowers: 1¼–2" (3–5 cm) wide; sepals 5–8, hairy
on back, petal-like; petals absent;
stamens many.

Leaves: 1½–3" (4–7.5 cm) wide, several at base,
3 in a whorl on stem beneath flower,
divided into narrow, crowded segments.

Fruit: Base seed-like, bearing a silvery plume
to 1½" (4 cm) long; many in a shaggy
round head.

Height: 8–24" (20–60 cm).

Flowering: May–September.

Habitat: Mountain slopes and meadows.

Range: British Columbia south to southern
Sierra Nevada and east to northeastern
Oregon and western Montana.

Comments: *Pasque* is the Old French word for Easter
or Passover and also refers to the pure
white of the sepals. Because Western

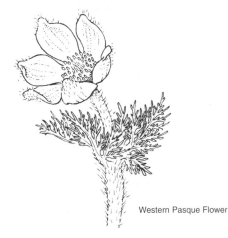

Western Pasque Flower

Pasque Flower grows at high elevations, it blooms later in the season than the related *Anemone* species, but it is still early among the plants in its area. Its flower structure is typical of pasque flowers.

575 Pasque Flower; Wild Crocus; Lion's Beard
Pulsatilla patens

Description: A hairy plant with 1 to many stems, each topped by *1 lavender, purple, or blue, deeply cup-shaped flower.*

Flowers: About 1½–2″ (4–5 cm) wide; sepals 5–7, petal-like, hairy on back; petals absent; stamens many, yellow.

Leaves: 1½–4″ (4–10 cm) wide, several at base, 3 in a whorl on stem below flower, repeatedly *divided into narrow lobes.*

Fruit: Base seed-like, bearing a silvery plume ¾–1¼″ (2–3 cm) long; many in a shaggy round head.

Height: To 14″ (35 cm).

Flowering: May–August.

Habitat: Well-drained soil from prairies to mountain slopes.

Range: Alaska south and east to eastern Canada, south to central Washington, Idaho, Utah, New Mexico, and Texas, and east across northern Great Plains to Illinois and Michigan.

Comments: This is South Dakota's state flower. Other common names are Prairie Anemone, Blue Tulip, and American Pulsatilla. As two of the common names suggest, the flower shape may resemble a tulip or crocus, but there is no close relationship to either. On some plants the sepals may be white; such plants are most easily distinguished from Western Pasque Flower *(P. occidentalis)* by their longer, less crowded leaf segments. Pasque flowers are often included in the genus *Anemone*.

50 Water Buttercup; Water Crowfoot
Ranunculus aquatilis

Description: Submerged and floating stems generally forming fairly dense beds with *white flowers held on stalks slightly above water.*

Flowers: ½–¾" (1.5–2 cm) wide; sepals dropping off as flower opens; petals 5, white, sometimes yellow at base.

Leaves: Submerged ones droop when stems lifted from water, with blades about 1" (2.5 cm) long, on stalks ½–¾" (1.5–2 cm) long, *finely divided into forked, hair-like segments;* floating ones less divided.

Height: Aquatic; flowers about 1" (2.5 cm) above water, stems to 3' (90 cm) long.

Flowering: May–August.

Habitat: Ponds and slow streams.

Range: Much of North America.

Comments: This plant is also found in Europe. The genus name, from the Latin *rana* ("frog"), refers to the wet habitat of some species.

203 Subalpine Buttercup
Ranunculus eschscholtzii

Description: A low plant bearing flowers with 5 *shiny, brilliant yellow petals;* flowers sometimes so numerous as to nearly hide foliage.

Flowers:	¾–1½" (2–4 cm) wide; sepals dropping off as flower opens.
Leaves:	¼–1¼" (6–31 mm) long, roundish to ovate, varying from 3 shallow lobes to highly divided into narrow segments.
Height:	2–10" (5–25 cm).
Flowering:	June–August.
Habitat:	Meadows and rocky slopes high in mountains.
Range:	Alaska south to southern California, east to Alberta, and south throughout Rocky Mountains to northern New Mexico.
Comments:	Subalpine Buttercup has the largest flowers of any North American *Ranunculus* species. There are many buttercups, most with shiny, yellow petals; most are difficult to distinguish from one another. Yellow Marsh Marigold *(Caltha asarifolia),* found in coastal bogs from Alaska to Oregon, resembles a buttercup but lacks green sepals.

202 Sagebrush Buttercup
Ranunculus glaberrimus

Description:	*A small fleshy plant* with most leaves at base and bearing *flowers with 5 shiny, yellow petals.*
Flowers:	¾–1¼" (2–3 cm) wide; sepals 5, purplish-tinged; petals 5–8, yellow; stamens and pistils many.
Leaves:	½–2" (1.5–5 cm) long, rather fleshy, blades varying from elliptical to nearly round, often with 3 lobes at end.
Fruit:	Seed-like, about half as thick as broad; in oval heads.
Height:	2–8" (5–20 cm).
Flowering:	March–June.
Habitat:	Mostly in sagebrush and open pinewoods.
Range:	British Columbia south to northern California and east to New Mexico, Colorado, Nebraska, and the Dakotas.
Comments:	This plant is among the first wildflowers to bloom in the spring. The very smooth, rather fleshy leaves are characteristic. Most buttercups are to some degree poisonous, but the toxin is unstable and is rendered harmless by drying or boiling the leaves.

377   Western Meadow Rue
Thalictrum occidentale

Description: Branched stems with *highly divided,
soft, thin leaves* and open branched
clusters of greenish-brown flowers.

Flowers: About ⅜" (9 mm) wide; sepals 4–5,
eventually dropping off; petals absent;
some plants bearing flowers with pistils
and no stamens; some plants bearing
flowers lacking pistils and with many
stamens hanging from purplish, thread-
like filaments.

Leaves: Leaflets each ½–1½" (1.5–4 cm) long,
about as wide, usually with 3 lobes,
shallowly notched and cleft.

Fruit: Seed-like, narrow, many per flower, each
spreading horizontally or pointing
downward.

Height: 1–3' (30–90 cm).

Flowering: May–July.

Habitat: Moist ground, often in shady woods.

Range: British Columbia south to northern
California and east to Montana,
Wyoming, and Utah.

Comments: The common name meadow rue
is given to *Thalictrum* species because
of their resemblance to European rues
(Ruta), which are grown for their
aromatic and medicinal properties.
The similar Fendler's Meadow Rue
(T. fendleri) has laterally flattened
fruit and occurs from Oregon and
Wyoming south to California, Texas,
and northern Mexico.

52   White Globeflower
Trollius laxus subsp. *albiflorus*

Description: 1 or several leafy stems, each topped by
1 *greenish-white or white, bowl-shaped
flower.*

Flowers: 1–1½" (2.5–4 cm) wide; sepals 5–9,
each ⅜–¾" (1–2 cm) long, broad, petal-
like, greenish-white or white; petals
15–25, yellow, one-half to two-thirds as
long as stamens after pollen shed;
stamens many.

Leaves: About 2″ (5 cm) long, about as wide, deeply cleft into 5 lobes, each jaggedly cut and toothed.

Fruit: Pod-like, nearly ½″ (1.5 cm) long, many from each flower, each with several seeds and a short beak at tip.

Height: 4–20″ (10–50 cm).

Flowering: May–August.

Habitat: Wet places in mountains.

Range: British Columbia and Alberta south to Oregon, Idaho, and Utah, and east to Montana, Wyoming, and Colorado.

Comments: The common name globeflower refers to the shape of the flower in cultivated species; native western plants have a much flatter flower. Western plants (subspecies *albiflorus*) differ from eastern plants (subspecies *laxus,* known as Yellow Globeflower) only in sepal color, eastern plants having yellow sepals.

BUCKTHORN FAMILY
Rhamnaceae

Shrubs, trees, or vines, usually with small flowers in clusters.

Flowers: Radially symmetrical. Sepals 5, rarely 4, separate; petals often 5, sometimes 4, separate, or absent; 1 stamen opposite each petal, or alternate with sepals if petals absent; all these parts attached near edge of a conspicuous disk surrounding ovary.
Leaves: Alternate or opposite, simple, unlobed.
Fruit: Capsule, with 2–3 chambers, or berry-like.

There are about 55 genera and 900 species, throughout the world. Edible fruits are obtained from the tropical Jujube *(Ziziphus jujuba),* and the bark of Cascara *(Rhamnus purshiana)* is collected for its purgative properties. Several species are grown as ornamentals.

143 Deer Brush
Ceanothus integerrimus

Description: An openly branched shrub with thin leaves, gray bark, and *tiny, white or pale blue flowers in conical clusters* at ends of flexible twigs.

Flowers:	Cluster 3–6″ (7.5–15 cm) long; sepals 5, petal-like, triangular, curving toward center; petals 5, spoon-shaped.
Leaves:	To 2½″ (6.5 cm) long, elliptical, with 3 main veins.
Fruit:	Small, 3-chambered capsule.
Height:	3–13′ (90–390 cm).
Flowering:	May–June.
Habitat:	Dry slopes in chaparral and open forests.
Range:	Eastern Washington southwest to southwestern Oregon and through most of California to Baja California, and east to western New Mexico.
Comments:	In the spring Deer Brush covers hillsides with a mixture of white and pale blue and fills the air with its sweet, spicy honey scent.

ROSE FAMILY
Rosaceae

Herbs, shrubs, or trees, often with prickly stems.

Flowers: Usually bisexual, radially symmetrical. Sepals 5; petals 5, separate, or sometimes absent; stamens usually numerous; all these parts attached at edge of a cup-like flower base (hypanthium) or at top of ovary; pistils 1 to many.

Leaves: Simple or compound; usually with small, leaf-like structures (stipules) at base of leafstalk.

Fruit: Dry or fleshy, sometimes opening at maturity; hip of *Rosa* species a fleshy receptacle enclosing numerous achenes.

There are about 100 genera and 3,000 species in this worldwide family. Several genera provide important fruits: apples and crab apples are from *Malus;* pears are from *Pyrus;* quinces are from *Cydonia;* cherries, plums, peaches, nectarines, and apricots are from *Prunus;* loquats are from *Eriobotrya;* blackberries and raspberries are from *Rubus;* and strawberries are from *Fragaria.* Roses *(Rosa),* cotoneasters *(Cotoneaster),* firethorns *(Pyracantha),* mountain ash *(Sorbus),* spiraeas *(Spiraea),* and hawthorns *(Crataegus)* are common ornamentals. It is estimated that there are 2,000 named varieties of apples and 5,000 of roses.

31 Western Serviceberry
Amelanchier alnifolia

Description: *A shrub bearing many white flowers* and
oval leaves with small teeth on edges.

Flowers: 1–2" (2.5–5 cm) wide; *sepals and petals 5
each, growing from rim of a little cup;*
stamens 20; styles 5.

Leaves: ¾–1½" (2–4 cm) long, hairless or
sparsely haired when old.

Fruit: Purplish, round, juicy berry, about ½"
(1.5 cm) long.

Height: 4–30' (1.2–9 m).

Flowering: April–July.

Habitat: Slopes, canyons, and open coniferous
woods from low to high elevations.

Range: Alaska south and east to Quebec, and
south to southern California, Nevada,
Utah, Colorado, Nebraska, and Iowa.

Comments: Serviceberries are variable, and the
species are not easily identified. The
berries produced by this species were
once used to make jelly and wine.

144 Western Goatsbeard;
Western Bride's Feather
Aruncus dioicus var. *acuminatus*

Description: *Large, narrow, elongated clusters of tiny
white flowers* nodding or arching atop
stems of a rather tall, leafy plant.

Flowers: Less than ⅛" (3 mm) wide; sepals 5;
petals 5, white, dropping off; some
plants bearing flowers with 3–5 pistils
and lacking stamens, some bearing
flowers with 15–20 stamens and lacking
pistils.

Leaves: Large, divided into ovate leaflets, each to
6" (15 cm) long, with many sharp teeth
on edges.

Height: 3–7' (90–210 cm).

Flowering: May–July.

Habitat: Moist places in woods.

Range: Alaska to northwestern California; also
south throughout much of East.

Comments: *Aruncus,* from the Greek *aryngos* ("goat's
beard"), refers to the long cluster of
white flowers. The species occurs around

the Northern Hemisphere. Our western plants once comprised a separate species, known as *A. sylvester,* among other names. Classification is still unsettled; some botanists consider western plants to be the variety *pubescens,* others consider them to be the variety *acuminatus.*

---

162 Sierran Mountain Misery
Chamaebatia foliolosa

Description: Few *white flowers* in open clusters just above *patches of fine, fern-like leaves with a resinous or balsamic odor.*

Flowers: Sepals 5; petals 5, each ¼–⅓" (6–8 mm) long, white, broadly ovate, growing from rim of a cup about ¼" (5 mm) wide.

Leaves: Obovate in outline, pinnately divided into very fine, tiny, densely arranged segments, each segment tipped by a minute hair with a round, glandular tip.

Fruit: ¼" (6 mm) long, hard, egg-shaped, 1-seeded, not opening.

Height: 8–24" (20–60 cm).

Flowering: May–July.

Habitat: Open forests.

Range: California in Cascade Range and Sierra Nevada.

Comments: The extensive patches of very finely divided leaves are unmistakable. Plants often grow in semi-open areas in poor soil disturbed several decades earlier, such as road banks; like many such plants, this species has nodules on the roots harboring bacteria, which makes atmospheric nitrogen available to the plant. Southern Mountain Misery *(C. australis),* a similar species growing in the mountains of southern California and northern Baja California, has leaves elliptical in outline, and the gland at the tip of each segment lacks hair; some populations are threatened by the clearing of land for avocado orchards. Fernbush *(Chamaebatiaria millefolium)* has fern-like leaves, white flowers with

five petals, and dry fruit about ¼″
(6 mm) long, with five sections, each
of which opens on the inner side; this
widespread species is found from
Oregon to Wyoming south to eastern
California and northern Arizona.

34 White Mountain Avens
Dryas octopetala

Description: A small *prostrate plant, often growing in
large patches,* with woody, rooting stems
and *1 cream or white flower* at end of each
erect, leafless stalk.

Flowers: About 1″ (2.5 cm) wide; calyx with
8–10 narrow, pointed lobes, hairy,
darkened by stalked glands; petals 8–10,
broad; stamens many.

Leaves: To 1¼″ (3 cm) long, lanceolate, often
very hairy on lower surface, edges
scalloped and rolled downward.

Fruit: Base seed-like, bearing a silvery plume
to 1½″ (4 cm) long; many in a shaggy
round head.

Height: Creeper; flower stalks 2–10″ (5–25 cm).

Flowering: June–August.

Habitat: Open, often rocky places from middle
elevations to above timberline.

Range: Across northern North America; in
West, south to northern Washington,
northeastern Oregon, central Idaho,
northern Utah, and Colorado.

Comments: This species, which also occurs in
northern Eurasia, often grows with
dwarf willows. Prostrate habits provide
both plants protection against cold
drying winds.

38 Apache Plume
Fallugia paradoxa

Description: A shrub with *white flowers* and *silvery
puffs of fruit heads* at tips of very dense,
intertangled, twiggy, slender branches.

Flowers: 1–1½″ (2.5–4 cm) wide; sepals 5; petals
5, round, growing from rim of a small
cup; stamens many.

Leaves:	½–1″ (1.5–2.5 cm) long, thick, *divided into 5 or 7 narrow lobes,* edges strongly curled downward.
Fruit:	Base seed-like, bearing a silvery plume ¾–2″ (2–5 cm) long; many in a shaggy round head.
Height:	To 7′ (2.1 m).
Flowering:	May–October.
Habitat:	Gravelly or rocky slopes and in washes from deserts to open pine forests.
Range:	Southeastern California and southern Nevada east to southern Colorado and western Texas, and south to northern Mexico.
Comments:	This rather thick shrub appears unkempt, but in full flower the white petals are attractive against the dark foliage. A shrub in full fruit, loaded with "Apache plumes," glistens silvery as sunlight passes through the feathery styles.

37 Beach Strawberry
Fragaria chiloensis

Description:	A low *plant connected to others by runners,* at least when young, often growing in patches, with *white flowers* on stalks slightly shorter than leaves.
Flowers:	About ¾″ (2 cm) wide; sepals 5, pointed, alternating with 5 smaller bracts; petals 5, broadly ovate, each with a short stalk at base; stamens many.
Leaves:	Compound, with *3 leaflets,* each ¾–2″ (2–5 cm) long, broad, leathery, toothed at end, shiny dark green above, hairy and grayish below, on stalk 2–8″ (5–20 cm) long.
Fruit:	Berry, ½–¾″ (1.5–2 cm) wide, enlarging from a cone-shaped flower center with many pistils.
Height:	Creeper; flower stalks 2–8″ (5–20 cm).
Flowering:	March–August.
Habitat:	Coastal dunes and bluffs.
Range:	Alaska south along Pacific Coast through northern two-thirds of California.

Comments: The word strawberry comes from
the Anglo-Saxon *streawberige,*
referring to the berries "strewing"
their runners out over the ground.
This plant also grows in South
America; Chilean plants of this
species were the parents in the
production of hybrid domestic
strawberries. Several species of
wild strawberries in the West
strongly resemble Beach Strawberry
but have thin leaflets.

190 Bigleaf Avens; Large-leaved Geum
Geum macrophyllum

Description: A leafy plant with 1 or several
stems topped by few *yellow flowers*
on branches.

Flowers: About ½" (1.5 cm) wide; sepals 5,
pointed, bent downward; petals 5, each
¼" (6 mm) long, broad; stamens and
pistils many, each with a slender style
consisting of a *persistent basal part hooked
at tip* and a terminal part dropping off.

Leaves: To 1' (30 cm) long, *pinnately compound,*
segments progressively larger from base
to tip, end segment by far the largest.

Fruit: Base seed-like, bearing a reddish hooked
beak about ⅛" (4 mm) long; many in a
dense round head.

Height: To 3' (90 cm).

Flowering: April–August.

Habitat: Moist woods and meadows from
low to high elevations.

Range: Alaska south to Baja California
and east to South Dakota and Rocky
Mountain region as far south as
northern New Mexico; also in eastern
Canada and northern portion of eastern
United States.

Comments: Geums with yellow flowers are
to distinguish from cinquefoils
(Potentilla), but in *Geum* the style is
divided into an upper and lower part,
and in most western species the leaves
are also narrow at the base and broad
at the tip.

478 Prairie Smoke; Purple Avens; Old Man's Whiskers
Geum triflorum

Description: Several *pink or reddish-pink, sometimes yellowish, bell-shaped flowers hanging* from long, reddish, branched stalks above thick clumps of mostly basal leaves.

Flowers: About ½" (1.5 cm) long; sepals 5, pointed, alternating with 5 narrow bracts; petals 5, tiny.

Leaves: 1¼–6" (3–15 cm) long, pinnately compound, blades jaggedly toothed.

Fruit: Base seed-like, bearing a reddish plume to 2" (5 cm) long; many in a shaggy round head.

Height: To 16" (40 cm).

Flowering: April–August.

Habitat: Sagebrush plains to mountain ridges and meadows.

Range: Across northern North America; south in West to central Sierra Nevada and in Rocky Mountain region to Utah and New Mexico; also in much of northern portion of eastern United States.

Comments: After fertilization, the bell-shaped flowers turn upward and plumes begin to grow from the pistils, ready to be caught by the wind or a passing animal, thus achieving seed dispersal.

Prairie Smoke

353 Gordon's Ivesia
Ivesia gordonii

Description: *Yellow flowers in a crowded, head-like*
cluster on each of several nearly leafless
stalks growing from *basal leaves.*

Flowers: Cluster ½–¾″ (1.5–2 cm) wide; petals
5, narrow, on small stalks, shorter than
narrowly triangular lobes of sepals;
stamens 5.

Leaves: ¾–4″ (2–10 cm) long, *pinnately*
compound, usually with more than 20
leaflets, each with 3–5 rounded
segments.

Height: To 8″ (20 cm).

Flowering: June–August.

Habitat: Open, gravelly or rocky places; at lower
elevations along riverbanks, at higher
elevations on open ridges.

Range: Central Washington south to central
Sierra Nevada and east to Utah,
northern Colorado, Wyoming, and
western Montana.

Comments: *Ivesia* is a western genus with mostly
yellow flowers; a few species have white
or pink flowers. The genus is closely
related to *Horkelia,* which has stamens
with broad filaments. Cinquefoils
(Potentilla) are similar but usually do not
have stalks at the base of the petals, and

Gordon's Ivesia

the three uppermost leaflets do not grow
together as they do in many *Ivesia* species.

---

109 Partridge Foot
Luetkea pectinata

Description: Erect stalks topped by *white flowers in
dense clusters* and growing from *dense
patches or mats of dark green, divided leaves.*

Flowers: Cluster 1–2″ (2.5–5 cm) long; sepals 5;
petals 5, each about ⅛″ (3 mm) long,
white; stamens about 20.

Leaves: Mostly crowded at base, on stalks to ½″
(13 mm) long; blades ¼–½″ (6–13 mm)
long; fan-shaped, dissected into very
narrow lobes.

Height: 2–6″ (5–15 cm).

Flowering: June–August.

Habitat: Usually well-drained soil high in
mountains where snow persists until late
in season.

Range: Alaska south to northern California,
eastern Idaho, and western Montana.

Comments: The common name refers to the divided
leaves, which are shaped like birds' feet.

---

135 Rocky Mountain Rockmat
Petrophyton caespitosum

Description: *Pinkish- or brownish-white flowers in dense
racemes above thick, impenetrable mats of
stems and leaves* resembling stone.

Flowers: Cluster ¾–1¼″ (2–3 cm) wide; sepals 5;
petals 5, each about ⅛″ (3 mm) long;
stamens 20.

Leaves: To ½″ (1.5 cm) long, narrow, crowded,
hairy, gray.

Height: Flower stalks 1–3″ (2.5–7.5 cm); mats
to about 3″ (7.5 cm) thick, 3′ (90 cm)
wide.

Flowering: June–August.

Habitat: Barren rock crevices.

Range: Northeastern Oregon south to southern
California and east to western Texas,
Colorado, South Dakota, and Montana.

Comments: This strange plant is found almost
exclusively in the inhospitable habitat

of barren rock, clinging by stout roots jammed in crevices. There are only two other species: Chelan Rockmat *(P. cinerascens),* found in central Washington, and Olympic Mountain Rockmat *(P. hendersonii),* found in the Olympic Mountains of northwestern Washington.

---

189 Common Silverweed
Potentilla anserina subsp. *anserina*

Description: A low, patch-forming plant with *silky leaves in tufts, connected by runners to other tufts,* and *1 yellow flower* atop each leafless stalk rising from leaf axil on runner.

Flowers: About ¾" (2 cm) wide; sepals 5; petals 5, broad; stamens 20–25.

Leaves: 4–12" (10–30 cm) long, pinnately compound, usually with 15–29 rounded, sharply toothed leaflets.

Height: Creeper; flower stalks 2–12" (5–30 cm), runners 3–6' (90–180 cm) long.

Flowering: May–August.

Habitat: Moist ground, meadows, and streambanks.

Range: Throughout West; in East, across Canada and south to much of northeastern United States.

Comments: This species, also occurring in Eurasia, is sometimes placed in the genus *Argentea* because of the solitary flower at the tip of the stalk. The very similar Pacific Silverweed *(P. anserina* subsp. *pacifica)* grows along the Pacific Coast from Alaska to southern California; the runners and stalks of its leaves lack hairs or have a few hairs that lie flat. In ancient times Common Silverweed was grown for food and medicine. The cooked root is purported to have the flavor of parsnips or sweet potatoes. An extract from the root has also been used to tan leather. The supposed medicinal properties of various species of *Potentilla* inspired the genus name, derived from the Latin *potens* ("powerful"), meaning "powerful little one." To treat scrofula, Pliny recommended an ointment made from certain *Potentilla,* honey, and axle grease.

188 Shrubby Cinquefoil
Potentilla fruticosa

Description: *A small shrub with reddish-brown, shredding bark* on young twigs and 1 *yellow flower* in each upper leaf axil, or few in clusters at branch ends.

Flowers: About 1″ (2.5 cm) wide; sepals 5; petals 5, broad; stamens 25–30.

Leaves: Pinnately divided, usually with 5 crowded leaflets, each ½–¾″ (1.5–2 cm) long, hairy and grayish, especially on underside.

Height: 6–36″ (15–90 cm).

Flowering: June–August.

Habitat: Ridges, open forests, and plains from low to high elevations.

Range: Across northern North America, and south throughout most of West; also in northern portion of eastern United States.

Comments: This handsome shrub, common in the West and also found in Eurasia, adapts well to cultivation. Among the many horticultural variants are dwarf, low-growing, and unusually large-flowered forms, some with white or yellowish-orange flowers.

187 Sticky Cinquefoil
Potentilla glandulosa

Description: A leafy plant with several stems, often reddish and *sticky with minute, glandular hairs,* topped by *yellow flowers in loose branched clusters.*

Flowers: ½–¾″ (1.5–2 cm) wide; sepals 5, pointed, alternating with 5 smaller bracts, all growing from rim of a nearly flat cup; petals 5, broad; stamens 25–40; pistils numerous; style attached to lower side of ovary, thickest in middle.

Leaves:	Pinnately compound, with 5–9 ovate leaflets, each ½–2″ (1.5–5 cm) long, with sharp teeth on edges.
Height:	To 20″ (50 cm).
Flowering:	May–July.
Habitat:	In dry or moist soil, generally in open sites.
Range:	British Columbia and Alberta south to southern California and east to Arizona, Colorado, Wyoming, South Dakota, and Montana.
Comments:	This attractive wildflower is common in the West and generally recognizable as a cinquefoil, a name ultimately deriving from Latin through French, meaning "five leaves"; some species have leaves with five leaflets. The genus differs from very similar-appearing species of buttercups *(Ranunculus)* in having a hypanthium. Some species hybridize; others reproduce asexually. Hybrids may reproduce asexually, and populations of intermediate plants are frequent. Identification of cinquefoil species is therefore difficult.

387 Red Cinquefoil
Potentilla thurberi

Description:	1 or several leafy branched stems bearing loose clusters of long-stalked, *rich, deep crimson flowers.*
Flowers:	About 1″ (2.5 cm) wide; sepals 5; petals 5, broad; stamens many.
Leaves:	Pinnately divided, with 5–7 closely adjacent, toothed leaflets, each 1–2″ (2.5–5 cm) long.
Height:	1–2½′ (30–75 cm).
Flowering:	July–October.
Habitat:	Rich soil in coniferous forests, damp meadows, and along streams.
Range:	Central Arizona east to central New Mexico and south to northern Mexico.
Comments:	The rich red, darkest in the flower's center, seems to have a velvety glow; the surface is dull but the color intense. A second *Potentilla* species with reddish flowers, Purple Cinquefoil *(P. palustris),*

is relatively humble, with tiny,
dark red petals between larger,
dull red sepals; it grows in bogs
across North America, extending
south in the West to northern
California and Wyoming.

461   Nootka Rose
Rosa nutkana

Description: *A thorny shrub* with *pale pink flowers;*
largest (often only) thorns in pairs near
leafstalks.

Flowers: 2–3″ (5–7.5 cm) wide; sepals 5,
slender, usually tapering from
base to narrow middle, then
expanding slightly near tip; petals 5,
broad; stamens many.

Leaves: Pinnately compound, with 5–9 ovate
leaflets, each ½–3″ (1.5–7.5 cm) long,
sharply toothed on edges.

Fruit: Berry-like, ½–¾″ (1.5–2 cm) long,
round, smooth, reddish purple.

Height: 2–13′ (60–390 cm).

Flowering: May–July.

Habitat: Woods and open places in mountains.

Range: Alaska south to northern California,
northeastern Oregon, northern Utah,
and Colorado.

Comments: The hips, or fruit, of any wild rose are
edible and are used to make tea and jams
and jellies. Sweetbrier *(R. eglanteria),* the
Eglantine of Shakespeare and Chaucer,
introduced in North America from
Europe, is now fairly common west of
the Cascade Range and the Sierra
Nevada; it has many down-curved
prickles on the stem and minute glands
on the leaves and sepals that give off a
pleasant rose aroma.

32   Dwarf Bramble
Rubus lasiococcus

Description: *Trailing, thornless, freely rooting, leafy stems*
and short erect stems bearing 1 leaf and
1–2 *white flowers.*

Flowers:	About ½″ (1.5 cm) wide; sepals 5; petals 5, broad; stamens many.
Leaves:	1–2½″ (2.5–6.5 cm) wide, about as long, cleft into 3 lobes, with toothed edges.
Fruit:	Small red raspberry.
Height:	Erect flower stems to 4″ (10 cm); trailing stems to 7′ (2.1 m) long.
Flowering:	June–August.
Habitat:	Thickets and woods.
Range:	British Columbia south to northern California.
Comments:	*Rubus* comes from the Roman word for "bramble"; species of this large and complicated genus are more often shrubs or formidable patches of thorny brambles than low creepers. There are perhaps 15 *Rubus* species throughout the West, variously called blackberries, raspberries, or thimbleberries. Through hybridization and selection, many horticultural varieties have improved the berries. However, berries found in the wild are equally sweet, juicy, and flavorful.

MADDER FAMILY
Rubiaceae

Herbs, shrubs, or trees, with flowers in branched clusters.

Flowers: Usually radially symmetrical. Sepals 4–5, or absent; petals 4–5, united at base; stamens 4–5; all these parts attached at top of ovary.

Leaves: Opposite, with bases connected by united stipules extending across node; or whorled, with stipules apparently lacking.

Fruit: Usually a berry or a 2-chambered capsule; or splitting into 2–4 seed-like sections, each 1-seeded.

There are about 450 genera and 6,500 species, primarily in tropical regions, where woody representatives are most frequent. A dye is obtained from Madder *(Rubia tinctoria),* coffee from species of *Coffea,* and quinine from species of *Cinchona. Gardenia* species are popular ornamentals in mild climates. Sweet-scented members of the genus *Galium* were once used as mattress stuffing, thus the common name bedstraw is often given to these species as well as to Rubiaceae as a whole.

417 Scarlet Bouvardia; Trompetilla
Bouvardia ternifolia

Description: *A shrub with brilliant scarlet, tubular flowers* in loose clusters at ends of numerous erect branches.

Flowers: Corolla ½–1¼″ (1.5–3 cm) long, with 4 short lobes at end; calyx 4-lobed.

Leaves: To 3″ (7.5 cm) long, ovate, 3–4 in a whorl on branches.

Height: To 3′ (90 cm).

Flowering: May–November.

Habitat: Dry rocky slopes and among boulders.

Range: Southern Arizona, southwestern New Mexico, and western Texas south to Mexico.

Comments: The spectacular red corolla attracts, and provides nectar for, hummingbirds. The Spanish name, Trompetilla, which means "little trumpet," refers to the corolla's shape.

106 Bedstraw
Galium boreale

Description: A leafy plant with *leaves in whorls of 4* on 4-sided stems, short branches often in leaf axils, and *many round-topped clusters of tiny white flowers* at branch ends.

Flowers: Sepals absent; petals 4, each less than ⅛″ (3 mm) long, spreading from top of ovary.

Leaves: To 2″ (5 cm) long, narrow, with 3 veins.

Height: 8–31″ (20–80 cm).

Flowering: June–August.

Habitat: Open moist areas from sea level to high in mountains.

Range: Throughout much of North America; in West, south to northern California, Arizona, New Mexico, and Texas.

Comments: This plant is also found in Eurasia. The genus name, from the Greek *gala* ("milk"), comes from the use of one species to curdle milk. Most *Galium* species have inconspicuous flowers borne singly or in small clusters, but the four spreading corolla lobes, the attachment of

flower parts above the ovary, and the
whorled leaves are consistent features.
Galium species bearing tiny hooks all
over the surface of the round fruits are
sometimes called cleavers, for the fruits
cleave to fabric or fur.

PITCHER PLANT FAMILY
Sarraceniaceae

Carnivorous herbs with tubular leaves and large, nodding,
long-stalked flowers, borne singly or in racemes.

Flowers: Radially symmetrical. Sepals 3–6, often petal-like;
petals 5; stamens at least 12; all these parts attached at
base of ovary; ovary topped by umbrella-like style and
stigma.
Leaves: Basal, long; commonly with a decorative opening to
a tubular base.
Fruit: Capsule, with 3–6 chambers.

There are 3 genera and 15 species, found in North America and northern South America; in the United States all
species but one are in the East. A few are grown as curiosities; collecting for this purpose and habitat destruction
threaten the rarest plants. Several species are classified as
endangered or threatened in many states.

4 **California Pitcher Plant; Cobra Plant;
Cobra Lily**
Darlingtonia californica

Description: Several *tubular leaves with hood-like tops*
in a cluster and *1 yellow-green and maroon
flower hanging at tip* of a leafless stalk.
Flowers: Sepals 5, each 1½–3½" (4–9 cm) long,
yellow-green, petal-like; petals 5,
maroon, shorter than sepals; ovary green,
bell-shaped.
Leaves: 4–20" (10–50 cm) long, with 2 long flat
appendages beneath hood.
Height: To 3' (90 cm).
Flowering: April–August.
Habitat: Coastal bogs and mountain streams and
seeps.
Range: Most of western Oregon south to
northwestern California and central
Sierra Nevada.

Comments: Insects or other small organisms, attracted to the nectar secreted by the leaf hood and appendages, enter the hole beneath the hood, are trapped by numerous down-pointing hairs, and are decomposed by microorganisms in the fluid in the tubular base. Nutrients thus released are absorbed by the plant.

LIZARD TAIL FAMILY
Saururaceae

Herbs, mostly of moist places, with small flowers often intermixed with colored bracts.

Flowers: Radially symmetrical; in a dense spike, raceme, or cluster often resembling 1 large flower. Sepals and petals absent; stamens 3, 6, or 8; pistils 3–4, sometimes partly joined at base.
Leaves: Simple.
Fruit: Seed-like or fleshy capsule.

There are 5 genera and 7 species, found in North America and eastern Asia.

91   **Yerba Mansa**
Anemopsis californica

Description: A grayish-green, patch-forming plant with *cone-shaped spikes, each resembling 1 white flower.*

Yerba Mansa

Flowers:	Spike 1–2″ (2.5–5 cm) long; several broad, white, petal-like bracts ½–1″ (1.5–2.5 cm) long at spike base; 1 small white bract beneath each tiny flower.
Leaves:	To 6″ (15 cm) long, mostly oblong, erect.
Height:	To 1′ (30 cm).
Flowering:	May–August.
Habitat:	Low, moist, saline or alkaline places.
Range:	Oregon, Nevada, Utah, Colorado, and Nebraska south through much of Southwest to Mexico.
Comments:	The aromatic root has been put to many medicinal uses: treatment of abrasions, cuts, and burns; a cure for a variety of gastrointestinal upsets; a poultice for rheumatism; and a tonic for blood purification.

SAXIFRAGE FAMILY
Saxifragaceae

Usually herbs with small flowers, borne singly or in raceme-like or branched clusters.

Flowers: Radially symmetrical. Sepals 5; petals usually 5 or 10, separate; stamens 5 or 10; all these parts attached to edge of a cup-like flower base (hypanthium), with ovary in center.
Leaves: Usually alternate, basal.
Fruit: Capsule, small pod, or berry.

There are about 40 genera and 700 species, mainly in cooler regions of the Northern Hemisphere. Species of *Saxifraga, Bergenia,* and *Astilbe* are commonly grown as ornamentals.

19 Coast Boykinia
Boykinia occidentalis

Description:	*Leaves mostly at base* and *openly branched clusters of small white flowers* tending to turn upward atop several reddish stems covered with minute, glandular hairs.
Flowers:	About ¼″ (6 mm) wide; calyx with 5 short pointed lobes in rim of a cup; petals 5, narrow, each with a narrow, stalk-like base; stamens 5.

Leaves: *Broadly heart-shaped or kidney-shaped, cleft into 5–7 lobes,* edges with sharp, irregular, bristle-tipped teeth; those near base on long stalks.

Height: 6–24″ (15–60 cm).

Flowering: June–August.

Habitat: Springs and seeps in moist woods and along streams.

Range: British Columbia south to western Washington, Oregon, and northern half of California.

Comments: There are several species of *Boykinia* in North America, most occurring in the West. The genus name honors an early-19th-century naturalist from the state of Georgia, Dr. Samuel Boykin.

523 Umbrella Plant
Darmera peltata

Description: Large masses of *nearly round, jaggedly toothed leaves on rough hairy stalks,* and *small pink flowers in large, round, branched clusters* on stalks slightly taller than leaves.

Flowers: Petals 5, each about ¼″ (6 mm) long, pink or white; stamens 10; pistil with 2 reddish-purple sections.

Leaves: To 16″ (40 cm) wide.

Height: 2–6′ (60–180 cm).

Flowering: April–June.

Habitat: In and along edges of cold streams.

Range: Central Oregon south to central California.

Comments: With its luxuriant foliage, this plant, usually anchored firmly among water-washed rocks, can give a verdant, almost tropical aspect to mountain streams. The peltate leafstalk (attaching near the middle of the blade) is an important identification feature and gave the genus its former name, *Peltiphyllum.*

316 Poker Heuchera; Poker Alumroot
Heuchera cylindrica

Description: *Leathery leaves,* varying from ovate to broadly heart-shaped, on *long stalks clustered at base* of flower stalks; upper plant densely covered with glandular hairs, especially in *narrow, greenish-yellowish flower cluster.*

Flowers: Sepals 5, round, forming rim of a cream or greenish-yellow cup ¼–½" (6–13 mm) deep, lower sepals slightly longer; petals 5 (sometimes fewer or absent), white, less than one-half as long as sepals; stamens 5.

Leaves: 1–3" (2.5–7.5 cm) wide.

Height: 6–36" (15–90 cm).

Flowering: April–August.

Habitat: Rocky flats, slopes, and cliffs.

Range: British Columbia and Alberta south to northeastern California and east to northern Nevada, Wyoming, and Montana.

Comments: The dense narrow flower cluster and the very short petals (or their absence) help distinguish this species from several others in the genus. Alumroot species are variable, making identification of many plants difficult.

403 Coral Bells
Heuchera sanguinea

Description: *Bright, coral-red bells hanging in a narrow cluster* from upper part of a nearly leafless stalk; leaves mostly basal.

Flowers: ¼–½" (6–13 mm) long; sepals 5, on rim of a colorful, bell-shaped cup; petals 5, as long as sepals; stamens 5.

Leaves: 1–3" (2.5–7.5 cm) wide, nearly round, leathery, most on long stalks.

Height: 10–20" (25–50 cm).

Flowering: March–October.

Habitat: Moist, shaded, rocky places.

Range: Southern Arizona and southwestern New Mexico south to northern Mexico; introduced in Pennsylvania.

Comments: The dainty bells and dark green leaves
make this a highly popular ornamental.
Several other western species have
smaller, pink or purplish flowers in
more open clusters.

179 Leatherleaf Saxifrage
Leptarrhena pyrolifolia

Description: *A dense roundish cluster of tiny white to
pinkish flowers* atop an erect, nearly
leafless stalk growing from a *basal rosette
of leaves.*
Flowers: Cluster ¾–1″ (2–2.5 cm) wide; calyx
with 5 erect lobes attached near rim of a
saucer-like base; petals 5, narrow, white;
stamens 10, slender, as long as or longer
than petals; pistil with 2 segments
attached to saucer-like base only at
bottom and not by sides.
Leaves: 1–6″ (2.5–15 cm) long, elliptical,
smooth, leathery, widest above middle,
scalloped on edges.
Fruit: Tiny, rusty red pods.
Height: 2–10″ (5–25 cm).
Flowering: June–August.
Habitat: Wet places along streams, in meadows,
or on mountain slopes.
Range: Alaska south to central Oregon,
northern Idaho, and western Montana.
Comments: This is the only species in the genus. Its
dark green, persistent foliage and rusty
red fruits that mature from the flowers
make it an attractive plant. It has pistils
totally separate from one another;
similar species of *Saxifraga* usually have
pistils joined to one another for at least
20 percent of their length or joined to
the calyx for a similar distance.

444 Prairie Star
Lithophragma parviflorum

Description: Flowers in open, slender racemes with
*white or pale pink petals cleft into 3 or 5
finger-like lobes;* leaves mostly at base and
lower part of stem.

Prairie Star

Flowers: ½–1″ (1.5–2.5 cm) wide; sepals 5, short, triangular, attached near rim of a bell-shaped base; petals 5; stamens 5.

Leaves: ½–1¼″ (1.5–3 cm) wide, roundish, deeply cleft into 3 or 5 sections, these less deeply divided into narrow lobes.

Height: To 20″ (50 cm).

Flowering: March–June.

Habitat: Prairies, in sagebrush, and in open forests at lower elevations.

Range: British Columbia south to northern California and east to western Nebraska, western South Dakota, Montana, and Alberta.

Comments: White or pinkish petals on star-like flowers in racemes are characteristic of this genus. Species that grow in woods are called woodland stars. Some species in the genus have tiny, maroon beads (bulblets) in leaf axils and in place of some flowers; these can grow into new plants.

10 **Five-point Bishop's Cap**
Mitella pentandra

Description: A small plant with *tiny, greenish flowers in slender racemes* and leaves in a basal cluster.

Flowers: About ¼″ (6 mm) wide; petals 5, each with a slender central rib from which

even finer strands project at right
angles, *each tiny petal like a fine double
comb with sparse slender teeth.*

Leaves: 1–3" (2.5–7.5 cm) wide, roundish, on
long stalks.

Height: 4–16" (10–40 cm).

Flowering: June–August.

Habitat: Damp woods, streambanks, and wet
meadows.

Range: Alaska and northwestern Canada south
to southern Sierra Nevada and east to
Colorado, Wyoming, western South
Dakota, Montana, and Alberta.

Comments: There are several species of *Mitella,* all
dainty little plants that grow in damp
shady places in the West. One species,
Bare-stem Mitella *(M. nuda),* has 10
stamens; others have half as many.

59 Fringed Grass-of-Parnassus
Parnassia fimbriata

Description: *1 white or yellowish, saucer-shaped flower*
atop each of several stems with most
leaves at base.

Flowers: About 1" (2.5 cm) wide; petals 5,
fringed on lower edges; stamens 5, with
a yellowish, fan-shaped structure with
gland-tipped "fingers" between each.

Leaves: To 2" (5 cm) wide, broadly heart-shaped
or kidney-shaped, with several major
veins arching from notched base to tip;
all long-stalked except leaf at midstem.

Height: 6–20" (15–50 cm).

Flowering: July–September.

Habitat: Wet places in mountains.

Range: Alaska south to central California and
east to Rocky Mountains from New
Mexico to Alberta.

Comments: Grass-of-Parnassus is the translation
of the Latin name of a European
species, *Gramen parnassi.* The word
gramen was used for many herbs, not
only grasses. Parnassus, in both
common and scientific names, is
probably a dedication of the plant to
the Muses; snowcapped Mount
Parnassus was celebrated as their

home. The fan-shaped structures
(staminodia) between the stamens of
Parnassia are distinctive.

356 Spotted Saxifrage
Saxifraga bronchialis

Description: A *matted plant,* resembling a small
evergreen or large moss, with *small
yellowish-white flowers* in an open,
branched, reddish cluster.

Flowers: About ⅜″ (9 mm) wide; petals 5,
spotted with maroon or orange;
stamens 10; ovary purplish.

Leaves: ¼–¾″ (6–20 mm) long, narrow,
rigid, mostly near base, with tiny
stiff hairs on edges.

Height: 2–6″ (5–15 cm).

Flowering: June–August.

Habitat: Open slopes, usually among rocks,
generally high in mountains.

Range: Alaska east to north-central Canada,
south to northern Oregon, and in Rocky
Mountain region to Idaho, Utah, and
New Mexico.

Comments: This is a common plant along mountain
trails. The genus name, from the Latin
saxum ("rock") and *frangere* ("to break"),
alludes to the species' rocky habitat;

Spotted Saxifrage

saxifrages grow in rock crevices, looking as if they have split the rock. Herbalists once used some species in a treatment for kidney stones in the urinary tract.

108 Merten's Saxifrage
Saxifraga mertensiana

Description: *Nearly circular leaves with hairy stalks in a basal cluster* around a taller, branched flower stalk bearing *tiny white flowers.*

Flowers: Nearly ¼" (6 mm) wide; petals 5, oblong; stamens 10, with club-like filaments and pink anthers; some flowers replaced by pink bulbs.

Leaves: Blades 1–4" (2.5–10 cm) wide, with lobed edges, larger lobes with roundish, shallow teeth; stalks to 4 times length of blade; membranous sheath around stem at stalk base.

Height: 4–16" (10–40 cm).

Flowering: April–August.

Habitat: Wet banks and along streams in coniferous woods.

Range: Alaska south to central California, northeastern Oregon, central Idaho, and western Montana.

Comments: The tiny bulbs that replace some flowers can grow into new plants when they drop to the ground.

20 Western Saxifrage
Saxifraga occidentalis

Description: A small clump of basal leaves surrounding an erect, *reddish-glandular stem with tiny white flowers in a branched cluster.*

Flowers: Cluster ¾–2" (2–5 cm) wide; petals 5, each about ⅛" (3 mm) long, ovate or oblong, sometimes with 2 yellow spots at base; stamens 10, with slender or club-shaped filaments; ovary with 2 nearly separate chambers.

Leaves: Blades to 2½" (6.5 cm) long, ovate, coarsely toothed, tapered to a short or long stalk.

Fruit:	Greenish or reddish capsule, nearly divided into 2 separate pod-like sections less than ¼″ (6 mm) long.
Height:	2–12″ (5–30 cm).
Flowering:	April–August.
Habitat:	Moist slopes, meadows, and among rocks.
Range:	British Columbia south to northwestern Oregon, eastern Nevada, Idaho, and northwestern Wyoming.
Comments:	This species has several varieties and intergrades with several other species, which are distinguished by technical features only.

457 Purple Saxifrage
Saxifraga oppositifolia

Description:	*A dense little cushion plant with oval leaves,* often tinged with maroon, and *bright pinkish- to reddish-lavender flowers.*
Flowers:	About ¼″ (6 mm) wide; petals 5, erect, spatula-shaped; stamens 10; pistil with 2 projections at top, each tipped with a tiny knob.
Leaves:	About ⅛″ (3 mm) long, opposite, in 4 rows on stem, strongly over lapping, edges with stiff short hairs.
Height:	About 2″ (5 cm); tuft to 8″ (20 cm) wide.
Flowering:	June–August.
Habitat:	Rocky areas and crevices in mountains.
Range:	Across northern North America; in West, south to northwestern Oregon, Idaho, eastern Nevada, Wyoming, and perhaps northern Colorado; in East, south to northeastern United States.
Comments:	In *Saxifraga,* white flowers are more common than this species' richly colored ones. The plant resembles Moss Pink *(Silene acaulis),* which is distinguished from it by three styles and generally a notch at the end of the slender petals.

178   Diamondleaf Saxifrage
Saxifraga rhomboidea

Description: 1 erect, *glandular-hairy stem* with a *tight cluster of tiny white flowers* growing from a *basal cluster of leaves.*

Flowers: Petals 5, each about ⅛" (3 mm) long, ovate; stamens 10, with filaments thickest near middle; ovary with 2–4 nearly separate chambers; cluster may resemble a round head about ¾" (2 cm) wide, or may be more openly branched with flowers grouped near branch ends.

Leaves: Blades ½–2" (1.5–5 cm) long, thick, with blunt teeth, diamond-shaped or nearly triangular, on broad flat stalks.

Height: 2–12" (5–30 cm).

Flowering: May–August.

Habitat: Moist places from sagebrush hills to high in mountains.

Range: British Columbia and Alberta south to Idaho, Nevada, northern Arizona, and northern New Mexico.

Comments: This plant belongs to a complex of closely similar species found in most parts of the West.

177   Alpine Saxifrage
Saxifraga tolmiei

Description: A low, *mat-forming plant with tiny white flowers in clusters* atop mostly leafless stems.

Flowers: Petals 5, each to ¼" (6 mm) long, white; stamens 10, with filaments thickest near tip, like tiny baseball bats.

Leaves: ⅛–½" (3–13 mm) long, narrow, crowded at base, becoming stiff and dry, remaining on stem when dead.

Fruit: Capsule, with usually 2 beak-like projections at tip.

Height: 1–3" (2.5–7.5 cm).

Flowering: July–August.

Habitat: Meadows and moist rocky areas in mountains.

Range: Alaska south to central California and east to western Montana, Idaho, and Nevada.

Comments: This attractive alpine plant has two varieties. The common one in California (variety *ledifolia*) has no hairs on its leaves, whereas the leaves of plants in other areas (variety *tolmiei*) usually have a few long hairs on the leaf bases.

458 Violet Suksdorfia
Suksdorfia violacea

Description: *A slender, delicate plant* with few branches at top bearing several *deep pink or violet, funnel-shaped flowers.*

Flowers: Petals 5, each ⅜" (9 mm) long, slender; stamens 5.

Leaves: To 1" (2.5 cm) wide, roundish, edges deeply lobed; those at base with long stalks; those on stem on shorter stalks with very broad bases, or with leaf-like flaps at base.

Height: 4–8" (10–20 cm).

Flowering: March–June.

Habitat: Moist, sandy, shaded areas, mossy banks, cliffs, and rock crevices.

Range: British Columbia south to northern Oregon and east to northern Idaho and northwestern Montana.

Comments: W. N. Suksdorf, whom the genus and common names honor, was one of the foremost plant collectors of the Pacific Northwest around the turn of the 20th century. The only other species, Buttercup-leaved Suksdorfia *(S. ranunculifolia),* found from British Columbia south to California and east to Montana, has white petals; its five stamens and broad leafstalk bases (especially of the stem leaves) distinguish it from similar species of *Saxifraga,* which have 10 stamens and narrow leafstalk bases.

127 Fringe Cups
Tellima grandiflora

Description: A plant growing in clumps with most leaves near base and *cream or pale pink, fringed flowers in several long racemes.*

Flowers:	About ½″ (1.5 cm) wide; sepals 5, short; petals 5, white or pink, fringed across end; sepals and petals attached to edge of a cup-like base; stamens 10.
Leaves:	1–4″ (2.5–10 cm) wide, roundish, hairy, shallowly lobed and scalloped; those at base on long stalks.
Height:	To 31″ (80 cm).
Flowering:	April–July.
Habitat:	Moist places in woods.
Range:	Alaska south to coastal central California and east to northern Idaho and western Montana.
Comments:	This species is a beautiful plant of shaded woods, the slender wands of flowers arching upward or standing erect above the rich green foliage. The unusual petals are at first white or cream but often become deep pink with age.

---

107 False Mitrewort; Foam Flower; Lace Flower
Tiarella trifoliata

Description:	*Tiny white flowers hanging in loose clusters in narrow branched racemes* atop leafy stems.
Flowers:	Calyx about ¼″ (6 mm) wide, with 5 lobes attached to a pale green, cup-like base about ¹⁄₁₆″ (2 mm) long, upper lobe largest; petals 5, each about ⅛″ (3 mm) long, white, hair-like; stamens 10, white, protruding.
Leaves:	Blades to 3½″ (9 cm) wide, lower ones on long stalks, rather triangular, indented and toothed or divided into 3 often deeply cut leaflets.
Fruit:	Capsule, opening by a split between unequal halves.
Height:	8–16″ (20–40 cm).
Flowering:	May–August.
Habitat:	Moist woods and streambanks.
Range:	Alaska south to central California and east to Idaho and western Montana.
Comments:	The form with the most highly cut leaf blades grows in western Washington. If the leaves are cut to the top of the leafstalk, this is the variety *trifoliata;* if

the leaves are lobed but not cut, then this is the variety *unifoliata.* The genus name is from the Greek *tiara,* an ancient Persian headdress, which the fruit resembles.

FIGWORT FAMILY
Scrophulariaceae

Mostly herbs, sometimes shrubs, rarely trees, often with showy flowers.

Flowers: Usually bilaterally symmetrical. Sepals united, usually forming calyx with 4–5 lobes; petals usually 4–5, united, usually forming corolla with an upper and lower lip; stamens usually 4, sometimes 2 or 5, when 5 the fifth often sterile and different; all these parts attached at base of ovary.

Leaves: Alternate, opposite, or whorled; simple or pinnately compound.

Fruit: Berry or 2-chambered capsule.

There are about 190 genera and 4,000 species, found nearly throughout the world. A cardiac drug is extracted from Foxglove *(Digitalis purpurea),* a handsome species also cultivated as an ornamental. Snapdragons *(Antirrhinum),* speedwells *(Veronica),* beardtongues *(Penstemon),* and slipper-flowers *(Calceolavia)* are other plants grown for their beauty. Scrophulariaceae has also been known as the snapdragon family.

114   White Snapdragon
Antirrhinum coulterianum

Description:	Slender, wand-like racemes of *white, bilaterally symmetrical flowers* on sparsely leaved stems; *slender tendrils in flower cluster* cling to other vegetation.
Flowers:	Corolla about ½″ (1.5 cm) long; upper corolla lip 2-lobed, bent upward; lower corolla lip 3-lobed, bent downward, hairy, lightly lined and spotted with violet on hump closing tube opening; stamens 4.
Leaves:	Few, lower ones 1–2½″ (2.5–6.5 cm) long, opposite, lanceolate.
Height:	To 4½′ (1.4 m).
Flowering:	April–June.

Habitat: Brushy flats and slopes in loose soil.
Range: Southern California and northern
Baja California.
Comments: This snapdragon's tall slender spires
are sparsely distributed and thus
never provide dense color displays.
The genus name, from the Greek *anti*
("against") and *rhinos* ("nose"), refers
to the way the snout-like corolla's
lower lip presses against the upper one.

288 Yellow Twining Snapdragon
Antirrhinum filipes

Description: *Many slender stems, twisting and
twining* through other vegetation, with
yellow, bilaterally symmetrical flowers on
thread-like stalks growing from leaf
axils.
Flowers: Corolla about ½" (1.5 cm) long; upper
corolla lip 2-lobed, bent upward; lower
corolla lip 3-lobed, bent downward,
dotted with black on hump closing tube
opening; stamens 4.
Leaves: To 2" (5 cm) long, lanceolate.
Height: Vine; stems to about 3' (90 cm) long.
Flowering: February–May.
Habitat: Sandy deserts.
Range: Southeastern Oregon to southern
California, southwestern Utah, and
western Arizona.
Comments: The flowers are brilliant yellow, but the
plant, hidden and tangled in low bushes,
is hard to find; its twining stems are
ordinarily obscured by leaves and twigs.

617 Alpine Besseya
Besseya alpina

Description: *A small pale plant, woolly* in younger
parts, bearing *pale bluish-violet flowers in
dense spikes* with conspicuous bracts.
Flowers: Calyx woolly; corolla about ¼" (6 mm)
long, bilaterally symmetrical; upper
corolla lip cupped forward; lower corolla
lip 3-lobed, bent down, middle lobe
shortest; stamens 2.

Leaves:	¾–2″ (2–5 cm) long, mostly at base, blades broadly ovate, edges scalloped; those on stem beneath spike much smaller, bract-like.
Height:	To 6″ (15 cm).
Flowering:	July–September.
Habitat:	High cold meadows and tundra.
Range:	Wyoming south to Utah and New Mexico.
Comments:	The several *Besseya* species have corollas varying from violet to yellow or white, or lacking entirely. The genus name honors the great American botanist Charles E. Bessey (1845–1915).

414   Desert Paintbrush
Castilleja angustifolia

Description:	Several erect *stems with bright orange to red sepals and bracts* clustered at tip.
Flowers:	Calyx bright reddish orange, as deeply cleft on upper side as lower, shallowly cleft on sides, the resulting 4 lobes bluntly pointed; corolla ¾–1¼″ (2–3 cm) long, bilaterally symmetrical, beak-like, very slender; lower corolla lip a green bump at about middle; upper corolla lip projecting as a beak, lightly hairy on top, usually pale with orange to red edges.
Leaves:	About 1–2″ (2.5–5 cm) long, lower ones very narrow and undivided, upper ones divided into 3 or 5 very narrow lobes; bracts in flower cluster similarly divided, bright reddish orange.
Height:	4–16″ (10–40 cm).
Flowering:	April–August.
Habitat:	Dry open soil, often in sagebrush.
Range:	Eastern Oregon east of mountains south to southern California, east to Utah, Wyoming, and Montana, and north into Alberta.
Comments:	This is one of the West's most common dryland paintbrushes. The genus is easily recognized, but many species are notoriously difficult to identify. The genus name (usually pronounced *cast-til-lay-yah*) honors the Spanish botanist Domingo Castillejo.

519   Common Owl's Clover; Escobita
Castilleja exserta

Description: An erect, little plant with a *rose and yellow or rose and white* flower cluster; *flowers and flower bracts velvety and rose-purple* on divided tips.

Flowers: Corolla ½–1¼" (1.5–3 cm) long, bilaterally symmetrical, strongly angled upward; lower corolla lip forming a white or yellow, 3-lobed pouch seeming to peer from bracts, with 3 tiny teeth at end; upper corolla lip short, hooked, velvety, rose-purple, forming a small beak above pouch.

Leaves: ½–2" (1.5–5 cm) long, divided into few very narrow segments.

Fruit: Capsule, about ½" (1.5 cm) long.

Height: 4–16" (10–40 cm).

Flowering: March–May.

Habitat: Fields, deserts, and open, wooded areas.

Range: Southern California to southern Arizona and northern Mexico.

Comments: Following a wet spring, acre upon acre is carpeted with this beautiful wildflower. The Spanish name, Escobita, means "little broom" and describes the flower cluster. The origin of the English common name is unknown, but it may refer to the swollen, head-like ends of the erect corollas that seem to peer from the bracts as owls peer from the leaves of a tree. Careful study has demonstrated that this plant is not an *Orthocarpus,* as previously classified *(O. purpurescens),* but instead belongs to a lineage of *Castilleja.*

---

413   Giant Red Paintbrush;
Scarlet Paintbrush
Castilleja miniata

Description: A leafy plant with a flower cluster resembling a *ragged, crimson or scarlet paintbrush;* calyx and bracts beneath each flower brightly colored.

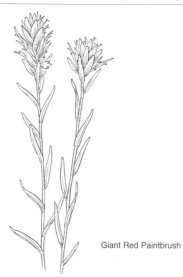

Giant Red Paintbrush

Flowers: Calyx conspicuous, tubular, with 4 pointed lobes, as deeply cleft between upper lobes as between lower lobes; corolla ¾–1½″ (2–4 cm) long, bilaterally symmetrical, relatively inconspicuous; lower corolla lip a green bump; upper corolla lip a pale yellow beak, at least as long as pale, tubular lower portion, with thin red edges.

Leaves: To about 4″ (10 cm) long, on stem, lanceolate, usually without lobes, some upper leaves and colorful bracts with 3 pointed lobes.

Height: 1–3′ (30–90 cm).

Flowering: May–September.

Habitat: Mountain meadows, thickets, and forest openings.

Range: Alaska south and east to Ontario, and south to northern California, Nevada, northern Arizona, northern New Mexico, and North Dakota.

Comments: Most paintbrushes are partial parasites on other plants, their roots connecting with roots of other species. For this reason they usually cannot be transplanted and are difficult to grow from seed.

214　Great Plains Paintbrush
Castilleja sessiliflora

Description: A hairy plant with clustered stems and *yellow to pinkish bracts and flowers with corollas protruding like long, pale, curved beaks.*

Flowers: Calyx same color as bracts, with 4 long narrow lobes; corolla 1¼–2½" (3–6.5 cm) long, bilaterally symmetrical, pale yellow to pale pink; upper corolla lip beak-like, about ½" (1.5 cm) long; lower corolla lip with 2 flared lobes, each about ¼" (6 mm) long.

Leaves: About 1–2" (2.5–5 cm) long, lower ones very narrow, upper ones usually with a pair of narrow lobes.

Height: 4–12" (10–30 cm).

Flowering: March–September.

Habitat: Dry, open, rocky or sandy knolls or slopes on plains and among piñon and juniper.

Range: Throughout Great Plains to western Texas and southeastern Arizona; also in northern Mexico.

Comments: In very dry areas with poor soil, this species forms diminutive tufts; where soil and moisture are better, plants are taller and more open.

314　Sulfur Paintbrush
Castilleja sulphurea

Description: A leafy plant with a flower cluster resembling *a ragged, pale yellow paintbrush;* calyx and bracts beneath each flower bright yellow.

Flowers: Calyx tubular, with 4 short pointed lobes; corolla ¾–1¼" (2–3 cm) long, bilaterally symmetrical, relatively inconspicuous; lower corolla lip a green bump on lower side well above middle; upper corolla lip pale, barely extending beyond calyx as a short beak.

Leaves: 1–3" (2.5–7.5 cm) long, lanceolate, usually not cleft or lobed; bracts of flower cluster similar but yellowish.

Height: 6–20" (15–50 cm).

Flowering: June–September.

Habitat: Moist meadows and slopes from moderate to high elevations.

Range: British Columbia and southwestern Alberta south through Rocky Mountain region to Idaho, Utah, northern New Mexico, and western South Dakota.

Comments: Most paintbrushes are bright red; this is one of the few yellow ones, as the species name suggests. It is sometimes considered to be a variety of the red-flowered Rosy Paintbrush *(C. rhexifolia).* The large genus is found primarily in western North America.

---

611 **Purple Chinese Houses; Innocence**
Collinsia heterophylla

Description: *Bilaterally symmetrical flowers in several widely spaced whorls* atop a sparsely leaved stem.

Flowers: Corolla about ¾" (2 cm) long; upper corolla lip 2-lobed, bent upward, *lavender, pale blue-violet, or white,* with many maroon dots at base; lower corolla lip 3-lobed, with *2 violet lobes projecting forward and a middle lobe folded between them,* hiding style and 4 stamens.

Leaves: To 2½" (6.5 cm) long, few, opposite, lanceolate, edges scalloped.

Height: 1–2' (30–60 cm).

Flowering: March–June.

Habitat: Sandy soil on shaded flats or slopes.

Range: Southern two-thirds of California and northern Baja California.

Comments: Few of California's spectacular wildflowers are as charming as this one. The flowers grow in perfect rings around the stem, together forming a fairy-tale pagoda, the "Chinese houses." There are about 20 *Collinsia* species, most found in California, distinguished from other genera by the corolla's folded middle lower lobe. In this respect it resembles members of the pea family (Fabaceae); however, pea flowers usually have 10 stamens rather than four, and the five petals are not all joined into a tubular base.

644 Maiden Blue-eyed Mary
Collinsia parviflora

Description: A small, widely branched plant with
an open cluster of *tiny, blue and white,
bilaterally symmetrical flowers* on slender
stalks.

Flowers: Corolla about ¼" (6 mm) wide; upper
corolla lip 2-lobed, bent upward, white,
often tinged with violet near tip; lower
corolla lip 3-lobed, with 2 blue-violet
lobes projecting forward and a middle
lobe folded between them, hiding style
and 4 stamens.

Leaves: To 2" (5 cm) long, usually much shorter,
narrowly lanceolate, opposite near base,
in whorls of 4 in flower cluster.

Height: 2–16" (5–40 cm).

Flowering: April–July.

Habitat: Open, gravelly flats and banks, often in
sparse grass.

Range: British Columbia south to southern
California and east to Colorado,
Michigan, and Ontario.

Comments: This *Collinsia* has among the smallest
flowers in the genus. The similar
Little Tonella *(Tonella tenella)*, found
from western Washington to northern
California, has a bilaterally symmetrical,
white corolla barely ⅛" (3 mm) long,
the five lobes tipped with violet and
not folded.

132 Saltmarsh Clubflower
Cordylanthus maritimus subsp. *maritimus*

Description: A softly hairy, loosely branched, low
plant bearing *flowers with a pinkish and
white, bilaterally symmetrical corolla nearly
hidden* within tubular calyx and leafy
racemes.

Flowers: Corolla ¾" (2 cm) long, lower end
a slender tube, upper end swollen
and blushed with pink or dull red-
violet, opening almost closed by
very short lips; upper corolla lip pale
yellow, beak-like; lower corolla lip
4-toothed; stamens 4.

Leaves:	¼–1″ (6–25 mm) long, broadly lanceolate.
Height:	8–16″ (20–40 cm).
Flowering:	May–September.
Habitat:	Coastal salt marshes.
Range:	Southern Oregon south along Pacific Coast to northern Baja California.
Comments:	*Cordylanthus* species have bracts surrounding each flower. The subspecies *maritimus* has inner bracts notched near the tip; the inner bracts of subspecies *canescens,* found on alkaline flats from southern Oregon to east-central California and east through Nevada to Utah, are not notched. The genus name, from the Greek *kordyle* ("club") and *anthos* ("flower"), describes the corolla's shape.

603 Wright's Birdbeak
Cordylanthus wrightii

Description:	An openly branched, spindly plant with *yellow or dull purplish, bilaterally symmetrical flowers resembling birds' beaks* in clusters at branch ends.
Flowers:	Calyx with a tubular base, 1 bract opposite 1 lobe giving effect of a 2-lobed calyx; corolla ¾–1¼″ (2–3 cm) long, with pointed upper and lower lips nearly equal in length, edges of upper lip flaring to side near base; outer bracts around flowers with up to 7 very slender lobes.
Leaves:	About 1–2″ (2.5–5 cm) long, divided into 3 or 5 very narrow segments.
Height:	2′ (60 cm).
Flowering:	July–October.
Habitat:	Open, sandy areas on plains and in pine forests.
Range:	Central Arizona east to western Texas.
Comments:	Most of the nearly 40 species of birdbeaks are found in western North America. The plants tend to grow in dry places, blooming late in the season when most other flowers have passed. The color of the corolla varies from white to dull violet, mauve, or yellow.

508 Foxglove
Digitalis purpurea

Description: Spectacular *spires of hanging flowers all
turned to one side* in long dense racemes
atop a tall leafy plant.

Flowers: Corolla bilaterally symmetrical, with a
flared, white to pinkish-lavender tube
1½–2½″ (4–6.5 cm) long, ¾″ (2 cm)
wide, conspicuously speckled with many
red or maroon dots on lower inside, tube
rimmed with 5 short lobes.

Leaves: To 1′ (30 cm) long, largest at base,
ovate, edges scalloped or toothed.

Height: 2–7′ (60–210 cm).

Flowering: June–July.

Habitat: Roadsides and other disturbed, open sites.

Range: British Columbia south to central
California mostly west of Cascade Range
and Sierra Nevada; also occurs sporadically
in other western states, and in East.

Comments: Foxglove is native to Europe. Unlike
many plants introduced from foreign
lands, it has not come to be considered
an unwelcome weed. It lends spectacular
columns of color to the green, brushy
and wooded slopes of the Pacific region.
The heart stimulant digitalis, toxic
when not properly administered, is
extracted from the species. Foxglove is
deadly toxic to livestock, but it is
usually avoided; however, if the plants
are mixed into hay, the results can be
fatal. Teas or salads made from the leaves
have been deadly to humans.

398 Red Shrubby Penstemon
Keckiella corymbosa

Description: *A low, dark green shrub with bright, brick
red, bilaterally symmetrical flowers* in
bunches at branch ends.

Flowers: Corolla 1–1½″ (2.5–4 cm) long; upper
corolla lip 2-lobed, projecting forward;
lower corolla lip 3-lobed, bent downward;
stamens 5, all but 1 with anthers hairy
only at base, the fifth sterile but with
golden hairs at tip and hairy throughout.

Leaves: ¾–1½″ (2–4 cm) long, *opposite,* leathery, ovate, often with small teeth.

Height: 12–20″ (30–50 cm).

Flowering: June–October.

Habitat: Open, rocky slopes and cliffs.

Range: Northwestern California south through northern Coast Ranges.

Comments: After the summer heat dries the low mountains, driving most wildflowers to seed and browning the grasses, Red Shrubby Penstemon begins to flower, providing a final source of nectar before the hummingbirds must seek food higher in the cooler mountains or, if late in the season, migrate south. This small genus was recently segregated from the larger genus *Penstemon;* its name honors David Keck, a student of *Penstemon* and California plants in general.

495 Texas Silverleaf; Purple Sage; Cenizo
Leucophyllum frutescens

Description: *A gray shrub* with leaves covered with silvery hairs and *bright pink-lavender, bilaterally symmetrical flowers* borne singly in crowded leaf axils.

Flowers: Corolla ¾–1″ (2–2.5 cm) long, about as wide, funnel-shaped, with 5 round lobes, lower lobes hairy inside; stamens 4.

Leaves: Usually about 1″ (2.5 cm) long, nearly oval, base long and tapered.

Height: To 8′ (2.4 m).

Flowering: June–November.

Habitat: Rocky, limestone plains, brushlands, and deserts.

Range: Southern Texas and northern Mexico.

Comments: As one travels east across northern Texas near the Mexican border, the olive green of Creosote Bush gives way to the gray of this species, with its display of bright pink-lavender flowers. These burst into bloom for only a few days at a time, in the summer and fall, depending on rainfall. This and other *Leucophyllum* species are popular water-conserving ornamentals in the Southwest.

305   Butter-and-eggs; Common Toadflax
Linaria vulgaris

Description: Erect stems in dense patches and
numerous mostly *yellow, bilaterally
symmetrical flowers all tipped upward in a
dense spike.*

Flowers: Corolla 1–1½" (2.5–4 cm) long; upper
corolla lip 2-lobed, pointing forward;
lower corolla lip 3-lobed, bent
downward, with an orange patch of hairs
on hump at base closing tube opening;
straight spur beneath each flower
projecting backward.

Leaves: To 4" (10 cm) long, many, narrow,
grayish green.

Height: 1–3′ (30–90 cm).

Flowering: June–September.

Habitat: Open, often disturbed places.

Range: Throughout much of Canada and
United States.

Comments: This species was introduced from
Eurasia. The name toadflax refers to the
opening of the corolla, which looks like
the mouth of a toad, and to the leaves,
which resemble those of flax *(Linum).*
The common name Butter-and-eggs
refers to the corolla's color combination.
A similar plant, Dalmatian Toadflax *(L.
genistifolia* subsp. *dalmatica),* also
introduced from Eurasia and spreading
geographically, has ovate leaves that
clasp the stem. As lovely as these species
appear, both can be aggressive and
unwelcome weeds.

596   Little Snapdragon Vine;
Violet Twining
Maurandya antirrhiniflora

Description: *Stems twining* through other vegetation,
with *pale blue-violet or reddish-lavender
flowers;* flower stalks and leafstalks
curved and twisted.

Flowers: Corolla ¾–1" (2–2.5 cm) long,
bilaterally symmetrical, with a hairy
cream patch at base of lower lip near
opening; upper corolla lip 2-lobed, bent

upward; lower corolla lip 3-lobed, bent downward.

Leaves: About 1″ (2.5 cm) long, arrowhead-shaped.

Height: Vine; stems to 7′ (2.1 m) long.

Flowering: June–September.

Habitat: Sandy or gravelly soil in deserts, sometimes on rock walls, and among piñon and juniper.

Range: Southeastern California east to western Texas and south to Mexico.

Comments: These little snapdragons, attractive and well worth cultivating, can be grown from seed. They produce small, scrambling vines that die back to the ground each winter.

595 Net-cup Snapdragon Vine
Maurandya wislizenii

Description: *A vine with rather arrowhead-shaped leaves and pale blue-violet flowers* in axils of bract-like leaves.

Flowers: Sepals enlarging as fruit matures, with a rigid, net-like pattern throughout, base of each sepal becoming swollen and pouch-like; corolla 1″ (2.5 cm) long, bilaterally symmetrical.

Leaves: To 2″ (5 cm) long, on stalks about as long.

Fruit: Capsule, about ½″ (1.5 cm) long.

Height: Vine; to 10′ (3 m) long.

Flowering: April–July.

Habitat: Among shrubs and on dunes.

Range: Southeastern Arizona east to western Texas and south to northern Mexico.

Comments: This species is much coarser in appearance than its close relative Little Snapdragon Vine *(M. antirrhiniflora).* Both make delightful ornamentals.

375 Orange Bush Monkeyflower
Mimulus aurantiacus

Description: Branched woody stems, covered with a sticky, varnish-like secretion, bearing *yellowish-orange to deep orange, bilaterally symmetrical flowers.*

Flowers:	Calyx smooth; corolla 1¼–2″ (3–5 cm) long; upper corolla lip 2-lobed, bent upward; lower corolla lip 3-lobed, bent downward.
Leaves:	To 3″ (7.5 cm) long, lanceolate, dark green above, pale and sparsely hairy on underside, edges with fine teeth.
Height:	2–4′ (60–120 cm).
Flowering:	March–August.
Habitat:	Slopes and banks in chaparral and open woods.
Range:	Southwestern Oregon south to southern California, inland as far as base of Sierra Nevada.
Comments:	Its long blooming season makes this species a reliable source of nectar for hummingbirds. At the end of the style, the two flaps of the stigma will slowly but visibly move together and close when touched by a pollen-laden insect or hummingbird, providing a protective chamber for the pollen to begin its growth. This movement can be seen by gently touching the stigma with a blade of grass.

487 Fremont's Monkeyflower
Mimulus fremontii

Description:	A small, branched, glandular-hairy, reddish plant with *slightly bilaterally symmetrical, rose-lavender flowers.*
Flowers:	Calyx with 5 prominent angles and 5 nearly equal triangular lobes; corolla ¾–1″ (2–2.5 cm) wide, with 5 nearly equal round lobes, base broadly tubular; stamens 4, hidden within.
Leaves:	½–1¼″ (1.5–3 cm) long, oblong, opposite.
Height:	1–8″ (2.5–20 cm).
Flowering:	April–June.
Habitat:	Recent burns, road banks, dry gullies, and other dry open places.
Range:	Southern California and Baja California west of desert.
Comments:	This species is abundant for a few years after a fire sweeps through the chaparral but decreases as the vegetation closes back in.

287 Seep-spring Monkeyflower; Common Monkeyflower
Mimulus guttatus

Description: A leafy, extremely variable plant, ranging from spindly and tiny to large and bushy, with *yellow, bilaterally symmetrical flowers* on slender stalks in upper leaf axils.

Flowers: Calyx swollen, angular, with 5 teeth at opening, upper tooth longest; corolla ½–1½" (1.5–4 cm) long, often with reddish spots near opening; upper corolla lip 2-lobed, bent upward; lower corolla lip 3-lobed, bent downward, with a hairy hump almost closing opening at base.

Leaves: ½–4" (1.5–10 cm) long, ovate, opposite, clasping stem, sharp teeth on edges.

Height: To 3' (90 cm).

Flowering: March–September.

Habitat: Wet places from sea level to mountains.

Range: Throughout western North America, from Alaska to Mexico; also in eastern Canada and northeastern United States.

Comments: In this large genus of several look-alikes with yellow corollas, this species is distinguished by the longer upper tooth on the angular calyx.

532 Lewis's Monkeyflower
Mimulus lewisii

Description: Showy, *deep pink to red, bilaterally symmetrical flowers* in profusion near top of a leafy, several-stemmed plant.

Flowers: Corolla 1¼–2" (3–5 cm) long, 5-lobed, 3 lobes bent downward, 2 lobes bent upward, marked with yellow patches of hairs and darker red-violet lines on lower side near opening.

Leaves: 1–4" (2.5–10 cm) long, opposite, edges toothed or plain.

Height: 1–3' (30–90 cm).

Flowering: June–August.

Habitat: Wet open places in mountains.

Range: Western Canada south to southern Sierra Nevada and higher mountains of

Nevada, Utah, Colorado, Wyoming, and
Montana.

Comments: This is among the handsomest of
mountain wildflowers, its deep pink to
red flowers attracting hummingbirds
during their summer stay in the
mountains.

590 Dwarf Purple Monkeyflower
Mimulus nanus

Description: A little plant, covered with glandular
hairs, bearing stems with 1 or many
branches and *rich reddish-lavender,
bilaterally symmetrical flowers* on short
stalks in upper leaf axils.

Flowers: Corolla ½–1″ (1.5–2.5 cm) long, 5-
lobed, 3 lobes bent downward, 2 lobes
bent upward, marked inside near
opening with yellow and deep red lines.

Leaves: To 1½″ (4 cm) long, lanceolate, opposite.

Height: To 4″ (10 cm).

Flowering: May–August.

Habitat: Dry open areas on sagebrush plains and
in open pine forests.

Range: Central Washington south to northern
California and east to northeastern
Nevada, northwestern Wyoming, and
southwestern Montana.

Comments: Like other desert annuals, in a year of
poor rainfall Dwarf Purple
Monkeyflower puts all its efforts into
producing a new crop of seeds to ensure
future generations. After growing only
about ¼″ (6 mm) tall, it flamboyantly
produces one comparatively huge flower
that seems to sit directly on the ground.
In years of ample moisture, plants will
be branched and up to 4″ (10 cm) tall,
bearing dozens of flowers.

290 Ghost Flower; Mojave Flower
Mohavea confertiflora

Description: An erect plant with *large, bilaterally
symmetrical, translucent, pale yellow flowers
tipped upward* in upper leaf axils.

Flowers:	Corolla about 1¼" (3 cm) long, with 5 ragged-edged lobes, lower lobes with maroon speckles inside and a maroon blotch at base; opening to base closed by a hairy bump on lower side; stamens 2.
Leaves:	2–4" (5–10 cm) long, hairy, narrowly lanceolate.
Height:	4–20" (10–50 cm).
Flowering:	March–April.
Habitat:	Desert washes and rocky slopes.
Range:	Southern Nevada south to western Arizona, southeastern California, and northwestern Mexico.
Comments:	The translucent, pale corolla gives the common name Ghost Flower. There is only one other species in the genus, Lesser Mohavea or Golden Desert Snapdragon *(M. breviflora),* which grows in the same region and has bilaterally symmetrical, lemon yellow corollas only about ½" (1.5 cm) long.

612 Blue Toadflax; Old-field Toadflax
Nuttallanthus canadensis

Description:	Slender, erect stems with short prostrate branches at base and *blue-violet, bilaterally symmetrical flowers* in a raceme.
Flowers:	Corolla about ½" (1.5 cm) long, with a slender spur about ¼" (6 mm) long projecting backward and curving downward; upper corolla lip 2-lobed, bent upward; lower corolla lip 3-lobed, extending forward, with 2 broad lobes hanging to sides of a central hump and 1 narrower lobe hanging at end.
Leaves:	Those at base small, mostly opposite, on rosette-like, trailing stems; those on stem to 1½" (3.5 cm) long, alternate, linear, smooth, shiny.
Height:	To 28" (70 cm).
Flowering:	March–June.
Habitat:	Open, sandy areas where moist in spring.
Range:	Throughout West; also in much of eastern United States and southern Canada.

Comments: This plant, once in the genus
             Linaria, has recently been placed
             in *Nuttallanthus.* Texas Toadflax
             (N. texanus), similar but less common
             in the Southwest, has larger flowers
             and seeds. *Nuttallanthus* species
             are often components of wildflower
             seed mixes, and some have escaped
             from cultivation, particularly in
             California.

313 Yellow Owl's Clover
Orthocarpus luteus

Description: *Many golden yellow flowers angled
              upward and protruding from glandular-
              hairy bracts* near top of an erect
              plant.
     Flowers: Corolla about ½″ (1.5 cm) long,
              bilaterally symmetrical; lower
              corolla lip forming a pouch with
              3 tiny teeth at end; upper corolla lip
              forming a short beak above pouch;
              stamens 4, hidden within.
      Leaves: ½–1½″ (1.5–4 cm) long, very
              narrow, sometimes divided into
              3 narrow lobes.
      Height: 4–16″ (10–40 cm).
   Flowering: July–September.
     Habitat: Plains and open woods.
       Range: British Columbia south to
              southeastern California, mostly
              east of Cascade Range and Sierra
              Nevada, and east to New Mexico,
              Colorado, Nebraska, Minnesota, and
              Ontario.
    Comments: There are about nine species of
              owl's clover, all found in western
              North America, several with a yellow
              corolla and some with a 3-lobed
              pouch. The origin of the common
              name is unknown; "owl's clover"
              may refer to the eye-like spots on
              the petals of some species or,
              picturesquely, to the swollen, head-
              like ends of the erect corollas that
              seem to peer from the bracts as owls
              peer from the leaves of a tree.

304 Yellow Parentucellia
Parentucellia viscosa

Description: An erect, leafy, *glandular-hairy plant with small, bilaterally symmetrical, yellow flowers* tucked among upper leaf-like bracts.

Flowers: Corolla about ¾" (2 cm) long, upper lip hood-like, lower lip 3-lobed and slightly bent downward.

Leaves: ½–1½" (1.5–4 cm) long, ovate, with toothed edges; at least the lower ones opposite.

Height: 4–28" (10–70 cm).

Flowering: June–August.

Habitat: Moist open areas.

Range: British Columbia south to northwestern California.

Comments: This species was introduced from Europe. It often grows in such profusion that grassy hillsides and flats acquire a yellow hue.

312 Towering Lousewort
Pedicularis bracteosa

Description: An erect plant with *divided, rather fern-like leaves* and *bilaterally symmetrical, beak-like flowers in a dense raceme.*

Flowers: Corolla ½–¾" (1.5–2 cm) long, varying from yellow to purple, maroon, or reddish; upper corolla lip narrow,

Towering Lousewort

arching outward like prow of an
overturned canoe; lower corolla lip
shorter, with 3 lobes projecting forward,
central lobe narrowest.

Leaves: 3–10″ (7.5–25 cm) long, divided into
narrow leaflets with jagged teeth; upper
leaves about as large as lower.

Height: To 3′ (90 cm).

Flowering: June–August.

Habitat: Moist woods and meadows in
mountains.

Range: British Columbia and Alberta south to
northern California, Idaho, Utah, and
western Colorado.

Comments: Western louseworts vary from plants 4′
(1.2 m) tall to miniature ones only 1″
(2.5 cm) tall. The common name
lousewort and the genus name, from the
Latin *pediculus* ("little louse"), allude to a
superstition that livestock would suffer
from an infestation of lice if they ate this
plant.

506 Elephant Heads; Little Red Elephants
Pedicularis groenlandica

Description: Dense racemes of *flowers resembling perfect,
little, pink elephant heads* on leafy stems.

Flowers: Corolla, exclusive of "trunk," about ½″
(1.5 cm) long, strongly bilaterally
symmetrical; upper corolla lip curving
forward well beyond lower lip, forming
"trunk"; lower corolla lip 3-lobed, side
lobes forming "ears," central lobe
forming lower "jaw."

Leaves: 2–10″ (5–25 cm) long, narrow,
pinnately divided into sharp-toothed
lobes.

Height: To 31″ (80 cm).

Flowering: June–August.

Habitat: Wet meadows and small cold streams.

Range: Throughout northern North America; in
West, south in mountains to California,
Arizona, and New Mexico.

Comments: The flower's charming structure
facilitates pollination, and at the same
time reduces the chances of
hybridization with other species. Little

Elephant Heads *(P. attollens),* only to 16″
(40 cm) tall, has a corolla marked with
white and rose, and its head proportions
are not so perfectly elephantine (the
"trunk," raised as if trumpeting, is only
as long as the lower lip); it grows from
the Cascade Range of Oregon to the
southern Sierra Nevada.

505 Sickletop Lousewort
Pedicularis racemosa

Description: A bushy, leafy plant with several stems
and *twisted, white or pink flowers* on short
branches in upper leaf axils.
Flowers: Corolla about ½″ (1.5 cm) long, white,
pale pink, or pink; upper corolla lip
narrow, an arched, beak-like hook
twisting to one side, touching lower lip;
lower corolla lip broad, 3-lobed, central
lobe smaller than side lobes.
Leaves: 2–4″ (5–10 cm) long, lanceolate, with
many tiny blunt teeth on edges.
Height: 6–20″ (15–50 cm).
Flowering: June–September.
Habitat: Coniferous woods and dry meadows in
mountains.
Range: British Columbia and Alberta south to
southern Sierra Nevada, Idaho, Utah,
and eastern New Mexico, and in Rocky
Mountains from Montana to New
Mexico.
Comments: The contorted beak of this common
mountain trailside plant's corolla is
distinctive, and the undivided leaves are
unusual among western louseworts.

291 Dwarf Lousewort
Pedicularis semibarbata

Description: A little plant with a short raceme of *pale
yellow, bilaterally symmetrical flowers
among fern-like leaves in a tuft.*
Flowers: Corolla about ¾″ (2 cm) long; upper
corolla lip resembling prow of an
overturned canoe; lower corolla lip 3-
lobed, about as long as upper lip.

Leaves:	To 6″ (15 cm) long, pinnately divided into many leaflets, with jagged lobes and teeth.
Height:	Less than 4″ (10 cm).
Flowering:	May–July.
Habitat:	Dry coniferous woods in mountains.
Range:	Southern Oregon south to southern California and western Nevada.
Comments:	This species is among the shortest of the many lardworts; its flowers often sit almost upon the ground.

416 Goldenbeard Penstemon
Penstemon barbatus

Description:	*Slender, bilaterally symmetrical, scarlet flowers hanging slightly* in a long open cluster above sparsely leaved stems.
Flowers:	Corolla 1–1½″ (2.5–4 cm) long; upper corolla lip projecting forward like a visor, with 2 small teeth at tip; lower corolla lip 3-lobed, bent downward and backward, with usually few yellow hairs near opening; stamens 5, the fifth sterile.
Leaves:	2–5″ (5–12.5 cm) long, smooth, gray-green, opposite, narrow.
Height:	To 3′ (90 cm).
Flowering:	June–September.
Habitat:	Dry rocky slopes in open forests.
Range:	Southern Colorado south to Arizona, New Mexico, western Texas, and Mexico.
Comments:	This species is one of several penstemons with scarlet corollas. The genus name, from the Greek *pen* ("almost") and *stemon* ("thread"), refers to the slender fifth, sterile stamen.

415 Scarlet Bugler
Penstemon centranthifolius

Description:	Few erect, sparsely leaved stems with *bright red, nearly radially symmetrical, tubular flowers* in a long, narrow, open cluster near top.

Flowers:	Corolla 1–1¼″ (2.5–3 cm) long, with 5 very short, barely spreading lobes with round tips; stamens 5, the fifth sterile.
Leaves:	1¼–3″ (3–7.5 cm) long, spatula-shaped or lanceolate, opposite.
Height:	1–4′ (30–120 cm).
Flowering:	April–July.
Habitat:	Dry open places in brush, commonly in disturbed soil.
Range:	Central California Coast Ranges and southern Sierra Nevada foothills to Baja California.
Comments:	This species sometimes produces extensive, nearly solid patches of brilliant red. The almost radially symmetrical corollas are unusual in the genus.

650 Platte River Penstemon
Penstemon cyananthus

Description:	An erect plant with several leafy stems and *rings of blue-violet, bilaterally symmetrical flowers* near top.
Flowers:	Corolla ¾–1¼″ (2–3 cm) long, smooth, with 5 blue lobes, tube violet and swollen; stamens 5, the fifth sterile but densely bearded with golden hairs at tip; anthers hairy on sides, not opening across region where joined to filament.
Leaves:	¾–4″ (2–10 cm) long, narrowly lanceolate or ovate, without stalks, opposite.
Height:	8–40″ (20–100 cm).
Flowering:	May–July.
Habitat:	Sagebrush hills and openings in mountain forests.
Range:	Southeastern Idaho, northern Utah, and western Wyoming.
Comments:	This is a common spring wildflower in its range, often covering disturbed ground with handsome patches of blue. Members of this genus are commonly known as beardtongues, referring to the bearded sterile stamen.

616   Davidson's Penstemon
Penstemon davidsonii

Description: *A matted plant* with a woody base
and stems, opposite, crowded leaves,
and *blue-lavender, bilaterally symmetrical
flowers* clustered on short erect stems.

Flowers: Corolla ¾–1¼″ (2–3 cm) long, hairy
inside at base of lower lip; upper
corolla lip 2-lobed, projecting
forward; lower corolla lip 3-lobed,
bent downward; stamens 5, all but 1
with long wool on anthers, the fifth
sterile but hairy at tip.

Leaves: ¼–¾″ (6–20 mm) long, thick, firm,
oval but tapered to stalk, with or
without small teeth; leaves nearer
flowers reduced to small bracts.

Height: 2–6″ (5–15 cm).

Flowering: June–August.

Habitat: On rock ledges and slopes from
moderate to high elevations.

Range: British Columbia south to northern
California and northern Nevada.

Comments: When in full flower, this species
forms spectacular lavender mats.
Plants in the southern part of the
range have toothless leaves; to the
north, toothed leaves are common.

113   Hot Rock Penstemon
Penstemon deustus

Description: Stems growing in clusters from a
woody base with *dingy white or cream,
bilaterally symmetrical flowers* in several
whorls in axils of leafy bracts.

Flowers: Corolla ½–¾″ (1.5–2 cm) long,
generally with fine purplish lines
inside; upper corolla lip with 2 round
lobes bent upward; lower corolla lip
with 3 lobes bent downward; stamens
5, the fifth sterile but sometimes hairy
at tip.

Leaves: To 3″ (7.5 cm) long, opposite, bright
green, ovate, with sharp teeth.

Height: 8–24″ (20–60 cm).

Flowering: May–July.
Habitat: Dry, open, rocky places from lowlands to mountains.
Range: Central Washington south to central California and east to northwestern Utah, westernWyoming, and southwestern Montana.
Comments: In a huge western genus of more than 200 species, this plant is representative of the few with white flowers. Most species have a mildly unpleasant odor, which is especially noticeable in Hot Rock Penstemon.

597 Lowbush Penstemon
Penstemon fruticosus

Description: A bushy plant, usually much broader than tall, with large, showy, *pale lavender or pale blue-violet, bilaterally symmetrical flowers* in crowded, narrow clusters at stem ends.
Flowers: Corolla 1–2″ (2.5–5 cm) long, plump, with long white hairs inside near base of lower lip; upper corolla lip 2-lobed, arching forward; lower corolla lip 3-lobed, bent downward; stamens 5, all but 1 with hairy anthers, the fifth sterile but with a bearded tip.
Leaves: To 2½″ (6.5 cm) long, opposite, lanceolate or ovate, edges with or without teeth.
Height: 6–16″ (15–40 cm).
Flowering: May–August.
Habitat: Rocky, open or wooded sites from foothills well into mountains.
Range: Southern British Columbia south to central Oregon and east to western Montana and western Wyoming.
Comments: In a genus with many beautiful species, this one may be the most spectacular. Bright green, leafy patches cascade down banks and between rocks, topped with a dense display of subtly shaded flowers that butterflies seem to find especially attractive.

649   Narrowleaf Penstemon
Penstemon linarioides

Description: *Bilaterally symmetrical, blue-violet flowers turned to one side* in a narrow, long, open cluster above a leafy base.

Flowers: Corolla about ¾″ (2 cm) long, with a very narrow, tubular base expanding abruptly into a broad throat lacking 2 ridges on lower inside; upper corolla lip 2-lobed, bent upward; lower corolla lip 3-lobed, bent downward; stamens 5, the fifth sterile but bearded at tip.

Leaves: ½–1″ (1.5–2.5 cm) long, *very narrow, grayish green, usually downy,* crowded near base.

Height: 6–16″ (15–40 cm).

Flowering: June–August.

Habitat: Open, often rocky soil at moderate elevations.

Range: Southern Utah and southwestern Colorado south to much of New Mexico and Arizona.

Comments: This is a common penstemon in dry open woodlands in the Southwest. Among the several species in this huge genus with beautiful blue-violet flowers and narrow leaves, some have two ridges inside the corolla.

496   Mountain Pride
Penstemon newberryi

Description: Short, erect, leafy stems, growing from a matted base, with *deep pink, bilaterally symmetrical flowers* usually all turned to one side in a short raceme.

Flowers: Corolla ¾–1¼″ (2–3 cm) wide, tube with 2 densely hairy ridges on lower inside; upper corolla lip 2-lobed, arching forward; lower corolla lip 3-lobed, bent downward; stamens 5, all but 1 with densely hairy anthers, the fifth sterile but densely bearded with golden hairs at tip.

Leaves: ½–1¼″ (1.5–3 cm) long, toothed, ovate, thick, opposite.

Height: 6–12″ (15–30 cm).

Flowering: June–August.

Habitat: Rocky places from moderate to high elevations.

Range: Southwestern Oregon south to southern Sierra Nevada and western Nevada.

Comments: This handsome species commonly adds bright swatches of color to roadsides in the rocky California mountains.

507 Balloon Flower
Penstemon palmeri

Description: Few sparsely leaved, erect, stout stems with *swollen, white to reddish-pink, bilaterally symmetrical flowers mostly turned to one side* in a long narrow cluster.

Flowers: Corolla 1–1½″ (2.5–4 cm) long, short tube at base abruptly expanding into a large swollen chamber with reddish lines on lower inside; upper corolla lip 2-lobed, bent sharply upward; lower corolla lip 3-lobed, bent downward; stamens 5, the fifth sterile but densely bearded with golden hairs at tip.

Leaves: Largest to 10″ (25 cm) long, lanceolate, opposite; bases of paired upper leaves often joined, with stem appearing to go through them.

Height: 2–7′ (60–210 cm).

Flowering: May–July.

Habitat: Open, rocky areas among sagebrush, piñon and juniper, and pinewoods.

Range: Southeastern California east across southern Nevada and much of Utah and Arizona to New Mexico; introduced in Idaho and perhaps also in eastern Washington.

Comments: This is one of the most delightful penstemons; its cheery, puffed-up flowers are exquisitely fragrant.

504 Parry's Penstemon
Penstemon parryi

Description: Several erect, sparsely leaved stems with *pinkish-lavender, bilaterally symmetrical flowers* in a long, open, interrupted cluster.

Flowers: Corolla about ¾″ (2 cm) long, glandular-hairy on outside, broadly funnel-shaped, with short round lobes; upper corolla lip 2-lobed, bent upward; lower corolla lip 3-lobed, bent downward; stamens 5, the fifth sterile but bearded at tip.

Leaves: 2–5″ (5–12.5 cm) long, lanceolate, without stalks, smooth, those at midstem broadest at base.

Height: To 4′ (1.2 m).

Flowering: March–May.

Habitat: Grassy or brushy slopes and flats.

Range: Southern Arizona and northwestern Mexico.

Comments: This handsome species is commonly included in highway seeding mixes, which has expanded its range. Along highways it may provide spectacular splashes of color against grasses still brown from winter.

494 Cliff Penstemon; Rock Penstemon
Penstemon rupicola

Description: Few large, *brilliant pink or rose, bilaterally symmetrical flowers in many racemes,* often forming a dense display, above thick mats of stems and leaves.

Flowers: Corolla 1–1½″ (2.5–4 cm) long; upper corolla lip 2-lobed, bent upward; lower corolla lip 3-lobed, bent downward; stamens 5, all but 1 with long wool on anthers, the fifth sterile but sometimes with few hairs at tip.

Leaves: ½–¾″ (1.5–2 cm) long, opposite, ovate, thick; edges with small, irregular teeth.

Height: Creeper; flower stalks to 4″ (10 cm).

Flowering: May–August.

Habitat: Rocky slopes, ledges, and cliffs.

Range: Central Washington south to northern California.

Comments: This is one of the West's most beautiful wildflowers. Although there are only a few flowers in any one raceme, there are many racemes, and in full bloom the plant is a swatch of bright, glowing pink.

613   Rydberg's Penstemon
Penstemon rydbergii

Description: *Small, pale purple to dark blue-violet,*
bilaterally symmetrical flowers forming 1 or
several dense whorls at or along upper part
of erect stems.

Flowers: Corolla ½–¾″ (1.5–2 cm) long,
narrowly funnel-shaped; upper corolla
lip 2-lobed, projecting forward; lower
corolla lip 3-lobed, spreading
downward, hairy near tube opening on
lower inside; stamens 5, the fifth sterile
but densely bearded at tip.

Leaves: 1½–3″ (4–7.5 cm) long, lanceolate,
opposite, those at midstem without
stalks.

Height: 8–24″ (20–60 cm).

Flowering: June–July.

Habitat: Open mountain slopes.

Range: Southeastern Washington south to
eastern California and east to northern
Arizona, northern New Mexico,
Colorado, Wyoming, and southwestern
Montana.

Comments: The dark blue-violet whorls of small
flowers help distinguish this common
penstemon from most other species.

614   Cascade Penstemon
Penstemon serrulatus

Description: Several erect, leafy stems topped with 1
or several whorls of *deep blue to dark*
purple, bilaterally symmetrical flowers.

Flowers: Corolla ¾–1″ (2–2.5 cm) long, lacking
hairs; upper corolla lip 2-lobed, bent
slightly upward; lower corolla lip 3-
lobed, spreading downward; stamens 5,
the fifth sterile but golden-hairy at tip.

Leaves: 1¼–3″ (3–7.5 cm) long, opposite,
broadly lanceolate or ovate, not hairy,
usually without stalks, edges sharply
toothed.

Height: 8–28″ (20–70 cm).

Flowering: June–August.

Habitat: Moist places from low to moderate
elevations.

Range: British Columbia south to southern
           Oregon.
Comments: This is one of the few penstemons
           occurring west of the Cascade Range.
           Serrulatus refers to the little, serrated
           teeth on the leaves.

---

615 Whipple's Penstemon
Penstemon whippleanus

Description: *Deep wine-lavender to black-purple,*
              bilaterally symmetrical flowers in several
              clusters on upper half of leafy stems.
Flowers: Corolla ¾–1¼" (2–3 cm) long, finely
              glandular-hairy outside, usually with
              sparse long hairs inside at base of lower
              lip, tubular base expanding abruptly to
              much broader middle portion; upper
              corolla lip arching forward; lower corolla
              lip projecting farther forward than
              upper; stamens 5, the fifth sterile but
              usually with a tuft of hair at tip.
Leaves: ½–6" (1.5–15 cm) long, ovate, opposite,
              edges smooth or with small teeth.
Height: 4–28" (10–70 cm).
Flowering: July–September.
Habitat: In meadows or on wooded slopes, often
              where moist.
Range: Southeastern Idaho and southwestern
              Montana south through Rocky
              Mountain region to northern Arizona
              and southern New Mexico.
Comments: This common mountain penstemon
              ordinarily can be recognized by its
              plump, dark purple, glandular-hairy
              corolla. However, phases with dingy
              yellow or white corollas blushed with
              brown, purple, or blue are frequent.

---

308 Yellow Rattle
Rhinanthus crista-galli

Description: An erect plant with *widely spaced, opposite*
              leaves on stem and *bilaterally symmetrical*
              flowers in spikes at top; *all flowers turned to*
              one side, each with a *yellow corolla*

protruding from a flat calyx (as if pressed from sides).

Flowers: Calyx oval, becoming larger as fruit develops, with 4 teeth at tip; corolla about ½" (1.5 cm) long; upper corolla lip hood-like, with 2 small round teeth; lower corolla lip smaller, with 3 round teeth projecting forward.

Leaves: To 2½" (6.5 cm) long, lanceolate, with toothed edges.

Height: 6–31" (15–80 cm).

Flowering: June–August.

Habitat: Meadows and moist slopes.

Range: Throughout Northern Hemisphere; in West, south to northwestern Oregon, Arizona, and New Mexico; in East, south to New York.

Comments: The scientific name means "snout-flower cock's comb," probably referring to the comb-like row of calyces (plural for calyx) and the snout-shaped corolla. The plant is unmistakable, but its technical classification is unsettled. Around the Northern Hemisphere there are numerous regional variants, many of which have been named as species that are accepted by some authorities but not by others.

Yellow Rattle

647 Mountain Kittentails
Synthyris missurica

Description: A generally low, erect plant with *dense racemes of bilaterally symmetrical, deep blue-violet flowers* above basal leaves.

Flowers: Corolla about ¼" (6 mm) long, with 4 somewhat spreading lobes; stamens 2.

Leaves: 1–3" (2.5–7.5 cm) wide, round, coarsely toothed, on long stalks.

Height: 4–24" (10–60 cm).

Flowering: April–July.

Habitat: Moist, open or shaded slopes from foothills to moderate elevations.

Range: Northern Idaho southwest to southeastern Washington and northeastern Oregon; also in south-central Oregon and northeastern California.

Comments: The intense blue-violet of the corolla seems to deepen in the shade, where this plant is often found. Although pretty, this species is surpassed in beauty by a close relative, Fringed Synthyris *(S. schizantha),* in which the edges of the corolla lobes are cut into many strips, forming a beautiful fringe; it grows only on a few moist shaded cliffs in northern Oregon and western Washington.

626 Snow Queen; Roundleaf Synthyris
Synthyris reniformis

Description: *Several weak leafless stems* curving upward from a cluster of long-stalked leaves and bearing *pale purple to deep blue-violet, slightly bilaterally symmetrical flowers* in short racemes.

Flowers: Corolla about ¼" (6 mm) long, with 4 slightly spreading lobes, 1 lobe broader than others; stamens 2.

Leaves: To 3" (7.5 cm) wide, heart-shaped, with rounded tip, edges irregularly scalloped.

Height: To 6" (15 cm).

Flowering: March–May.

Habitat: Coniferous woods.
Range: Southwestern Washington south to central California.
Comments: This is one of the humbler, early-flowering *Synthyris* species; in the dim light of the early spring woods, its low dark flowers are easily overlooked.

301 Moth Mullein
Verbascum blattaria

Description: Slender spires of *pale yellow flowers* atop erect, leafy stems.
Flowers: Corolla about 1″ (2.5 cm) wide, almost radially symmetrical, with 5 round lobes of about equal length; stamens 5, with red-purple hairs on filaments.
Leaves: 2–6″ (5–15 cm) long, edges variously lobed or toothed; largest ones in a rosette at base; those on stem becoming progressively smaller up stem.
Height: 1–5′ (30–150 cm).
Flowering: May–September.
Habitat: Roadsides, fields, and vacant lots.
Range: Throughout much of Canada and United States.
Comments: This species was introduced from Eurasia. It sometimes has white corollas. The common name alludes to the resemblance of the flowers to moths resting on the stem.

302 Woolly Mullein; Common Mullein; Flannel Mullein
Verbascum thapsus

Description: A spike, resembling a *stout pole,* of *densely packed, yellow flowers* above a leafy stem.
Flowers: Corolla ¾–1″ (2–2.5 cm) wide, almost radially symmetrical, with 5 round lobes spreading out flat; stamens 5, upper 3 with yellow hairs on filaments.
Leaves: 4–16″ (10–40 cm) long, ovate, covered with felt-like, gray hair.
Height: 2–7′ (60–210 cm).
Flowering: June–August.
Habitat: Open places.

Range: Throughout much of Canada and United States.

Comments: No one wishes to claim a weed; a wildflower book written near the turn of the 20th century cites that Europeans called this species American Velvet Plant, despite the fact that the plant is of Old World origin. Although only a few of the 360 Eurasian *Verbascum* species have crossed the seas to North America, this one makes up for the lack of variety in the genus by sheer number of individual plants; in some states it is now considered a noxious weed. Ancient Greeks and Romans dipped the stalks in tallow for funeral torches. In medieval Europe it was called Hag Taper because it was supposedly used by witches. Children have been known to hurl the dried stalks as javelins, the light weight and pointed root hurtling them far and straight.

656 American Brooklime
Veronica americana

Description: Erect or leaning, leafy stems with *an open raceme of small blue flowers* in each of several upper leaf axils.

Flowers: Corolla ¼–½" (6–13 mm) wide, with 4 lobes joined at base, lower lobe narrowest; stamens 2.

Leaves: ½–3" (1.5–7.5 cm) long, opposite, short-stalked, broadly lanceolate, edges toothed or nearly smooth.

Fruit: 2-lobed capsule, ⅛" (3 mm) long.

Height: 4–40" (10–100 cm).

Flowering: May–July.

Habitat: Wet places.

Range: Throughout much of Canada and United States south to Mexico.

Comments: This species also occurs in Asia. The plant spreads from rhizomes shallowly buried in the mud and can quickly form dense patches in slow-moving or still water. The genus name may commemorate Saint Veronica.

646 Cusick's Speedwell
Veronica cusickii

Description: Small patches of erect stems with *deep blue-violet, flat flowers* in racemes on hair-like stalks.

Flowers: Corolla about ½″ (1.5 cm) wide, 4-lobed, lowest lobe narrowest; stamens 2, spreading apart; style more than ¼″ (6 mm) long.

Leaves: ½–1″ (1.5–2.5 cm) long, opposite, shiny, ovate.

Fruit: 2-lobed capsule, ¼″ (5 mm) long.

Height: 2–8″ (5–20 cm).

Flowering: July–August.

Habitat: Open moist areas in mountains.

Range: Western Washington southeast to northeastern Oregon and central Sierra Nevada, and east to northern Idaho and western Montana.

Comments: This perky little wildflower is common along mountain trails. The structure of flowers and leafy stems is distinctive. In other *Veronica* species, some of which are weeds in lawns or ditches, the corolla varies from nearly white to clear blue.

NIGHTSHADE FAMILY
Solanaceae

Herbs, shrubs, vines, or trees with often showy flowers, generally in branched clusters.

Flowers: Usually radially symmetrical. Sepals 5, united; petals 5, united; stamens usually 5, sometimes fewer; all these parts attached at base of ovary.

Leaves: Alternate or rarely opposite; usually simple, sometimes compound.

Fruit: Berry or 2-chambered capsule.

There are about 85 genera and 2,800 species, found in tropical and warm temperate regions, especially in Central and South America. Several are poisonous, but others supply food such as chiles and bell peppers *(Capsicum),* tomatoes *(Lycopersicon esculentum),* potatoes *(Solanum tuberosum),* eggplant *(Solanum melongena),* and groundcherries (also known as husk tomatoes or tomatillos, in *Physalis).* Commercial tobacco is obtained from *Nicotiana tabacum.* Painted

Tongue *(Salpiglossis sinuata)*, petunias *(Petunia)*, and butterfly flowers *(Schizanthus)* are grown as ornamentals.
Solanaceae has also been known as the potato family.

225   Dingy Chamaesaracha
Chamaesaracha sordida

Description: A low, dull green plant, covered with
fine, glandular hairs, with a *flat, round,
dingy whitish-green flower* in each upper
axil.

Flowers: Corolla about ½" (1.5 cm) wide, with 5
pale bands radiating from center to tips
of 5 low lobes; hairy, greenish-yellow
pads alternating with bases of 5 slender
stamens near center of flower.

Leaves: To 1½" (4 cm) long, pointed at tip,
tapering to base, edges usually wavy
and sometimes with low lobes.

Fruit: Berry, ⅛–⅜" (4–8 mm) wide, tightly
enveloped by calyx.

Height: Creeper; stems to 1' (30 cm) long,
mostly hugging ground.

Flowering: May–September.

Habitat: Plains and deserts.

Range: Southern Arizona east to western Texas
and south to northern Mexico.

Comments: This and other *Chamaesaracha* species
are frequent but rarely very conspicuous.
The corollas are dull, and the foliage
often has an earthen hue.

71   Southwestern Thorn Apple
Datura wrightii

Description: Large, *trumpet-shaped, white flowers,*
generally withered by mid-morning,
protruding from *coarse foliage* of a
stout, branched, rank-smelling plant.

Flowers: Corolla 6" (15 cm) long, flared portion
with 5 slender teeth on rim.

Leaves: To 6" (15 cm) long, ovate, covered
with minute low hairs.

Fruit: 1½" (4 cm) wide, spherical, hanging
down, surface prickly, with many
slender spines less than ½" (1 cm)
long.

Height:	To 5′ (1.5 m).
Flowering:	May–November.
Habitat:	Loose sand in arroyos and on plains.
Range:	Central California south to northern Mexico and east to Colorado, New Mexico, and Texas.
Comments:	Technical references disagree as to whether there are one or two species in this complex. *D. wrightii* has short, down-curved hairs on the stem less than ¹⁄₅₀″ (0.5 mm) long, whereas Thorn Apple *(D. innoxia)* has spreading hairs, straight or twisted, ¹⁄₂₅″ (1 mm) long. Extracts from these plants and their relatives are narcotic and, when improperly prepared, lethal. The narcotic properties have been recorded throughout history. They once figured importantly in religious ceremonies of southwestern Native Americans. Among several species, all with round thorny fruits, is the wide-ranging Jimsonweed *(D. stramonium);* the fruit has many small spines and does not hang, and the corolla is only about 3″ (7.5 cm) long. Originally from Mexico, Jimsonweed was carried throughout much of the world for medicinal use; the common name is a corruption of Jamestown Weed, so named because the plant grew near the homes of the Jamestown colonists. In all species corollas may be tinged to varying degrees with violet.

236 Tree Tobacco
Nicotiana glauca

Description:	An open *shrub or small tree* with few branches and *yellow, trumpet-shaped flowers* tending to spread or hang on slender branches.
Flowers:	Corolla 1¼–2″ (3–5 cm) long; stamens 5.
Leaves:	2–7″ (5–17.5 cm) long, smooth, ovate, gray-green.
Height:	To 26′ (8 m).
Flowering:	April–November.
Habitat:	Roadsides, slopes, and washes.

Range: Central California, southern Arizona, and western Texas south into Mexico; introduced in a few eastern states.

Comments: This native of South America is now widespread in the world. It is a common and conspicuous plant along roadsides in southern California. All species of *Nicotiana* contain the highly toxic alkaloid nicotine. An effective insecticide against aphids can be prepared by steeping the leaves of *Nicotiana* species, including commercial tobacco, in water and spraying the solution on affected parts of the plant. Tree Tobacco contains an even more potent poison for aphids, anabasine.

81   Desert Tobacco; Tabaquillo
Nicotiana obtusifolia

Description: *Sticky-glandular stems and leaves,* and *trumpet-shaped, white flowers* in a loosely branched cluster at top.

Flowers: Corolla ½–¾" (1.5–2 cm) long, with 5 low, bluntly pointed lobes at flared end; stamens 5.

Leaves: 2–6" (5–15 cm) long, broadly lanceolate; lower ones on broad flat stalks; upper ones stalkless, with ear-like lobes at base on either side of stem.

Height: 1–3' (30–90 cm).

Flowering: November–June in western part of range, March–November in eastern part.

Habitat: Sandy areas and washes.

Range: Southeastern California and southern Nevada east to western Texas and south to northwestern New Mexico.

Comments: The Spanish name, Tabaquillo (pronounced *tah-bah-kee-yoh*), means "little tobacco." It was also once called Punche ("a punch") by Spanish Americans, who carefully tended it for tobacco and medicinal use, and it is still smoked by Native Americans in traditional ceremonies. Coyote Tobacco *(N. attenuata),* found from British Columbia south to Baja California and east to New Mexico, Colorado, and northern Idaho, has fewer glands, short, triangular calyx lobes, and dingy white, trumpet-shaped corollas 1–1½″ (2.5–4 cm) long. All wild tobaccos are poisonous, but they are so strong-smelling and distasteful that livestock usually avoid them.

226 Ivyleaf Groundcherry
Physalis hederifolia

Description: *Flattish, rather pentagonal, pale yellow flowers,* usually with 5 *deeper yellow patches near center,* protruding from lightly hairy foliage.

Flowers: Corolla about ½″ (1.5 cm) wide, abruptly flaring from tube about ¼″ (6 mm) long.

Leaves: Blades ½–1½″ (1.5–4 cm) long, ovate-triangular to more or less heart-shaped, stalks about as long as blades; hairy, hairs sometimes with round, glandular tips making plant slightly sticky.

Fruit: Round, smooth, greenish-yellow berry, about ½″ (1.5 cm) wide; hidden within a swollen, papery, 10-ribbed, lantern-shaped calyx to 1¼″ (3 cm) long, 1″ (2.5 cm) wide.

Height: 4–10″ (10–25 cm).

Flowering: March–September.

Habitat: Dry sandy, gravelly, or rocky areas on plains, in brush, and in open woodlands.

Range: Southeastern California east across southern Nevada, Utah, and Arizona to western Texas, and north through Plains states to eastern Wyoming, western South Dakota, and perhaps southeastern Montana.

Comments: As the fruit matures the calyx enlarges, becoming inflated and papery. This also occurs in Tomatillo *(P. philadelphica),* a species with a fruit to almost 3″ (7.5 cm) wide, popular in Mexican and southwestern cuisine and a tangy addition to salads. Prior to preparation, the husk (calyx) is removed from the green, tomato-like fruit (*tomatillo* means "little tomato"). There are more than a dozen species of groundcherry in the West, all recognizable by the inflated calyx. Some have branched hairs on the leaves; others have longer flower stalks than *P. hederifolia* or flowers that are more bell-shaped. Caution is advised; the unripe berries of some *Physalis* are poisonous.

---

564   **Purple Groundcherry**
Quincula lobata

Description: *Blue-violet or violet, saucer-shaped flowers* on slender stalks in leaf axils of short erect stems growing from a rosette of leaves, or on longer, leafy stems lying on ground with upturned ends.

Flowers: Calyx enlarging as fruit matures, forming a 5-sided bladder ¾" (2 cm) long; corolla about ¾" (2 cm) wide; hairy pads alternating with bases of 5 slender stamens near center of flower; anthers resembling small yellow knobs.

Leaves: To 4" (10 cm) long, lanceolate, pinnately lobed or divided.

Fruit: Berry, about ¼" (6 mm) wide, enclosed in calyx.

Height: Reclining stems to 20" (50 cm) long; erect stems to about 6" (15 cm).

Flowering: March–September.

Habitat: Open areas on desert plains; frequent in agricultural areas.

Range: Southeastern California east across southern Nevada to southeastern Utah, eastern Colorado, and western Kansas, and south to western Texas, New Mexico, Arizona, and northern Mexico.

Comments: The berry is edible, but caution is advised, for the flower resembles some of those of *Solanum,* a genus with both edible and deadly berries. Purple Groundcherry was formerly placed in the genus *Physalis,* but the purple flower and the flat, scale-like hairs on the leaves are considered distinctive.

582 Bittersweet; Climbing Nightshade
Solanum dulcamara

Description: *Long stems climbing or scrambling* over other vegetation, with *blue or deep violet, star-like flowers* in roundish, open clusters.

Flowers: ½–¾″ (1.5–2 cm) wide; corolla with 5 points often bent backward; 5 long yellow anthers usually forming narrow blunt cone in center of flower.

Leaves: To 3″ (7.5 cm) long, heart-shaped or ovate with 2 lobes at base.

Fruit: Red shiny berry, about ½″ (1.5 cm) wide.

Height: Vine; stems to 10′ (3 m) long.

Flowering: May–September.

Habitat: Thickets, cleared areas, open woods, and fencerows.

Range: Throughout much of Canada and United States, but infrequent or absent in arid regions.

Comments: This plant is native to northern Eurasia. *Solanum* species are expensive pests in agricultural regions because the foliage and fruit of several are mildly poisonous. Truckloads of dried beans have been discarded because agricultural inspectors found a few *Solanum* berries harvested along with the crop, a necessary precaution even though not all plants in the genus are poisonous. Potatoes and eggplants are among the nonpoisonous and economically important plants in this huge genus. Among the poisonous species is Belladonna *(Atropa belladonna),* also known as Deadly Nightshade, which has black berries and is an occasional weed west of the Cascade Range.

569 White Horsenettle; Silver Horsenettle; Silverleaf Nightshade
Solanum elaeagnifolium

Description: Stems growing in patches and bearing *fine prickles, bluish-gray, lanceolate leaves, and bluish-violet, violet, or lavender, star-like flowers.*

Flowers: ¾–1¼″ (2–3 cm) wide; corolla with 5 points; long anthers forming slender,

yellow cone in center of flower,
especially when young.

Leaves: 1–4″ (2.5–10 cm) long, usually with
wavy edges.

Fruit: Shiny, yellow berry, ½″ (1.5 cm) wide.

Height: To 3′ (90 cm).

Flowering: May–September.

Habitat: Dry open areas; common along roads, in
old lots, and in agricultural regions.

Range: Across southern half of United States
and in northern Mexico; in West, north
to Washington, Idaho, Colorado, and
Nebraska.

Comments: The lavender, star-shaped flowers with
yellow centers are beautifully set off by
the silvery foliage, and large patches of
the plant in full bloom are striking.
However, the plant is an aggressive,
poisonous weed, spreading steadily from
deep rootstocks; in a few states it is
classified as a noxious weed. The genus
name, from the Latin *solamen*
("quieting"), alludes to the narcotic
properties of many species.
Southwestern Native Americans used
the crushed berries to curdle milk in
making cheese, and the berries have also
been used in various preparations for
treating sore throat and toothache. This
species is also known as Bullnettle.

16, 224   Buffalo Bur
Solanum rostratum

Description: A leafy plant with dense, *golden yellow
prickles* covering stems and calyx of each
yellow, star-like flower.

Flowers: Corolla ¾–1″ (2–2.5 cm) wide, with 5
points; unequal anthers forming a
slender, irregular, blunt cone in center of
flower.

Leaves: 2–6″ (5–15 cm) long, including stalks,
blades deeply parted into irregularly
pinnate lobes, stalks and backs of veins
covered with prickles.

Fruit: Berry, enclosed by spiny, tight-fitting
calyx; about 1″ (2.5 cm) wide including
spines.

Height: 16–31″ (40–80 cm).
Flowering: May–September.
Habitat: Roadsides, edges of fields, and old lots.
Range: Throughout much of southern Canada and United States; in West, probably more common in southern part; also in northern Mexico.
Comments: Abundant prickles help to discourage livestock from grazing on this highly toxic plant. Melonleaf Nightshade *(S. citrullifolium),* an equally prickly species of about the same habit, has blue-violet corollas; it is found from New Mexico east to the southern Great Plains, and in a few eastern states.

CACAO FAMILY
Sterculiaceae

Trees, shrubs, or herbs, often covered with star-like hairs, sometimes with large showy flowers.

Flowers: Usually bisexual, radially symmetrical. Sepals 3 or 5, joined at base, often petal-like; petals 5, small, or absent; stamens separate and in a single whorl, or in 2 whorls and united by filaments; all these parts attached at base of ovary.
Leaves: Simple or pinnately compound.
Fruit: Leathery or fleshy, with at least 4 chambers.

There are about 50 genera and 1,500 species, mostly in warm regions of the world. Chocolate comes from fermented seeds of Cacao *(Theobroma cacao).*

198 Flannel Bush; Fremontia
Fremontodendron californicum

Description: A spreading shrub with many *large, saucer-shaped, yellow-orange flowers.*
Flowers: 1½–2½″ (4–6.5 cm) wide; sepals petal-like, ovate, with long hairs in pits at base; petals absent; stamens 5, united at base into tube.
Leaves: ½–3″ (1.5–7.5 cm) long, dark green, with *3 shallow lobes,* 1–3 veins.
Height: 5–30′ (1.5–9 m).
Flowering: May–June.
Habitat: Dry slopes in brush or pine forests.

Range: Much of California south to Baja
California and east to central Arizona.
Comments: The flowers bloom in showy masses,
making this a popular ornamental.
The similar Mexican Fremontia
(*F. mexicanum*), found along the
California–Mexico border, has
flowers hidden among the leaves
and 5–7 veins at the base of the
leaves.

VALERIAN FAMILY
Valerianaceae

Leafy herbs with small flowers in branched or head-like clusters.

Flowers: Bisexual or unisexual, bilaterally symmetrical.
Calyx barely developed, often feathery when present;
corolla with 5 united petals, often bearing a backward-
projecting spur; stamens 1–4; all these parts attached at
top of ovary.
Leaves: Opposite or basal, often pinnately divided.
Fruit: Seed-like.

There are about 13 genera and 400 species, found in the
northern temperate region and the Andes. Red Valerian
(*Centranthus ruber*) is grown as an ornamental.

160   Downy-fruited Valerian
Valeriana acutiloba

Description: *Small, slightly bilaterally symmetrical,
white flowers* in branched clusters atop a
stem *with largest leaves at base.*
Flowers: About ¼″ (6 mm) long; corolla with 5
roundish lobes sharply bent outward,
lower side of tubular portion slightly
swollen; stamens 3, protruding.
Leaves: Blades to 3″ (7.5 cm) long, ovate; those
at base usually not divided, tapering to a
long stalk; those on stem pinnately
divided into 1–2 pairs of lobes, without
stalks.
Fruit: Seed-like, with short hairs; numerous
plume-like bristles unrolling at top
when fruit matures.
Height: 4–24″ (10–60 cm).
Flowering: June–July.

Habitat: Open, rocky slopes in mountains, often near water or snowbanks.

Range: Southwestern Montana southwest to northern California, southern Sierra Nevada, northern Arizona, and New Mexico.

Comments: The mostly undivided, basal leaves help distinguish this from other similar species, which have divided leaves. This species is variable, and by some botanists is divided into at least three species: Cordilleran Valerian *(V. acutiloba),* the more southwestern, has hairless leaves and stems; Downy-fruited Valerian *(V. pubicarpa),* more western, has hairless leaves but hairy stems; California Valerian *(V. californica),* also western, has hairy leaves and stems. *Valeriana* comes from the Latin *valere* ("to be strong") and refers to the medicinal qualities of the plants. Extracts were used as a nerve tonic and are said, under certain circumstances, to relax better than opium. Valerian was one of 72 ingredients Mithridates, king of Pontus in the second century B.C., compounded as an antidote to poison, using poisoned slaves as test subjects.

VERBENA FAMILY
Verbenaceae

Herbs, shrubs, or trees, usually with flowers in spike-like or branched clusters or in heads.

Flowers: Bilaterally symmetrical. Sepals 5, united; petals 5, united, forming corolla with a slender tube and an abruptly flared top; stamens usually 4; all these parts attached at base of ovary.

Leaves: Opposite or whorled, simple.

Fruit: Often separating into 4 hard sections (nutlets), each 1-seeded.

There are about 100 genera and 2,600 species, mostly in tropical and warm temperate regions. A highly prized furniture wood is obtained from Teak *(Tectona grandis).* Vervains *(Verbena),* lantanas *(Lantana),* lippias (also known as frog fruits, in *Phyla*), and Chaste Tree *(Vitex agnus-castus)* are grown as ornamentals. Verbenaceae has also been known as the vervain family.

524   Western Pink Vervain; Moradilla
Glandularia bipinnatifida

Description: *Gently rounded clusters of bilaterally symmetrical, pink, lavender, or pale purple flowers* atop stems with highly divided leaves.

Flowers: Calyx glandular-hairy, with 5 narrow lobes with teeth about ⅛" (3 mm) long; corolla ¼–½" (6–13 mm) wide, tubular base 1–1½ times as long as calyx.

Leaves: ¾–2½" (2–6.5 cm) long, pinnately divided, main divisions again pinnately divided, final divisions lanceolate.

Height: 8–16" (20–40 cm).

Flowering: February–October.

Habitat: Open fields and weedy areas.

Range: Arizona east to Oklahoma and Texas, and south to northern Mexico.

Comments: The Spanish name, Moradilla, comes from *morado* ("purple") and means "little purple one." This plant often forms brilliant displays of pink or light purple, covering acres of ground. It is a variable complex, with some plants tall and pink-flowered, others more matted and with lavender or purple flowers; the two forms are usually found in separate areas. The genus *Glandularia* is closely related to *Verbena,* differing conspicuously in its round-topped clusters of showy flowers; in some references, this species is listed as *Verbena ambrosifolia.*

605   New Mexico Vervain
Verbena macdougalii

Description: A harshly hairy plant with 4-sided stems and thick, dense, long, erect spikes, each with a *ring of small, lavender to blue-violet, bilaterally symmetrical flowers.*

Flowers: Corolla ¼" (6 mm) wide, 5-lobed, lower 3 lobes bent downward, middle lobe largest, upper 2 lobes bent upward.

Leaves: Blades to 4" (10 cm) long, opposite, ovate, edges with coarse, irregular teeth.

Fruit: Separating into 4 long, seed-like nutlets.

Height: To 3' (90 cm).

New Mexico Vervain

Flowering: June–October.

Habitat: Valleys and open flats from moderate to high elevations.

Range: Southern Wyoming and southern Utah south to Arizona, New Mexico, and western Texas.

Comments: This species resembles members of the mint family (Lamiaceae) but lacks the aromatic odor. There are several species of tall vervains, with thick or slender spikes of flowers, which are usually not easy to distinguish from one another. New Mexico Vervain has relatively thick spikes; it is common in the southern Rocky Mountain region.

VIOLET FAMILY
Violaceae

Herbs with often colorful flowers in the United States, but often shrubby and less showy elsewhere.

Flowers: Bilaterally or radially symmetrical. Sepals 5, separate; petals 5, separate, lower petal often largest and bearing a backward-projecting spur; stamens 5, loosely united around ovary; all these parts attached at base of ovary.

Leaves: Simple, sometimes deeply lobed.

Fruit: Berry or explosively opening capsule.

There are about 16 genera and 800 species, found nearly throughout the world. Many species of *Viola* are cultivated for their attractive flowers.

642   Blue Violet
Viola adunca

Description:	A small plant with pansy-like, *blue-violet flowers* hanging at tips of slender stalks.
Flowers:	½–¾" (1.5–2 cm) wide; petals 5; upper 2 petals bent upward; lower 3 petals white at base, outer ones with white hairs; *slender spur extending backward beneath flower.*
Leaves:	Blades ½–1¼" (1.5–3 cm) long, with stalks, dark green, rather thick, ovate or heart-shaped, finely scalloped on edges; in tufts at base.
Height:	To 4" (10 cm).
Flowering:	April–August.
Habitat:	Meadows, open woods, and open slopes from sea level to timberline.
Range:	Across much of Canada and northern United States; in West, south to southern California, Arizona, New Mexico, and South Dakota.
Comments:	Violets are very popular wildflowers and garden plants, romantically described as "shrinking" because of the way the petals fold in. Species are often difficult to identify, as they may hybridize, producing intermediate forms. These hybrids may in turn reproduce by means of self-fertilization, with the inconspicuous flowers at the base of the plant (often even underground) producing seeds without opening.

588   Western Pansy Violet; Beckwith Violet; Great Basin Violet
Viola beckwithii

Description:	*Bilaterally symmetrical, two-tone flowers hanging and facing outward* on leafless stalks growing from a low tuft of leaves.

Flowers:	½–¾" (1.5–2 cm) wide; petals 5; upper 2 petals reddish purple; lower 3 petals mauve with yellowish patches and reddish-purple lines near base, outer ones with yellow hairs, middle one with a pouch behind it.
Leaves:	Blades about 1" (2.5 cm) long, grayish green, divided into 3 main sections, these again divided into narrow segments, all attached to a long stalk.
Height:	2–5" (5–12.5 cm).
Flowering:	March–May.
Habitat:	In sagebrush and open pinewoods.
Range:	Northeastern Oregon south to southeastern California and east to Utah and Idaho.
Comments:	This species is as pretty as the garden Pansy *(V. arvensis),* a violet native to Europe. Sagebrush Violet or Desert Pansy *(V. trinervata),* found in eastern Washington and northeastern Oregon, is very similar but has leaves with 3-veined, leathery segments.

97 Canada Violet
Viola canadensis

Description:	*White, bilaterally symmetrical flowers hanging and facing outward* at tips of short stalks growing from axils of heart-shaped leaves.

Canada Violet

Flowers:	Nearly 1″ (2.5 cm) wide; petals 5, almost all white, yellow at base; upper 2 petals bent upward, purplish on back; lower 3 petals with purple lines near base, outer ones hairy at base, middle one with a short spur projecting beneath flower.
Leaves:	Blades 1–3″ (2.5–7.5 cm) long, on slender stalks to 1′ (30 cm) long.
Height:	4–16″ (10–40 cm).
Flowering:	May–July.
Habitat:	Moist woodlands.
Range:	Across much of Canada and northern United States; in West, south to Oregon, Idaho, Arizona, New Mexico, and northern Mexico; widespread in eastern United States.
Comments:	This lovely species is distinguishable from other white-flowered violets by its yellow petal bases on flowers growing from upper leaf axils.

279 Douglas's Violet
Viola douglasii

Description:	*Bilaterally symmetrical, orangish-yellow flowers hanging and facing outward* atop leafless stalks growing from a low tuft of leaves.
Flowers:	½–¾″ (1.5–2 cm) wide; petals 5; upper 2 petals maroon on back; lower 3 petals with purple lines near base, middle one with a short pouch behind it.
Leaves:	Blades ¾–2″ (2–5 cm) long, pinnately divided into several main divisions, these again divided into narrow segments, all attached to a comparatively long stalk.
Height:	2–6″ (5–15 cm).
Flowering:	March–May.
Habitat:	Dry, open, gravelly slopes at low elevations.
Range:	Southern Oregon and northern two-thirds of California.
Comments:	This violet grows on very sparsely vegetated banks, often in rather sterile soil, the perky little flowers peering from the bank like golden faces among the grayish foliage. As summer

progresses, the soil becomes hard and
crusty and the plants wither, the stout
roots preserving life until the next
flowering season.

280 Stream Violet; Pioneer Violet; Smooth Yellow Violet
Viola glabella

Description: Slender, leaning or erect stems with
leaves only in upper one-third; *bilaterally
symmetrical, yellow flowers facing outward*
and hanging from slender stalks.

Flowers: ½–¾″ (1.5–2 cm) wide; petals 5; upper
2 petals yellow on back; lower 3 petals
with fine maroon lines at base, outer
ones bearded, middle one with a short
pouch projecting backward beneath
flower.

Leaves: Blades 1¼–3½″ (3–9 cm) long, heart-
shaped, with finely toothed edges, on
long stalks.

Height: 2–12″ (5–30 cm).

Flowering: March–July.

Habitat: In moist woods and along streams.

Range: Alaska south to southern Sierra Nevada
and east to Idaho and western Montana.

Comments: This is a very common species in moist
shaded places in woods. Most western
violets have yellow rather than purple
corollas, but all have the perky little
flower with a spur or pouch behind the
lowermost petal. This petal forms a
landing platform for insects seeking
nectar within the spur.

283 Yellow Wood Violet; Pine Violet
Viola lobata

Description: Leaves and *bright yellow, bilaterally
symmetrical flowers* crowded near top of
stem.

Flowers: ¾–1″ (2–2.5 cm) wide; petals 5, yellow;
upper 2 petals brown on back; lower 3
petals with fine brown lines at base,
larger middle one with a pouch barely
extending backward beneath flower.

Leaves:	1–4″ (2.5–10 cm) wide, palmately cleft into 3–9 narrow lobes, or broadly heart-shaped and irregularly scalloped.
Height:	4–14″ (10–35 cm).
Flowering:	April–July.
Habitat:	Dry slopes in open woods.
Range:	Southwestern Oregon south to southern California.
Comments:	Phases of this species with unlobed leaves occur in the same region as those with deeply lobed leaves. However, in southwestern Oregon and northwestern California, the phase with lobed leaves is rare.

589 Larkspur Violet
Viola pedatifida

Description:	*Bilaterally symmetrical, blue-violet flowers facing outward* and hanging atop leafless stalks barely taller than tufted leaves.
Flowers:	½–¾″ (1.5–2 cm) wide; petals 5; outer lower petals with hairs at base, middle lower petal with a prominent spur.
Leaves:	¾–2¾″ (2–7 cm) long, on long stalks, blades divided into 1–2 main sections, these again divided into narrow lobes.
Height:	3–8″ (7.5–20 cm).
Flowering:	May–June.
Habitat:	Forest openings, valleys, and plains.
Range:	Alberta east to Ontario, south in Rocky Mountains to Arizona and New Mexico, south in Plains states to Oklahoma and Arkansas, and east to Ohio.
Comments:	The deep blue-violet flowers and divided leaves resemble those of larkspurs *(Delphinium),* hence the common name.

281 Goosefoot Violet
Viola purpurea

Description:	*Bilaterally symmetrical, yellow flowers facing outward and hanging at tips of slender stalks* growing from axils of *purplish-green leaves.*

Flowers: ½–¾" (1.5–2 cm) wide; petals 5, often with a purplish or brownish tinge; lower 3 petals with brownish lines near base, middle petal with a very short spur extending beneath flower.

Leaves: Blades ½–2" (1.5–5 cm) long, lanceolate to nearly round, thick, fleshy, with veins deeply impressed on upper surface and raised on lower, edges with shallow or deep rounded teeth.

Height: 2–6" (5–15 cm).

Flowering: May–August.

Habitat: In open or partly shaded places from lowlands to high mountains.

Range: Eastern British Columbia and eastern Washington south to southern California and east to Arizona, Colorado, Wyoming, and Montana.

Comments: The leaves of this variable violet often have a purplish hue and are prominently veined. The shape of some leaves is reminiscent of a goose's foot, hence the common name.

282 Redwood Violet; Evergreen Violet
Viola sempervirens

Description: Stems creeping across ground and producing *mats of thick, leathery, broadly heart-shaped leaves; bilaterally symmetrical, clear yellow flowers* facing outward and hanging on short stalks barely as tall as leaves.

Flowers: About ½" (1.5 cm) wide; petals 5; upper 2 petals bent upward; lower 3 petals with maroon veins near base, middle one with a short spur.

Leaves: ½–1¼" (1.5–3 cm) wide, edges finely scalloped and toothed, on long stalks.

Height: Creeper; flower stalks 1–5" (2.5–12.5 cm), stems to 1′ (30 cm) long.

Flowering: March–June.

Habitat: Moist woods.

Range: British Columbia south to southern Oregon west of Cascade Range, and in Coast Ranges south to central California.

Comments: This is one of the most common
wildflowers within the dim redwood
forest, lining many of the trails in the
parks of the region. The mats of leaves
persist throughout the winter, giving
the common name Evergreen Violet and
making this a choice plant for the
woodland garden.

CALTROP FAMILY
Zygophyllaceae

Herbs or shrubs, rarely trees, with flowers borne singly or in
branched clusters.

Flowers: Usually bisexual, radially symmetrical. Sepals usually 5, separate; petals 5, separate; stamens 5, 10, or 15,
often with scale-like appendages on stalks; all these parts
attached at base of ovary.
Leaves: Opposite, pinnately compound.
Fruit: Usually a 5-chambered capsule.

There are about 30 genera and 250 species, mostly in
warm temperate or tropical regions. Creosote Bush *(Larrea
tridentata)* is a common shrub in southwestern deserts. The
densest of well-known commercial woods, lignum vitae, is
obtained from tropical trees in the genus *Guaicum.*

429   Fagonia
Fagonia laevis

Description: A low, round, open plant with green,
*forking, angular stems and scattered flowers
like pale lavender stars* at branch ends.
Flowers: About ½" (1.5 cm) wide; petals 5,
narrow; ovary 5-lobed.
Leaves: Opposite, divided into 3 lanceolate
leaflets, each ⅛–½" (3–13 mm) long.
Height: 8–24" (20–60 cm).
Flowering: March–May; sometimes
November–January, depending on
rains.
Habitat: Rocky slopes and washes in deserts.
Range: Southern Utah south through western
Arizona and southeastern California to
northwestern Mexico.
Comments: This plant is so open that it hardly
casts a shadow. The stems and small

leaves present little surface area to
the sun and hot dry air, an adaptation
to desert conditions that conserves
precious water.

---

371 **Desert Poppy; Summer Poppy;
Arizona Poppy**
Kallstroemia grandiflora

Description: *Brilliant orange, bowl-shaped flowers,
crimson in center,* facing upward on
stalks above sprawling, forked, hairy
stems.

Flowers: 2″ (5 cm) wide; petals 5, broad;
stamens 10; ovary 5-lobed.

Leaves: ¾–2½″ (2–6.5 cm) long, opposite,
pinnately compound.

Height: Creeper; erect flowering stems to
1½′ (45 cm), sprawling stems to 3′
(90 cm) long.

Flowering: May–November.

Habitat: Open, sandy areas in deserts.

Range: Southern Arizona east to western
Texas and south through much of
Mexico; introduced in southeastern
California.

Comments: This is not a true poppy, or even a
close relative, but the resemblance is
there; large patches provide a display
as brilliant and spectacular as those of
California Poppy *(Eschscholzia californica).*
This is one of the handsomest wildflowers
in the Southwest and is frequently seen
along roadsides. There are several other
Kallstroemia species, all found in the
Southwest, that can be recognized
by their opposite, pinnately compound
leaves on trailing stems; they have
corollas only about ½″ (1.5 cm)
wide. Small-flowered Carpetweed *(K.
parviflora)* has orange flowers, and a
beak on the fruit that is longer than the
round body. Two have yellow flowers
and short beaks: Hairy Carpetweed
(K. hirsutissima) has sepals that do not
drop off, and the base of the fruit's beak
is bristly-hairy; California Carpetweed
(K. californica) has sepals that usually

drop off after the flower opens and has either no hairs or only small ones at the base of the beak.

204 Goat's Head; Caltrop; Puncture Weed
Tribulus terrestris

Description: A plant with sprawling stems, often forming mats, and *small yellow flowers* on short stalks in leaf axils.

Flowers: ¼–½" (6–13 mm) wide; petals 5, broad; stamens 10.

Leaves: 1–2" (2.5–5 cm) long, opposite, pinnately compound, with 4–8 pairs of leaflets, each ¼–½" (6–13 mm) long.

Fruit: Hard, star-shaped capsule, dividing into 5 sharply 2-horned segments.

Height: Creeper; rarely more than 8" (20 cm), forming mats to 3' (90 cm) wide.

Flowering: April–November.

Habitat: Weedy, open areas.

Range: Throughout much of United States; also in southern Canada; widespread in Mexico.

Comments: A native of the Mediterranean region, this is one of the West's most unloved weeds; it is classified as a noxious weed in several states. The sharp spines on the fruit segments (the "goat's head") cause painful injury to bare feet and to livestock and easily pierce bicycle tires, hence the common name Puncture Weed; it is also known as Puncture Vine. The foliage is poisonous to livestock.

PART III
APPENDICES

GLOSSARY

Achene   A small, dry, hard, seed-like fruit that does not open and contains one seed.

Adventive   A plant that has been introduced from one region into another but has not become fully naturalized. *See also* Introduced.

Air plant   A plant growing on another plant but deriving no nutrition from it; an epiphyte.

Alternate leaves   Leaves rising singly along the stem, not in pairs or whorls.

Annual   Having a life cycle completed in one year or season.

Anther   The sac-like, pollen-containing part of a stamen.

Aquatic   A plant growing in water.

Axil   The angle formed by the upper side of a leaf and the stem from which the leaf grows.

Banner   The broad upper petal in a pea flower; also called the standard.

Basal leaves   Leaves at the base of the stem.

Bearded   Bearing a tuft or ring of long or stiff hairs.

Berry   A fleshy fruit with one to many seeds, developed from a single ovary.

Biennial   Growing vegetatively during the first year and flowering, fruiting, and dying during the second.

Bilaterally symmetrical   A flower that can be divided into equal halves by only one line through the middle; often called bilateral or irregular. *See also* Radially symmetrical.

Bisexual   A flower with both female (pistil) and male (stamen) parts.

Blade   The flat portion of a leaf, petal, or sepal.

Bloom   A whitish, powdery or waxy coating giving a frosted appearance, usually easily rubbed off (e.g., the bloom on a plum).

Bract   A modified leaf, usually smaller than the foliage leaves, often situated at the base of a flower or an inflorescence.

Bractlet   A small bract.

Bud   An undeveloped leaf, stem, or flower, often enclosed in scales; an incompletely opened flower.

Bulb   A short, underground stem, the swollen portion consisting mostly of fleshy, food-storing, modified leaves (e.g., an onion).

Bulblet   A small bulb; most often referring to one borne in a leaf axil or in an inflorescence.

Calyx   Collective term for the sepals of a flower.

Capsule   A dry, usually thin-walled fruit with one or more compartments, splitting open along two or more lines.

Carnivorous   Subsisting partly on nutrients obtained from the breakdown of animal tissue; with regard to plants, usually referring to insect tissue.

Catkin   A scaly-bracted, deciduous spike composed of very small, unisexual flowers.

Clasping leaf   A leaf with its base wholly or partly surrounding the stem.

Claw   The narrow, stalk-like base of a petal.

Compound leaf   A leaf divided into leaflets.

Compound umbel   A flower cluster consisting of small umbels joined by their stalks to a common point. *See also* Umbel.

Corolla   Collective term for the petals of a flower.

Corona   A crown-like structure between corolla and stamens on some flowers.

Creeper   Technically, a trailing shoot that takes root at the nodes; used here to denote any trailing, prostrate plant.

Cross-pollination   The transfer of pollen from one plant to another.

Deciduous   Shedding leaves seasonally; the shedding of certain parts after a period of growth.

Disk   The fleshy development of the base of the flower around the base of the ovary; in reference to members of the aster family, the swollen, often dome-like top of the flower stalk, bearing the disk flowers.

Disk flower   Each of the small, tubular, radially symmetrical flowers making up the central part of the flower head in many members of the aster family, or making up the entire head in some members.

Dissected leaf   A deeply cut leaf, the cleft not reaching to the midrib; same as a divided leaf.

Divided leaf   A deeply cut leaf, the cleft not reaching to the midrib; same as a dissected leaf.

Drupe   A fleshy fruit with a single seed enveloped by a hard covering (e.g., a peach); also called a stone fruit.

Emergent   An aquatic plant with its lower part submerged and its upper part extending above water.

Epiphyte   A plant growing on another plant but deriving no nutrition from it; an air plant.

Escaped   A plant that has spread beyond the confines of a deliberate planting, as from a garden.

Family   A group of closely related genera.

Female flower   A flower with one or more pistils but lacking stamens; a pistillate flower.

Fertile stamen   A stamen with a pollen-producing anther.

Filament   The stalk of a stamen, usually slender and thread-like.

Follicle   A dry, one-chambered fruit developed from a single ovary, usually opening along one line (e.g., a milkweed fruit).

Fruit   The seed-bearing, ripened ovary or pistil, often with attached parts.

Genus (plural, Genera)   A group of closely related species.

Gland   A small structure secreting some substance, usually oil or nectar.

Glandular   Bearing glands.

Head   A crowded cluster of flowers on very short stalks or without stalks; in reference to members of the aster family, the composite of ray and disk flowers resembling a single flower.

Herb   A plant producing little or no woody tissue, as opposed to a shrub or a tree.

Humus   A brown or black, complex, variable material resulting from partial decomposition of plant or animal matter and forming the organic portion of soil.

Hypanthium   A cup- or saucer-shaped or tubular base to certain flowers, composed of the united and modified bases of calyx, corolla, and stamens; sepals, petals, and stamens grow from the rim.

Inflorescence   A flower cluster on a plant or, especially, the arrangement of flowers on a plant.

Introduced   A plant that has been either accidentally or deliberately brought from one region into another; may or may not become naturalized.

Involucre   A whorl or circle of bracts beneath a flower or flower cluster.

Irregular flower   A flower with petals that are not uniform in size or shape but often form an upper and lower lip; usually used in reference to a bilaterally symmetrical flower.

Keel   A sharp ridge or rib; in a pea flower, the two lowest petals joined by lower edges and shaped like the prow of a boat.

Lanceolate Lance-shaped, much longer than wide and pointed at the end, usually with the widest portion below the middle.

Leaflet One of the leaf-like parts of a compound leaf.

Linear Long, narrow, with parallel sides.

Lip petal The lower petal of some bilaterally symmetrical flowers, often larger and/or more showy than the other petals.

Lobed Indented on the edges, with the indentations not reaching to the center or base.

Local A plant occurring sporadically but sometimes common where found.

Male flower A flower with stamens but lacking pistils; a staminate flower.

Naturalized A plant that has been introduced from one region into another where it has become established in the wild and reproduces as though native.

Node The place on a stem from which a leaf or a branch grows.

Obovate More or less egg-shaped; in reference to a leaf, one with the stalk attached at the narrow end of the leaf.

Opposite leaves Leaves occurring in pairs at a node, with one leaf on either side of the stem.

Ovary The swollen base of a pistil, within which seeds develop.

Ovate More or less egg-shaped, pointed at the top, and broadest near the base or below the middle; in reference to a leaf, one with the stalk attached at the broad end of the leaf.

Palmate leaf A leaf with three or more divisions or lobes, much like the outspread fingers of a hand.

Panicle A branched, open inflorescence in which the main branches are again branched.

Pappus Bristles, scales, hairs, or a crown atop the seed-like fruits of various members of the aster family.

Parasite A plant deriving its nutrition from another organism.

Pea flower A bilaterally symmetrical flower with the corolla consisting of one broad upper petal (banner or standard), two lateral petals (wings), and two joined bottom petals (keel).

Perennial Present at all times of the year; in reference to a plant, one that lives for more than two years, usually producing flowers, fruits, and seeds annually.

Perianth Collective term for the calyx and corolla of a flower; in a flower lacking either sepals or petals, simply the outer whorl.

Petal The basic unit of the corolla; flat, usually broad, and brightly colored or white.

Petiole The stalk-like part of a leaf, attaching it to the stem.

Pinnate leaf   A leaf with leaflets along the sides of a common central stalk, much like a feather.

Pistil   The female organ of a flower, composed of an ovary, style, and stigma.

Pistillate flower   A flower with one or more pistils but lacking stamens; a female flower.

Pith   A spongy material present in the center of stems of certain plants.

Pod   A dry fruit that opens at maturity to release its seeds.

Pollen   The mass of dust-like grains produced in the anther of a stamen.

Pollen sac   The terminal, pollen-containing portion of a stamen; the anther.

Pollination   The transfer of pollen from an anther to a stigma by various agents (insects, birds, wind, water, etc.).

Raceme   An unbranched, often elongated flower cluster in which each flower is attached by its stalk directly to a central stem; flowers bloom in sequence from bottom to top.

Radially symmetrical   A flower with the symmetry of a wheel; often called radial or regular. *See also* Bilaterally symmetrical.

Ray flower   Each of the bilaterally symmetrical flowers around the edge of the central disk in many members of the aster family, or making up the entire head in some members; each ray flower resembles a single petal.

Recurved   Curving backward or downward.

Reflexed   Abruptly bent backward or downward.

Regular flower   A flower with petals and/or sepals of equal size and shape arranged around the center, much like the spokes of a wheel; always radially symmetrical.

Rhizome   A horizontal, underground stem, often enlarged by food storage, distinguished from a root by the presence of nodes and sometimes scale-like leaves.

Root   A specialized structure that absorbs water and nutrients from the soil and transports these substances to a plant's stem; lacks nodes.

Rose hip   A smooth, rounded, fruit-like structure consisting of a cup-shaped calyx enclosing seed-like fruits in certain members of the rose family.

Rosette   A crowded cluster of leaves; usually basal, circular, and appearing to grow directly out of the ground.

Runner   A stem that grows on the surface of the ground, often developing leaves, roots, and new plants at the nodes or tip.

Sap   A general term for the liquid contained within the parts of a plant.

Saprophyte   A plant lacking chlorophyll and living on dead organic matter.

Scale   A small, flattened, thin, usually green structure; the scales of a grass spikelet, among which the flowers develop, or the scales (much reduced leaves) in a flower cluster.

Self-pollination   The transfer of pollen from a stamen of one flower to the stigma of the same flower or of another flower on the same plant.

Sepal   The basic unit of the calyx; often green, sometimes colored and petal-like.

Sessile   Without a stalk; in reference to a leaf, one lacking a petiole, with the blade attached directly to the stem.

Sheath   A more or less tubular structure surrounding a part, as the lower portion of a leaf surrounding the stem.

Shoot   A young stem or branch with its leaves and flowers not yet mature.

Shrub   A woody, relatively low plant with several to many stems arising from the base.

Simple leaf   A leaf that is not compound.

Spadix   A dense spike of tiny flowers, usually enclosed in a spathe.

Spathe   A bract or pair of bracts, often large, enclosing the flowers.

Spatulate   More or less spatula- or spoon-shaped, with a rounded tip and tapering to the base.

Species (plural, Species)   A fundamental category of taxonomic classification, ranking below a genus; individuals within a species usually reproduce among themselves and are more closely related than to individuals of other species.

Spike   An elongated, unbranched flower cluster in which each flower lacks a stalk.

Spikelet   A tiny spike; in reference to members of the grass family, a structure consisting of overlapping scales enclosing small flowers lacking petals or sepals.

Spur   In reference to a flower, a slender, usually hollow projection.

Stalk   A general and less precise term for the stem; used here to describe a supporting structure, such as a leafstalk or flower stalk.

Stamen   The male organ of a flower, composed of a filament topped by an anther; usually several in each flower.

Staminate flower   A flower with stamens but lacking pistils; a male flower.

Standard   The broad upper petal in a pea flower; also called the banner.

Stem   The main axis of a plant or of its branches, responsible for supporting the leaves and flowers.

Sterile stamen   A stamen that does not produce pollen; usually lacks an anther.

Stigma   The tip of the pistil where the pollen lands and begins its development in the style.

Stipule   A small, often leaf-like appendage on either side of some petioles at the base.

Style   The narrow part of the pistil, connecting ovary and stigma.

Succulent   Fleshy and thick, storing water; a plant with fleshy, water-storing stems or leaves.

Tendril   A slender, coiling structure that helps support climbing plants.

Toothed   Having a sawtooth edge.

Tuber   A fleshy, enlarged part of an underground stem, serving as a storage organ (e.g., a potato).

Umbel   A flower cluster in which the individual flower stalks grow from the same point, much like the ribs of an umbrella.

Unisexual   A flower with only female (pistil) or male (stamen) parts.

Whorl   A circle of three or more leaves, branches, or flower stalks at a node.

Wing   A thin flat extension or ridge found at the edges of a seed or leafstalk or along the stem; in a pea flower, each of the two lateral petals.

PHOTO CREDITS

1 Ron Boender/
   Butterfly World
2 Don Eastman
2 (inset) Harry M. Walker
3 Wolfgang Kaehler
3 Jessie M. Harris
3 (inset) Jessie M. Harris
4 Walt Anderson
4 (inset) Joy Spurr
5 Rob & Ann Simpson
5 (inset) Rob & Ann
   Simpson
6 Tim Reeves
6 (inset) Don Eastman
7 Jessie M. Harris
7 (inset) Jessie M. Harris
8 Derrick Ditchburn/
   Visuals Unlimited
8 (inset) Derrick Ditchburn/
   Visuals Unlimited
9 Jessie M. Harris
10 Don Eastman
10 (inset) Joy Spurr
11 Jessie M. Harris
12 Jessie M. Harris
13 Priscilla Alexander
   Eastman
14 Jon M. Stewart
15 Ernest H. Rogers/
   Sea Images
16 Bill Johnson
17 Virginia P. Weinland/
   Photo Researchers, Inc.
18 Gerald & Buff Corsi/
   Focus on Nature, Inc.
19 Don Eastman

20 Mark Turner
21 Lee Rentz
22 Mark Turner
23 Jessie M. Harris
24 Don Eastman
24 (inset) Don Eastman
25 E. R. Degginger/
   Color-Pic, Inc.
26 Kevin Adams
26 (inset) Kevin Adams
27 Gerald & Buff Corsi/
   Visuals Unlimited
28 Steve Junak
29 Janet Horton
30 Jessie M. Harris
31 Joy Spurr
31 (inset) Ronald J. Taylor
32 Mark Turner
33 Don Eastman
34 Joanne Pavia
35 David Ransaw
36 Geoff Bryant/Photo
   Researchers, Inc.
37 Mark Turner
37 (inset) Mark Turner
38 Rob & Ann Simpson
38 (inset) Stephen Ingram
39 Joy Spurr
39 (inset) Joy Spurr
40 Dr. Richard Spellenberg
41 Gerald & Buff Corsi/
   Focus on Nature, Inc.
41 (inset) Stephen G.
   Maka
42 Steve Junak
43 Charles Mann

44 Gerald & Buff Corsi/
    Focus on Nature, Inc.
45 John Shaw
46 Herbert Clarke
47 Gerald & Buff Corsi/
    Focus on Nature, Inc.
47 (inset) Gerald & Buff
    Corsi/Focus on Nature, Inc.
48 Karl H. Switak/Photo
    Researchers, Inc.
48 (inset) Karl H. Switak/
    Photo Researchers, Inc.
49 Mark Turner
50 Charles Webber/California
    Academy of Sciences
50 (inset) J. E. (Jed) &
    Bonnie McClellan/
    California Academy
    of Sciences
51 Michael T. Stubben/
    Visuals Unlimited
52 Tom Branch/Photo
    Researchers, Inc.
53 Calvin Larsen/Photo
    Researchers, Inc.
54 Larry Kimball
55 Joy Spurr
56 Don Eastman
57 Francis E. Caldwell
58 Rod Planck
59 Gerald & Buff Corsi/
    Focus on Nature, Inc.
59 (inset) Gerald & Buff
    Corsi/Focus on Nature, Inc.
60 Jessie M. Harris
60 (inset) Jessie M. Harris
61 Jessie M. Harris
62 Janet Horton
63 Mark Turner
64 Janet Horton
65 Gerald & Buff Corsi/
    Focus on Nature, Inc.
66 E. R. Degginger/
    Color-Pic, Inc.
66 (inset) E. R. Degginger/
    Color-Pic, Inc.
67 Betty Randall
68 Barbara Magnuson
68 (inset) Barbara Magnuson

69 Gerald & Buff Corsi/
    Focus on Nature, Inc.
70 C. K. Lorenz/Photo
    Researchers, Inc.
71 Rod Planck/Photo
    Researchers, Inc.
72 Dr. Eckhart Pott/
    OKAPIA/Photo
    Researchers, Inc.
73 Jessie M. Harris
73 (inset) Jessie M. Harris
74 Steve Junak
74 (inset) Steve Junak
75 Joy Spurr
76 Joy Spurr
76 (inset) Joy Spurr
77 Joy Spurr
78 F. H. Kolwicz/Visuals
    Unlimited
78 (inset) F. H. Kolwicz/
    Visuals Unlimited
79 Jon M. Stewart
79 (inset) Jon M. Stewart
80 Rob & Ann Simpson
81 Walt Anderson
81 (inset) Walt Anderson
82 Joy Spurr
83 Jon M. Stewart
83 (inset) Jon M. Stewart
84 Jessie M. Harris
84 (inset) Jessie M. Harris
85 Jessie M. Harris
85 (inset) Jessie M. Harris
86 Joy Spurr
87 C. K. Lorenz/Photo
    Researchers, Inc.
88 Charles Mann
89 Gerald & Buff Corsi/
    Focus on Nature, Inc.
90 Gerald & Buff Corsi/
    Focus on Nature, Inc.
90 (inset) Gerald &
    Buff Corsi/Focus
    on Nature, Inc.
91 Jerry Pavia
91 (inset) Jerry Pavia
92 Jon M. Stewart
92 (inset) Jon M. Stewart
93 Larry Kimball

195 Steve Junak
196 Rob & Ann Simpson
197 Gail Jankus/Photo
     Researchers, Inc.
198 Steve Junak
199 Mark Turner
200 Don Eastman
201 Jessie M. Harris
202 Joy Spurr
203 Jessie M. Harris
204 Don Eastman
204 (inset) Don Eastman
205 Jerry Pavia
206 Stephen Ingram
207 Carlyn Galati/Visuals
     Unlimited
207 (inset) Carlyn Galati/
     Visuals Unlimited
208 Dan Guravich/Photo
     Researchers, Inc.
209 Steve Junak
209 (inset) Steve Junak
210 Gerald & Buff Corsi/
     Focus on Nature, Inc.
211 Charles Mann
212 Rod Barbee/Visuals
     Unlimited
213 E. R. Degginger/
     Color-Pic, Inc.
213 (inset) E. R. Degginger/
     Color-Pic, Inc.
214 Shan Cunningham
215 Gerald & Buff Corsi/
     Focus on Nature, Inc.
216 Andrew J. Martinez/
     Photo Researchers, Inc.
217 Gerald & Buff Corsi/
     Focus on Nature, Inc.
218 Gerald & Buff Corsi/
     Focus on Nature, Inc.
219 Thomas K. Todsen
220 Gerald & Buff Corsi/
     Focus on Nature, Inc.
221 Jon M. Stewart
221 (inset) Jon M. Stewart
222 Emily Johnson
223 Larry Sansone
224 Bill Johnson
225 Dr. Richard Spellenberg

226 Michael T. Stubben/
     Visuals Unlimited
227 Don Eastman
228 Jon M. Stewart
228 (inset) Jon M. Stewart
229 Gerald & Buff Corsi/
     Focus on Nature, Inc.
230 Walt Anderson
231 Jessie M. Harris
232 Robert E. Barber
233 Jessie M. Harris
233 (inset) Jessie M. Harris
234 Larry Sansone
235 Gerald & Buff Corsi/
     Focus on Nature, Inc.
235 (inset) Gerald &
     Buff Corsi/Focus
     on Nature, Inc.
236 Jerry Pavia
236 (inset) A. Kerstitch/
     Visuals Unlimited
237 Ralph Lee Hopkins
238 Gerald & Buff Corsi/
     Focus on Nature, Inc.
239 Bruce Clendenning/
     Visuals Unlimited
240 Gerald & Buff Corsi/
     Focus on Nature, Inc.
241 Michael T. Stubben/
     Visuals Unlimited
242 Jerry Pavia
243 Jon M. Stewart
244 Gerald & Buff Corsi/
     Focus on Nature, Inc.
245 Jessie M. Harris
246 Jessie M. Harris
247 Dennis Flaherty
248 Scott T. Smith
249 Alan & Linda Detrick/
     Photo Researchers, Inc.
250 Mark Turner
251 Frank S. Balthis
252 Jon M. Stewart
253 Jessie M. Harris
254 Don Eastman
254 (inset) Don Eastman
255 Michael T. Stubben/
     Visuals Unlimited
256 Don Eastman

INDEX